STUDY GUIDE

KAREN C. TIMBERLAKE
Los Angeles Valley College

GENERAL, ORGANIC, AND BIOLOGICAL CHEMISTRY
Structures of Life

KAREN C. TIMBERLAKE

Third Edition

Prentice Hall
New York Boston San Francisco
London Toronto Sydney Tokyo Singapore Madrid
Mexico City Munich Paris Cape Town Hong Kong Montreal

Project Editor: Jessica Neumann
Acquisitions Editor: Dawn Giovanniello
Editor in Chief, Chemistry and Geosciences: Nicole Folchetti
Marketing Manager: Scott Dustan
Managing Editor, Chemistry and Geosciences: Gina M. Cheselka
Project Manager, Science: Shari Toron
Full Service Vendor: Elm Street Publishing
Composition: Integra
Operations Specialist: Amanda Smith
Supplement Cover Manager: Paul Gourhan
Supplement Cover Designer: Tina Krivoshein
Cover Photo Credits: FoodCollection/Getty Images, Inc.

© 2010 Pearson Education, Inc.
Pearson Prentice Hall
Pearson Education, Inc.
Upper Saddle River, NJ 07458

All rights reserved. No part of this book may be reproduced, in any form or by any means, without permission in writing from the publisher.

Pearson Prentice Hall™ is a trademark of Pearson Education, Inc.

The author and publisher of this book have used their best efforts in preparing this book. These efforts include the development, research, and testing of the theories and programs to determine their effectiveness. The author and publisher make no warranty of any kind, expressed or implied, with regard to these programs or the documentation contained in this book. The author and publisher shall not be liable in any event for incidental or consequential damages in connection with, or arising out of, the furnishing, performance, or use of these programs.

This work is protected by United States copyright laws and is provided solely for teaching courses and assessing student learning. Dissemination or sale of any part of this work (including on the World Wide Web) will destroy the integrity of the work and is not permitted. The work and materials from it should never be made available except by instructors using the accompanying text in their classes. All recipients of this work are expected to abide by these restrictions and to honor the intended pedagogical purposes and the needs of other instructors who rely on these materials.

Printed in the United States of America

10 9 8 7 6 5 4 3 2 1

ISBN-13: 978-0-321-58755-8
ISBN-10: 0-321-58755-3

Prentice Hall
is an imprint of

www.pearsonhighered.com

Table of Contents

Preface

This Study Guide is intended to accompany *General, Organic, and Biological Chemistry: Structures of Life*, Third Edition. The purpose of this Study Guide is to provide students with additional learning resources that increase their understanding of the concepts. Each section in this Study Guide is correlated with a chapter section in the text. Within each section, there for Learning Goals, Guides to Problem Solving, Learning Exercises and Answers that focus on problem solving and promote an understanding of the chemical principles of that Learning Goal. A checklist of learning goals and a multiple-choice Practice Test provide a study of the entire chapter content. The Answers and complete Solutions to the odd-numbered problems in the text are now provided in a separate supplement, *Students Solutions* Manual.

I hope that this Study Guide will help in the learning of chemistry. If you wish to make comments or corrections, or ask questions, you can send me an e-mail message at khemist@aol.com.

Karen C. Timberlake

To the Student

"One must learn by doing the thing;
though you think you know it, you have
no certainty until you try."
—*Sophocles*

Here you are in a chemistry class with your textbook in front of you. Perhaps you have already been assigned some reading or some problems to do in the book. Looking through the chapter, you may see words, terms, and pictures that are new to you. This may very well be your first experience with a science class like chemistry. At this point you may have some questions about what you can do to learn chemistry. This Study Guide is written with that consideration in mind.

Learning chemistry is similar to learning a new sport such as tennis or skiing or driving. If I asked you how you learn to play tennis or ski or drive a car, you would probably tell me that you would need to practice often. It is the same with learning chemistry, where understanding the chemical ideas and successfully solving the problems depends on the time and effort you invest in it. If you practice every day, you will find that learning chemistry is an exciting experience and a way to understand the current issues of the environment, health, and medicine.

Manage Your Study Time

I often recommend a study system to students: read one section of the text and immediately practice the questions and problems that go with it. In this way, you concentrate on a small amount of information and actively use what you learned to answer questions. This helps you to organize and review the information without being overwhelmed by the entire chapter. It is important to understand each section because they build like steps. Information presented in each chapter proceeds from the basic to the more complex. Perhaps you can only study three or four sections of the chapter. As long as you also practice doing some problems at the same time, the concepts and problem solving strategies will stay with you.

Form a Study Group

I highly recommend that you form a study group in the first week of your chemistry class. Working with your peers will help you use the language of chemistry. By scheduling a time to meet each week helps you study and prepare to discuss problems. You will be able to teach some things to the other students in the group, and sometimes they will help you understand a topic that puzzles you. You won't always understand a concept right away. Your group will help you see your way through it. Most of all, a study group creates a strong support system whereby students like you get together to help each other complete the class successfully.

Go to Office Hours

Try to go to your professor's or teaching assistant's office hours. Your professor wants you to understand and enjoy learning this material and should have office hours. Often a tutor is assigned to a class or there are tutors available at your college. Don't be intimidated. Going to see a tutor or your professor is one of the best ways to clarify what you need to learn in chemistry.

Using this Study Guide

Now you are ready to sit down and study chemistry. Let's go over some methods that can help you learn chemistry. This Study Guide is written specifically to help you understand and practice the chemical concepts that are presented in your class and in your text. Some of the exercises teach basic skills; others encourage you to extend your scientific curiosity. The following features are part of this Study Guide.

1. Study Goals

The Study Goals give you an overview of what the chapter is about and what you can expect to accomplish when you complete your study and learning of a chapter.

2. Think About It

Each chapter in the Study Guide has a group of questions that encourage you to think about some of the ideas and practical applications of the chemical concepts you are going to study. You may find that you already have knowledge of chemistry in some of the areas. That will be helpful to you. Other questions give you an overview of the chemistry ideas you will be learning.

3. Key Terms

Each chapter in the Study Guide introduces Key Terms. As you complete the description of the Key Terms, you will have an overview of the topics you will be studying in that chapter. Because many of the Key Terms may be new to you, this is an opportunity to review their meaning.

4. Chapter Sections

Each section of the chapter begins with the Key Concepts to illustrate the important ideas in that section. The summary of concepts is written to guide you through each of the learning activities. When you are ready to begin your study, read the matching section in the textbook and review the sample exercises in the text.

5. Learning Exercises

The Learning Exercises give you an opportunity to practice problem solving related to the chemical principles in the chapter. Each set of Learning Exercises reviews one chemical principle. At various times, you will notice some essay questions that illustrate the concepts. I believe that writing out your ideas is a very important way of learning new content. The answers are found immediately following each exercise. Check your answers right away. If they don't match the answer in the Study Guide, review that section of the text again. It is important to make corrections before you go on. In learning tennis, you hit the ball a lot from the baseline before you learn to volley or serve. Chemistry, too, involves a layering of skills such that each one is understood before the next one can be learned.

6. Checklist

Use the Checklist to check your understanding of the Study Goals. This gives you an overview of the major topics in the section. If something does not sound familiar, go back and review. One aspect of being a strong problem-solver is the ability to check your knowledge and understanding as you study.

7. Practice Test

A Practice Test is found at the end of each chapter. When you have learned the material in a chapter, you can apply your understanding to the Practice Test. If the results of this test indicate that you know the material, you are ready to proceed to the next chapter. If, however, the results indicate further study is needed, you can repeat the Learning Exercises in the sections. Answers for all of the questions are included at the end of the Practice Test.

Prologue
Chemistry in Our Lives

Study Goals

- Define the term chemistry and identify substances as chemicals.
- Describe the activities that are part of the scientific method.
- Develop a study plan for learning chemistry.

Think About It

1. Why can we say that the salt and sugar we use on food are chemicals?

2. How can the scientific method help us make decisions?

3. What are some things you can do to help you study and learn chemistry?

Key Terms

Match each of the following key terms with the correct definition:

1. scientific method **2.** experiment **3.** hypothesis

4. theory **5.** chemistry

a. ______________ An explanation of nature validated by many experiments

b. ______________ The study of substances and how they interact

c. ______________ A possible explanation of a natural phenomenon

d. ______________ The process of making observations, writing a hypothesis, and testing with experiments

e. ______________ A procedure used to test a hypothesis

Answers **a.** 4 **b.** 5 **c.** 3 **d.** 1 **e.** 2

P.1 Chemistry and Chemicals

- A chemical is any material used in or produced by a chemical process.
- A substance is a chemical that contains material with the same composition and properties.
- In the sciences, physical quantities are described in units of the metric or International System (SI).

◆ Learning Exercise P.1

Indicate if each of the following is a chemical:

a. ______ aluminum
b. ______ heat
c. ______ sodium fluoride in toothpaste
d. ______ ammonium nitrate in fertilizer
e. ______ time

Answers **a.** yes **b.** no **c.** yes **d.** yes **e.** no

P.2 Scientific Method: Thinking Like a Scientist

- The scientific method is a process of making observations, writing a hypothesis, and testing the hypothesis with experiments.
- A theory develops when experiments that validate a hypothesis are repeated by many scientists with consistent results.

MasteringChemistry

Tutorial: Scientific Notation

◆ Learning Exercise P.2

Identify each of the following as an observation (O), hypothesis (H), or experiment (E):

a. _____ Sunlight is necessary for the growth of plants.
b. _____ Plants in the shade were shorter than plants in the sun.
c. _____ Plant leaves are covered with aluminum foil and their growth measured.
d. _____ Fertilizer is added to plants.
e. _____ Ozone slows plant growth by interfering with photosynthesis.
f. _____ Ozone causes brown spots on plant leaves.

Answers **a.** H **b.** O **c.** E **d.** E **e.** H **f.** O

P.3 A Study Plan for Learning Chemistry

- Components of the text that promote learning include *Looking Ahead, Learning Goals, Concept Checks, Sample Problems, Guides to Problem Solving (GPS), Study Checks, Health Notes, Green Chemistry Notes, Environmental Notes, Explore Your World, Questions and Problems, Concept Maps, Chapter Reviews, Key Terms, Understanding the Concepts, Additional Questions and Problems, Challenge Problems*, and *Answers to Selected Questions and Problems.*
- An active learner continually interacts with chemical concepts while reading the text and attending lecture.
- Working with a study group clarifies ideas and illustrates problem solving.

◆ Learning Exercise P.3

Which of the following activities are included in a successful study plan for learning chemistry?

a._______ attending lecture once in a while

b._______ working problems with friends from class

c. _______ attending review sessions

d._______ planning a regular study time

e. _______ not doing the assigned problems

f. _______ going to the instructor's office hours

Answers **a.** no **b.** yes **c.** yes
d. yes **e.** no **f.** yes

Checklist for Prologue

You are ready to take the *Practice Test* for the Prologue. Be sure you have accomplished the following learning goals for this chapter. If you are not sure, review the section listed at the end of the goal. Then apply your new skills and understanding to the Practice Test.

After studying the Prologue, I can successfully:

____ Describe a substance as a chemical (P.1).

____ Identify the components of the scientific method (P.2).

____ Design a study plan for successful learning chemistry (P.3).

Practice Test for Prologue

1. Which of the following would be described as a chemical?
A. sleeping **B.** salt **C.** singing
D. listening to a concert **E.** energy

2. Which of the following is not a chemical?
A. wool **B.** sugar **C.** feeling cold
D. salt **E.** vanilla

For questions 3–7, identify each statement as an observation (O), hypothesis (H), or experiment (E):

3. ____ More sugar dissolves in 50 mL of hot water than in 50 mL of cold water.

4. ____ Samples containing 20 g of sugar each are placed separately in a glass of cold water and a glass of hot water.

5. ____ Sugar consists of white crystals.

6. ____ Water flows downhill.

7. ____ Drinking ten glasses of water a day will help me lose weight.

For questions 8–12, answer yes or no:

To learn chemistry I will

8. ____ work the problems in the chapter and check answers.

9. ____ attend some lectures, but not all.

10. ____ form a study group.

11. ____ set up a regular study time.

12. ____ wait until the night before the exam to start studying.

Answers to the Practice Test

1. B **2.** C **3.** O **4.** E **5.** O
6. O **7.** H **8.** yes **9.** no **10.** yes
11. yes **12.** no

1
Measurements

Study Goals

- Learn the units and abbreviations for the metric (SI) system.
- Distinguish between measured numbers and exact numbers.
- Determine the number of significant figures in a measurement.
- Convert a standard number to scientific notation.
- Use prefixes to change a unit to a larger or smaller unit.
- Form conversion factors from units in an equality.
- Use metric units, U.S. units, a percentage, ppm or ppb, and density as conversion factors.
- In problem solving, convert the initial unit of a measurement to another unit.
- Round off a calculator answer to report an answer with the correct number of significant figures.
- Calculate the density or specific gravity of a substance.
- Use density or specific gravity to calculate the mass or volume of a substance.

Think About It

1. What kind of device would you use to measure each of the following: your height, your weight, and the quantity of water to make soup?
2. When you make a measurement, why should you write down a number and a unit?
3. Why does oil float on water?

Key Terms

Match each the following key terms with a statement below:

a. metric system	**b.** exact number	**c.** significant figures
d. conversion factor	**e.** density	**f.** scientific notation

1. ____ all the numbers recorded in a measurement including the estimated digit

2. ____ a fraction that gives the quantities of an equality in the numerator and denominator

3. ____ a form of writing a number using a coefficient and a power of ten

4. ____ the relationship of the mass of an object to its volume usually expressed as g/mL

5. ____ a number obtained by counting items or from a definition

6. ____ a decimal system of measurement used throughout the world

Answers **1.** c **2.** d **3.** f **4.** e **5.** b **6.** a

1.1 Units of Measurement

- In the sciences, physical quantities are described in units of the metric or International System (SI).
- Length or distance is measured in meters (m), volume in liters (L), mass in grams (g), time in seconds (s), and temperature in Celsius degrees (°C) or kelvins (K).

◆ Learning Exercise 1.1

Indicate the type of measurement in each of the following:

1. length **2.** mass **3.** volume **4.** temperature **5.** time

a. _____ 45 g **b.** _____ 8.2 m **c.** _____ 215 °C **d.** _____ 50 s

e. _____ 45 L **f.** _____ 825 K **g.** _____ 8.8 g **h.** _____ 2.0 L

Answers **a.** 2 **b.** 1 **c.** 4 **d.** 5 **e.** 3 **f.** 4 **g.** 2 **h.** 3

1.2 Scientific Notation

- A value written in scientific notation has two parts: a number 1 to 9 called a *coefficient* followed by a power of 10.
- For numbers greater than 10, the decimal point is moved to the left to give a positive power of ten.
- For numbers less than 1, the decimal point is moved to the right to give a negative power of ten.

MasteringChemistry

Tutorial: Scientific Notation

Study Note

1. For a number greater than 10, the decimal point is moved to the left to give a coefficient 1 to 9 and a positive power of ten. For a number less than 1, the decimal point is moved to the right to give a coefficient 1 to 9 and a negative power of ten.
2. The number 2.5×10^3 means that 2.5 is multiplied by 10^3 (1000).
   $2.5 \times 1000 = 2500$
3. The number 8.2×10^{-2} means that 8.2 is multiplied by 10^{-2} (0.01).
   $8.2 \times 0.01 = 0.082$

◆ Learning Exercise 1.2A

Write the following measurements in scientific notation:

a. 240 000 cm _______________ **b.** 825 m _______________

c. 230 000 kg _______________ **d.** 53 000 y _______________

e. 0.002 m _______________ **f.** 0.000 0015 g _______________

g. 0.08 kg _______________ **h.** 0.000 15 s _______________

Answers **a.** 2.4×10^5 cm **b.** 8.25×10^2 m **c.** 2.3×10^5 kg **d.** 5.3×10^4 y
e. 2×10^{-3} m **f.** 1.5×10^{-6} g **g.** 8×10^{-2} kg **h.** 1.5×10^{-4} s

◆ Learning Exercise 1.2B

Circle the larger number in each pair.

a. 2500 or 2.5×10^2 **b.** 0.04 or 4×10^{-3}

c. 65 000 or 6.5×10^5 **d.** 0.000 35 or 3.5×10^{-3}

e. 300 000 or 3×10^6 **f.** 0.002 or 2×10^{-4}

Answers **a.** 2500 **b.** 0.04 **c.** 6.5×10^5
d. 3.5×10^{-3} **e.** 3×10^6 **f.** 0.002

◆ Learning Exercise 1.2C

Write each of the following in standard form:

Example: 2×10^2 m = 200 m and 3×10^{-4} g = 0.0003 g

a. 4×10^3 m ____________ **b.** 5.2×10^4 g ____________

c. 1.8×10^5 g ____________ **d.** 8×10^{-3} L ____________

e. 6×10^{-2} kg ____________ **f.** 3.1×10^{-5} g ____________

Answers **a.** 4 000 m **b.** 52 000 g **c.** 180 000 g
d. 0.008 L **e.** 0.06 kg **f.** 0.000 031 g

1.3 Measured Numbers and Significant Figures

- A measured number is obtained when you use a measuring device to determine an amount of some item.
- An exact number is obtained by counting items or from a definition that relates units in the same measuring system.
- There is uncertainty in every measured number, but not in exact numbers.
- Significant figures in a measured number are all the reported figures including the estimated digit.
- Zeros written in front of a nonzero number or zeros that are used as placeholders in a large number without a decimal point are not significant digits.

◆ Learning Exercise 1.3A

Are the numbers in each of the following statements measured (M) or exact (E)?

a. ____There are 7 days in one week. **b.** ____A concert lasts for 73 minutes.

c. ____There are 1000 g in 1 kg. **d.** ____The potatoes have a mass of 2.5 kg.

e. ____A student has 26 CDs. **f.** ____The snake is 1.2 m long.

Answers **a.** E (counted) **b.** M (use a watch) **c.** E (metric definition)
d. M (use a balance) **e.** E (counted) **f.** M (use a metric ruler)

MasteringChemistry

Self Study Activity: Significant Figures

Tutorial: Counting Significant Figures

Study Note

Significant figures (SFs) are all the numbers reported in a measurement including the estimated digit. Zeros are significant unless they are placeholders appearing at the beginning of a decimal number or in a large number without a decimal point.

4.255 g (4 SFs) 0.0042 m (2 SFs) 46 500 L (3 SFs)

◆ Learning Exercise 1.3B

State the number of significant figures in the following measured numbers:

a. 35.24 g ______ **b.** 0.000 080 m ______

c. 55 000 m ______ **d.** 805 mL ______

e. 5.025 L ______ **f.** 0.006 kg ______

g. 268 200 mm ______ **h.** 25.0 °C ______

Answers	**a.**	4	**b.**	2	**c.**	2	**d.**	3
	e.	4	**f.**	1	**g.**	4	**h.**	3

1.4 Significant Figures in Calculations

- In multiplication or division, the final answer must have the same number of significant digits as in the measurement with the fewest significant figures.
- In addition or subtraction, the final answer must have the same number of decimal places as the measurement with the fewest decimal places.
- When evaluating a calculator answer, it is important to count the significant figures in the measurements and round the calculator answer properly.
- Answers in chemical calculations rarely use all the numbers that appear in the calculator. Exact numbers are not included in the determination of the number of significant figures in an answer.

Study Note

1. To round a number, when the first digit to be dropped is less than 5, keep the digits you need and drop all the digits that follow.
   Round 42.8254 to 3 SFs ⟶ 42.8 (drop 254)
2. To round a number, when the first number dropped is 5 or greater, keep the proper number of digits and increase the last retained digit by 1.
   Round 8.4882 to 2 SFs ⟶ 8.5
3. In large numbers, maintain the value of the answer by adding nonsignificant zeros.
   Round 356 835 to 3 SFs ⟶ 357 000

◆ Learning Exercise 1.4A

Round each of the following to give **two** significant figures:

a. 88.75 m ______ **b.** 0.002 923 g ______

c. 50.525 g ______ **d.** 1.672 m ______

e. 0.001 055 8 kg ______ **f.** 82 080 mL ______

Answers **a.** 89 m **b.** 0.0029 g **c.** 51 g
d. 1.7 m **e.** 0.0011 kg **f.** 82 000 mL

Study Note

1. An answer from multiplying and dividing has the same number of significant figures as the measurement that has the smallest number of significant figures.

   1.5 × 32.546 = 48.819 ⟶ 49 *Answer rounded to 2 SFs*
   2 SFs *5 SFs*

2. An answer from adding or subtracting has the same number of decimal places as the initial number with the fewest decimal places.

   82.223 + 4.1 = 86.323 ⟶ 86.3 *Answer rounded to one decimal place*
   3 decimal places *1 decimal place*

MasteringChemistry

Tutorial: Significant Figures in Calculations

◆ Learning Exercise 1.4B

Solve each problem and give the answer with the correct number of significant figures or decimal places:

a. $1.3 \times 71.5 =$ **b.** $\dfrac{8.00}{4.00} =$

c. $\dfrac{0.082 \times 25.4}{0.116 \times 3.4} =$ **d.** $\dfrac{3.05 \times 1.86}{118.5} =$

e. $\dfrac{376}{0.0073} =$ **f.** $38.520 - 11.4 =$

g. $4.2 + 8.15 =$ **h.** $102.56 + 8.325 - 0.8825 =$

Answers **a.** 93 **b.** 2.00 **c.** 5.3 **d.** 0.0479
e. 52 000 **f.** 27.1 **g.** 12.4 **h.** 110.00

1.5 Prefixes and Equalities

- In the metric system, larger and smaller units use prefixes to change the size of the unit by factors of 10. For example, a prefix such as *centi* or *milli* preceding the unit meter gives a smaller length than a meter. A prefix such as *kilo* added to gram gives a unit that measures a mass that is 1000 times greater than a gram.
- An equality contains two units that measure the *same* length, volume, or mass.
- Some common metric equalities are: 1 m = 100 cm; 1 L = 1000 mL; 1 kg = 1000 g.
- Some useful metric-U.S. equalities are: 2.54 cm = 1 in.; 1 kg = 2.20 lb; 946 mL = 1 quart
- Some of the common metric (SI) prefixes are:

Prefix	Symbol	Numerical Value	Scientific Notation
Prefixes That Increase the Size of the Unit			
peta	P	1 000 000 000 000 000	10^{15}
tera	T	1 000 000 000 000	10^{12}
giga	G	1 000 000 000	10^{9}
mega	M	1 000 000	10^{6}
kilo	k	1 000	10^{3}
deci	d	0.1	10^{-1}
centi	c	0.01	10^{-2}
milli	m	0.001	10^{-3}
micro	μ	0.000 001	10^{-6}
nano	n	0.000 000 001	10^{-9}
pico	p	0.000 000 000 001	10^{-12}
femto	f	0.000 000 000 000 001	10^{-15}

MasteringChemistry

Self Study Activity: Metric System

◆ Learning Exercise 1.5A

Match the items in column A with those from column B.

A		B
1. _____	megameter	**a.** nanometer
2. _____	1000 meters	**b.** decimeter
3. _____	0.1 m	**c.** 10^{-6} m
4. _____	millimeter	**d.** kilometer
5. _____	centimeter	**e.** 0.01 m
6. _____	10^{-9} m	**f.** 1000 m
7. _____	micrometer	**g.** 10^{-3} m
8. _____	kilometer	**h.** 10^{6} m

Answers **1.** h **2.**d **3.** b **4.** g **5.** e **6.** a **7.** c **8.** f

◆ Learning Exercise 1.5B

Place the following units in order from smallest to largest:

a. kilogram milligram gram ____________________

b. centimeter kilometer millimeter ____________________

c. dL mL L ____________________

d. kg pg mg μg ____________________

Answers **a.** milligram, gram, kilogram **b.** millimeter, centimeter, kilometer
c. mL, dL, L **d.** pg, μg, mg, kg

◆ Learning Exercise 1.5C

Complete the following metric relationships:

a. 1 L = ________ mL		**b.** 1 L = ________ dL
c. 1 m = ________ cm		**d.** 1 dL = ________ mL
e. 1 kg = ________ g		**f.** 1 cm = ________ mm
g. 1 mg = ________ µg		**h.** 1 dL = ________ L
i. 1 m = ________ mm		**j.** 1 cm = ________ m

Answers **a.** 1000 **b.** 10 **c.** 100 **d.** 100 **e.** 1000
f. 10 **g.** 1000 **h.** 0.1 **i.** 1000 **j.** 0.01

1.6 Writing Conversion Factors

- Conversion factors are used in a calculation to change from one unit to another. Each factor represents an equality that is expressed in the form of a fraction.
- Two forms of a conversion factor can be written for any equality. For example, the metric–U.S. equality 2.54 cm = 1 inch (in.) can be written as follows:

$$\frac{2.54\text{ cm}}{1\text{ in.}} \text{ and } \frac{1\text{ in.}}{2.54\text{ cm}}$$

Study Note

Metric conversion factors are obtained from metric prefixes. For example, the metric equality 1 m = 100 cm is written as two factors:

$$\frac{1\text{ m}}{100\text{ cm}} \text{ and } \frac{100\text{ cm}}{1\text{ m}}$$

◆ Learning Exercise 1.6A

Write two conversion factors for each of the following pairs of units:

a. millimeters and meters **b.** kilograms and grams

c. kilograms and pounds

d. inches and centimeters

e. centimeters and meters

f. milliliters and quarts

g. deciliters and liters

h. millimeters and centimeters

Answers

a. $\frac{1000 \text{ mm}}{1 \text{ m}}$ and $\frac{1 \text{ m}}{1000 \text{ mm}}$

b. $\frac{1000 \text{ g}}{1 \text{ kg}}$ and $\frac{1 \text{ kg}}{1000 \text{ g}}$

c. $\frac{2.20 \text{ lb}}{1 \text{ kg}}$ and $\frac{1 \text{ kg}}{2.20 \text{ lb}}$

d. $\frac{2.54 \text{ cm}}{1 \text{ in.}}$ and $\frac{1 \text{ in.}}{2.54 \text{ cm}}$

e. $\frac{100 \text{ cm}}{1 \text{ m}}$ and $\frac{1 \text{ m}}{100 \text{ cm}}$

f. $\frac{946 \text{ mL}}{1 \text{ qt}}$ and $\frac{1 \text{ qt}}{946 \text{ mL}}$

g. $\frac{10 \text{ dL}}{1 \text{ L}}$ and $\frac{1 \text{ L}}{10 \text{ dL}}$

h. $\frac{10 \text{ mm}}{1 \text{ cm}}$ and $\frac{1 \text{ cm}}{10 \text{ mm}}$

Study Note

1. Sometimes, a statement within a problem gives an equality that is only true for that problem. Then conversion factors can be written that are true only for that problem. For example, a problem states that there are 50 mg of vitamin B in a tablet. The conversion factors are

$$\frac{1 \text{ tablet}}{50 \text{ mg of vitamin B}} \text{ and } \frac{50 \text{ mg of vitamin B}}{1 \text{ tablet}}$$

2. If a problem gives a percentage (%), it can be stated as parts per 100 parts. For example, a candy bar contains 45% by mass chocolate. This percentage (%) equality can be written with factors using the same mass unit such as grams.

$$\frac{45 \text{ g of chocolate}}{100 \text{ g of candy bar}} \text{ and } \frac{100 \text{ g of candy bar}}{45 \text{ g of chocolate}}$$

3. When a problem gives ppm or ppm, it can be stated as parts per million (ppm), which is mg/kg or parts per billion (ppb), which is μg/kg. For example, the level of nitrate in the Los Angeles water is 2.5 ppm. This ppm can be written as conversion factors using mg/kg.

$$\frac{2.5 \text{ mg of nitrate}}{1 \text{ kg of water}} \text{ and } \frac{1 \text{ kg of water}}{2.5 \text{ mg of nitrate}}$$

◆ Learning Exercise 1.6 B

Write two conversion factors for each of the following statements:

a. A cheese contains 55% fat by mass.

b. In the city, a car gets 14 miles to the gallon.

c. A 125-g steak contains 45 g of protein.

d. 18-carat pink gold contains 25% copper by mass.

e. A cadmium level of 1.8 ppm in food causes liver damage in rats.

f. A water sample contains 5.4 ppb of arsenic.

Answers

a. $\frac{55\text{ g fat}}{100\text{ g cheese}}$ and $\frac{100\text{ g cheese}}{55\text{ g fat}}$ **b.** $\frac{14\text{ mi}}{1\text{ gal}}$ and $\frac{1\text{ gal}}{14\text{ mi}}$

c. $\frac{45\text{ g protein}}{125\text{ g steak}}$ and $\frac{125\text{ g steak}}{45\text{ g protein}}$ **d.** $\frac{25\text{ g copper}}{100\text{ g pink gold}}$ and $\frac{100\text{ g pink gold}}{25\text{ g copper}}$

e. $\frac{1.8\text{ mg cadmium}}{1\text{ kg food}}$ and $\frac{1\text{ kg food}}{1.8\text{ mg cadmium}}$ **f.** $\frac{5.4\ \mu\text{g arsenic}}{1\text{ kg water}}$ and $\frac{1\text{ kg water}}{5.4\ \mu\text{g arseni}}$

1.7 Problem Solving

- Conversion factors from metric and/or U.S. relationships and percent can be used to change a quantity expressed in one unit to a quantity expressed in another unit.
- The process of solving a problem with units requires the change of the initial unit using one or more conversion factors until the final unit of the answer is obtained.

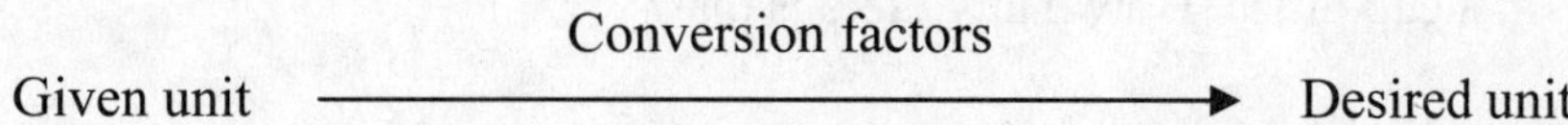

Example: How many liters is 2850 mL?

STEP 1: **Given:** 2850 mL **Need:** L

STEP 2: **Plan:** milliliters $\xrightarrow{\text{Metric factor}}$ liters

STEP 3: **Equality/Conversion factors:** 1 L = 1000 mL

$$\frac{1\text{ L}}{1000\text{ mL}} \text{ and } \frac{1000\text{ mL}}{1\text{ L}}$$

STEP 4: **Set Up Problem:** $2850\ \cancel{\text{mL}} \times \dfrac{1\text{ L}}{1000\ \cancel{\text{mL}}} = 2.85\text{ L}$

Guide to Problem Solving Using Conversion Factors	
STEP 1	State the given unit and the needed unit.
STEP 2	Write a plan to convert the given unit to the final unit.
STEP 3	State the equalities and conversion factors needed to cancel units.
STEP 4	Set up problem to cancel units and calculate answer.

MasteringChemistry

Tutorial: Metric Conversions

Tutorial: Using Percentage as a Conversion Factor

◆ Learning Exercise 1.7A

Use metric–metric conversion factors to solve the following problems:

a. 189 mL = ________ L **b.** 2.7 cm = ________ mm

c. 0.0025 L = ________ mL **d.** 76 mg = ________ g

e. How many meters tall is a person whose height is 175 cm?

f. There are 285 mL in a cup of tea. How many liters is that?

g. An 18–carat ring contains 75.0% gold by mass. If the total mass of the ring is 13 500 mg, how many grams of gold does the ring contain?

h. You walked 1.5 km on the treadmill at the gym. How many meters did you walk?

Answers	**a.** 0.189 L	**b.** 27 mm	**c.** 2.5 mL	**d.** 0.076 g
	e. 1.75 m	**f.** 0.285 L	**g.** 10.1 g	**h.** 1500 m

◆ Learning Exercise 1.7B

Use metric–U.S. conversion factors to solve the following problems:

a. 18 inches = _____cm

b. 4.0 qt = _____L

c. 275 mL = _____qt

d. 1300 mg = _____lb

e. 150 lb = _____kg

f. 840 g = _____lb

g. 15 ft = _____cm

h. 8.50 oz = _____g

Answers	**a.** 46 cm	**b.** 3.8 L	**c.** 0.291 qt	**d.** 0.0029 lb
	e. 68 kg	**f.** 1.9 lb	**g.** 460 cm	**h.** 241 g

MasteringChemistry

Tutorial: Determining the Correct Dosage

Tutorial: Using Percentage as a Conversion Factor

Study Note

1. For setups that require a series of conversion factors, it is helpful to write out the unit plan first. Work from the given unit to the needed unit. Then use a conversion factor for each unit change.
   Given unit ⟶ unit (1) ⟶ unit (2) = needed unit
2. To convert from unit to another, select conversion factors that cancel the given unit and provide a unit or the needed unit for the problem. Several factors may be needed to arrive at the needed unit.

$$\text{\sout{Given unit}} \times \frac{\text{\sout{unit (1)}}}{\text{\sout{given unit}}} \times \frac{\text{unit (2)}}{\text{\sout{unit (1)}}} = \text{needed unit (2)}$$

◆ Learning Exercise 1.7C

Use conversion factors to solve the following problems:

a. A piece of plastic tubing measures 120 mm. What is the length of the tubing in inches?

b. A statue weighs 242 pounds. What is the mass of the statue in kilograms?

c. Your friend has a height of 6 feet 3 inches. What is your friend's height in meters?

d. In a triple-bypass surgery, a patient requires 3.00 pints of whole blood. How many mL of blood were given?

e. A doctor orders 0.450 g of a sulfa drug. On hand are 150-mg tablets. How many tablets are needed?

f. A mouthwash contains 22% alcohol by volume. How many milliliters of alcohol are in a 1.05-pt bottle of mouthwash?

g. An 18-karat gold bracelet has a mass of 2.0 oz. If 18-karat gold contains 75% pure gold, how many grams of pure gold are in the bracelet?

Answers	**a.** 4.7 in.	**b.** 110 kg	**c.** 1.9 m	**d.** 1420 mL
	e. 3 tablets	**f.** 110 mL	**g.** 43 g	

1.8 Density

- The density of a substance is a ratio of its mass to its volume, usually in units of g/mL or g/cm^3
- (1 mL is equal to 1 cm^3). For example, the density of sugar is 1.59 g/mL and silver is 10.5 g/mL.

$$\text{Density} = \frac{\text{mass of substance}}{\text{volume of substance}}$$

- Specific gravity (sp gr) is a unitless relationship of the density of a substance divided by the density of water, 1.00 g/mL. We can calculate the specific gravity of sugar as

$$\frac{1.59\ \cancel{\text{g/mL}}\ \text{(density of sugar)}}{1.00\ \cancel{\text{g/mL}}\ \text{(density of water)}} = 1.59\ \text{(sp gr of sugar)}$$

Guide to Calculating Density	
STEP 1	State the given and needed quantities.
STEP 2	Write the density expression.
STEP 3	Express mass in grams and volume in milliliters as g/mL.
STEP 4	Substitute mass and volume into density expression and solve.

Study Note

Density can be used as a factor to convert between the mass (g) and volume (mL) of a substance. The density of silver is 10.5 g/mL. What is the mass of 6.0 mL of silver?

$$6.0\ \cancel{\text{mL silver}} \times \underbrace{\frac{10.5\ \text{g silver}}{1\ \cancel{\text{mL silver}}}}_{\textit{Density factor}} = 63\ \text{g of silver}$$

What is the volume of 25 g of olive oil (D= 0.92 g/mL)?

$$25\ \cancel{\text{g olive oil}} \times \underbrace{\frac{1\ \text{mL olive oil}}{0.92\ \cancel{\text{g olive oil}}}}_{\textit{Density factor inverted}} = 27\ \text{mL of olive oil}$$

Guide to Using Density	
STEP 1	State the given and needed quantities.
STEP 2	Write a plan to calculate the needed quantity.
STEP 3	Write equalities and their conversion factors including density.
STEP 4	Set up problem to solve for the needed quantity.

◆ Learning Exercise 1.8

Calculate the density or specific gravity, or use density as a conversion factor to solve each of the following:

a. What is the density (g/mL) of glycerol if a 200.0 mL sample has a mass of 252 g?

b. A person with diabetes may produce 5 to 12 liters of urine per day. Calculate the specific gravity of a 100.0 mL urine sample that has a mass of 100.2 g.

c. A small solid has a mass of 5.5 oz. When placed in a graduated cylinder with the water level at 25.2 mL, the object causes the water level to rise to 43.8 mL. What is the density of the object in g/mL?

d. A sugar solution has a density of 1.20 g/mL. What is the mass, in grams, of 0.250 L of the solution?

e. A piece of pure gold weighs 0.26 pound. If gold has a density of 19.3 g/mL, what is the volume, in mL, of the piece of gold?

f. Diamond has a density of 3.52 g/mL. What is the specific gravity of diamond?

g. A salt solution has a specific gravity of 1.15 and a volume of 425 mL. What is the mass, in grams, of the solution?

h. A 50.0-g sample of a glucose solution has a density of 1.28 g/mL. What is the volume, in liters, of the sample?

Answers	**a.** 1.26 g/mL	**b.** 1.002	**c.** 8.4 g/mL	**d.** 300. g
	e. 6.1 mL	**f.** 3.52	**g.** 489 g	**h.** 0.0391 L

Checklist for Chapter 1

You are ready to take the *Practice Test* for Chapter 1. Be sure that you have accomplished the following learning goals for this chapter. If you are not sure, review the section listed at the end of the goal. Then apply your new skills and understanding to the Practice Test.

After studying Chapter 1, I can successfully:

____ Write the names and abbreviations for the metric (SI) units of measurement (1.1).

____ Write large or small numbers using scientific notation (1.2).

____ Identify a number as a measured number or an exact number (1.3).

____ Count the number of significant figures in measured numbers (1.3).

____ Report an answer with the correct number of significant figures (1.4).

____ Write a metric equality from the numerical values of metric prefixes (1.5).

____ Write two forms of a conversion factor for an equality (1.6).

____ Use conversion factors to change from one unit to another unit (1.7).

____ Calculate the density of a substance, or use the density to calculate the mass or volume (1.8).

Practice Test for Chapter 1

1. Which of the following is a metric measurement of volume?
A. kilogram **B.** kilowatt **C.** kiloliter **D.** kilometer **E.** kiloquart

2. The measurement 24 000 g written in scientific notation is:
A. 24 g **B.** 24×10^3 g **C.** 2.4×10^3 g **D.** 2.4×10^{-3} g **E.** 2.4×10^4 g

3. The measurement 0.005 m written in scientific notation is:
A. 5 m **B.** 5×10^{-3} m **C.** 5×10^{-2} m **D.** 0.5×10^{-4} m **E.** 5×10^3 m

4. The measured number in the following is:
A. 1 book **B.** 2 cars **C.** 4 flowers **D.** 5 rings **E.** 45 g

5. The number of significant figures in 105.4 m is:
A. 1 **B.** 2 **C.** 3 **D.** 4 **E.** 5

6. The number of significant figures in 0.00082 g is:
A. 1 **B.** 2 **C.** 3 **D.** 4 **E.** 5

7. The calculator answer 5.78052 rounded to two significant figures is:
A. 5 B. 5.7 C. 5.8 D. 5.78 E. 6.0

8. The calculator answer 3486.512 rounded to three significant figures is:
A. 4000 B. 3500 C. 349 D. 3487 E. 3490

9. The reported answer for the problem 16.0 ÷ 8.0 is:
A. 2 B. 2.0 C. 2.00 D. 0.2 E. 5.0

10. The reported answer for the problem 58.5 + 9.158 is:
A. 67 B. 67.6 C. 67.7 D. 67.66 E. 67.658

11. The reported answer for the problem $\dfrac{2.5 \times 3.12}{4.6}$ is:
A. 0.54 B. 7.8 C. 0.85 D. 1.7 E. 1.69

12. Which of these prefixes has the largest value?
A. centi B. deci C. kilo D. giga E. mega

13. What is the decimal equivalent of the prefix *centi*?
A. 0.001 B. 0.01 C. 0.1 D. 10 E. 100

14. Which of the following is the smallest unit of measurement?
A. gram B. milligram C. kilogram D. decigram E. centigram

15. Which volume is the largest?
A. mL B. dL C. cm^3 D. L E. kL

16. Which of the following is a conversion factor?
A. 12 in. B. 3 ft C. 20 ms D. $\dfrac{1000\,\text{g}}{1\,\text{kg}}$ E. 2 cm^3

17. Which is the correct conversion factor that relates milliliters and liters?
A. $\dfrac{1000\,\text{mL}}{1\,\text{L}}$ B. $\dfrac{100\,\text{mL}}{1\,\text{L}}$ C. $\dfrac{10\,\text{mL}}{1\,\text{L}}$ D. $\dfrac{0.01\,\text{mL}}{1\,\text{L}}$ E. $\dfrac{0.001\,\text{mL}}{1\,\text{L}}$

18. Which is the correct conversion factor that relates millimeters and centimeters?
A. $\dfrac{1\,\text{mm}}{1\,\text{cm}}$ B. $\dfrac{10\,\text{mm}}{1\,\text{cm}}$ C. $\dfrac{100\,\text{cm}}{1\,\text{mm}}$ D. $\dfrac{100\,\text{mm}}{1\,\text{cm}}$ E. $\dfrac{10\,\text{cm}}{1\,\text{mm}}$

19. The length of 294 mm is equal to:
A. 2940 m B. 29.4 m C. 2.94 m D. 0.294 m E. 0.0294 m

20. The handle on a tennis racket measures 4.5 inches. What is that size in centimeters?
A. 11 cm B. 1.8 cm C. 0.56 cm D. 450 cm E. 15 cm

21. What is the volume of 65 mL in liters?
A. 650 L B. 65 L C. 6.5 L D. 0.65 L E. 0.065 L

22. What is the mass, in kg, of a 22-lb turkey?
A. 10. kg B. 48 kg C. 10 000 kg D. 0.048 kg E. 22,000 kg

23. The number of milliliters in 2 deciliters is:
A. 20 mL B. 200 mL C. 2000 mL D. 20 000 mL E. 500 000 mL

24. A person who is 5 feet 4 inches tall would be:
A. 64 m **B.** 25 m **C.** 14 m **D.** 1.6 m **E.** 1.3 m

25. How many oz are in 1500 g? (1 lb = 16 oz)
A. 94 oz **B.** 53 oz **C.** 24 000 oz **D.** 33 oz **E.** 3.3 oz

26. How many quarts of orange juice are in 255 mL of juice?
A. 0.255 qt **B.** 270 qt **C.** 236 qt **D.** 0.270 qt **E.** 0.400 qt

27. An order for a patient calls for 0.020 g of medication. On hand are 4-mg tablets. How many tablets are needed for the patient?
A. 2 tablets **B.** 4 tablets **C.** 5 tablets **D.** 8 tablets **E.** 200 tablets

28. A doctor orders 1500 mg of a sulfa drug. Tablets in stock are 0.500 g. How many tablets are needed?
A. 1 tablet **B.** 1½ tablets **C.** ⅓ tablet **D.** 2½ tablets **E.** 3 tablets

29. What is the density of a bone with a mass of 192 g and a volume of 120 cm^3?
A. 0.63 g/mL **B.** 1.4 g/cm^3 **C.** 1.6 g/cm^3 **D.** 1.9 g/cm^3 **E.** 2.8 g/cm^3

30. How many milliliters of a salt solution with a density of 1.8 g/mL are needed to provide 400 g of salt solution?
A. 220 mL **B.** 22 mL **C.** 720 mL **D.** 400 mL **E.** 4.5 mL

31. The density of a solution is 0.85 g/mL. Its specific gravity is:
A. 222 mL **B.** 8.5 **C.** 0.85 mL **D.** 1.2 **E.** 0.85

32. Three liquids have densities of 1.15 g/mL, 0.79 g/mL and 0.95 g/mL. When the liquids, which do not mix, are poured into a graduated cylinder, the liquid at the top is the one with a density of
A. 1.15 g/mL **B.** 1.00 g/mL **C.** 0.95 g/mL **D.** 0.79 g/mL **E.** 0.16 g/mL

33. A sample of oil has a mass of 65 g and a volume of 80. mL. What is the specific gravity of the oil?
A. 1.5 **B.** 1.4 **C.** 1.2 **D.** 0.90 **E.** 0.81

34. What is the mass of a 10.0 mL sample of urine with a specific gravity of 1.04?
A. 104 g **B.** 10.4 g **C.** 1.04 g **D.** 1.40 g **E.** 9.62 g

35. Ethyl alcohol has a density of 0.790 g/mL. What is the mass of 0.250 L of the alcohol?
A. 198 g **B.** 158 g **C.** 3.95 g **D.** 0.253 g **E.** 0.160 g

Answers to the Practice Test

1. C	**2.** E	**3.** B	**4.** E	**5.** D
6. B	**7.** C	**8.** E	**9.** B	**10.** C
11. D	**12.** D	**13.** B	**14.** B	**15.** E
16. D	**17.** A	**18.** B	**19.** D	**20.** A
21. E	**22.** A	**23.** B	**24.** D	**25.** B
26. D	**27.** C	**28.** E	**29.** C	**30.** A
31. E	**32.** D	**33.** E	**34.** B	**35.** A

2
Energy and Matter

Study Goals

- Describe potential and kinetic energy.
- Calculate temperatures values in degrees Celsius, degrees Fahrenheit, and kelvins.
- Calculate the calories lost or gained by a specific amount of a substance for a specific temperature change.
- Determine the kilocalories for food samples.
- Classify matter as a pure substance or a mixture.
- Classify a pure substance as an element or a compound.
- Identify the states of matter.
- Describe the types of forces that hold particles together in liquids and solids.
- Determine the energy lost or gained during a change of state at the melting or boiling point.
- Identify the states of matter and changes of state on a heating or cooling curve.

Think About It

1. What kinds of activities did you do today that used *kinetic* energy?
2. Why is the energy in your breakfast cereal *potential* energy?
3. Why is the high specific heat of water important to our survival?
4. How does perspiring during a workout help to keep you cool?

Key Terms

Match the following terms with the statements below:

a. change of state	**b.** kinetic energy	**c.** potential energy
d. calorie	**e.** kilojoule	**f.** matter

1. ____ the amount of heat needed to raise the temperature of 1 g of water by 1 °C

2. ____ water boiling at 100 °C

3. ____ the energy of motion

4. ____ stored energy

5. ____ anything that has mass and occupies space

6. ____ the amount of energy equal to 1000 joules

Answers	**1.** d	**2.** a	**3.** b
	4. c	**5.** f	**6.** e

2.1 Energy

- Energy is the ability to do work.
- Potential energy is stored energy; kinetic energy is the energy of motion.
- The SI unit of energy is the joule (J).

◆ Learning Exercise 2.1A

State whether the following statements describe potential (P) or kinetic (K) energy:

1. ____ a potted plant sitting on a ledge
2. ____ breakfast cereal in a bowl
3. ____ logs sitting in a fireplace
4. ____ a piece of candy
5. ____ an arrow shot from a bow
6. ____ a ski jumper at the top of the ski jump
7. ____ a jogger running
8. ____ a sky diver waiting to jump
9. ____ water flowing down a stream
10. ____ a bowling ball striking the pins

Answers **1.** P **2.** P **3.** P **4.** P **5.** K
6. P **7.** K **8.** P **9.** K **10.** K

> ***MasteringChemistry***
>
> **Tutorial: Elements and Symbols in the Periodic Table**
>
> **Tutorial: Energy Conversions**

◆ Learning Exercise 2.1B

Match the words in column A with the descriptions in column B.

A	B
1. ____ calorie	**a.** 1000 calories.
2. ____ joule	**b.** the SI unit of heat
3. ____ kilocalorie	**c.** a unit of heat equal to 4.184 J

Answers **1.** c **2.** b **3.** a

◆ Learning Exercise 2.1C

Make the following conversions:

a. 58 000 cal to kcal

b. 450 J to cal

c. 2.8 kJ to cal

d. 15 200 cal to kJ

Answers **a.** 58 kcal **b.** 825 cal **c.** 670 cal **d.** 63.6 kJ

2.2 Temperature

- In the sciences, temperature is measured in Celsius degrees, °C, or kelvins, K.
- In the United States, the Fahrenheit scale, °F or T_F, is still in use.
- The equation $T_F = 1.8(T_C) + 32$ is used to convert a Celsius temperature to a Fahrenheit temperature. When the equation is rearranged for T_C, it used to convert from T_F to T_C.

$$T_C = \frac{(T_F - 32)}{1.8}$$

- The temperature on the Celsius scale is related to the kelvin scale: $T_K = T_C + 273$.

◆ Learning Exercise 2.2

Calculate the temperatures in the following problems:

a. To prepare yogurt, milk is warmed to 68 °C. What Fahrenheit temperature is needed to prepare the yogurt?

b. On a cold day in Alaska, the temperature drops to −12 °C. What is that temperature on a Fahrenheit thermometer?

c. A patient has a temperature of 39.5 °C. What is that temperature in °F?

d. On a hot summer day, the temperature is 95 °F. What is the temperature on the Celsius scale?

e. A pizza is cooked at a temperature of 425 °F. What is the °C temperature?

f. A research experiment requires the use of liquid nitrogen to cool the reaction flask to –45 °C. What temperature will this be on the Kelvin scale?

Answers **a.** 154 °F **b.** 10 °F **c.** 103.1 °F **d.** 35 °C **e.** 218 °C **f.** 228 K

2.3 Specific Heat

- Specific heat is the amount of energy required to raise the temperature of 1 g of a substance by 1 °C.
- The specific heat for liquid water is 1.00 calorie/g °C or 4.184 joules/g °C.

Study Note

The heat lost or gained by a substance is calculated from the mass, temperature change, and specific heat of the substance.

Heat (calories) = **mass** (g) × **temperature change** (ΔT) × **specific heat** (cal/g °C)

There are 4.184 joules in one calorie. The conversion factors for heat are:

$$\frac{4.184\text{ J}}{1\text{ cal}} \text{ and } \frac{1\text{ cal}}{4.184\text{ J}}$$

MasteringChemistry

Tutorial: Heat

Tutorial: Specific Heat Calculations

Guide to Calculations Using Specific Heat	
STEP 1	List the given and the needed data.
STEP 2	Calculate temperature change.
STEP 3	Write the equation for heat. Heat = mass x ΔT x SH and rearrange for the unknown.
STEP 4	Substitute given values and solve, making sure units cancel.

◆ Learning Exercise 2.3A

Calculate the specific heat for each of the following:

a. A 15.2 g sample of a metal that absorbs 231 J when its temperature rises from 84.5 °C to 125.3 °C.

b. A 31.8 g sample of a metal that absorbs 816 J when its temperature rises from 23.7 °C to 56.2 °C.

c. A 38.2 g sample of a metal that absorbs 125 J when its temperature rises from 62.1 °C to 68.4 °C.

Answers **a.** 0.372 J/g °C **b.** 0.790 J/g °C **c.** 0.52 J/g °C

◆ Learning Exercise 2.3B

Calculate the joules (J) and calories (cal) gained or released during the following:

1. heating 20 g of water from 22 °C to 77 °C

2. heating 18 g of water from 12 °C to 97 °C

3. cooling 4.00 kg of water from 80.0 °C to 35.0 °C

4. cooling 125 g of water from 45.0 °C to 72.0 °C

Answers
1. 4600 J; 1100 cal
2. 6400 J; 1500 cal
3. 753 000; 180 000 cal
4. 14 100 J; 3380 cal

◆ Learning Exercise 2.3C

Study Note

The mass of a substance is calculated by rearranging the following heat equation:

$$\text{Heat (joules)} = \textbf{Mass} \text{ (g)} \times \text{temperature change } (\Delta T) \times \text{specific heat (J/g °C)}$$

$$\textbf{Mass(g)} = \frac{\text{Heat (joules)}}{\Delta T \times SH(\text{J}/g\,°\text{C})}$$

a. Copper has a specific heat of 0.386 J/g °C. When 1250 J are added to a copper sample, its temperature rises from 24.6 °C to 61.3 °C. What is the mass of the copper sample?

b. A sample of aluminum has a specific heat of 0.897 J/g °C. When 785 J are added to an aluminum sample, its temperature rises from 14 °C to 106 °C. What is the mass of the aluminum sample?

Answers **a.** 88.2 g of copper **b.** 9.5 g of aluminum

2.4 Energy and Nutrition

- A nutritional Calorie is the same amount of energy as 1 kcal or 1000 calories.
- When a substance is burned in a calorimeter, the water that surrounds the reaction chamber absorbs the heat given off. The calories absorbed by the water are calculated and the caloric value (energy per gram) is determined for the substance.

MasteringChemistry

Tutorial: Nutritional Energy

Case Study: Calories from Hidden Sugar

◆ Learning Exercise 2.4A

State the caloric value, in kcal/g and kJ/g, associated with each of the following:

a. lard ____________ **b.** protein ____________

c. sugar ____________ **d.** sucrose ____________

e. oil ____________ **f.** fat ____________

g. starch ____________ **h.** glucose ____________

Answers **a.** 9 kcal/g; 38 kJ/g **b.** 4 kcal/g; 17 kJ/g
c. 4 kcal/g; 17 kJ/g **d.** 4 kcal/g; 17 kJ/g
e. 9 kcal/g; 38 kJ/g **f.** 9 kcal/g; 38 kJ/g
g. 4 kcal/g; 17 kJ/g **h.** 4 kcal/g; 17 kJ/g

Study Note

The caloric content of a food is the sum of calories from carbohydrate, fat, and protein. It is calculated by using their number of grams in a food and the caloric values of 4 kcal/g (17 kJ/g) for carbohydrate and protein, and 9 kcal/g (38 kJ/g) for fat.

◆ Learning Exercise 2.4B

Calculate the kilojoules (kJ) and the kilocalories (kcal) for each of the following foods (round the final answer to the tens place):

Food	Carbohydrate	Fat	Protein	kJ	kcal
a. Peas, green, cooked	19 g	1 g	9 g	_____	_____
b. Potato chips, 10 chips	10 g	8 g	1 g	_____	_____
c. Cream cheese, 8 oz	5 g	86 g	18 g	_____	_____
d. Hamburger, lean, 3 oz	0	10 g	23 g	_____	_____
e. Salmon, canned	0	5 g	17 g	_____	_____
f. Banana, 1	26 g	0	1 g	_____	_____

Answers **a.** 510 kJ; 120 kcal **b.** 490 kJ; 120 kcal **c.** 3700 kJ; 870 kcal
d. 770 kJ; 180 kcal **e.** 480 kJ; 110 kcal **f.** 460 kJ; 110 kcal

◆ Learning Exercise 2.4 C

Use caloric values to solve each of the following:

1. How many kcal are in a single serving of pudding that contains 5 g of protein, 31 g of carbohydrate, and 5 g of fat (round kcal to the tens place)?

2. One serving of peanut butter (2 tbsp) has a caloric value of 190 kcal. If there are 8 g of protein and 10 g of carbohydrate, how many grams of fat are contained in one serving of peanut butter (round kcal to the tens)?

3. A serving of breakfast cereal provides 220 kcal. In this serving, there are 8 g of protein and 6 g of fat. How many grams of carbohydrates are in the cereal (round kcal to the tens)?

4. Complete the following table listing ingredients for a peanut butter sandwich (tbsp = tablespoon; tsp = teaspoon) (round kcal to the tens place):

	Protein	**Carbohydrate**	**Fat**	**kcal**
2 slices of bread	5 g	30 g	0 g	____
2 tbsp of peanut butter	8 g	10 g	13 g	____
2 tsp of jelly	0 g	10 g	0 g	____
1 tsp of margarine	0 g	0 g	7 g	____
			Total kcal in sandwich	____

Answers

1. protein = 20 kcal; carbohydrate = 120 kcal; fat = 50 kcal; total = 190 kcal
2. protein = 30 kcal; carbohydrate = 40 kcal; then 190 kcal – 30 kcal – 40 kcal = 120 kcal of fat; converting 120 kcal of fat to g of fat: 120 kcal fat (1g fat/9 kcal fat) = 13 g of fat
3. protein = 30 kcal; fat = 50 kcal = 80 kcal from protein and fat; 220 kcal – 80 kcal = 140 kcal due to carbohydrate; 140 kcal(1 g carbohydrate/4 kcal) = 35 g of carbohydrate
4. bread = 140 kcal; peanut butter = 190 kcal; jelly = 40 kcal; margarine = 60 kcal; total kcal in sandwich = 430 kcal (4.3×10^2 kcal)

2.5 Classification of Matter

- Matter is anything that has mass and occupies space.
- A pure substance, element or compound, has a definite composition.
- Elements are the simplest type of matter; compounds consist of a combination of two or more elements.
- Mixtures contain two or more substances that are physically, not chemically, combined.
- Mixtures are classified as homogeneous or heterogeneous.

MasteringChemistry

Tutorial: Classification of Matter

◆ Learning Exercise 2.5A

Identify each of the following as an element (E) or compound (C):

1. _____ iron **2.** _____ carbon dioxide

3. _____ potassium iodide **4.** _____ gold

5. _____ aluminum **6.** _____ table salt (sodium chloride)

Answers **1.** E **2.** C **3.** C
4. E **5.** E **6.** C

◆ Learning Exercise 2.5B

Identify each of the following as a pure substance (P) or mixture (M):

1._____ bananas and milk **2.** _____ sulfur

3._____ silver **4.** _____ a bag of raisins and nuts

5._____ water **6.** _____ sand and water

Answers **1.** M **2.** P **3.** P **4.** M
5. P **6.** M

◆ Learning Exercise 2.5C

Identify each of the following mixtures as homogeneous (Ho) or heterogeneous (He):

1._____ chocolate milk **2.** _____ sand and water

3._____ lemonade **4.** _____ a bag of raisins and nuts

5._____ air **6.** _____ vinegar

Answers **1.** Ho **2.** He **3.** Ho **4.** He
5. Ho **6.** Ho

2.6 States and Properties of Matter

- The states of matter are solid, liquid, and gas.
- Physical properties are those characteristics of a substance that can change without affecting the identity of the substance.
- A substance undergoes a physical change when its shape, size, or state changes, but the type of substance itself does not change.
- Chemical properties are those characteristics of a substance that change when a new substance is produced.
- A chemical change occurs when the atoms of the initial substances rearrange to form new substances.

MasteringChemistry
Tutorial: Heat, Energy, and Changes of State

◆ Learning Exercise 2.6A

State whether the following statements describe a gas (G), a liquid (L), or a solid (S):

1. _____ There are no attractions among the molecules.
2. _____ Particles are held close together in a definite pattern.
3. _____ The substance has a definite volume, but no definite shape.
4. _____ The particles are moving extremely fast.
5. _____ This substance has no definite shape and no definite volume.
6. _____ The particles are very far apart.
7. _____ This material has its own volume, but takes the shape of its container.
8. _____ The particles of this material bombard the sides of the container with great force.
9. _____ The particles in this substance are moving very, very slowly.
10. _____ This substance has a definite volume and a definite shape.

Answers	**1.** G	**2.** S	**3.** L	**4.** G	**5.** G
	6. G	**7.** L	**8.** G	**9.** S	**10.** S

◆ Learning Exercise 2.6B

Classify each of the following as a physical (P) or chemical (C) property:

a. ______ Silver is shiny. **b.** ______ Water fills a glass.
c. ______ Wood burns. **d.** ______ Mercury is a very dense liquid.
e. ______ Helium is not reactive. **f.** ______ Ice cubes float in water.

Answers	**a.** P	**b.** P	**c.** C	**d.** P
	e. C	**f.** P		

◆ Learning Exercise 2.6C

Classify each of the following as a physical (P) or chemical change (C):

a. ______ Sodium melts at 98 °C.

b. ______ Iron forms rust in air and water.

c. ______ Water condenses on a cold window.

d. ______ Fireworks explode when ignited.

e. ______ Gasoline burns in a car engine.

f. ______ Paper is cut to make confetti.

Answers **a.** P **b.** C **c.** P **d.** C **e.** C **f.** P

◆ Learning Exercise 2.6D

Identify each of the following as a physical (P) or a chemical (C) change:

1. ______ tearing a piece of paper
2. ______ burning paper
3. ______ rusting iron
4. ______ digesting of food
5. ______ dissolving salt in water
6. ______ boiling water
7. ______ chewing gum
8. ______ removing tarnish with silver polish

Answers **1.** P **2.** C **3.** C **4.** C **5.** P **6.** P **7.** P **8.** C

2.7 Changes of State

- When a substance is changing state (melting or freezing, boiling or condensing, subliming or depositing), the temperature remains constant.
- A substance melts/freezes at its melting (freezing) point; boils (condenses) at its boiling point.
- The *heat of fusion* is the heat energy required to change 1 g of solid to liquid. For water to freeze at 0 °C, the heat of fusion is 80. cal (334 J). This is also the amount of heat lost when 1 g of water freezes at 0 °C.
- When water boils at 100 °C, 540 cal (2260 J), the *heat of vaporization* is required to change 1 g of liquid to gas (steam); it is also the amount of heat released when 1 g of water vapor condenses at 100 °C.
- A heating or cooling curve illustrates the changes in temperature and state as heat is added to or removed from a substance.

◆ Learning Exercise 2.7A

Identify each of the following as

1. melting **2.** freezing **3.** sublimation

a. _____ A liquid changes to a solid.

b. _____ Ice forms on the surface of a lake in winter.

c. _____ Dry ice in an ice cream cart changes to a gas.

d. _____ Butter in a hot pan turns to liquid.

Answers **a.** 2 **b.** 2 **c.** 3 **d.** 1

Study Note
The amount of heat needed or released during melting or freezing can be calculated using the heat of fusion: Heat (cal) = mass (g) × heat of fusion

Guide to Calculations Using Heat of Fusion/Vaporization	
STEP 1	List grams of substance change of state.
STEP 2	Write the plan to convert grams to heat and desired unit.
STEP 3	Write the heat conversion factor and metric unit, if needed.
STEP 4	Set up the problem with factors.

◆ Learning Exercise 2.7B

Calculate the energy required or released when the following substances melt or freeze:

a. How many calories are needed to melt 15 g of ice at 0 °C?

b. How much heat, in kilojoules, is released when 325 g of water freezes at 0 °C?

c. How many grams of ice would melt when 4 000 calories of heat were absorbed?

Answers **a.** 1200 cal **b.** 109 kJ **c.** 50 g

◆ Learning Exercise 2.7C

Calculate the energy required or released for the following substances undergoing boiling or condensation:

a. How many calories are needed to completely change 10 g of water to vapor at 100 °C?

b. How many kilojoules are released when 515 g of steam at 100 °C condense to form liquid water at 100 °C?

c. How many grams of water can be converted to steam at 100 °C when 155 kJ of energy is absorbed?

Answers **a.** 5400 cal **b.** 1160 kJ **c.** 68.6 g

◆ Learning Exercise 2.7D

On each heating or cooling curve, indicate the portion that corresponds to a solid, liquid, or gas, and the changes in state.

1. Draw a heating curve for water that begins at –20 °C and ends at 120 °C. Water has a melting point of 0 °C and a boiling point of 100 °C.

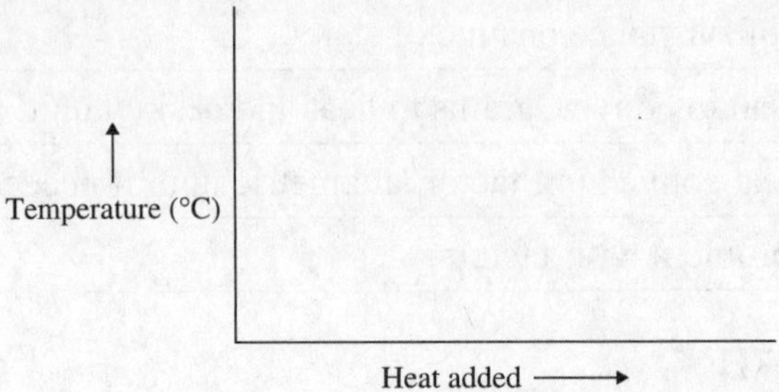

2. Draw a heating curve for bromine from –25 °C to 75 °C. Bromine has a melting point of –7 °C and a boiling point of 59 °C.

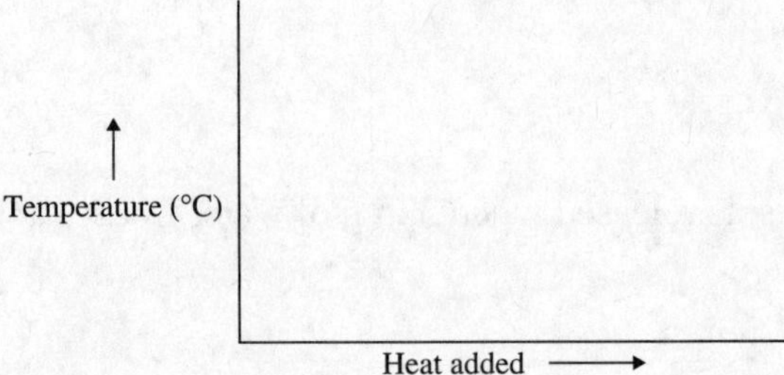

3. Draw a cooling curve for sodium from 1000 °C to 0 °C. Sodium has a freezing point of 98 °C and a boiling (condensation) point of 883 °C.

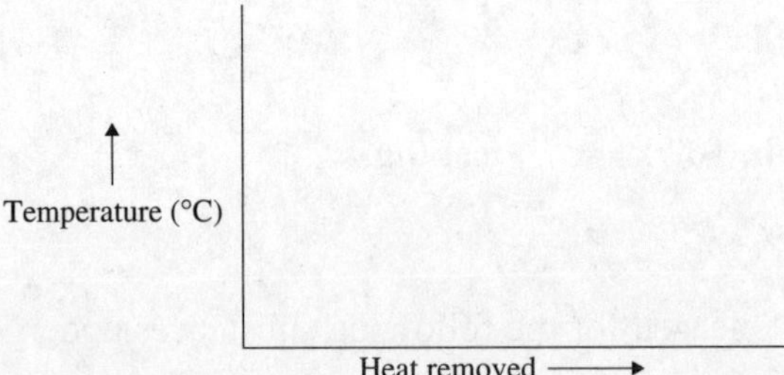

Answers

1.

120
100
Temperature (°C)
0
–20
Gas
Boils
Liquid
Melts
Solid
Heat added

2.

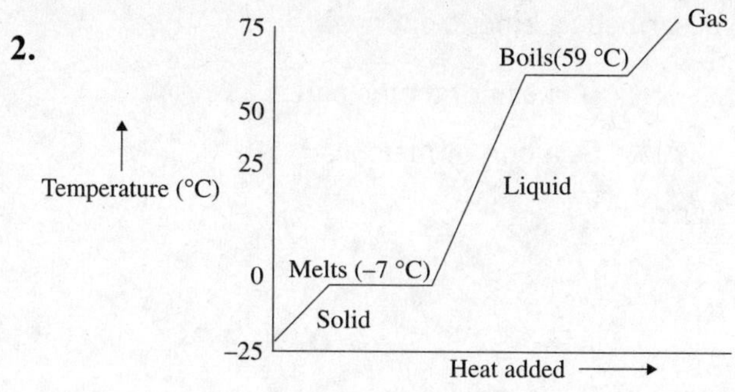

3.

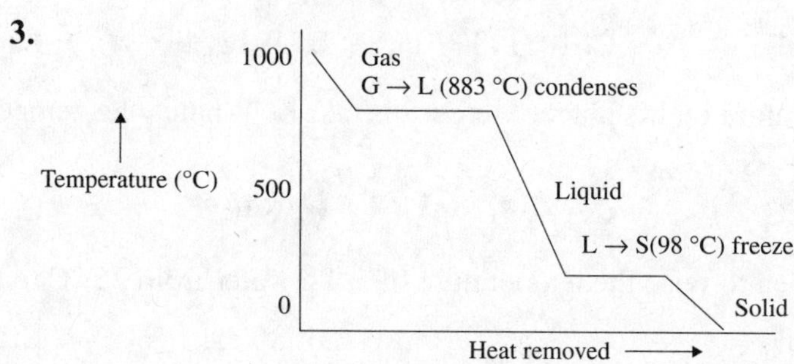

Checklist for Chapter 2

You are ready to take the *Practice Test* for Chapter 2. Be sure that you have accomplished the following learning goals for this chapter. If you are not sure, review the section listed at the end of the goal. Then apply your new skills and understanding to the Practice Test.

After studying Chapter 2, I can successfully:

____ Describe kinetic and potential energy (2.1).

____ Given a temperature, calculate a corresponding temperature on a different scale (2.2).

____ Given the mass of a sample, specific heats, and the temperature change, calculate the heat lost or gained (2.3).

____ Using the caloric values, calculate the kilocalories or kilojoules for a food sample (2.4).

____ Classify pure substances as elements or compounds (2.5).

____ Identify mixtures as heterogeneous or homogeneous (2.5).

____ Identify the physical state of a substance as a solid, liquid, or gas (2.6).

____ Identify a change in properties as a physical change or chemical change (2.6).

____ Calculate the heat change for the melting or boiling of a specific amount of a substance (2.7).

____ Draw heating and cooling curves using the melting and boiling points of a substance (2.7).

Practice Test for Chapter 2

1. Which of the following would be described as potential energy?

A. a car going around a racetrack **B.** a rabbit hopping
C. oil in an oil well **D.** a moving merry-go-round
E. a bouncing ball

2. Which of the following would be described as kinetic energy?

A. a car battery
B. a can of tennis balls
C. gasoline in a car fuel tank
D. a box of matches
E. a tennis ball crossing over the net

3. 105 °F = ____ °C

A. 73 °C **B.** 41 °C **C.** 58 °C **D.** 90 °C **E.** 189 °C

4. The melting point of gold is 1064 °C. The Fahrenheit temperature needed to melt gold is:

A. 129 °C **B.** 623 °F **C.** 1031 °F **D.** 1913 °F **E.** 1947 °F

5. The average daytime temperature on the planet Mercury is 683 K. What is this temperature on the Celsius scale?

A. 956 °C **B.** 715 °C **C.** 680 °C **D.** 410. °C **E.** 303 °C

6. The number of calories needed to raise the temperature of 5.0 g water from 25 °C to 55 °C is:

A. 5 cal **B.** 30 cal **C.** 5 cal **D.** 80 cal **E.** 150 cal

7. The number of kilocalories (kcal) released when 150 g of water cools from 58 °C to 22 °C is:

A. 1.1 kcal **B.** 4.2 kcal **C.** 5.4 kcal **D.** 6.9 kcal **E.** 8.7 kcal

For questions 8 through 10, consider a cup of milk that contains 2 g of fat, 12 g of carbohydrate, and 9 g of protein. (Round to the tens place.)

8. The number of kcal provided by the carbohydrate is:

A. 4 kcal **B.** 20 kcal **C.** 40 kcal **D.** 50 kcal **E.** 80 kcal

9. The number of kcal provided by the fat is:

A. 4 kcal **B.** 20 kcal **C.** 40 kcal **D.** 50 kcal **E.** 80 kcal

10. The number of kilojoules provided by the protein is:

A. 20 kJ **B.** 80 kJ **C.** 150 kJ **D.** 200 kJ **E.** 320 kJ

For questions 11 through 14, classify each of the following as a pure substance (P) or a mixture (M):

11. toothpaste _____
12. platinum _____
13. chromium _____
14. mouthwash _____

For questions 15 through 18, classify each of the following mixtures as homogeneous (Ho) or heterogeneous (He):

15. noodle soup _____
16. mineral water _____
17. chocolate chip cookie _____
18. mouthwash _____

19. Which of the following is a chemical property?

A. dynamite explodes
B. a shiny metal
C. a melting point of 110 °C
D. rain on a cool day
E. breaking up cement

20. Which of the following is a chemical property of silver?

A. density of 10.5 g/mL **B.** shiny **C.** melts at 961 °C

D. good conductor of heat **E.** reacts to form tarnish

21. Which of the following is a physical property of silicon?

A. burns in chlorine **B.** has a black to gray color

C. reacts with nitric acid **D.** reacts with oxygen to form sand

E. used to form silicone

For questions 22 through 26, classify each of the following as a physical (P) or chemical change (C):

22. ____ butter melts in a hot pan

23. ____ iron forms rust with oxygen

24. ____ baking powder forms bubbles (CO_2) during baking of a cake

25. ____ water boils

26. ____ propane burns in a camp stove

27. Which of the following describes a liquid?

A. a substance that has no definite shape and no definite volume

B. a substance with particles that are far apart

C. a substance with a definite shape and a definite volume

D. a substance containing particles that are moving very fast

E. a substance that has a definite volume, but takes the shape of its container

For questions 28 through 31, match the terms A to D with each of the definitions that follows:

A. evaporation **B.** heat of fusion

C. heat of vaporization **D.** boiling

28. the energy required to convert a gram of solid to liquid _____

29. the heat needed to boil a liquid _____

30. the conversion of liquid molecules to gas at the surface of a liquid _____

31. the formation of a gas within the liquid as well as on the surface _____

32. Ice cools down a drink because

A. the ice is colder than the drink and heat flows into the ice cubes

B. heat is absorbed from the drink to melt the ice cubes

C. the heat of fusion of the ice is higher than the heat of fusion for water

D. both A and B

E. None of the above

33. The number of kilocalories needed to convert 75 g of ice to liquid at 0 °C is

A. 1.0 kcal **B.** 3.0 kcal**C.** 4.0 kcal

D. 6.0 kcal **E.** 80. kcal

For questions 34 through 37, consider the heating curve below for p-toluidine. Answer the following questions when heat is added to p-toluidine at 20 °C where toluidine is below its melting point.

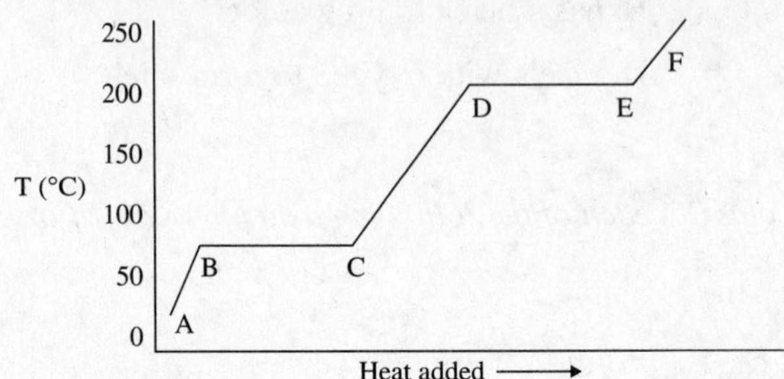

34. On the heating curve, segment BC indicates

A. solid **B.** melting **C.** liquid **D.** boiling **E.** gas

35. On the heating curve, segment CD shows toluidine as

A. solid **B.** melting **C.** liquid **D.** boiling **E.** gas

36. The boiling point of toluidine would be

A. 20 °C **B.** 45 °C **C.** 100 °C **D.** 200 °C **E.** 250 °C

37. On the heating curve, segment EF shows toluidine as

A. solid **B.** melting **C.** liquid **D.** boiling **E.** gas

Answers to the Practice Test

1. C	**2.** E	**3.** B	**4.** E	**5.** D
6. E	**7.** C	**8.** D	**9.** B	**10.** C
11. M	**12.** P	**13.** P	**14.** M	**15.** He
16. Ho	**17.** He	**18.** Ho	**19.** A	**20.** E
21. B	**22.** P	**23.** C	**24.** C	**25.** P
26. C	**27.** E	**28.** B	**29.** C	**30.** A
31. D	**32.** D	**33.** D	**34.** B	**35.** C
36. D	**37.** E			

3
Atoms and Elements

Study Goals

- Given the name of an element, write its correct symbol; from the symbol, write the name.
- Use the periodic table to identify the group and the period of an element and decide whether it is a metal, nonmetal, or metalloid.
- Describe the electrical charge and location in an atom for a proton, a neutron, and an electron.
- Describe the electrical charge and location in an atom for a proton, a neutron, and an electron.
- Describe Rutherford's gold-foil experiment and how it led to the current model of the atom.
- Use the periodic table to write orbital diagrams and electron configurations.
- Use the electron configurations of elements to explain periodic trends.

Think About It

1. Name some of the elements you have seen today.

2. How are the symbols of the elements related to their names?

3. What are some elements that are part of your vitamins?

4. On a dry day, you walk across a carpet and touch a doorknob. You feel a spark. What happened?

Key Terms

Match each the following key terms with the correct definition:

a. element **b.** atom **c.** atomic number
d. mass number **e.** isotope

1. _____ the number of protons and neutrons in the nucleus of an atom

2. _____ the smallest particle of an element

3. _____ a primary substance that cannot be broken down into simpler substances

4. _____ an atom that has a different number of neutrons than another atom of the same element

5. _____ the number of protons in an atom

Answers **1.** d **2.** b **3.** a **4.** e **5.** c

3.1 Elements and Symbols

- Elements are the primary substances of matter.
- Chemical symbols are one- or two-letter abbreviations for the names of the elements.

MasteringChemistry

Tutorial: Elements and Symbols in the Periodic Table

Study Note

Now is the time to learn the names of the elements and their symbols. Practice saying and writing the names of the elements on the periodic table with atomic numbers 1-54 and Cs, Ba, Hg, Au, and Pb. Cover the symbols in the lists of elements and practice writing the symbols for the elemental names.

◆ Learning Exercise 3.1A

Write the symbol for each of the following elements:

1. carbon _______ **2.** iron _______ **3.** sodium _______

4. phosphorus _______ **5.** oxygen _______ **6.** nitrogen _______

7. iodine _______ **8.** sulfur _______ **9.** potassium _______

10. lead _______ **11.** calcium _______ **12.** gold _______

13. copper _______ **14.** neon _______ **15.** chlorine _______

Answers

1. C **2.** Fe **3.** Na **4.** P **5.** O
6. N **7.** I **8.** S **9.** K **10.** Pb
11. Ca **12.** Au **13.** Cu **14.** Ne **15.** Cl

◆ Learning Exercise 3.1B

Write the name of the element represented by each of the following symbols:

1. Mg _______________ **2.** K _______________

3. Au _______________ **4.** F _______________

5. Cu _______________ **6.** Be _______________

7. Ag _______________ **8.** Br _______________

9. Zn _______________ **10.** Al _______________

11. Ba _______________ **12.** Li _______________

Answers

1. magnesium **2.** potassium **3.** gold
4. fluorine **5.** copper **6.** beryllium
7. silver **8.** bromine **9.** zinc
10. aluminum **11.** barium **12.** lithium

3.2 The Periodic Table

- The periodic table is an arrangement of the elements by increasing atomic number.
- Each vertical column contains a *group* of elements that have similar properties.
- A horizontal row of elements is called a *period.*
- On the periodic table, the *metals* are located on the left of the heavy zigzag line, the *nonmetals* are to the right, and metalloids are next to the zigzag line.
- Main group or representative elements are: 1A, 2A (1 and 2) and 3A to 8A (13 to 18). Transition elements are B-group elements (3–12).

Study Note

1. The periodic table consists of horizontal rows called *periods* and vertical columns called *groups.*
2. Elements in Group 1A (1) are the *alkali metals.* Elements in Group 2A (2) are the *alkaline earth metals*, and Group 7A (17) contains the *halogens.* Elements in Group 8A (18) are the *noble gases.*

◆ Learning Exercise 3.2A

Indicate whether each of the following elements is in a group (G), period (P), or neither (N):

a. Li, C, and O ________ **b.** Br, Cl, and F ________

c. Al, Si, and Cl ________ **d.** C, N, and O ________

e. Mg, Ca, and Ba ________ **f.** C, S and Br ________

g. Li, Na and K ________ **h.** K, Ca and Br ________

Answers **a.** P **b.** G **c.** P **d.** P
e. G **f.** N **g.** G **h.** P

◆ Learning Exercise 3.2B

Complete the list of elements, group numbers, and period numbers in the following table:

Element and Symbol	Group Number	Period Number
	2A (2)	3
Silicon, Si		
	5A (15)	2
Aluminum, Al		
	4A (14)	5
	1A (1)	6

Answers

Element and Symbol	Group Number	Period Number
Magnesium, Mg	2A (2)	3
Silicon, Si	4A (14)	3
Nitrogen, N	5A (15)	2
Aluminum, Al	3A (13)	3
Tin, Sn	4A (14)	5
Cesium, Cs	1A (1)	6

◆ Learning Exercise 3.2C

Identify each of the following elements as a metal (M), nonmetal (NM), or metalloid (ML):

1. Cl _____ **2.** N _____ **3.** Fe _____ **4.** K _____ **5.** Sb _____

6. C _____ **7.** Ca _____ **8.** Ge _____ **9.** Ag _____ **10.** Mg _____

Answers	**1.** NM	**2.** NM	**3.** M	**4.** M	**5.** ML
	6. NM	**7.** M	**8.** ML	**9.** M	**10.** M

◆ Learning Exercise 3.2D

Match the names of the chemical groups with the elements, K, Cl, He, Fe, Mg, Ne, Li, Cu, and Br.

1. halogens ____________

2. noble gases ____________

3. alkali metals ____________

4. alkaline earth metals ____________

5. transition elements ____________

Answers	**1.** Cl, Br	**2.** He, Ne	**3.** K, Li
	4. Mg	**5.** Fe, Cu	

3.3 The Atom

- An atom is the smallest particle that retains the characteristics of an element.
- Atoms are composed of three types of subatomic particles. Protons have a positive charge (+), electrons carry a negative charge (–), and neutrons are electrically neutral.
- The protons and neutrons, each with a mass of about 1 amu, are found in the tiny, dense nucleus. The electrons are located outside the nucleus.

MasteringChemistry
Tutorial: The Anatomy of Atoms

◆ Learning Exercise 3.3A

True (T) or false (F): Each of the following statements is consistent with atomic theory:

1. All matter is composed of atoms. _______

2. All atoms of an element are identical. _______

3. Atoms combine to form compounds. _______

4. Most of the mass of the atom is in the nucleus. _______

Answers **1.** T **2.** F **3.** T **4.** T

◆ Learning Exercise 3.3B

Match the following terms with the correct statements:

a. proton **b.** neutron **c.** electron **d.** nucleus

1. ____ found in the nucleus of an atom

2. ____ has a 1– charge

3. ____ found outside the nucleus

4. ____ has a mass of about 1 amu

5. ____ the small, dense center of the atom

6. ____ is neutral

Answers **1.** a and b **2.** c **3.** c
4. a and b **5.** d **6.** b

3.4 Atomic Number and Mass Number

- The *atomic number* is the number of protons in every atom of an element. In neutral atoms, the number of electrons is equal to the number of protons.
- The *mass number* is the total number of protons and neutrons in an atom.

MasteringChemistry

Tutorial: Atomic Number and Mass Number

Tutorial: Atomic Mass Calculations

Study Note

1. The *atomic number* is the number of protons in every atom of an element. In neutral atoms, the number of electrons equals the number of protons.
2. The *mass number* is the total number of neutrons and protons in the nucleus of an atom.
3. The number of neutrons is *mass number – atomic number.*

◆ Learning Exercise 3.4A

Give the number of protons in each of the following neutral atoms:

a. an atom of carbon ________

b. an atom of the element with atomic number 15 ________

c. an atom with a mass number of 40 and atomic number 19 ________

d. an atom with 9 neutrons and a mass number of 19 ________

e. a neutral atom that has 18 electrons ________

Answers **a.** 6 **b.** 15 **c.** 19 **d.** 10 **e.** 18

◆ Learning Exercise 3.4B

Find the number of neutrons in each of the following atoms:

a. a mass number of 42 and atomic number 20 ________

b. a mass number of 10 and 5 protons ________

c. $^{30}_{14}Si$ ________

d. a mass number of 9 and atomic number 4 ________

e. a mass number of 22 and 10 protons ________

f. a zinc atom with a mass number of 66 ________

Answers **a.** 22 **b.** 5 **c.** 16 **d.** 5 **e.** 12 **f.** 36

Study Note

In the atomic symbol for a particular atom, the mass number appears in the upper left corner and the atomic number in the lower left corner.

Mass Number → 32
Atomic Number → 16 $^{32}_{16}S$

◆ Learning Exercise 3.4C

Complete the following table for neutral atoms:

Atomic Symbol	Atomic Number	Mass Number	Number of Protons	Number of Neutrons	Number of Electrons
	12			12	
			20	22	
		55		29	
	35			45	
		35	17		
$^{120}_{50}Sn$					

Answers

Atomic Symbol	Atomic Number	Mass Number	Number of Protons	Number of Neutrons	Number of Electrons
$^{24}_{12}Mg$	12	24	12	12	12
$^{42}_{20}Ca$	20	42	20	22	20
$^{55}_{26}Fe$	26	55	26	29	26
$^{80}_{35}Br$	35	80	35	45	35
$^{35}_{17}Cl$	17	35	17	18	17
$^{120}_{50}Sn$	50	120	50	70	50

3.5 Isotopes and Atomic Mass

- Atoms that have the same number of protons but different numbers of neutrons are called isotopes.
- The atomic mass of an element is the average mass of all the isotopes in a naturally occurring sample of that element.

◆ Learning Exercise 3.5A

Identify the sets of atoms that are isotopes.

A. ${}^{20}_{10}X$ **B.** ${}^{20}_{11}X$ **C.** ${}^{21}_{11}X$ **D.** ${}^{19}_{10}X$ **E.** ${}^{19}_{9}X$

Answer Atoms A and D are isotopes (atomic number 10); atoms B and C are isotopes (atomic number 11).

◆ Learning Check 3.5B

Essay Copper has two naturally occurring isotopes, ${}^{63}_{29}Cu$ and ${}^{65}_{29}Cu$. Why is the atomic mass of copper listed as 63.55 on the periodic table?

Answer Copper in nature consists of two isotopes with different atomic masses. The atomic mass is the average of the individual masses of the two isotopes and their percent abundance in the sample. The atomic mass does not represent the mass of any individual atom.

3.6 Electron Energy Levels

- Energy levels, which are indicated by the principal quantum number, n, contain electrons of similar energies.
- Within each energy level, electrons with identical energy are grouped in *sublevels*: an s sublevel can accommodate 2 electrons, a p sublevel can accommodate 6 electrons, a d sublevel can accommodate 10 electrons, and an f sublevel can accommodate 14 electrons.
- An orbital is a region in an atom where there is the greatest probability of finding an electron of certain energy. An orbital can hold a maximum of two electrons, which have opposite spins.
- An s orbital is spherical, and p orbitals have two lobes along an axis. The d and f orbitals have more complex shapes.
- Each sublevel consists of a set of orbitals: an s sublevel consists of one orbital; a p sublevel consists of three orbitals; a d sublevel consists of five orbitals; and an f sublevel consists of seven orbitals.

MasteringChemistry

Tutorial: Energy Levels

◆ Learning Exercise 3.6

State the maximum number of electrons for each of the following:

a. 3*p* sublevel ______ **b.** 3*d* sublevel ______

c. 2*s* orbital ______ **d.** energy level 4 ______

e. 1*s* sublevel ______ **f.** 4*p* orbital ______

g. 5*p* sublevel ______ **h.** 4*f* sublevel ______

Answers **a.** 6 **b.** 10 **c.** 2 **d.** 32
e. 2 **f.** 2 **g.** 6 **h.** 14

3.7 Electron Configurations

- An orbital diagram represents the orbitals in an atom that contain electrons.
- The electron configuration shows the number of electrons in each sublevel in order of increasing energy.
- The abbreviated electron configuration uses the symbol of the previous noble gas and only shows the configuration of the electrons in the higher energy levels.

◆ Learning Exercise 3.7A

Write the orbital diagram for each of the following elements.

a. beryllium ____________________ **b.** carbon ____________________

c. sodium ____________________ **d.** nitrogen ____________________

e. fluorine ____________________ **f.** magnesium ____________________

Answers

a. [↑↓] [↑↓]
1*s* 2*s*

b. [↑↓] [↑↓] [↑|↑|]
1*s* 2*s* 2*p*

c.
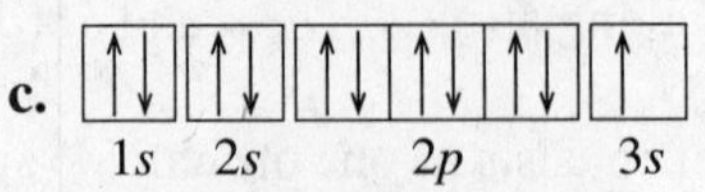
1*s* 2*s* 2*p* 3*s*

d.
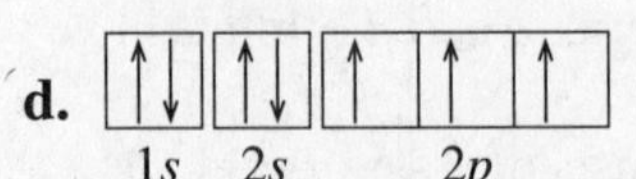
1*s* 2*s* 2*p*

e. [↑↓][↑↓][↑↓|↑↓|↑]
1*s* 2*s* 2*p*

f. [↑↓][↑↓][↑↓|↑↓|↑↓][↑↓]
1*s* 2*s* 2*p* 3*s*

MasteringChemistry

Tutorial: Electron Configurations

◆ Learning Exercise 3.7B

Write the electron configuration ($1s^22s^22p^6$ etc.) for each of the following elements:

a. carbon ______________________

b. magnesium ______________________

c. iron ______________________

d. silicon ______________________

e. chlorine ______________________

f. phosphorus ______________________

Answers
a. $1s^22s^22p^2$ **b.** $1s^22s^22p^63s^2$ **c.** $1s^22s^22p^63s^23p^64s^23d^6$
d. $1s^22s^22p^63s^23p^2$ **e.** $1s^22s^22p^63s^23p^5$ **f.** $1s^22s^22p^63s^23p^3$

◆ Learning Exercise 3.7C

Write the abbreviated electron configuration for each of the elements in 3.7B:

a. carbon ______________________

b. magnesium ______________________

c. iron ______________________

d. silicon ______________________

e. chlorine ______________________

f. phosphorus ______________________

Answers
a. [He]$2s^22p^2$ **b.** [Ne]$3s^2$ **c.** [Ar]$4s^23d^6$
d. [Ne]$3s^23p^2$ **e.** [Ne]$3s^23p^5$ **f.** [Ne]$3s^23p^3$

◆ Learning Exercise 3.7D

Name the element with an electron configuration ending with each of the following notations:

a. $3p^5$ ______________ **b.** $2s^1$ ______________

c. $3d^8$ ______________ **d.** $4p^1$ ______________

e. $5p^5$ ______________ **f.** $3p^2$ ______________

g. $1s^1$ ______________ **h.** $6s^2$ ______________

Answers
a. chlorine **b.** lithium **c.** nickel **d.** gallium
e. iodine **f.** silicon **g.** hydrogen **h.** barium

3.8 Periodic Trends

- The changes in the physical and chemical properties of elements going across a period are repeated in each successive period.
- Representative elements in a group have similar behavior.
- The group number of an element gives the number of valence electrons.
- The electron–dot symbol shows each valence electron as a dot placed around the atomic symbol.
- The atomic radius of representative elements generally increases going down a group and decreases going across a period.
- The ionization energy generally decreases going down a group and increases going across a period.

MasteringChemistry

Tutorial: Ionization Energy

Tutorial: Patterns in the Periodic Table

◆ Learning Exercise 3.8A

State the number of electrons in the outermost energy level, the group number of each element, and draw the electron–dot symbol for each of the following elements:

Element	Valence Electrons	Group Number	Electron–Dot Symbol
a. sulfur	________	________	________
b. oxygen	________	________	________
c. magnesium	________	________	________
d. hydrogen	________	________	________
e. fluorine	________	________	________
f. aluminum	________	________	________

Answers

Element	Valence Electrons	Group Number	Electron–Dot Symbol
a. sulfur	$6e^-$	Group 6A (16)	$\cdot\ddot{\underset{\cdot\cdot}{S}}:$
b. oxygen	$6e^-$	Group 6A (16)	$\cdot\ddot{\underset{\cdot}{O}}:$
c. magnesium	$2e^-$	Group 2A (2)	$\text{Mg}\cdot$ (with one dot above)
d. hydrogen	$1e^-$	Group 1A (1)	$\text{H}\cdot$
e. fluorine	$7e^-$	Group 7A (17)	$\cdot\ddot{\underset{\cdot\cdot}{F}}:$
f. aluminum	$3e^-$	Group 3A (13)	$\cdot\dot{\text{Al}}\cdot$

◆ Learning Exercise 3.8B

Indicate the element that has the larger atomic radius.

a. _____ **Mg or Ca** b. _____ **Si or Cl**

c. _____ **Sr or Rb** d. _____ **Br or Cl**

e. _____ **Li or Cs** f. _____ **Li or N**

g. _____ **N or P** h. _____ **As or Ca**

Answers **a.** Ca **b.** Si **c.** Rb **d.** Br
e. Cs **f.** Li **g.** P **h.** Ca

◆ Learning Exercise 3.8C

Indicate the element in each set that has the lower ionization energy:

a. _____ Mg or Na **b.** _____ P or Cl

c. _____ K or Rb **d.** _____ Br or F

e. _____ Li or O **f.** _____ Sb or N

g. _____ K or Br **h.** _____ S or Na

Answers **a.** Na **b.** P **c.** Rb **d.** Br
e. Li **f.** Sb **g.** K **g.** Na

Checklist for Chapter 3

You are ready to take the *Practice Test* for Chapter 3. Be sure that you have accomplished the following learning goals for this chapter. If you are not sure, review the section listed at the end of the goal. Then apply your new skills and understanding to the Practice Test.

After studying Chapter 3, I can successfully:

____ Write the correct symbol or name for an element (3.1).

____ Use the periodic table to identify the group and period of an element, and describe it as a metal or nonmetal (3.2).

____ State the electrical charge, mass, and location of the protons, neutrons, and electrons in an atom (3.3).

____ Given the atomic number and mass number of an atom, state the number of protons, neutrons, and electrons (3.4).

____ Identify an isotope and calculate the atomic mass of an element (3.5).

____ State the maximum number of electrons in orbitals and sublevels (3.6).

____ Write the electron dot symbol for a representative element (3.7).

____ Write the electron configuration for elements using sublevel notation (3.8).

____ Determine which of two elements has a larger atomic size (3.8).

____ Determine which of two elements has a higher ionization energy (3.8).

Practice Test for Chapter 3

Write or select the correct answer for each of the following questions:

In questions 1 through 5, write the correct symbol for each of the elements listed:

1. potassium ________ **2.** phosphorus ________

3. calcium ________ **4.** carbon ________

5. sodium ________

In questions 6 through 10, write the correct name for each of the symbols listed:

6. Fe ________________ **7.** Cu ________________

8. Cl ________________ **9.** Pb ________________

10. Ag ________________

11. The elements C, N, and O are part of a

A. period **B.** group **C.** neither

12. The elements Li, Na, and K are part of a

A. period **B.** group **C.** neither

13. What is the classification of an atom with 15 protons and 17 neutrons?

A. metal **B.** nonmetal **C.** transition element
D. noble gas **E.** halogen

14. What is the group number of the element with atomic number 3?

A. 1 **B.** 2 **C.** 3 **D.** 7 **E.** 8

For questions 15 through 18, consider an atom with 12 protons and 13 neutrons:

15. This atom has an atomic number of

A. 12 **B.** 13 **C.** 23 **D.** 24 **E.** 25

16. This atom has a mass number of

A. 12 **B.** 13 **C.** 23 **D.** 24.3 **E.** 25

17. This is an atom of

A. carbon **B.** sodium **C.** magnesium **D.** aluminum **E.** manganese

18. The number of electrons in this atom is

A. 12 **B.** 13 **C.** 23 **D.** 24 **E.** 25

For questions 19 through 22, consider an atom of calcium with a mass number of 42:

19. This atom of calcium has an atomic number of

A. 20 **B.** 22 **C.** 40 **D.** 41 **E.** 42

20. The number of protons in this atom of calcium is

A. 20 **B.** 22 **C.** 40 **D.** 41 **E.** 42

21. The number of neutrons in this atom of calcium is

A. 20 **B.** 22 **C.** 40 **D.** 41 **E.** 42

22. The number of electrons in this atom of calcium is

A. 20 **B.** 22 **C.** 40 **D.** 41 **E.** 42

23. Platinum, ${}^{195}_{78}Pt$ has

A. $78p^+$, $78e^-$, $78n$ **B.** $195p^+$, $195e^-$, $195n$ **C.** $78p^+$, $78e^-$, $195n$
D. $78p^+$, $78e^-$, $117n$ **E.** $78p^+$, $117e^-$, $117n$

For questions 24 and 25, use the following list of atoms:

${}^{14}_{7}V$ ${}^{16}_{8}W$ ${}^{19}_{9}X$ ${}^{16}_{7}Y$ ${}^{18}_{8}Z$

24. Which atoms(s) are isotopes of an atom with 8 protons and 9 neutrons?

A. W **B.** W, Z **C.** X, Y **D.** X **E.** Y

25. Which atom(s) are isotopes of an atom with 7 protons and 8 neutrons?

A. V **B.** W **C.** V, Y **D.** W, Z **E.** none

26. Which element would you expect to have properties most like oxygen?

A. nitrogen **B.** carbon **C.** chlorine **D.** argon **E.** sulfur

27. Which of the following is an isotope of nitrogen?

A. ${}^{14}_{8}N$ **B.** ${}^{7}_{3}N$ **C.** ${}^{10}_{5}N$ **D.** ${}^{4}_{2}He$ **E.** ${}^{15}_{7}N$

28. Except for helium, the number of electrons in the outer shells of the noble gases is

A. 3 **B.** 5 **C.** 7 **D.** 8 **E.** 12

29. The electron configuration for an oxygen atom is

A. $2s^22p^4$ **B.** $1s^22s^42p^4$ **C.** $1s^22s^6$ **D.** $1s^22s^22p^23s^2$ **E.** $1s^22s^22p^4$

30. The electron configuration for aluminum is

A. $1s^22s^22p^9$ **B.** $1s^22s^22p^63p^5$ **C.** $1s^22s^22p^63s^23p^1$ **D.** $1s^22s^22p^83p^1$ **E.** $1s^22s^22p^63p^3$

For questions 31 through 35, match the final notation in the electron configuration with one of the following:

A. As **B.** Rb **C.** Na **D.** N **E.** Rn

31. $4p^3$_____ **32.** $5s^1$______ **33.** $3s^1$______

34. $6p^6$_____ **35.** $2p^3$______

36. Which element has a larger atomic radius, Mg or P? _____

37. Which element has a larger atomic radius, Ar or Xe? _____

38. Which element has a higher ionization energy, N or F? _____

39. Which element has a higher ionization energy, Br or F? _____

Answers for the Practice Test

1. K	**2.** P	**3.** Ca	**4.** C	**5.** Na
6. iron	**7.** copper	**8.** chlorine	**9.** lead	**10.** silver
11. A	**12.** B	**13.** B	**14.** A	**15.** A
16. E	**17.** C	**18.** A	**19.** A	**20.** A
21. B	**22.** A	**23.** D	**24.** B	**25.** C
26. E	**27.** E	**28.** D	**29.** E	**30.** C
31. A	**32.** B	**33.** C	**34.** E	**35.** D
36. Mg	**37.** Xe	**38.** F	**39.** F	

4
Nuclear Radiation

Study Goals

- Identify the types of radiation as alpha particles, beta particles, positrons, or gamma radiation.
- Describe the methods required for proper shielding for each type of radiation.
- Write an equation for an atom that undergoes radioactive decay.
- Calculate the amount of radioisotope that remains after a given number of half-lives.
- Identify some radioisotopes used in nuclear medicine.
- Describe nuclear fission and fusion.

Think About It

1. What is nuclear radiation?

2. In nuclear medicine, iodine-125 is used for detecting a tumor in the thyroid. What does the number 125 indicate?

3. How are living cells damaged by radiation?

4. How does nuclear fission differ from nuclear fusion?

5. Why is there a concern about radon in our homes?

Key Terms

Match each the following key terms with the correct definition:

a. radioactive nucleus **b.** half-life **c.** curie **d.** nuclear fission **e.** alpha particle

1. ____ a particle identical to a helium nucleus produced in a radioactive nucleus

2. ____ the time required for one-half of a radioactive sample to undergo radioactive decay

3. ____ a unit of radiation measurement equal to 3.7×10^{10} disintegrations per second

4. ____ a process in which large nuclei split into smaller nuclei with the release of energy

5. ____ a nucleus that spontaneously emits radiation

Answers **1.** e **2.** b **3.** c **4.** d **5.** a

4.1 Natural Radioactivity

- Radioactive isotopes have unstable nuclei that break down (decay) spontaneously emitting alpha (α), beta (β), and gamma (γ) radiation.
- An alpha particle is the same as a helium nucleus; it contains two protons and two neutrons. A beta particle is a high-energy electron and a gamma ray is high-energy radiation.
- Because radiation can damage the cells in the body, proper protection must be used: shielding, time limitation, and distance.

MasteringChemistry

Self Study Activity: Nuclear Chemistry

Self Study Activity: Radiation and Its Biological Effects

Tutorial: Types of Radiation

Study Note

It is important to learn the symbols for the radiation particles in order to describe the different types of radiation:

$^{1}_{1}\text{H}$ or p	$^{1}_{0}\text{n}$ or n	$^{0}_{-1}e$ or β	$^{4}_{2}\text{He}$ or α	$^{0}_{+1}e$ or β^{+}	$^{0}_{0}\gamma$ or γ
proton	neutron	beta particle	alpha particle	positron	gamma ray

◆ Learning Exercise 4.1A

Match the description in column B with the terms in column A:

A	B
1. ____ $^{18}_{8}\text{O}$	**a.** beta particle
2. ____ γ	**b.** alpha particle
3. ____ $^{0}_{+1}e$	**c.** positron

4. ____ $^{4}_{2}He$ **d.** atom of oxygen

5. ____ β **e.** gamma radiation

Answers **1.** d **2.** e **3.** c **4.** b **5.** a

◆ Learning Check 4.1B

Discuss some things you can do to minimize the amount of radiation received if you work with a radioactive substance. Describe how each method helps to limit the amount of radiation you would receive.

Answer

Three ways to minimize exposure to radiation are: (1) use shielding, (2) keep time short in the radioactive area, and (3) keep as much distance as possible from the radioactive materials. Shielding such as clothing and gloves stops alpha and beta particles from reaching your skin, whereas lead or concrete will absorb gamma rays. Limiting the time spent near radioactive samples reduces exposure time. Increasing the distance from a radioactive source reduces the intensity of radiation. Wearing a film badge will monitor the amount of radiation you receive.

◆ Learning Exercise 4.1C

What type(s) of radiation (alpha, beta, and/or gamma) would each of the following shielding materials protect you from?

a. clothing ____________ **b.** skin ____________

c. paper ____________ **d.** concrete ____________

e. lead wall ____________

Answers **a.** alpha, beta **b.** alpha **c.** alpha
d. alpha, beta, gamma **e.** alpha, beta, gamma

4.2 Nuclear Equations

- A balanced nuclear equation is used to represent the changes that take place in the nuclei of the reactants and products.
- The new isotopes and the type of radiation emitted can be determined from the symbols that show the mass numbers and atomic numbers of the isotopes in the nuclear reaction.

Radioactive nucleus ⟶ new nucleus + radiation

Total of the mass numbers are equal

$$^{11}_{6}C \longrightarrow {}^{7}_{4}Be + {}^{4}_{2}He$$

Total of the atomic numbers are equal

Guide to Completing a Nuclear Equation	
STEP 1	Write the incomplete nuclear equation.
STEP 2	Determine the missing mass number.
STEP 3	Determine the missing atomic number.
STEP 4	Determine the symbol of the new nucleus.
STEP 5	Complete the nuclear equation.

MasteringChemistry

Tutorial: Writing Nuclear Equations

Tutorial: Alpha, Beta, and Gamma Emitters

Study Note

When balancing nuclear equations for radioactive decay, be sure that

1. the mass number of the reactant equals the sum of the mass numbers of the products.

2. the atomic number of the reactant equals the sum of the atomic numbers of the products.

◆ Learning Check 4.2

Write a nuclear symbol that completes each of the following nuclear equations:

a. ${}^{66}_{29}\text{Cu} \longrightarrow {}^{66}_{30}\text{Zn} + ?$ **a.** ________

b. ${}^{127}_{53}\text{I} \longrightarrow {}^{1}_{0}n + ?$ **b.** ________

c. ${}^{40}_{19}\text{K} \longrightarrow {}^{40}_{18}\text{Ar} + ?$ **c.** ________

d. ${}^{24}_{11}\text{Na} \longrightarrow {}^{0}_{-1}e + ?$ **d.** ________

e. $? \longrightarrow {}^{30}_{14}\text{Si} + {}^{0}_{-1}e$ **e.** ________

Answers **a.** ${}^{0}_{-1}e$ **b.** ${}^{126}_{53}\text{I}$ **c.** ${}^{0}_{+1}e$ **d.** ${}^{24}_{12}\text{Mg}$ **e.** ${}^{30}_{13}\text{Al}$

4.3 Radiation Measurement

- A Geiger counter is used to detect radiation. When radiation passes through the gas in the counter tube, some atoms of gas are ionized producing an electrical current.
- The activity of a radioactive sample measures the number of nuclear transformations per second. The curie (Ci) is equal to 3.7×10^{10} disintegrations in 1 second. The becquerel (Bq) is equal to 1 disintegration per second.
- The radiation dose absorbed by a gram of body tissue is measured in units of rads or the Gray.
- The biological damage of different types of radiation on the body is measured in radiation units of rems or sieverts.

MasteringChemistry

Case Study: Food Irradiation

◆ Learning Exercise 4.3

Match each type of measurement unit with the radiation process measured:

a. curie **b.** becquerel **c.** rad **d.** gray **e.** rem

1. ____ an activity of one disintegration per second

2. ____ the amount of radiation absorbed by one gram of material

3. ____ an activity of 3.7×10^{10} disintegrations per second

4. ____ the biological damage caused by different kinds of radiation

5. ____ a unit of absorbed dose equal to 100 rads

Answers **1.** b **2.** c **3.** a **4.** e **5.** d

4.4 Half-Life of a Radioisotope

- The half-life of a radioactive sample is the time required for one–half of the sample to decay (emit radiation).
- Most radioisotopes used in medicine, such as Tc-99m and I–131, have short half-lives. By comparison, many naturally occurring radioisotopes, such as C–14, Ra–226, and U–238, have long half-lives. For example, potassium–42 has a half-life of 12 h, whereas, potassium–40 takes 1.3×10^9 y for one-half of the radioactive sample to decay.

MasteringChemistry

Tutorial: Radioactive Half-Lives

◆ Learning Exercise 4.4

a. Suppose you have an 80-mg sample of iodine–125. If iodine–125 has a half-life of 60 days, how many milligrams are radioactive?

1. after one half-life?

2. after two half-lives?

3. after 240 days?

b. ${}^{99m}_{43}Tc$ has a half-life of 6 hours. If a technician picked up a 16-mg sample at 8 A.M., how much of the radioactive sample remained at 8 P.M. that same day?

c. Phosphorus–32 has a half-life of 14 days. How much of a 240-μg sample will be radioactive after 56 days?

d. Iodine–131 has a half-life of 8 days. How many days will it take for 80 mg of I–131 to decay to 5 mg?

e. Suppose an archaeologist digs up a piece of a wooden boat at an ancient site. When a sample of the wood is analyzed for C–14, scientists determine that 12.5% or 1/8 of the original amount of C–14 remains. If the half-life of carbon–14 is 5730 y, how long ago, in years, was the boat made?

Answers **a. 1.** 40 mg **2.** 20 mg **3.** 5 mg
b. 4.0 mg **c.** 15 μg **d.** 32 days **e.** 17 200 years ago

4.5 Medical Applications Using Radioactivity

- In nuclear medicine, radioactive isotopes are given that go to specific sites in the body.
- For diagnostic work, radioisotopes are used that emit gamma rays and produce nonradioactive products.
- By detecting the radiation emitted by medical radioisotopes, evaluations can be made about the location and extent of an injury, disease, or tumor, blood flow, or level of function of a particular organ.

◆ Learning Check 4.5

Write the nuclear symbol for each of the following radioactive isotopes:

a. ______ iodine–131 used to study thyroid gland activity

b. ______ phosphorus–32 used to locate brain tumors

c. ______ sodium–24 used to determine blood flow and to locate a blood clot or embolism

d. ______ nitrogen–13 used in positron emission tomography

Answers **a.** $^{131}_{53}\text{I}$ **b.** $^{32}_{15}\text{P}$ **c.** $^{24}_{11}\text{Na}$ **d.** $^{13}_{7}\text{N}$

4.6 Nuclear Fission and Fusion

- In fission, a large nucleus breaks apart into smaller pieces releasing one or more types of radiation and a great amount of energy.
- In fusion, small nuclei combine to form a larger nucleus, which releases great amounts of energy.

MasteringChemistry

Tutorial: Fission and Fusion

◆ Learning Exercise 4.6

Discuss the nuclear processes of fission and fusion for the production of energy.

Answer *Nuclear fission* is a splitting of the atom into two or more nuclei accompanied by the release of large amounts of energy and radiation. In the process of *nuclear fusion*, two or more nuclei combine to form a heavier nucleus and release a large amount of energy. However, fusion requires a considerable amount of energy to initiate the process.

Checklist for Chapter 4

You are ready to take the *Practice Test* for Chapter 4. Be sure that you have accomplished the following learning goals for this chapter. If you are not sure, review the section listed at the end of the goal. Then apply your new skills and understanding to the Practice Test.

After studying Chapter 4, I can successfully:

____ Describe alpha, beta, positron, and gamma radiation (4.1).

____ Write a nuclear equation showing the balance of mass numbers and atomic numbers for radioactive decay (4.2).

____ Describe the detection and measurement of radiation (4.3).

____ Using its half-life value, calculate the amount of a radioisotope remaining after one or more half-lives (4.4).

____ Describe the use of radioisotopes in medicine (4.5).

____ Describe the processes of nuclear fission and fusion (4.6).

Practice Test for Chapter 4

1. The correctly written symbol for an atom of sulfur would be

A. $^{30}_{16}Su$ **B.** $^{14}_{30}Si$ **C.** $^{30}_{16}S$ **D.** $^{30}_{15}Su$ **E.** $^{16}_{30}S$

2. Alpha particles are composed of

A. protons **B.** neutrons **C.** electrons **D.** protons and electrons **E.** protons and neutrons

3. Gamma radiation is a type of radiation that

A. originates in the electron shells.
B. is most dangerous.
C. is least dangerous.
D. is the heaviest.
E. goes the shortest distance.

4. The charge on a positron is

A. 1– **B.** 1+ **C.** 2– **D.** 2+ **E.** 4+

5. Beta particles formed in a radioactive nucleus are

A. protons **B.** neutrons **C.** electrons **D.** protons and electrons **E.** protons and neutrons

For questions 6 through 10, select from the following:

A. $^{0}_{-1}X$ **B.** $^{4}_{2}X$ **C.** $^{1}_{1}X$ **D.** $^{1}_{0}X$ **E.** $^{0}_{+1}X$

6. An alpha particle

7. A beta particle

8. A positron

9. A proton

10. A neutron

11. Shielding from gamma rays is provided by

A. skin **B.** paper **C.** clothing **D.** lead **E.** air

12. The skin will provide shielding from

A. alpha particles **B.** beta particles **C.** gamma rays **D.** ultraviolet rays **E.** X-rays

13. The radioisotope iodine-131 is used as a radioactive tracer for studying thyroid gland activity. The symbol for iodine-131 is

A. I **B.** $_{131}I$ **C.** $^{131}_{53}I$ **D.** $^{53}_{131}I$ **E.** $^{78}_{53}I$

14. When an atom emits an alpha particle, its atomic mass

A. increases by 1 **B.** increases by 2 **C.** increases by 4
D. decreases by 4 **E.** does not change

15. When a nucleus emits a beta particle, the atomic number of the new nucleus

A. increases by 1 **B.** increases by 2 **C.** decreases by 1
D. decreases by 2 **E.** does not change

16. When a nucleus emits a gamma ray, the atomic number of the new nucleus

A. increases by 1 **B.** increases by 2 **C.** decreases by 1
D. decreases by 2 **E.** does not change

For questions 17 through 20, select the particle that completes each of the equations.

A. neutron **B.** alpha particle **C.** beta particle **D.** positron

17. $^{126}_{50}Sn \longrightarrow ^{126}_{51}Sb + ?$

18. $^{69}_{30}Zn \longrightarrow ^{69}_{31}Ga + ?$

19. $^{121}_{53}I \longrightarrow ^{121}_{52}Te + ?$

20. $^{149}_{62}Sm \longrightarrow ^{145}_{60}Nd + ?$

21. What symbol completes the following reaction?

$^{14}_{7}N + ^{1}_{0}n \longrightarrow ? + ^{1}_{1}H$

A. $^{15}_{8}O$ **B.** $^{15}_{6}C$ **C.** $^{14}_{8}O$ **D.** $^{14}_{6}C$ **E.** $^{15}_{7}N$

22. To complete the following nuclear equation, you need to write:

$^{54}_{26}Fe + ? \longrightarrow ^{57}_{28}Ni + ^{1}_{0}n$

A. an alpha particle **B.** a beta particle **C.** gamma ray **D.** a neutron **E.** a proton

23. The name of the unit used to measure the number of disintegrations per second is

A. curie **B.** rad **C.** rem **D.** RBE **E.** MRI

24. The rem and the sievert are units used to measure

A. activity of a radioactive sample
B. biological damage of different types of radiation
C. radiation absorbed
D. background radiation
E. all of the above

25. Radiation can cause

A. nausea **B.** a lower white cell count **C.** fatigue **D.** hair loss **E.** all of these

26. Radioisotopes used in medical diagnosis

A. have short half-lives. **B.** emit only gamma rays. **C.** locate in specific organs.
D. produce nonradioactive nuclei. **E.** all of these

27. The imaging technique that uses the energy emitted by exciting the nuclei of hydrogen atoms is

A. computed tomography (CT)
B. positron emission tomography (PET)
C. radioactive tracer
D. magnetic resonance imaging (MRI)
E. radiation

28. The imaging technique that detects the absorption of x-rays by the body tissues is

A. computed tomography (CT)
B. positron emission tomography (PET)
C. radioactive tracer
D. magnetic resonance imaging (MRI)
E. radiation

29. The time required for a radioisotope to decay is measured by its

A. half-life **B.** protons **C.** activity **D.** fusion **E.** radioisotope

30. Oxygen–15, which is used in PET imaging, has a half-life of 2 min. How many half-lives occurr in the 10 min it takes to prepare the sample?

A. 2 **B.** 3 **C.** 4 **D.** 5 **E.** 6

31. Iodine–131 has a half-life of 8 days. How long does it take for a 160-mg sample to decay to 10 mg?

A. 8 days **B.** 16 days **C.** 32 days **D.** 40 days **E.** 48 days

32. Phosphorus–32 has a half-life of 14 days. After 28 days, how many milligrams of a 100-mg sample will still be radioactive?

A. 75 mg **B.** 50 mg **C.** 40 mg **D.** 25 mg **E.** 12.5 mg

33. The "splitting" of a large nucleus to form smaller particles accompanied by a release of energy is called

A. radioisotope **B.** fission **C.** fusion **D.** rem **E.** half-life

34. The process of combining small nuclei to form larger nuclei is

A. radioisotope **B.** fission **C.** fusion **D.** rem **E.** half-life

35. The fusion reaction

A. occurs in the sun.
B. forms larger nuclei from smaller nuclei.
C. requires extremely high temperatures.
D. releases a large amount of energy.
E. all of the these

Answers to the Practice Test

1. C	**2.** E	**3.** B	**4.** B	**5.** C
6. B	**7.** A	**8.** E	**9.** C	**10.** D
11. D	**12.** A	**13.** C	**14.** D	**15.** A
16. E	**17.** C	**18.** C	**19.** D	**20.** B
21. D	**22.** A	**23.** A	**24.** B	**25.** E
26. E	**27.** D	**28.** A	**29.** A	**30.** D
31. C	**32.** D	**33.** B	**34.** C	**35.** E

5

Compounds and Their Bonds

Study Goals

- Use the octet rule to determine the ionic charge of ions for representative elements.
- Use charge balance to write an ionic formula.
- Draw the electron-dot formula for covalent compounds.
- Write the correct names for ionic and covalent compounds.
- Use electronegativity values to identify polar and nonpolar covalent bonds.
- Write ionic formulas and names of compounds with polyatomic ions.
- Use VSEPR theory to determine the shape and polarity of a molecule.
- Write resonance structures for compounds with double bonds that are equivalent.
- Describe the types of forces that hold particles together in liquids and solids.

Think About It

1. What is the octet rule?

2. How does a compound differ from an element?

3. When is an electron-dot formula written with multiple bonds?

Key Terms

Match each the following key terms with the correct definition:

a. polar covalent bond	**b.** multiple bond	**c.** VSEPR theory
d. nonpolar covalent bond	**e.** resonance structures	**f.** dipole–dipole attraction

1. ____ equal sharing of valence electrons by two atoms

2. ____ occurs when two or more electron-dot formulas can be written for the same compound

3. ____ the unequal attraction for shared electrons in a covalent bond

4. ____ the atoms in a molecule are arranged to minimize repulsion between electrons

5. ____ the sharing of two or three pairs of electrons by two atoms

6. ____ interaction between the positive end of a polar molecule and the negative end of another

Answers **1.** d **2.** e **3.** a **4.** c **5.** b **6.** f

5.1 Octet Rule and Ions

- The stability of the noble gases is associated with an electron configuration of 8 electrons (s^2p^6), an octet, in their outer energy level. Helium is stable with 2 electrons in the outer energy level.

He	$1s^2$	Ne	$1s^22s2p^6$
Ar	$1s^22s^22p^63s^23p^6$	Kr	$1s^22s^22p^63s^23p^64s^23d^{10}4p^6$

- Atoms of elements other than the noble gases achieve stability by losing, gaining, or sharing valence electrons with other atoms in the formation of compounds.
- Metals of the representative elements in Groups 1A (1), 2 (2A), and 3A (13) achieve a noble gas electron configuration by losing their valence electron(s) to form positively charged cations with a charge of 1+, 2+, or 3+.
- Nonmetals gain valence electrons to achieve an octet forming negatively charged ions with a charge of 3–, 2–, or 1–.

MasteringChemistry

Tutorial: Octet Rule and Ions

Study Note

When an atom loses or gains electrons, it acquires the electron configuration of its nearest noble gas. For example, sodium loses 1 electron, which gives the Na^+ ion a configuration like neon. An oxygen atom gains 2 electrons to give an oxide ion O^{2-} with the same electron configuration as neon.

◆ Learning Exercise 5.1A

The following elements lose electrons when they form ions. Indicate the group number, the number of electrons lost, and the ion (symbol and charge) for each of the following:

Element	Group Number	Electrons Lost	Ion Formed
Magnesium			
Sodium			
Calcium			
Potassium			
Aluminum			

Answers

Element	Group Number	Electrons Lost	Ion Formed
Magnesium	2A (2)	2	Mg^{2+}
Sodium	1A (1)	1	Na^{+}
Calcium	2A (2)	2	Ca^{2+}
Potassium	1A (1)	1	K^{+}
Aluminum	3A (13)	3	Al^{3+}

Study Note

The valence electrons are the electrons in the outermost energy level of an atom. For representative elements, you can determine the number of valence electrons by looking at the group number.

◆ Learning Exercise 5.1B

The following elements gain electrons when they form ions. Indicate the group number, the number of electrons gained, and the ion (symbol and charge) for each of the following:

Element	Group Number	Electrons Gained	Ion Formed
Chlorine			
Oxygen			
Nitrogen			
Fluorine			
Sulfur			

Answers

Element	Group Number	Electrons Gained	Ion Formed
Chlorine	7A (17)	1	Cl^{-}
Oxygen	6A (16)	2	O^{2-}
Nitrogen	5A (15)	3	N^{3-}
Fluorine	7A (17)	1	F^{-}
Sulfur	6A (16)	2	S^{2-}

5.2 Ionic Compounds

- In the formulas of ionic compounds, the total positive charge is equal to the total negative charge. For example, the compound magnesium chloride, $MgCl_2$, contains Mg^{2+} and $2Cl^-$. The sum of the charges is zero: $1(2+) + 2(1-) = 0$.
- When two or more ions are needed for charge balance, that number is indicated by subscripts in the formula.

MasteringChemistry
Tutorial: Ionic Compounds

◆ Learning Exercise 5.2A

For this exercise, you may want to cut pieces of paper that represent typical positive and negative ions as shown below. Place the pieces together (positive ion first) adding more positive ions or negative ions to complete a geometric shape. Write the number of positive ions and negative ions as the subscripts for the formula.

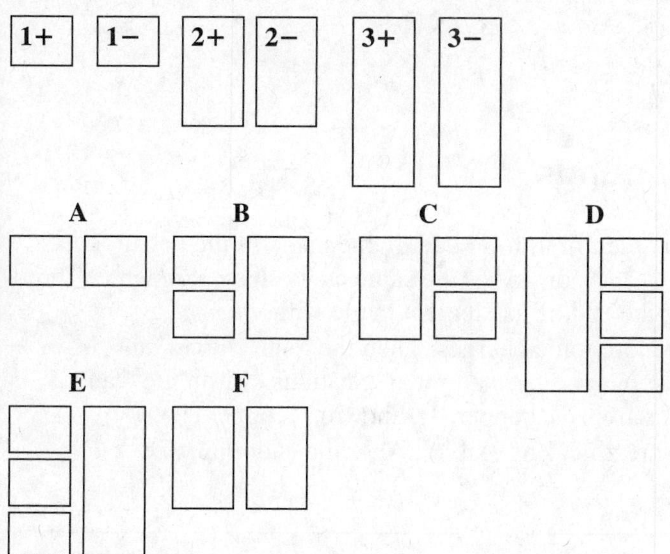

Give the letter (A, B, C, etc.) that matches the arrangement of ions in the following compounds:

Compound	Combination	Compound	Combination
1. $MgCl_2$	________	**2.** Na_2S	________
3. LiCl	________	**4.** CaO	________
5. K_3N	________	**6.** $AlBr_3$	________
7. MgS	________	**8.** $BaCl_2$	________

Answers **1.** C **2.** B **3.** A **4.** F **5.** E **6.** D **7.** F **8.** C

Study Note

You can check that the formula you write is electrically neutral by multiplying each of the ionic charges by their subscripts. When added together, their sum should equal zero. For example, the formula Na_2O gives $2(1+) + 1(2-) = (2+) + (2-) = 0$.

◆ Learning Exercise 5.2B

Write the correct formula of the ionic compound formed from each of the following pairs of ions:

1. Na^+ and Cl^- ________ **2.** K^+ and S^{2-} ________

3. Al^{3+} and O^{2-} ________ **4.** Mg^{2+} and Cl^- ________

5. Ca^{2+} and S^{2-} ________ **6.** Al^{3+} and Cl^- ________

7. Li^+ and N^{3-} ________ **8.** Ba^{2+} and P^{3-} ________

Answers **1.** NaCl **2.** K_2S **3.** Al_2O_3 **4.** $MgCl_2$
5. CaS **6.** $AlCl_3$ **7.** Li_3N **8.** Ba_3P_2

5.3 Naming and Writing Ionic Compounds

- In naming ionic compounds, the positive ion is named first, followed by the name of the negative ion. The name of a representative metal ion (Group 1A, 2A, or 3A) is the same as its elemental name. The name of a nonmetal ion is obtained by replacing the end of its element name with *ide.*
- Most transition metals form cations with two or more ionic charges. Then the ionic charge must be written as a Roman numeral after the name of the metal. For example, the cations of iron, Fe^{2+} and Fe^{3+}, are iron(II) and iron(III). The ions of copper are Cu^+, copper (I), and Cu^{2+}, copper (II).
- The only transition elements with fixed charges are zinc, Zn^{2+}, silver, Ag^+, and cadmium, Cd^{2+}.

MasteringChemistry

Tutorial: Writing Ionic Formulas

Guide to Naming Ionic Compounds with Metals that Form a Single Ion	
STEP 1	Identify the cation and anion.
STEP 2	Name the cation by its element name.
STEP 3	Name the anion by using the first syllable of its element name followed by *ide.*
STEP 4	Write the name of the cation first and the anion second.

◆ Learning Exercise 5.3A

Write the ions and the correct formula for each of the following ionic compounds:

Formula	Ions		Name
1. Cs_2O	______	______	____________________
2. $BaBr_2$	______	______	____________________
3. Mg_3P_2	______	______	____________________
4. Na_2S	______	______	____________________

Answers
1. Cs^+, O^{2-}, cesium oxide
2. Ba^{2+}, Br^-, barium bromide
3. Mg^{3+}, P^{3-}, magnesium phosphide
4. Na^+, S^{2-}, sodium sulfide

◆ Learning Exercise 5.3B

Write the names of each of the following ions:

1. Cl^-	____________	2. Fe^{2+}	____________
3. Cu^+	____________	4. Ag^+	____________
5. O^{2-}	____________	6. Ca^{2+}	____________
7. S^{2-}	____________	8. Al^{3+}	____________
9. Fe^{3+}	____________	10. Ba^{2+}	____________
11. Cu^{2+}	____________	12. N^{3-}	____________

Answers
1. chloride 2. iron(II) 3. copper(I) 4. silver
5. oxide 6. calcium 7. sulfide 8. aluminum
9. iron(III) 10. barium 11. copper(II) 12. nitride

◆ Learning Exercise 5.3C

Most of the transition metals form two or more ions with positive charge. Complete each of the following with the symbol or name of the ion:

Name of Ion	Symbol of Ion	Name of Ion	Symbol of Ion
1. iron(III)	____________	2. ____________	Cu^{2+}
3. zinc	____________	4. ____________	Fe^{2+}
5. copper(I)	____________	6. ____________	Ag^+
7. tin(IV)	____________	8. ____________	Cr^{2+}

Answers
1. Fe^{3+} 2. copper(II) 3. Zn^{2+} 4. iron(II)
5. Cu^+ 6. silver 7. Sn^{4+} 8. chromium(II)

Guide to Writing Formulas from the Name of An Ionic Compound	
STEP 1	Identify the cation and anion.
STEP 2	Balance the charges.
STEP 3	Write the formula, cation first, using subscripts from charge balance.

◆ Learning Exercise 5.3C

Write the ions and the correct formula for each of the following ionic compounds:

Compound	Positive Ion	Negative Ion	Formula of Compound
Aluminum sulfide			
Copper(II) chloride			
Magnesium oxide			
Iron(II) bromide			
Silver oxide			

Answers

Compound	Positive Ion	Negative Ion	Formula of Compound
Aluminum sulfide	Al^{3+}	S^{2-}	Al_2S_3
Copper(II) chloride	Cu^{2+}	Cl^-	$CuCl_2$
Magnesium oxide	Mg^{2+}	O^{2-}	MgO
Iron(II) bromide	Fe^{2+}	Br^-	$FeBr_2$
Silver oxide	Ag^+	O^{2-}	Ag_2O

Guide to Naming Ionic Compounds with Variable Charge Metals	
STEP 1	Determine the charge of the cation from the anion.
STEP 2	Name the cation by its element name and use a Roman numeral in parentheses for the charge.
STEP 3	Name the anion by using the first syllable of its element name followed by *ide*.
STEP 4	Write the name of the cation first and the name of the anion second.

Study Note

The ionic charge of a metal that forms more than one positive ion is determined from the total negative charge in the formula. For example, the formula $FeCl_3$ indicates $3Cl^-$ or 3(–). Then, the iron ion must have an ionic charge of 3+ or Fe^{3+}, which is named iron(III).

◆ Learning Exercise 5.3D

Write the ions and a correct name for each of the following ionic compounds:

Formula	Ions		Name
1. $BaCl_2$	______	______	____________________
2. $FeBr_3$	______	______	____________________
3. Na_3P	______	______	____________________
4. Al_2O_3	______	______	____________________
5. CuO	______	______	____________________
6. Mg_3N_2	______	______	____________________

Answers
1. Ba^{2+}, Cl^-, barium chloride
2. Fe^{3+}, Br^-, iron(III) bromide
3. Na^+, P^{3-}, sodium phosphide
4. Al^{3+}, O^{2-}, aluminum oxide
5. Cu^{2+}, O^{2-}, copper(II) oxide
6. Mg^{2+},N^{3-}, magnesium nitride

5.4 Polyatomic Ions

- A polyatomic ion is a group of nonmetal atoms that carries an electrical charge, usually negative, 1−, 2−, or 3−.
- Polyatomic ions cannot exist alone, but are combined with an ion of the opposite charge.
- Ionic compounds containing three elements (polyatomic ions) usually end with *ate* or *ite.*

MasteringChemistry

Tutorial: Polyatomic Ions

Study Note

By learning the most common polyatomic ions such as nitrate NO_3^-, carbonate CO_3^{2-}, sulfate SO_4^{2-}, and phosphate PO_4^{3-}, you can derive their related polyatomic ions. For example, the nitrite ion, NO_2^-, has one oxygen atom less than the nitrate ion: NO_3^-, nitrate and NO_2^-, nitrite

◆ Learning Exercise 5.4A

Write the polyatomic ion (symbol and charge) for each of the following:

1. sulfate ion	____________	**2.** hydroxide ion	____________
3. carbonate ion	____________	**4.** sulfite ion	____________
5. ammonium ion	____________	**6.** phosphate ion	____________
7. nitrate ion	____________	**8.** nitrite ion	____________

Answers
1. SO_4^{2-} **2.** OH^- **3.** CO_3^{2-} **4.** SO_3^{2-}
5. NH_4^+ **6.** PO_4^{3-} **7.** NO_3^- **8.** NO_2^-

◆ Learning Exercise 5.4B

Write the formula of the ions, and the correct formula for each of the following:

Compound	Positive Ion	Negative Ion	Formula
Sodium phosphate			
Iron(II) hydroxide			
Ammonium carbonate			
Silver bicarbonate			
Iron(III) sulfate			
Copper(II) nitrate			
Potassium sulfite			
Barium phosphate			

Answers

Compound	Positive Ion	Negative Ion	Formula
Sodium phosphate	Na^+	PO_4^{3-}	Na_3PO_4
Iron (II) hydroxide	Fe^{2+}	OH^-	$Fe(OH)_2$
Ammonium carbonate	NH_4^+	CO_3^{2-}	$(NH_4)_2CO_3$
Silver bicarbonate	Ag^+	HCO_3^-	$AgHCO_3$
Iron(III) sulfate	Fe^{3+}	SO_4^{2-}	$Fe_2(SO_4)_3$
Copper(II) nitrate	Cu^{2+}	NO_3^-	$Cu(NO_3)_2$
Potassium sulfite	K^+	SO_3^{2-}	K_2SO_3
Barium phosphate	Ba^{2+}	PO_4^{3-}	$Ba_3(PO_4)_2$

Guide to Naming Ionic Compounds with Polyatomic Ions	
STEP 1	Identify the cation and polyatomic ion (anion)
STEP 2	Name the cation, using a Roman numeral in parentheses, if needed.
STEP 3	Name the polyatomic ion usually ending in *ite* or *ate*.
STEP 4	Write the name of the compound, cation first and the polyatomic ion second.

◆ Learning Exercise 5.4C

Write the ions and a correct name for each of the following ionic compounds:

Formula **Ions** **Name**

1. $Ba(NO_3)_2$ ________ ________ ______________________________

2. $FeSO_4$ ________ ________ ______________________________

3. Na_3PO_3 ________ ________ ______________________________

4. $Al(ClO_3)_3$ _______ _______ ______________________________

5. $(NH_4)_2CO_3$ _______ _______ ______________________________

6. $Cr(OH)_2$ _______ _______ ______________________________

Answers

1. Ba^{2+}, NO_3^-, barium nitrate
2. Fe^{2+}, SO_4^{2-}, iron (II) sulfate
3. Na^+, PO_3^{3-}, sodium phosphate
4. Al^{3+}, ClO_3^-, aluminum chlorate
5. NH_4^+, CO_3^{2-}, ammonium carbonate
6. Cr^{2+}, OH^-, chromium(II) hydroxide

5.5 Covalent Compounds

- In a covalent bond, atoms of nonmetals share electrons to achieve an octet. For example, oxygen with six valence electrons shares electrons with two hydrogen atoms to form the covalent compound water (H_2O).

```
   ..
H: O :
   ..
   H
```

- In a double bond, two pairs of electrons are shared between the same two atoms. In a triple bond, three pairs of electrons are shared.
- Covalent compounds are composed of nonmetals bonded together to give discrete units called molecules.
- When two or more equivalent electron-dot formulas can be written, they are **resonance structures**,

MasteringChemistry

Self Study Activity: Covalent Bonds

Tutorial: Covalent Molecules and the Octet Rule

Tutorial: Writing Electron-Dot Formulas

◆ Learning Exercise 5.5A

List the number of bonds typically formed by the following atoms in covalent compounds:

a. N ______ **b.** S ______ **c.** P ______ **d.** C ______

e. Cl ______ **f.** O ______ **g.** H ______ **h.** F ______

Answers **a.** 3 **b.** 2 **c.** 3 **d.** 4 **e.** 1 **f.** 2 **g.** 1 **h.** 1

Guide to Writing Electron-Dot Formulas	
STEP 1	Determine the arrangement of atoms.
STEP 2	Determine the total number of valence electrons.
STEP 3	Attach each bonded atom to the central atom with a pair of electrons.
STEP 4	Place the remaining electrons as lone pairs to complete octets (two for H, six for B).

Study Note

An electron-dot formula for SCl_2 can be written as follows:

STEP 1: Arrange atoms around the central atom.

Cl S Cl

STEP 2: Determine the total number of valence electrons:

1 S and 2 Cl = $1\,(6e^-) + 2(7e^-) = 20e^-$

STEP 3: Attach the central atom to each bonded atom by one pair of electrons (single bond):

Cl–S–Cl $20e^- - 4e^- = 16e^-$ remain (8 pairs)

STEP 4: Arrange the remaining electrons as lone pairs to complete octets:

:C̤̈l–S̤̈–C̤̈l:

◆ Learning Exercise 5.5B

Write the electron–dot formulas for the following covalent compounds (the central atom is underlined):

H_2	<u>N</u>Cl_3	HCl
Cl_2	H_2<u>S</u>	<u>C</u>Cl_4

Answers H:H   :C̤̈l:N̤̈:C̤̈l: (with :C̤l̤: below N)   H:C̤̈l: :C̤̈l:C̤̈l: H:S̤̈: (with H below S)   :C̤̈l:C̤̈:C̤̈l: (with :C̈l: above C and :C̤l̤: below C)

Study Note

An electron–dot formula for CO_2 can be written with double bonds as follows:

STEP 1: Arrange atoms around the central atom.

O C O

STEP 2: Determine the total number of valence electrons.

1 C and 2 O = $1(4e^-) + 2(6e^-) = 16e^-$

STEP 3: Attach the central atom to each bonded atom by one pair of electrons (single bond).

O—C—O $16e^- - 4e^- = 12e^-$ remain (6 pairs)

STEP 4: Arrange remaining valence electrons as lone pairs to complete octets.

:Ö̤–C–Ö̤:

When octets cannot be completed with available valence electrons, one or more lone pairs are shared between the central atom and bonded atoms.

:Ö=C=Ö: double bonds

◆ Learning Exercise 5.5C

Write the electron–dot formulas for each of the following compounds, which contain one or more multiple bonds:

a. CS_2

b. HCN

c. H_2CCH_2

d. HONO

Answers

a. :S̈::C::S̈:

b. H : C ::: N:

c. H:C̈::C̈:H (with H above each C)

d. H:Ö:N̈::Ö:

◆ Learning Exercise 5.5D

Write two or more resonance structures for each of the following:

a. SO_2

b. CO_3^{2-}

Answers

a. :Ö–S̈=Ö: :Ö=S̈–Ö:

b. $\left[\begin{array}{c}:\ddot{O}:\\|\\:\ddot{O}–C=\ddot{O}:\end{array}\right]^{2-}$ $\left[\begin{array}{c}:O:\\||\\:\ddot{O}–C–\ddot{O}:\end{array}\right]^{2-}$ $\left[\begin{array}{c}:\ddot{O}:\\||\\:\ddot{O}=C–\ddot{O}:\end{array}\right]^{2-}$

5.6 Naming and Writing Covalent Formulas

- The name of a covalent compound is written using the element name of the first nonmetal in the formula name followed by the name of the second nonmetal with the suffix *ide.* Prefixes indicate the number of atoms of each nonmetal in the formula.
- The formula of a covalent compound is written using the symbols of the nonmetals in the name followed by subscripts given by the prefixes.

MasteringChemistry
Tutorial: Naming Covalent Compounds

Guide to Naming Covalent Compounds with Two Nonmetals	
STEP 1	Name the first nonmetal by its element name.
STEP 2	Name the second nonmetal by using the first syllable of its element name followed by *ide.*
STEP 3	Add prefixes to indicate the number of atoms (subscripts).

Study Note

Two nonmetals can form two or more different covalent compounds. In their names, prefixes are used to indicate the subscript in the formula. Some typical prefixes are mono (1), di (2), tri (3), tetra (4), and penta (5). The ending of the second nonmetal is changed to *ide.*

◆ Learning Exercise 5.6A

Use the appropriate prefixes to name the following covalent compounds:

1. CS_2 ______________________________ **2.** CCl_4 ______________________________

3. CO ______________________________ **4.** SO_2 ______________________________

5. N_2O_4 ______________________________ **6.** PCl_3 ______________________________

Answers **1.** carbon disulfide **2.** carbon tetrachloride **3.** carbon monoxide
4. sulfur dioxide **5.** dinitrogen tetroxide **6.** phosphorus trichloride

Guide to Writing Formulas for Covalent Compounds	
STEP 1	Write the symbols in the order of the elements in a name.
STEP 2	Write any prefixes as subscripts.

◆ Learning Exercise 5.6B

Write the formula of each of the following covalent compounds:

1. dinitrogen oxide ______________ **2.** silicon tetrabromide ______________

3. nitrogen trichloride ______________ **4.** carbon dioxide ______________

5. sulfur hexafluoride ______________ **6.** oxygen difluoride ______________

Answers **1.** N_2O **2.** $SiBr_4$ **3.** NCl_3 **4.** CO_2 **5.** SF_6 **6.** OF_2

Summary of Writing Formulas and Names

- In both ionic and covalent compounds containing *two* different elements, the name of the element written first is named as the element. The ending of the name of the second element is replaced by *ide.* For example, $BaCl_2$ is named *barium chloride*. If the metal forms two or more positive ions, a Roman numeral is added to its name to indicate the ionic charge in the compound. For example, $FeCl_3$ is named *iron(III) chloride*.

- In naming covalent compounds, a prefix before the name of an element indicates the numerical value of a subscript. For example, N_2O_3 is named *dinitrogen trioxide*.
- In ionic compounds with three or more elements, a group of atoms is named as a polyatomic ion. The names of negative polyatomic ions end in *ate* or *ite*, except for hydroxide. For example, Na_2SO_4 is named *sodium sulfate*.
- When a polyatomic ion occurs two or three times in a formula, its formula is placed inside parenthesis, and the number of ions are shown as a subscript after the parenthesis $Ca(NO_3)_2$.

◆ Learning Exercise 5.6C

Indicate the type of compound (ionic or covalent) formed from each pair of elements. If it is an ionic compound, write the ions; if covalent, write the electron-dot formula of the molecule. Then give a formula and name for each:

Components	Ionic or Covalent?	Ions or Electron–Dot Formula	Formula	Name
Mg and Cl				
N and Cl				
K and SO_4				
Li and O				
C and Cl				
Na and PO_4				
H and S				
Ca and HCO_3				

Answers

Components	Ionic or Covalent?	Ions or Electron–Dot Formula	Formula	Name
Mg and Cl	Ionic	Mg^{2+}, Cl^-	$MgCl_2$	Magnesium chloride
N and Cl	Covalent	:Cl:N:Cl: :Cl:	NCl_3	Nitrogen trichloride
K and SO_4	Ionic	K^+, SO_4^{2-}	K_2SO_4	Potassium sulfate
Li and O	Ionic	Li^+, O^{2-}	Li_2O	Lithium oxide
C and Cl	Covalent	:Cl: :Cl:C:Cl: :Cl:	CCl_4	Carbon tetrachloride
Na and PO_4	Ionic	Na^+, PO_4^{3-}	Na_3PO_4	Sodium phosphate
H and S	Covalent	:H:S: H	H_2S	Dihydrogen sulfide
Ca and HCO_3	Ionic	Ca^{2+}, HCO_3^-	$Ca(HCO_3)_2$	Calcium hydrogen carbonate (bicarbonate)

5.7 Electronegativity and Bond Polarity

- Electronegativity values indicate the ability of an atom to attract electrons. In general, metals have low electronegativity values and nonmetals have high values.
- Electrons are shared unequally in polar covalent bonds because they are attracted to the more electronegative atom.
- An electronegativity difference of 0 to 0.4 indicates a nonpolar covalent bond, whereas a difference of 0.5 to 1.7 indicates a polar covalent bond. An electronegativity difference of 1.8 or greater indicates a bond that is ionic.
- A polar bond with its charge separation is called a dipole; the positive end is marked as δ^+ and the negative end as δ^-.
- Nonpolar molecules can have polar bonds when the dipoles are in a symmetric arrangement.
- In polar molecules, the dipoles do not cancel each other.

MasteringChemistry

Self Study Activity: Electronegativity

Self Study Activity: Bonds and Bond Polarity

◆ Learning Exercise 5.7

Identify the bonding between the following pairs of elements as (I) ionic, (P) polar covalent, (C) nonpolar covalent, or none.

1. H and N ______ **2.** P and O ______ **3.** Mg and O ______

4. Li and F ______ **5.** H and Cl ______ **6.** Cl and Cl ______

7. S and F ______ **8.** He and He ______

Answers **1.** P **2.** P **3.** I **4.** I
5. P **6.** C **7.** P **8.** none

5.8 Shapes and Polarity of Molecules

- Valence-shell electron-pair repulsion (VSEPR) theory predicts the geometry of a molecule by placing the electron pairs around a central atom as far apart as possible.
- A central atom with two electron groups has a linear arrangement (180°); three electron groups gives a trigonal planar arrangement (120°); and four electron pairs gives a tetrahedral arrangement (109°).
- The number of bonded atoms determines the shape of a molecule. A linear molecule has a central atom bonded to two atoms and no lone pairs. A trigonal planar molecule has a central atom bonded to three atoms and no lone pairs. A bent molecule at 120° has a central atom bonded to two atoms and one lone pair.
- A tetrahedral molecule has a central atom bonded to four atoms and no lone pairs. In a trigonal pyramidal molecule (109°), a central atom is bonded to three atoms and one lone pair. In a bent molecule at 109°, a central atom is bonded to two atoms and two lone pairs.
- A polar bond with its charge separation is called a dipole; the positive end is marked as δ^+ and the negative end as δ^-.
- Nonpolar molecules can have polar bonds when the dipoles are in a symmetrical arrangement that cancels.
- In polar molecules, the dipoles do not cancel each other.

MasteringChemistry

Self Study Activity: Polar Attraction

Tutorial: Molecular Shapes

Guide for Predicting Molecular Shape (VSEPR Theory)	
STEP 1	Write the electron-dot formula for the molecule.
STEP 2	Arrange the electron groups around the central atom to minimize repulsion.
STEP 3	Use the atoms bonded to the central atom to determine the molecular shape.

◆ Learning Exercise 5.8A

Match the shape of a molecule with the following descriptions of the electron groups around the central atoms and the number of bonded atoms.

A. linear **B.** trigonal planar **C.** tetrahedral
D. trigonal pyramidal **E.** bent (120 °) **F.** bent (109 °)

1. three electron groups with three bonded atoms ________

2. two electron groups with two bonded atoms ________

3. four electron groups with three bonded atoms ________

4. three electron groups with two bonded atoms ________

5. four electron groups with four bonded atoms ________

6. four electron groups with two bonded atoms ________

Answers **1.** B **2.** A **3.** D **4.** E **5.** C **6.** F

◆ Learning Exercise 5.8B

For each of the following, write the electron-dot formula, state the number of electron groups and bonded atoms, and predict the shape and angles of the molecule or ion:

Molecule or Ion	Electron-Dot Formula	Number of Electron Groups	Number of Bonded Atoms	Shape and Angle
CH_4				
PCl_3				
SO_3				
H_2S				

Answers

Molecule or Ion	Electron-Dot Formula	Number of Electron Groups	Number of Bonded Atoms	Shape and Angle
CH_4	H H:C:H H (with bonding pairs between C and each H)	4	4	Tetrahedral, 109°
PCl_3	:Cl:P:Cl: :Cl: (with lone pairs on each Cl and on P)	4	3	Trigonal pyramidal, 109°
SO_3	:O:S::O: :O: (with lone pairs on each O)	3	3	Trigonal planar, 120°
H_2S	H:S: H (with lone pairs on S)	4	2	Bent, 109°

◆ Learning Exercise 5.8C

Write the symbols δ^+ and δ^- over the atoms in polar bonds.

1. H—O **2.** N—N **3.** C—Cl

4. O—F **5.** N—F **6.** P—Cl

Answers

1. $\overset{\delta^+}{\text{H}}$—$\overset{\delta^-}{\text{O}}$ **2.** N—N *nonpolar* **3.** $\overset{\delta^+}{\text{C}}$—$\overset{\delta^-}{\text{Cl}}$

4. $\overset{\delta^+}{\text{O}}$—$\overset{\delta^-}{\text{F}}$ **5.** $\overset{\delta^+}{\text{N}}$—$\overset{\delta^-}{\text{F}}$ **6.** $\overset{\delta^+}{\text{P}}$—$\overset{\delta^-}{\text{Cl}}$

◆ Learning Exercise 5.8D

Indicate the dipoles in each of the following and determine whether the molecule is polar or nonpolar:

1. CF_4 **2.** HCl

3. NH_3 **4.** OF_2

Answers

1. CF_4

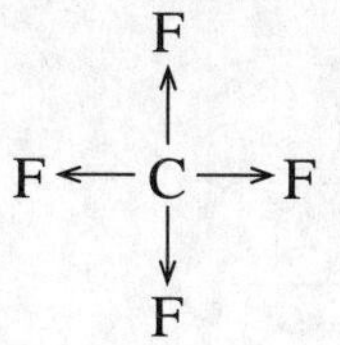

$$\begin{array}{c} F \\ \uparrow \\ F \leftarrow C \rightarrow F \\ \downarrow \\ F \end{array}$$ dipoles cancel, nonpolar

2. HCl $\overset{\delta^+}{H} \rightarrow \overset{\delta^-}{Cl}$ $\longmapsto$ dipoles do not cancel, polar

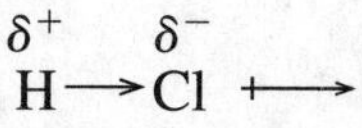

3. NH_3 $H \rightarrow \ddot{N} \leftarrow N$, $\uparrow H$ $\updownarrow$ dipoles do not cancel, polar

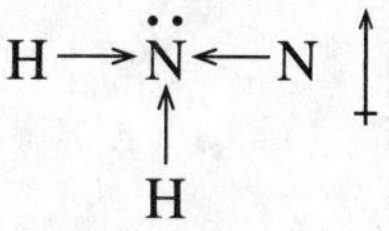

4. OF_2 $:\ddot{O} \rightarrow F$, $\downarrow F$ $\searrow$ dipoles do not cancel, polar

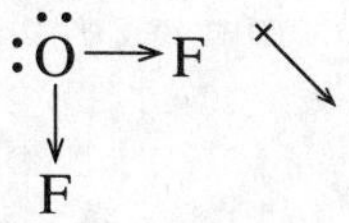

5.9 Attractive Forces in Compounds

- Ionic solids have high melting points due to strong ionic interactions between positive and negative ions.
- In polar substances, dipole-dipole attractions occur between the positive end of one molecule and the negative end of another.
- Hydrogen bonding, a type of dipole-dipole attraction, occurs between partially positive hydrogen atoms and strongly electronegative atoms of F, O, or N.
- Dispersion forces occur when temporary dipoles form within the nonpolar molecules causing attractions to other nonpolar molecules.

MasteringChemistry

Tutorial: Forces Between Molecules

◆ Learning Exercise 5.9A

Indicate the major type of interactive force that occurs in each of the following substances:

A. ionic bonds **B.** dipole–dipole attractions
C. hydrogen bonds **D.** dispersion forces

1. _____ KCl **2.** _____ NCl_3

3. _____ SBr_2 **4.** _____ Cl_2

5. _____ HF **6.** _____ H_2O

7. _____ C_4H_{10} **8.** _____ Na_2O

Answers **1.** A **2.** B **3.** B **4.** D **5.** C **6.** C **7.** D **8.** A

◆ Learning Exercise 5.9B

Identify the substance in each pair that would have the higher boiling point:

1. NaCl or HCl ________ **2.** Br_2 or HBr ________

3. H_2O or H_2S ________ **4.** C_2H_6 or CO_2 ________

5. $MgCl_2$ or OCl_2 ________ **6.** NH_3 or PH_3 ________

Answers

1. NaCl (ionic bonds) **2.** HBr (dipole-dipole attractions)

3. H_2O (hydrogen bonds) **4.** CO_2 (dipole-dipole attractions)

5. $MgCl_2$ (ionic) **6.** NH_3 (hydrogen bonding)

Checklist for Chapter 5

You are ready to take the *Practice Test* for Chapter 5. Be sure that you have accomplished the following learning goals for this chapter. If you are not sure, review the section listed at the end of the goal. Then apply your new skills and understanding to the Practice Test.

After studying Chapter 5, I can successfully:

____ Illustrate the octet rule for the formation of ions (5.1).

____ Write the formulas of compounds containing the ions of metals and nonmetals of representative elements (5.2).

____ Use charge balance to write an ionic formula (5.3).

____ Write the name of an ionic compound (5.3).

____ Write the name and formula of compounds containing polyatomic ions (5.4).

____ Write the electron-dot formula of a covalent compound (5.5).

____ Write the resonance structures of a covalent compound that has two or more possible electron-dot formulas (5.5).

____ Write the name and formula of a covalent compound (5.6).

____ Use electronegativity values to classify a bond as nonpolar covalent, polar covalent, or ionic (5.7).

____ Predict the shape and bond angles for a molecule (5.8).

____ Classify a molecule as polar or nonpolar (5.8).

____ Describe the types of forces that hold particles together in liquids and solids (5.9).

____ Identify the attractive forces in nonpolar covalent, polar covalent, or ionic compounds (5.9).

Practice Test for Chapter 5

For questions 1 through 4, consider an atom of phosphorus.

1. It is in group

A. 2A (2) **B.** 3A (13) **C.** 5A (15) **D.** 7A (17) **E.** 8A (18)

2. How many outer level electrons does it have?

A. 2 **B.** 3 **C.** 5 **D.** 8 **E.** 15

3. To achieve an octet, the phosphorus atom will

A. lose 1 electron **B.** lose 2 electrons **C.** lose 5 electrons
D. gain 2 electrons **E.** gain 3 electrons

4. As an ion, it has an ionic charge (valence) of

A. 1+ **B.** 2+ **C.** 5+ **D.** 2– **E.** 3–

5. To achieve an octet, a calcium atom

A. loses 1 electron **B.** loses 2 electrons **C.** loses 3 electrons
D. gains 1 electron **E.** gains 2 electrons

6. To achieve an octet, a chlorine atom

A. loses 1 electron **B.** loses 2 electrons **C.** loses 3 electrons
D. gains 1 electron **E.** gains 2 electrons

7. Another name for a positive ion is

A. anion **B.** cation **C.** proton **D.** positron **E.** sodium

8. The correct ionic charge (valence) for a calcium ion is

A. 1+ **B.** 2+ **C.** 1– **D.** 2– **E.** 3–

9. The silver ion has a charge of

A. 1+ **B.** 2+ **C.** 1– **D.** 2– **E.** 3–

10. The correct ionic charge (valence) for a phosphate ion is

A. 1+ **B.** 2+ **C.** 1– **D.** 2– **E.** 3–

11. The correct ionic charge (valence) for fluoride is

A. 1+ **B.** 2+ **C.** 1– **D.** 2– **E.** 3–

12. The correct ionic charge (valence) for a sulfate ion is

A. 1+ **B.** 2+ **C.** 1– **D.** 2– **E.** 3–

13. When the elements magnesium and sulfur are mixed

A. an ionic compound forms
B. a covalent compound forms
C. no reaction occurs
D. the two repel each other and will not combine
E. none of the above occurs

14. An ionic bond typically occurs between

A. two different nonmetals
B. two of the same type of nonmetals
C. two noble gases
D. two different metals
E. a metal and a nonmetal

15. A nonpolar covalent bond typically occurs between

A. two different nonmetals
B. two of the same type of nonmetals
C. two noble gases
D. two different metals
E. a metal and a nonmetal

16. A polar covalent bond typically occurs between

A. two different nonmetals
B. two of the same type of nonmetals
C. two noble gases
D. two different metals
E. a metal and a nonmetal

17. The formula for a compound between carbon and chlorine is

A. Cl **B.** CCl_2 **C.** C_4Cl **D.** CCl_4 **E.** C_4Cl_2

18. The formula for a compound between sodium and sulfur is

A. SoS **B.** NaS **C.** Na_2S **D.** NaS_2 **E.** Na_2SO_4

19. The formula for a compound between aluminum and oxygen is

A. AlO **B.** Al_2O **C.** AlO_3 **D.** Al_2O_3 **E.** Al_3O_2

20. The formula for a compound between barium and sulfur is

A. BaS **B.** Ba_2S **C.** BaS_2 **D.** Ba_2S_2 **E.** $BaSO_4$

21. The correct formula for iron (III) chloride is

A. $FeCl$ **B.** $FeCl_2$ **C.** Fe_2Cl **D.** Fe_3Cl **E.** $FeCl_3$

22. The correct formula for ammonium sulfate is

A. AmS **B.** $AmSO_4$ **C.** $(NH_4)_2S$ **D.** NH_4SO_4 **E.** $(NH_4)_2SO_4$

23. The correct formula for copper (II) chloride is

A. $CoCl$ **B.** $CuCl$ **C.** $CoCl_2$ **D.** $CuCl_2$ **E.** Cu_2Cl

24. The correct formula for lithium phosphate is

A. $LiPO_4$ **B.** Li_2PO_4 **C.** Li_3PO_4 **D.** $Li_2(PO_4)_3$ **E.** $Li_3(PO_4)_2$

25. The correct formula for silver oxide is

A. AgO **B.** Ag_2O **C.** AgO_2 **D.** Ag_3O_2 **E.** Ag_3O

26. The correct formula for magnesium carbonate is

A. $MgCO_3$ **B.** Mg_2CO_3 **C.** $Mg(CO_3)_2$ **D.** $MgCO$ **E.** $Mg_2(CO_3)_3$

27. The correct formula for copper (I) sulfate is

A. $CuSO_3$ **B.** $CuSO_4$ **C.** Cu_2SO_3 **D.** $Cu(SO_4)_2$ **E.** Cu_2SO_4

28. The name of $AlPO_4$ is

A. aluminum phosphide
B. alum phosphate
C. aluminum phosphate
D. aluminum phosphorus oxide
E. aluminum phosphite

29. The name of CuS is

A. copper sulfide
B. copper (I) sulfate
C. copper (I) sulfide
D. copper (II) sulfate
E. copper (II) sulfide

30. The name of $FeCl_2$ is

A. iron chloride
B. iron (II) chlorine
C. iron (II) chloride
D. iron chlorine
E. iron (III) chloride

31. The name of $ZnCO_3$ is

A. zinc (III) carbonate
B. zinc (II) carbonate
C. zinc bicarbonate
D. zinc carbon trioxide
E. zinc carbonate

32. The name of Al_2O_3 is

A. aluminum oxide
B. aluminum (II) oxide
C. aluminum trioxide
D. dialuminum trioxide
E. aluminum oxygenate

33. The name of NCl_3 is

A. nitrogen chloride
B. nitrogen trichloride
C. trinitrogen chloride
D. nitrogen chlorine three
E. nitrogen chloride (III)

34. The name of CO is

A. carbon monoxide
B. carbonic oxide
C. cobalt
D. carbonious oxide
E. carboxide

For questions 35 through 40, indicate the type of bond expected between the following:

A. ionic
B. nonpolar covalent
C. polar covalent
D. none

35. _____silicon and oxygen

36. _____barium and chlorine

37. _____aluminum and chlorine

38. _____chlorine and chlorine

39. _____sulfur and oxygen

40. _____neon and oxygen

For questions 41 through 45, determine the shape and angles of each of the following as:

A. linear, 180°
B. trigonal planar, 120°
C. bent, 120°
D. tetrahedral, 109°
E. trigonal pyramidal, 109°
F. bent, 109°

41. PCl_3

42. CBr_4

43. H_2S

44. BCl_3

45. $BeBr_2$

For questions 46 through 50, indicate the major type of interactive force that occurs in each of the following substances as:

A. ionic bonds **B.** dipole-dipole attractions **C.** hydrogen bonds **D.** dispersion forces

46. PBr_3

47. $CH_3\text{-}OH$

48. N_2

49. KCl

50. SO_2

Answers to the Practice Test

1. C	**2.** C	**3.** E	**4.** E	**5.** B
6. D	**7.** B	**8.** B	**9.** A	**10.** E
11. C	**12.** D	**13.** A	**14.** E	**15.** B
16. A	**17.** D	**18.** C	**19.** D	**20.** A
21. E	**22.** E	**23.** D	**24.** C	**25.** B
26. A	**27.** E	**28.** C	**29.** E	**30.** C
31. E	**32.** A	**33.** B	**34.** A	**35.** C
36. A	**37.** A	**38.** B	**39.** C	**40.** D
41. E	**42.** D	**43.** F	**44.** B	**45.** A
46. B	**47.** C	**48.** D	**49.** A	**50.** B

6

Chemical Reactions and Quantities

Study Goals

- Show that a balanced equation has an equal number of atoms of each element on the reactant side and the product side.
- Write a balanced equation for a chemical reaction when given the formulas of the reactants and products.
- Classify an equation as a combination, decomposition, single replacement, or double replacement.
- Describe the features of oxidation and reduction in an oxidation-reduction reaction.
- Determine the number of particles in a given number of moles of an element or compound.
- Calculate the molar mass of a compound using its formula and the atomic masses on the periodic table.
- Use the molar mass to convert between the grams of a substance and the number of moles.
- Using a given number of moles and a mole-mole conversion factor, determine the corresponding number of moles for a reactant or a product.
- Using a given mass of a substance in a reaction and the appropriate mole-mole factor and molar masses, calculate the mass of a reactant or a product.
- Given the actual yield of a product, calculate the percent yield.
- Determine the limiting reactant and calculate the amount of product formed.
- Given the heat of reaction, describe a reaction as an exothermic reaction or endothermic reaction.
- Given the heat of reaction, calculate the loss or gain of heat for an exothermic or endothermic reaction.

Think About It

1. What causes a slice of apple or avocado to turn brown?

2. How is a recipe like a chemical equation?

3. Why is the digestion of food a series of chemical reactions?

4. Why is energy released in an exothermic reaction?

Key Terms

Match each of the following terms with one of the statements below:

a. chemical change | **b.** chemical equation | **c.** combination reaction
d. mole | **e.** molar mass | **f.** physical change

1. ____ The amount of a substance that contains 6.02×10^{23} particles.

2. ____ A change that alters the composition of a substance producing a new substance with new properties.

3. ____ The mass, in grams, of an element or compound that is equal numerically to its atomic mass or the sum of atomic masses.

4. ____ The type of reaction in which the reactants combine to form a single product.

5. ____ A shorthand method of writing a chemical reaction with the formulas of the reactants written on the left side of an arrow and the formulas of the products on the right side.

Answers **1.** d **2.** a **3.** e **4.** c **5.** b

6.1 Chemical Reactions

- A chemical equation shows the formulas of the reactants on the left side of the arrow and the formulas of the products on the right side.
- In a balanced equation, *coefficients* in front of the formulas provide the same number of atoms for each kind of element on the reactant and product sides.
- A chemical equation is balanced by placing coefficients in front of the symbols or formulas in the equation.

Example: Balance the following equation:

$$N_2(g) + H_2(g) \longrightarrow NH_3(g)$$

1. Write an equation using the correct formulas of the reactants and products.

$$N_2(g) + H_2(g) \longrightarrow NH_3(g)$$

2. Count the atoms of N and H on the reactant side and on the product side.

$$N_2(g) + H_2(g) \longrightarrow NH_3(g)$$

2N, 2H   1N, 3H

3. Balance the N atoms by placing a coefficient of 2 in front of NH_3. (This increases the H atoms too.) Recheck the number of N atoms and the number of H atoms.

$$N_2(g) + H_2(g) \longrightarrow \mathbf{2}NH_3(g)$$

2N, 2H   2N, 6H

Balance the H atoms by placing a coefficient of 3 in front of H_2.

$$N_2(g) + \mathbf{3}H_2(g) \longrightarrow \mathbf{2}NH_3(g)$$

4. Recheck the number of N atoms and the number of H atoms.

$$N_2(g) + \mathbf{3}H_2(g) \longrightarrow \mathbf{2}NH_3(g)$$

2N, 6H   2N, 6H   *The equation is balanced.*

MasteringChemistry

Tutorial: Balancing Chemical Equations

Guide to Balancing a Chemical Equation	
STEP 1	Write an equation using the correct formulas of the reactants and products.
STEP 2	Count the atoms or ions of each element in reactants and products.
STEP 3	Use coefficients to balance each element.
STEP 4	Check the final equation for balance.

◆ Learning Exercise 6.1A

State the number of atoms of each element on the reactant side and on the product side for each of the following balanced equations:

a. $CaCO_3(s) \longrightarrow CaO(s) + CO_2(g)$

Element	Atoms on reactant side	Atoms on product side
Ca		
C		
O		

b. $2Na(s) + H_2O(l) \longrightarrow Na_2O(s) + H_2(g)$

Element	Atoms on reactant side	Atoms on product side
Na		
H		
O		

c. $C_5H_{12}(g) + 8O_2(g) \longrightarrow 5CO_2(g) + 6H_2O(g)$

Element	Atoms on reactant side	Atoms on product side
C		
H		
O		

d. $2AgNO_3\,(aq) + K_2S\,(aq) \longrightarrow 2KNO_3\,(aq) + Ag_2S\,(s)$

Element	Atoms on reactant side	Atoms on product side
Ag		
N		
O		
K		
S		

e. $2Al(OH)_3(aq) + 3H_2SO_4(aq) \longrightarrow Al_2(SO_4)_3(s) + 6H_2O(l)$

Element	Atoms on reactant side	Atoms on product side
Al		
O		
H		
S		

Answers

a. $CaCO_3(s) \longrightarrow CaO(s) + CO_2(g)$

Element	Atoms on reactant side	Atoms on product side
Ca	1	1
C	1	1
O	3	3

b. $2Na(s) + H_2O(l) \longrightarrow Na_2O(s) + H_2(g)$

Element	Atoms on reactant side	Atoms on product side
Na	2	2
H	2	2
O	1	1

c. $C_5H_{12}(g) + 8O_2(g) \longrightarrow 5CO_2(g) + 6H_2O(g)$

Element	Atoms on reactant side	Atoms on product side
C	5	5
H	12	12
O	16	16

d. $2AgNO_3(aq) + K_2S(aq) \longrightarrow 2KNO_3(aq) + Ag_2S(s)$

Element	Atoms on reactant side	Atoms on product side
Ag	2	2
N	2	2
O	6	6
K	2	2
S	1	1

e. $2Al(OH)_3(s) + 3H_2SO_4(aq) \longrightarrow Al_2(SO_4)_3(aq) + 6H_2O(l)$

Element	Atoms on reactant side	Atoms on product side
Al	2	2
O	18	18
H	12	12
S	3	3

◆ Learning Exercise 6.1B

Balance each of the following equations by placing coefficients in front of the formulas as needed:

a. ________ $MgO(s) \longrightarrow$ _____ $Mg(s) +$ _____ $O_2(g)$

b. ________ $Zn(s) +$ _____ $HCl(aq) \longrightarrow$ _____ $ZnCl_2(aq) +$ _____ $H_2(g)$

c. ________ $Al(s) +$ _____ $CuSO_4(aq) \longrightarrow$ _____ $Cu(s) +$ _____ $Al_2(SO_4)_3(aq)$

d. ________ $Al_2S_3(s) +$ _____ $H_2O(l) \longrightarrow$ _____ $Al(OH)_3(aq) +$ _____ $H_2S(g)$

e. ________ $BaCl_2(aq) +$ _____ $Na_2SO_4(aq) \longrightarrow$ _____ $BaSO_4(s) +$ _____ $NaCl(aq)$

f. ________ $CO(g) +$ _____ $Fe_2O_3(s) \longrightarrow$ _____ $Fe(s) +$ _____ $CO_2(g)$

g. ________ $K(s) +$ _____ $H_2O(l) \longrightarrow$ _____ $K_2O(s) +$ _____ $H_2(g)$

h. ________ $Fe(OH)_3(s) \longrightarrow$ _____ $Fe_2O_3(s) +$ _____ $H_2O(l)$

Answers

a. $2MgO(s) \longrightarrow 2Mg(s) + O_2(g)$

b. $Zn(s) + 2HCl(aq) \longrightarrow ZnCl_2(aq) + H_2(g)$

c. $2Al(s) + 3CuSO_4(aq) \longrightarrow 3Cu(s) + Al_2(SO_4)_3(aq)$

d. $Al_2S_3(s) + 6H_2O(l) \longrightarrow 2Al(OH)_3(s) + 3H_2S(g)$

e. $BaCl_2(aq) + Na_2SO_4(aq) \longrightarrow BaSO_4(s) + 2NaCl(aq)$

f. $3CO(g) + Fe_2O_3(s) \longrightarrow 2Fe(s) + 3CO_2(g)$

g. $2K(s) + H_2O(l) \longrightarrow K_2O(s) + H_2(g)$

h. $2Fe(OH)_3(s) \longrightarrow Fe_2O_3(s) + 3H_2O(l)$

6.2 Types of Reactions

- Reactions are classified as combination, decomposition, single replacement, and double replacement.
- In a *combination* reaction, reactants are combined. In a *decomposition* reaction, a reactant splits into simpler products.
- In *single (or double) replacement* reactions, one (or two) elements in the reacting compounds are replaced with the element(s) from the other reactant(s).

Study Note

Combination reactions combine reactants. *Decomposition reactions* split compounds into simpler products. In *single replacement reactions*, one of the elements in the reactants is replaced with an element(s) from the other reactant. In *double replacement reactions*, two of the elements in the reactants switch places.

MasteringChemistry

Self Study Activity: Chemistry Reactions and Equations

◆ Learning Exercise 6.2A

Match each of the following reactions with the type of reaction:

a. combination **b.** decomposition
c. single replacement **d.** double replacement

1. ________ $N_2(g) + 3H_2(g) \longrightarrow 2\,NH_3(g)$

2. ________ $BaCl_2(aq) + K_2CO_3(aq) \longrightarrow BaCO_3(s) + 2\,KCl(aq)$

3. ________ $2H_2O_2(aq) \longrightarrow 2H_2O(l) + O_2(g)$

4. ________ $CuO(s) + H_2(g) \longrightarrow Cu(s) + H_2O(l)$

5. ________ $N_2(g) + 2O_2(g) \longrightarrow 2NO_2(g)$

6. ________ $2NaHCO_3(s) \longrightarrow Na_2O(s) + 2CO_2(g) + H_2O(l)$

7. ________ $PbCO_3(s) \longrightarrow PbO(s) + CO_2(g)$

8. ________ $Al(s) + Fe_2O_3(s) \longrightarrow Fe(s) + Al_2O_3(s)$

Answers	**1.** a	**2.** d	**3.** b	**4.** c
	5. a	**6.** b	**7.** b	**8.** c

◆ Learning Exercise 6.2B

1. One way to remove tarnish from silver is to place the silver object on a piece of aluminum foil and add boiling water and some baking soda. The unbalanced equation is the following:

$$Al(s) + Ag_2S(s) \longrightarrow Ag(s) + Al_2S_3(s)$$

a. What is the balanced equation?

b. What type of reaction takes place?

2. Octane, C_8H_{18}, a compound in gasoline, burns in oxygen to produce carbon dioxide and water.

a. What is the balanced equation for the reaction?

b. What type of reaction takes place?

Answers

1a. $2Al(s) + 3Ag_2S(s) \longrightarrow 6Ag(s) + Al_2S_3(s)$ **1b.** single replacement

2a. $2C_8H_{18}(l) + 25O_2(g) \longrightarrow 16CO_2(g) + 18H_2O(l)$ **2b.** combustion

6.3 Oxidation-Reduction Reactions

- In an oxidation-reduction reaction, there is a loss and gain of electrons. In an oxidation, electrons are lost. In a reduction, electrons are gained.
- An oxidation must always be accompanied by a reduction. The number of electrons lost in the oxidation reaction is equal to the number of electrons gained in the reduction reaction.
- In biological systems, the term oxidation describes the gain of oxygen or the loss of hydrogen. The term reduction is used to describe a loss of oxygen or a gain of hydrogen.

MasteringChemistry

Tutorial: Identifying Oxidation-Reduction Reactions

◆ Learning Exercise 6.4

For each of the following reactions, indicate whether the underlined element is *oxidized or reduced.*

a. $4\underline{Al}(s) + 3O_2(g) \longrightarrow 2Al_2O_3(s)$ Al is ________________

b. $\underline{Fe}^{3+}(aq) + 1e^- \longrightarrow Fe^{2+}(aq)$ Fe^{3+} is ________________

c. $\underline{Cu}O(s) + H_2(g) \longrightarrow Cu(s) + H_2O(l)$ Cu^{2+} is ________________

d. $2\underline{Cl}^-(aq) \longrightarrow Cl_2(g) + 2e^-$ Cl^- is ________________

e. $2H\underline{Br}(aq) + Cl_2(g) \longrightarrow 2HCl(aq) + Br_2(g)$ Br^- is ________________

f. $2\underline{Na}(s) + Cl_2(g) \longrightarrow 2NaCl(s)$ Na is ________________

g. $\underline{Cu}Cl_2(aq) + Zn(s) \longrightarrow ZnCl_2(aq) + Cu(s)$ Cu^{2+} is ________________

Answers

a. Al is oxidized to Al^{3+}; loss of electrons (addition of O)
b. Fe^{3+} is reduced to Fe^{2+}; gain of electrons
c. Cu^{2+} is reduced to Cu; gain of electrons (loss of O)

d. $2Cl^-$ is oxidized to Cl_2; loss of electrons
e. $2Br^-$ is oxidized to Br_2; loss of electrons
f. Na is oxidized to Na^+; loss of electrons
g. Cu^{2+} is reduced to Cu; gain of electrons

6.4 The Mole

- A mole of any element contains Avogadro's number, 6.02×10^{23}, of atoms; a mole of any compound contains 6.02×10^{23} molecules or formula units.
- The subscripts in a formula indicate the number of moles of each element in one mole of the compound.

Guide to Calculating the Atoms or Molecules of a Substance	
STEP 1	Determine the given number of moles.
STEP 2	Write a plan to convert moles to atoms or molecules.
STEP 3	Use Avogadro's number to write conversion factors.
STEP 4	Set up problem to convert given moles to atoms or molecules.

MasteringChemistry

Tutorial: Using Avogadro's Number

Tutorial: Moles and the Chemical Formulas

◆ Learning Exercise 6.4A

Calculate each of the following:

a. number of P atoms in 1.50 moles of P

b. number of H_2S molecules in 0.0750 mole of H_2S

c. moles of Ag in 5.4×10^{24} atoms of Ag

d. moles of C_3H_8 in 8.25×10^{24} molecules of C_3H_8

Answers
a. 9.03×10^{23} P atoms
b. 4.52×10^{22} H_2S molecules
c. 9.0 moles of Ag
d. 13.7 moles of C_3H_8

Study Note

The subscripts in the formula of a compound indicate the number of moles of each element in one mole of that compound. For example, consider the formula Mg_3N_2:

1 mole of Mg_3N_2 = 3 moles of Mg atoms and 2 moles of N atoms

Some conversion factors for the moles of elements can be written as follows:

$$\frac{3 \text{ moles Mg atoms}}{1 \text{ mole } Mg_3N_2} \text{ and } \frac{1 \text{ mole } Mg_3N_2}{3 \text{ moles Mg atoms}} \qquad \frac{2 \text{ moles N atoms}}{1 \text{ mole } Mg_3N_2} \text{ and } \frac{1 \text{ mole } Mg_3N_2}{2 \text{ moles N atoms}}$$

◆ Learning Exercise 6.4B

Vitamin C (ascorbic acid) has the formula $C_6H_8O_6$.

a. How many moles of carbon are in 2.0 moles of vitamin C?

b. How many moles of hydrogen are in 5.0 moles of vitamin C?

c. How many moles of oxygen are in 1.5 moles of vitamin C?

Answers **a.** 12 moles of carbon (C) **b.** 40. moles of hydrogen (H)
c. 9.0 moles of oxygen (O)

◆ Learning Exercise 6.4C

For the compound ibuprofen ($C_{13}H_{18}O_2$) used in Advil and Motrin, determine the moles of each of the following:

a. moles of carbon (C) atoms in 2.20 moles of ibuprofen

b. moles of hydrogen (H) in 0.5 mole of ibuprofen

c. moles of oxygen (O) in 0.75 mole of ibuprofen

d. moles of ibuprofen that contain 36 moles of hydrogen (H)

Answers

	a. 28.6 moles of C	**b.** 9 moles of H
	c. 1.5 moles of O	**d.** 2 moles of ibuprofen

6.5 Molar Mass

- The molar mass (g/mole) of an element is numerically equal to its atomic mass in grams.
- The molar mass (g/mole) of a compound is the sum of the mass (grams) for each element in the formula. $MgCl_2$ has a molar mass that is the sum of the mass of 1 mole of Mg (24.3 g) and 2 moles of Cl (2×35.5 g) = 95.3 g/mole.
- The molar mass is useful as a conversion factor to change a given quantity in moles to grams.

$$\cancel{\text{Moles of substance}} \times \frac{\text{grams}}{1\ \cancel{\text{mole of substance}}} = \text{grams}$$

Guide to Calculating Molar Mass	
STEP 1	Obtain the molar mass of each element.
STEP 2	Multiply each molar by the number of moles (subscript) in the formula.
STEP 3	Calculate the molar mass by adding the masses of the elements.

Study Note

Example: What is the molar mass of silver nitrate, $AgNO_3$?

1 mole of Ag	× 107.9 g/mole =	107.9 g
1 mole of N	× 14.0 g/mole =	14.0 g
3 moles of O	× 16.0 g/mole =	48.0 g
	Molar mass of $AgNO_3$ =	169.9 g

MasteringChemistry

Self Study Activity: Stoichiometry

Tutorial: Converting Between Moles and Grams

◆ Learning Exercise 6.5A

Determine the molar mass for each of the following:

a. K_2O

b. $AlCl_3$

c. $C_{13}H_{18}O_2$ (ibuprofen)

d. C_4H_{10}

e. $Ca(NO_3)_2$

f. Mg_3N_2

g. $FeCO_3$

h. $(NH_4)_3PO_4$

Answers	**a.** 94.2 g	**b.** 133.5 g	**c.** 206.0 g	**d.** 58.0 g
	e. 164.1 g	**f.** 100.9 g	**g.** 115.9 g	**h.** 149.0 g

Guide to Calculating the Moles (or Grams) of a Substance from Grams (or Moles)	
STEP 1	Determine the given number of moles (or grams).
STEP 2	Write a plan to convert moles to grams (or grams to moles).
STEP 3	Determine the molar mass and write conversion factors.
STEP 4	Set up problem to convert given moles to grams (or grams to moles)

Study Note

Use molar mass as a conversion factor to change the number of moles of a substance to its mass in grams. Find the mass in grams of 0.250 mole of Na_2CO_3.

Molar mass

Grams ⟷ Moles

Example: $0.250\ \cancel{\text{mole } Na_2CO_3} \times \dfrac{106.0\text{ g } Na_2CO_3}{1\ \cancel{\text{mole } Na_2CO_3}} = 26.5\text{ g of } Na_2CO_3$

◆ Learning Exercise 6.5B

Find the number of grams in each of the following quantities:

a. 0.100 mole of SO_2

b. 0.100 mole of H_2SO_4

c. 2.50 moles of NH_3

d. 1.25 moles of O_2

e. 0.500 mole of Mg

f. 5.00 moles of H_2

g. 10.0 moles of PCl_3

h. 0.400 mole of S

Answers **a.** 6.41 g **b.** 9.81 g **c.** 42.5 g **d.** 40.0 g
e. 12.2 g **f.** 10.0 g **g.** 1380 g **h.** 12.8 g

Study Note

When the grams of a substance are given, the molar mass is used to calculate the number of moles of substance present.

$$\cancel{\text{grams of substance}} \times \frac{\text{1 mole of substance}}{\cancel{\text{grams of substance}}} = \text{moles of substance}$$

Example: How many moles of NaOH are in 4.0 g of NaOH?

$$4.0\ \cancel{\text{g NaOH}} \times \frac{\text{1 mole NaOH}}{40.0\ \cancel{\text{g NaOH}}} = 0.10 \text{ mole of NaOH}$$

Molar mass (inverted)

MasteringChemistry

Tutorial: Moles of Reactants and Products

◆ Learning Exercise 6.5C

Calculate the number of moles in each of the following quantities:

a. 32.0 g of CH_4

b. 391 g of K

c. 8.00 g of C_3H_8

d. 25.0 g of Cl_2

e. 0.220 g of CO_2

f. 5.00 g of Al_2O_3

g. The methane burned in a gas heater has a formula of CH_4. If 725 grams of methane are used in 1 month, how many moles of methane were burned?

h. There is 18 mg of iron in a vitamin tablet. If there are 100 tablets in a bottle, how many moles of iron are contained in the vitamins in the bottle?

Answers

a. 2.00 moles	**b.** 10.0 moles	**c.** 0.182 mole
d. 0.352 mole	**e.** 0.00500 mole	**f.** 0.0490 mole
g. 45.3 moles	**h.** 0.032 mole	

6.6 Mole Relationships in Chemical Equations

- The coefficients in a balanced chemical equation describe the moles of reactants and products in the reactions.
- Using the coefficients, mole-mole conversion factors are written for any two substances in the equation.
- For the reaction of oxygen forming ozone, $3O_2(g) \longrightarrow 2O_3(g)$, the mole–mole conversion factors are the following:

$$\frac{3 \text{ moles } O_2}{2 \text{ moles } O_3} \text{ and } \frac{2 \text{ moles } O_3}{3 \text{ moles } O_2}$$

Guide to Using Mole-Mole Factors	
STEP 1	Write the given and needed moles.
STEP 2	Write a plan to convert the given to the needed moles.
STEP 3	Use coefficients to write relationships and mole–mole factors.
STEP 4	Set up problem using the mole–mole factor that cancels given moles.

MasteringChemistry

Tutorial: Moles of Reactants and Products

◆ Learning Exercise 6.6A

Write the mole-mole factors that are possible from the following equation: $N_2(g) + O_2(g) \longrightarrow 2NO(g)$

Answers

For N_2 and O_2:

$$\frac{1 \text{ mole } N_2}{1 \text{ mole } O_2} \text{ and } \frac{1 \text{ mole } O_2}{1 \text{ mole } N_2}$$

For N_2 and NO:

$$\frac{1 \text{ mole } N_2}{2 \text{ moles NO}} \text{ and } \frac{2 \text{ moles NO}}{1 \text{ mole } N_2}$$

For NO and O_2:

$$\frac{1 \text{ mole } O_2}{2 \text{ moles NO}} \text{ and } \frac{2 \text{ moles NO}}{1 \text{ mole } O_2}$$

Study Note

The appropriate mole-mole factor is used to change the number of moles of the given to moles of a product.

Example: Using the equation, $N_2(g) + O_2(g) \longrightarrow 2NO(g)$, calculate the moles of NO obtained from 3 moles N_2.

$$3 \cancel{\text{moles } N_2} \times \frac{2 \text{ moles NO}}{1 \cancel{\text{mole } N_2}} = 6 \text{ moles of NO}$$

Mole-mole factor

◆ Learning Exercise 6.6B

Use the equation below to answer the following questions:

$$C_3H_8(g) + 5O_2(g) \longrightarrow 3CO_2(g) + 4\,H_2O(g)$$

a. How many moles of O_2 are needed to react with 2.00 moles of C_3H_8?

b. How many moles CO_2 are produced when 4.00 moles of O_2 react?

c. How many moles of C_3H_8 react with 3.00 moles of O_2?

d. How many moles of H_2O are produced from 0.50 mole of C_3H_8?

Answers **a.** 10.0 moles of O_2 **b.** 2.40 moles of CO_2
c. 0.600 mole of C_3H_8 **d.** 2.0 moles of H_2O

6.7 Mass Calculations for Reactions

- The grams of a substance in an equation are converted to grams of another substance using their molar masses and mole-mole factors.
- Suppose that a problem asks for the number of grams of O_3 (ozone) produced from 8.0 g of O_2. The equation is $3O_2(g) \longrightarrow 2O_3(g)$.

STEP 1 Molar mass of O_2 | **STEPS 2 and 3** Mole-mole factor from coefficients | **STEP 4** Molar mass of O_3

$$8.0\text{ g of }O_2 \xrightarrow{\text{Molar mass of }O_2} \text{moles of }O_2 \xrightarrow{\text{Mole-mole factor from coefficients}} \text{moles of }O_3 \xrightarrow{\text{Molar mass of }O_3} \text{g of }O_3$$

$$8.0\ \cancel{\text{g }O_2} \times \frac{1\ \cancel{\text{mole }O_2}}{32.0\ \cancel{\text{g }O_2}} \times \frac{2\ \cancel{\text{moles }O_3}}{3\ \cancel{\text{moles }O_2}} \times \frac{48.0\text{ g }O_3}{1\ \cancel{\text{mole }O_3}} = 8.0\text{ g of }O_3$$

Guide to Calculating the Masses of Reactants and Products in a Chemical Reaction	
STEP 1	Use molar mass to convert grams of given to moles (if necessary).
STEP 2	Write a mole-mole factor from the coefficients in the equation.
STEP 3	Convert moles of given to moles of needed substance using mole–mole factor.
STEP 4	Convert moles of needed substance to grams using molar mass.

MasteringChemistry

Tutorial: Masses of Reactants and Products

◆ Learning Exercise 6.7

Consider the following equation for the questions stated below:

$$2C_2H_6(g) + 7O_2(g) \longrightarrow 4CO_2(g) + 6H_2O(g)$$

a. How many grams of oxygen (O_2) are needed to react with 4.00 moles of C_2H_6?

b. How many grams of C_2H_6 are needed to react with 115 g of O_2?

c. How many grams of C_2H_6 react if 2.00 L of CO_2 gas are produced at STP?

d. How many grams of CO_2 are produced when 2.00 moles of C_2H_6 react with sufficient oxygen?

e. How many grams of water are produced when 82.5 g of O_2 react with sufficient C_2H_6?

Answers **a.** 448 g of O_2 **b.** 30.8 g of C_2H_6 **c.** 1.34 g of C_2H_6
d. 176 g of CO_2 **e.** 39.8 g of H_2O

6.8 Percent Yield and Limiting Reactants

- Theoretical yield is the maximum amount of product calculated for a given amount of a reactant.
- Percent yield is the ratio of the actual amount (yield) of product obtained to the theoretical yield.
- In a limiting reactant problem, the availability of one of the reactants limits the amount of product.
- The reactant that is used up is the limiting reactant; the reactant that remains is the excess reactant.
- The limiting reactant produces the smaller number of moles of product.

Study Note

The percent yield is the ratio of the actual yield obtained to the theoretical yield, which is calculated for a given amount of starting reactant. If we calculate that the reaction of 35.5 g of N_2 can theoretically produce 43.1 g of NH_3, but the actual yield is 26.0 g of NH_3, the percent yield is

$$\frac{26.0 \text{ g of NH}_3 \text{ (actual mass produced)}}{43.1 \text{ g of NH}_3 \text{ (theoretical mass)}} \times 100\% = 60.3\% \text{ Percent yield}$$

Guide to Calculations for Percent Yield

STEP 1	Write the given and needed quantities.
STEP 2	Write a plan to calculate the theoretical yield and the percent yield.
STEP 3	Write the molar mass for the reactant and the mole-mole factor from the balanced equation.
STEP 4	Solve for percent yield ratio by dividing the actual yield (given) by the theoretical yield and multiplying by 100%.

MasteringChemistry

Tutorial: What will Run Out First?

◆ Learning Exercise 6.8A

Consider the following reaction: $2H_2S(g) + 3O_2(g) \longrightarrow 2SO_2(g) + 2H_2O(g)$

a. If 60.0 g of H_2S reacts with sufficient oxygen and produces 45.5 g of SO_2, what is the percent yield for SO_2?

b. If 25.0 g of O_2 reacting with H_2S produces 18.6 g of SO_2, what is the percent yield for SO_2?

Consider the reaction: $2C_2H_6(g) + 7O_2(g) \longrightarrow 4CO_2(g) + 6H_2O(g)$
Ethane

c. If 125 g of C_2H_6 reacting with sufficient oxygen produces 175 g of CO_2, what is the percent yield for CO_2?

d. When 35.0 g of O_2 reacts with sufficient ethane to produce 12.5 g of H_2O, what is the percent yield of water?

Answers **a.** 40.3% **b.** 55.7% **c.** 47.7% **d.** 74.0%

Study Note

The amount of product possible from a mixture of two reactants is determined by calculating the moles of product each will produce. The limiting reactant produces the smaller amount of product.
In the reaction, $S(l) + 3F_2(g) \longrightarrow SF_6(g)$, how many grams of SF_6 are possible when 5.00 moles of S is mixed with 12.0 moles of F_2?

Find the limiting reactant:

$$5.00 \text{ moles S} \times \frac{1 \text{ mole } SF_6}{1 \text{ mole S}} = 5.00 \text{ moles of } SF_2$$

$$12.0 \text{ moles } F_2 \times \frac{1 \text{ mole } SF_6}{3 \text{ moles } F_2} = 4.00 \text{ moles of } SF_2$$ = **limiting reactant** (smaller number of moles)

Calculate the grams of 4.0 mole of SF_6 produced by the limiting reactant:

$$4.0 \text{ moles } SF_6 \times \frac{146.1 \text{ g } SF_6}{1 \text{ mole } SF_6} = 584 \text{ g of } SF_6$$

◆ Learning Exercise 6.8B

a. How many grams of Co_2S_3 can be produced in the reaction of 2.20 moles of Co and 3.60 moles of S?
$2Co(s) + 3S(s) \longrightarrow Co_2S_3(s)$

b. How many grams of NO_2 can be produced from the reaction of 32.0 g of NO and 24.0 g of O_2?
$2NO(g) + O_2(g) \longrightarrow 2NO_2(g)$

Answers **a.** 236 g **b.** 49.1 g

6.9 Energy Changes in Chemical Reactions

- In a reaction, molecules (or atoms) must collide with energy equal to or greater than the energy of activation.
- The heat of reaction is the energy difference between the energy of the reactants and the products.
- In exothermic reactions, the heat of reaction is the energy released. In endothermic reactions, the heat of reaction is the energy absorbed.
- The rate of a reaction (the speed at which products form) can be increased by adding more reacting molecules, raising the temperature of the reaction, or by adding a catalyst.

MasteringChemistry
Tutorial: Heat of Reaction

Guide to Calculations Using Heat of Reaction (ΔH)	
STEP 1	List given and needed data for the equation.
STEP 2	Write a plan using heat of reaction and any molar mass needed.
STEP 3	Write the conversion factors including heat of reaction.
STEP 4	Set up the problem.

◆ Learning Exercise 6.9A

Indicate whether each of the following is an endothermic or exothermic reaction:

1. $2H_2(g) + O_2(g) \longrightarrow 2H_2O(g) + 582\text{ kJ}$ ______________

2. $C_2H_4(g) + 42.1\text{ kcal} \longrightarrow H_2(g) + C_2H_2(g)$ ______________

3. $2C(s) + O_2(g) \longrightarrow 2CO(g) + 53\text{ kcal}$ ______________

4. $C_6H_{12}O_6(s) + 6O_2(g) \longrightarrow 6CO_2(g) + 6H_2O(l) + 1350\text{ kcal}$ ______________
Glucose

5. $C_2H_4(g) + H_2O(g) \longrightarrow C_2H_5OH(l) + 21\text{ kcal}$ ______________

Answers **1.** exothermic **2.** endothermic **3.** exothermic
4. exothermic **5.** exothermic

◆ Learning Exercise 6.9B

Consider the following reaction:

$$C_6H_{12}O_6(s) + 6O_2(g) \longrightarrow 6CO_2(g) + 6H_2O(l) + 1350\text{ kcal}$$

How much heat, in kcal and kJ, is produced when 50.0 g of CO_2 is formed?

Answer 256 kcal; 1070 kJ

◆ Learning Exercise 6.9C

Consider each of the following reactions and calculate the kilojoules absorbed or released for each:

1. $C_2H_4(g) + 176\ kJ \longrightarrow H_2(g) + C_2H_2(g)$

a. 3.50 moles of C_2H_2 is produced

b. 75.0 g of C_2H_4 reacts

2. $2H_2(g) + O_2(g) \longrightarrow 2H_2O(g) + 582\ kJ$

a. 0.820 mole of H_2 reacts

b. .25 g of H_2O is produced

Answers **1a.** 616 kJ absorbed **1b.** 471 kJ absorbed
2a. 239 kJ released **2b.** 36.4 kJ released

Checklist for Chapter 6

You are ready to take the practice test for Chapter 6. Be sure that you have accomplished the following learning goals for this chapter. If you are not sure, review the section listed at the end of the goal. Then apply your new skills and understanding to the practice test.

After studying Chapter 6, I can successfully:

____ Identify a chemical and physical change (6.1).

____ State a chemical equation in words and calculate the total atoms of each element in the reactants and products (6.1).

____ Write a balanced equation for a chemical reaction from the formulas of the reactants and products (6.2).

____ Identify a reaction as a combination, decomposition, single, or double replacement (6.2).

____ Identify an oxidation and reduction reaction (6.3).

____ Calculate the number of particles in a mole of a substance (6.4).

____ Calculate the molar mass given the formula of a substance (6.5).

____ Convert the grams of a substance to moles; moles to grams (6.5).

____ Use mole-mole factors for the mole relationships in an equation to calculate the moles of another substance in an equation for a chemical reaction (6.6).

____ Calculate the mass of a substance in an equation using mole-mole factors and molar masses (6.7).

____ Calculate the percent yield, given the actual yield of a product (6.8).

____ Given the mass of reactants, find the limiting reactant and calculate the amount of product formed (6.8).

____ Given the heat of reaction, describe a reaction as exothermic or endothermic (6.9).

____ Calculate the heat, in kcal or kilojoules, released or absorbed by a chemical reaction(6.9)

Practice Test for Chapter 6

For each of the unbalanced equations in questions 1 through 5, balance and indicate the correct coefficient for the component in the equation written in ***boldface type****.*

A. 1 **B.** 2 **C.** 3 **D.** 4 **E.** 5

1. ____ $Sn(s) + \mathbf{Cl_2}(g) \longrightarrow SnCl_4(s)$

2. ____ $Al(s) + H_2O(l) \longrightarrow Al_2O_3(s) + \mathbf{H_2}(g)$

3. ____ $C_3H_8(g) + \mathbf{O_2}(g) \longrightarrow CO_2(g) + H_2O(g)$

4. ____ $\mathbf{NH_3}(g) + O_2(g) \longrightarrow N_2(g) + H_2O(g)$

5. ____ $N_2O(g) \longrightarrow N_2(g) + \mathbf{O_2}(g)$

For questions 6 through 10, classify each reaction as one of the following:

A. combination **B.** decomposition **C.** single replacement **D.** double replacement

6. ____ $S(s) + O_2(g) \longrightarrow SO_2(g)$

7. ____ $Fe_2O_3(s) + 3C(s) \longrightarrow 2Fe(s) + 3CO(g)$

8. ____ $CaCO_3(s) \longrightarrow CaO + CO_2(g)$

9. ____ $Mg(s) + 2AgNO_3(aq) \longrightarrow Mg(NO_3)_2(aq) + 2Ag(s)$

10. ____ $Na_2S(aq) + Pb(NO_3)_2(aq) \longrightarrow PbS(s) + 2NaNO_3(aq)$

For questions 11 through 15, identify each reaction as an (A) oxidation or a (B) reduction.

11. $Ca \longrightarrow Ca^{2+} + 2e^-$ ____

12. $Fe^{3+} + 3e^- \longrightarrow Fe$ ____

13. $Al^{3+} + 3e^- \longrightarrow Al$ ____

14. $Br_2 + 2e^- \longrightarrow 2Br^-$ ____

15. $Sn^{2+} \longrightarrow Sn^{4+} + 2e^-$ ____

16. The moles of oxygen (O) in 2.0 moles of $Al(OH)_3$ is

A. 1.0 **B.** 2.0 **C.** 3.0 **D.** 4.0 **E.** 6.0

17. What is the molar mass of Li_2SO_4?

A. 55.1 g **B.** 62.1 g **C.** 100.1 g **D.** 109.9 g **E.** 103.1 g

18. What is the molar mass of $NaNO_3$?

A. 34.0 g **B.** 37.0 g **C.** 53.0 g **D.** 75.0 g **E.** 85.0 g

19. The number of grams in 0.600 mole of Cl_2 is

A. 71.0 g **B.** 118 g **C.** 42.6 g **D.** 84.5 g **E.** 4.30 g

20. How many grams are in 4.00 moles of NH_3?

A. 4.00 g **B.** 17.0 g **C.** 34.0 g **D.** 68.0 g **E.** 0.240 g

21. How many moles is 8.0 g of NaOH?

A. 0.10 mole **B.** 0.20 mole **C.** 0.40 mole **D.** 2.0 moles **E.** 4.0 moles

22. The number of moles of aluminum in 54 g of Al is

A. 0.50 mole **B.** 1.0 mole **C.** 2.0 moles **D.** 3.0 moles **E.** 4.0 moles

23. The number of moles of water in 36 g of H_2O is

A. 0.50 mole **B.** 1.0 mole **C.** 2.0 moles **D.** 3.0 moles **E.** 4.0 moles

24. What is the number of moles in 2.2 g of CO_2?

A. 2.0 moles **B.** 1.0 mole **C.** 0.20 mole **D.** 0.050 mole **E.** 0.010 mole

25. 0.20 g of H_2 = _____ mole of H_2

A. 0.10 mole **B.** 0.20 mole **C.** 0.40 mole **D.** 0.040 mole **E.** 0.010 mole

For questions 26 through 30, use the reaction: $\underset{\text{Ethanol}}{C_2H_5OH}(l) + 3O_2(g) \longrightarrow 2CO_2(g) + 3H_2O(l)$

26. How many grams of oxygen are needed to react with 1.0 mole of ethanol?

A. 8.0 g **B.** 16 g **C.** 32 g **D.** 64 g **E.** 96 g

27. How many moles of water are produced when 12 moles of oxygen react?

A. 3.0 moles **B.** 6.0 moles **C.** 8.0 moles **D.** 12 moles **E.** 36 moles

28. How many grams of carbon dioxide are produced when 92.0 g of ethanol react?

A. 22.0 g **B.** 44.0 g **C.** 88.0 g **D.** 92.0 g **E.** 176 g

29. How many moles of oxygen would be needed to produce 44 g of CO_2?

A. 0.67 mole **B.** 1.0 mole **C.** 1.5 moles **D.** 2.0 moles **E.** 3.0 moles

30. How many grams of water will be produced if 23 g of ethanol react?

A. 54 g **B.** 27 g **C.** 18 g **D.** 9.0 g **E.** 6.0 g

31. In the reaction, $N_2(g) + 3H_2(g) \longrightarrow 2NH_3(g)$, a 25.0-g sample of N_2 is reacted. If the actual yield of NH_3 is 20.8 g, the percent yield of NH_3 is

A. 68.4% **B.** 20.8% **C.** 25.0% **D.** 82.5% **E.** 100.%

For questions 32 and 33, use the reaction: $C_3H_8(g) + 5O_2(g) \longrightarrow 3CO_2(g) + 4H_2O(g)$

32. If 50.0 g of C_3H_8 and 150. g of O_2 react, the limiting reactant is:

A. C_3H_8 **B.** O_2 **C.** both **D.** neither **E.** CO_2

33. If 50.0 g of C_3H_8 and 150. g of O_2 react, the mass of CO_2 formed is:

A. 150. g **B.** 206 g **C.** 200. g **D.** 124 g **E.** 132 g

Consider the following equation and heat of reaction for Questions 34–37.

$$C_2H_6O(l) + 3O_2(g) \longrightarrow 2CO_2(g) + 3H_2O(l) + 1420\text{ kJ}$$

34. The reaction is

A. thermic **B.** endothermic **C.** exothermic **D.** nonthermic **E.** subthermic

35. How much heat, in kilojoules, is released when 0.500 mole of C_2H_6O reacts?

A. 710 kJ **B.** 1420 kJ **C.** 2130 kJ **D.** 2840 kJ **E.** 4260 kJ

36. How many grams of CO_2 are produced if 355 kJ heat are released?

A. 11.0 g **B.** 22.0 g **C.** 33.0 g **D.** 44.0 g **E.** 88.0 g

37. How much heat, in kilojoules, is released when 16.0 g of O_2 reacts?

A. 4260 kJ **B.** 1420 kJ **C.** 710 kJ **D.** 237 kJ **E.** 118 kJ

Answers to the Practice Test

1. B	**2.** C	**3.** E	**4.** D	**5.** A
6. A	**7.** C	**8.** B	**9.** C	**10.** D
11. A	**12.** B	**13.** B	**14.** B	**15.** A
16. E	**17.** D	**18.** E	**19.** C	**20.** D
21. B	**22.** C	**23.** C	**24.** D	**25.** A
26. E	**27.** D	**28.** E	**29.** C	**30.** B
31. A	**32.** B	**33.** D	**34.** C	**35.** A
36. B	**37.** D			

7

Gases

Study Goals

- Describe the kinetic molecular theory of gases and the properties of gases.
- Describe the units of measurement used for pressure, and change from one unit to another.
- Use the pressure-volume relationship (Boyle's law) to determine the new pressure or volume of a certain amount of gas at a constant temperature.
- Use the temperature-volume relationship (Charles's law) to determine the new temperature or volume of a certain amount of gas at a constant pressure.
- Use the temperature-pressure relationship (Gay-Lussac's law) to determine the new temperature or pressure of a certain amount of gas at a constant volume.
- Use the combined gas law to find the new pressure, volume, or temperature of a gas when changes in two of these properties are given.
- Describe the relationship (Avogadro's law) between the amount of a gas and its volume, and use this relationship in calculations.
- Use the ideal gas law to solve for P, V, T, or n of a gas when given three of the four values in the ideal gas equation.
- Calculate the quantity of a reactant or product in a chemical reaction involving a gas.
- Use the gas laws to calculate the molar mass of a gas.
- Use partial pressures to calculate the total pressure of a mixture of gases.

Think About It

1. How does a barometer work?

2. What happens to the pressure on a person who is scuba diving?

3. Why are airplanes pressurized?

4. Why does a bag of chips expand when you take it to a higher altitude?

Key Terms

Match the key terms with the statements shown below.

a. kinetic molecular theory   **b.** pressure   **c.** Boyle's law
d. Charles's law   **e.** partial pressure

1. ____ the volume of a gas varies directly with the Kelvin temperature (P and n constant)

2. ____ a force exerted by gas particles when they collide with the sides of a container

3. ____ the pressure exerted by the individual gases in a gas mixture

4. ____ the volume of a gas varies inversely with the pressure of a gas (T and n constant)

5. ____ the model that explains the behavior of gaseous particles

Answers **1.** d **2.** b **3.** e **4.** c **5.** a

7.1 Properties of Gases

- In a gas, particles are so far apart and moving so fast that they are not attracted to each other.
- A gas is described by the physical properties of pressure (P), volume (V), temperature (T), and amount in moles (n).

MasteringChemistry

Self Study Activity: Properties of Gases

◆ Learning Exercise 7.1

True or *false*:

a. ____ Gases are composed of small particles.

b. ____ Gas molecules are usually close together.

c. ____ Gas molecules move rapidly because they are strongly attracted.

d. ____ The distances between gas molecules are great.

e. ____ Gas molecules travel in straight lines until they collide.

Answers **a.** T **b.** F **c.** F **d.** T **e.** T

7.2 Gas Pressure

- A gas exerts pressure, which is the force of the gas particles on the surface of a container.
- Metric and SI units of gas pressure include torr, mmHg, atmosphere, and Pascal.

> ***MasteringChemistry***
>
> **Self Study Activity: Properties of Gases**
>
> **Case Study: Scuba Diving and Blood Gases**

◆ Learning Exercise 7.2

Complete each of the following:

a. 1.50 atm = __________ mmHg

b. 550 mmHg = __________ atm

c. 725 mmHg = __________ torr

d. 1520 mmHg = __________ atm

e. 30.5 psi = __________ mmHg

f. During the weather report on TV, the pressure was given as 98.7 kilopascals. What is this pressure in mmHg? In atm?

Answers **a.** 1140 mmHg **b.** 0.72 atm **c.** 725 torr
d. 2.00 atm **e.** 1580 mmHg **f.** 740 mmHg; 0.974 atm

7.3 Pressure and Volume (Boyle's Law)

- According to Boyle's law, pressure increases if volume decreases; pressure decreases if volume increases.
- The volume (V) of a gas changes inversely with the pressure (P) of the gas when T and n are held constant: $P_1V_1 = P_2V_2$.

Guide to Using the Gas Laws	
STEP 1	Organize the data in a table of initial and final conditions.
STEP 2	Rearrange the gas law to solve for the unknown quantity.
STEP 3	Substitute values into the gas law equation to solve for the unknown.

> ***MasteringChemistry***
>
> **Tutorial: Pressure and Volume**

◆ Learning Exercise 7.3A

Complete with *increases* or *decreases*:

1. Gas pressure increases (*T* constant) when volume ________________.

2. Gas volume increases at constant *T* when pressure ________________.

Answers **1.** decreases **2.** decreases

◆ Learning Exercise 7.3B

Calculate the variable in each of the following gas problems using Boyle's law:

a. Four (4.0) liters of helium gas have a pressure of 800 mmHg. What is the new pressure when the volume is reduced to 1.0 liter (*n* and *T* constant)?

b. A gas occupies a volume of 360 mL at 750 mmHg. What volume does it occupy at a pressure of (1) 1500 mmHg? (2) 375 mmHg (*n* and *T* constant)?

c. A gas sample at a pressure of 5.0 atm has a volume of 3.00 L. If the gas pressure is changed to 760 mmHg, what volume will the gas occupy (*n* and *T* constant)?

d. A sample of 250 mL of nitrogen is initially at a pressure of 2.50 atm. If the pressure changes to 825 mmHg, what is the new volume in milliliters?

Answers **a.** 3200 mmHg **b.** (1) 180 mL (2) 720 mL **c.** 15 L **d.** 576 mL

7.4 Temperature and Volume (Charles's Law)

- The volume (*V*) of a gas is directly related to its Kelvin temperature (*T*) when there is no change in the pressure of the gas:

$$\frac{V_1}{T_1} = \frac{V_2}{T_2}$$

- According to *Charles's law,* temperature increases if the volume of the gas increases; temperature decreases if volume decreases.

MasteringChemistry

Tutorial: Temperature and Volume

◆ Learning Exercise 7.4A

Complete with *increases* or *decreases*:

a. When the temperature of a gas increases at constant pressure, its volume ___________

b. When the volume of a gas decreases at constant pressure, its temperature ___________

Answers: **a.** increases **b.** decreases

◆ Learning Exercise 7.4B

Use *Charles's law* to solve the following gas problems:

a. A large balloon has a volume of 2.5 L at a temperature of 0 °C. What is the new volume of the balloon when the temperature rises to 120 °C and the pressure remains constant?

b. Consider a balloon filled with helium to a volume of 6600 L at a temperature of 223 °C. To what temperature must the gas be cooled to decrease the volume to 4800 L (*P* constant)?

c. A sample of 750 mL of neon is heated from 120 °C to 350 °C. If pressure is kept constant, what is the new volume?

d. What is the final temperature, in degrees Celsius, of 350 mL of oxygen gas at 22 °C when its volume increases to 0.80 L (*P* constant)?

Answers **a.** 3.6 L **b.** 88 °C **c.** 1200 mL **d.** 401 °C

7.5 Temperature and Pressure (Gay-Lussac's Law)

- The pressure (P) of a gas is directly related to its Kelvin temperature (T).

$$\frac{P_1}{T_1} = \frac{P_2}{T_2}$$

- This means that an increase in temperature increases the pressure of a gas, or a decrease in temperature decreases the pressure, as long as the volume stays constant.
- Vapor pressure is the pressure of the gas that forms when a liquid evaporates. At the boiling point of a liquid, the vapor pressure equals the atmospheric pressure.

MasteringChemistry
Tutorial: Temperature and Pressure
Tutorial: Vapor Pressure and Boiling Point

◆ Learning Exercise 7.5A

Solve the following gas law problems using *Gay-Lussac's law*:

a. A sample of helium gas has a pressure of 860 mmHg at a temperature of 225 K. At what pressure (mmHg) will the helium sample reach a temperature of 675 K (V constant)?

b. A balloon contains a gas with a pressure of 580 mmHg and a temperature of 227 °C. What is the new pressure (mmHg) of the gas when the temperature drops to 27 °C (V constant)?

c. A spray can contains a gas with a pressure of 3.0 atm at a temperature 17 °C. What is the pressure (atm) in the container if the temperature inside the can rises to 110 °C (V constant)?

d. A gas has a pressure of 1200 mmHg at 300 °C. What will the temperature (°C) be when the pressure falls to 1.10 atm (V constant)?

Answers **a.** 2580 mmHg **b.** 348 mmHg **c.** 4.0 atm **d.** 126 °C

◆ Learning Exercise 7.5B

Explain how a liquid can have a boiling point of 80 °C at sea level and a boiling point of 74 °C at an altitude of 1000 m.

Answer The vapor pressure required for boiling is lower at higher altitude because the atmospheric pressure is lower. As a result, the substance boils at a lower temperature.

7.6 The Combined Gas Law

- The gas laws can be combined into a relationship of pressure (P), volume (V) and temperature (T).

$$\frac{P_1V_1}{T_1} = \frac{P_2V_2}{T_2}$$

MasteringChemistry

Tutorial: The Combined Gas Law

◆ Learning Exercise 7.6

Solve the following using the combined gas law:

a. A 5.0-L sample of nitrogen gas has a pressure of 1200 mmHg at 220 K. What is the pressure of the sample when the volume increases to 20.0 L at 440 K?

b. A 10.0-L sample of gas is emitted from a volcano with a pressure of 1.20 atm and a temperature of 150.0 °C. What is the volume of the gas when its pressure is 0.900 atm and the temperature is −40.0 °C?

c. A 25.0-mL bubble forms at the ocean depths where the pressure is 10.0 atm and the temperature is 5.0 °C. What is the volume of that bubble at the ocean surface where the pressure is 760.0 mmHg and the temperature is 25 °C?

d. A 35.0-mL sample of argon gas has a pressure of 1.0 atm and a temperature of 15 °C. What is the final volume if the pressure goes to 2.0 atm and the temperature to 45 °C?

e. A weather balloon with a volume of 315 L is launched at the Earth's surface where the temperature is 12 °C and the pressure is 0.93 atm. What is the volume of the balloon in the upper atmosphere where the pressure is 116 mmHg and the temperature is −35 °C?

Answers **a.** 600 mmHg **b.** 7.34 L **c.** 268 mL **d.** 19 mL **e.** 1600 L

7.7 Volume and Moles (Avogadro's Law)

- Avogadro's law states that equal volumes of gases at the same temperature and pressure contain the same number of moles. The volume (V) of a gas is directly related to the number of moles of the gas when the pressure and temperature of the gas do not change.

$$\frac{V_1}{n_1} = \frac{V_2}{n_2}$$

- If the number of moles of gas increases, the volume increases; if the number of moles of gas decreases, the volume decreases.
- At STP conditions, standard pressure (1 atm) and temperature (0 °C), one mole of a gas occupies a volume of 22.4 L.
- The molar volume at STP can be used to determine the mass or volume of a gas in a chemical reaction.

MasteringChemistry

Tutorial: Volume and Moles

Study Note

At STP, the molar volume factor 22.4 L/mole converts between volume and moles of a gas.
Example: How many liters would 2.00 moles of N_2 occupy at STP?

Solution: $$2.00\ \cancel{\text{moles } N_2} \times \frac{22.4\text{ L (STP)}}{1\ \cancel{\text{mole } N_2}} = 44.8\text{ L of } N_2\text{(STP)}$$

◆ Learning Exercise 7.7A

Use Avogadro's law to solve the following gas problems:

a. A gas containing 0.50 mole of helium has a volume of 4.00 L. What is the new volume, in liters, when 1.0 mole of nitrogen gas is added to the container when pressure and temperature remain constant?

b. A balloon containing 1.00 mole of oxygen gas has a volume of 15 L. What is the new volume, in liters, of the balloon when 2.00 moles of helium gas are added (*T* and *P* constant)?

c. What is the volume, in liters, occupied by 28.0 g of nitrogen gas (N_2) at STP?

d. What is the volume, in liters, of a container that holds 6.40 g of O_2 gas at STP?

Answers **a.** 12 L **b.** 45 L **c.** 22.4 L **d.** 4.48 L

◆ Learning Exercise 7.7B

Use gas laws to determine the quantity of a reactant or product in each of the following chemical reactions:

a. How many liters of hydrogen gas at STP are produced when 12.5 g of magnesium reacts?

$$Mg(s) + 2HCl(aq) \longrightarrow MgCl_2(aq) + H_2(g)$$

b. How many liters of Cl_2 gas at STP are required to completely react 8.50 g of potassium?

$$2K(s) + Cl_2(g) \longrightarrow 2KCl(s)$$

c. How many grams of $KClO_3$ must be heated to produce 12.6 L of O_2 gas at STP?

$$2KClO_3(s) \longrightarrow 2KCl(s) + 3O_2(g)$$

d. How many liters of NO gas at STP can be produced when 55.8 L of O_2 react at STP?

$$4NH_3(g) + 5O_2(g) \longrightarrow 4NO(g) + 6H_2O(l)$$

Answers **a.** 11.5 L of H_2 **b.** 2.43 L of Cl_2 **c.** 46.0 g of $KClO_3$ **d.** 44.6 L of NO

7.8 The Ideal Gas Law

- The ideal gas law $PV = nRT$ gives the relationship between the four variables: pressure, volume, moles, and temperature. When any three variables are given, the fourth can be calculated.
- R is the universal gas constant: 0.0821 L·atm/mole·K *or* 62.4 L·mmHg/mole·K
- The ideal gas law can be used to determine the mass or volume of a gas in a chemical reaction.
- The molar mass of a gas can be determined using the ideal gas law.

Guide to Using the Gas Laws	
STEP 1	Organize data given for the gas.
STEP 2	Solve the ideal gas law to solve for the unknown quantity.
STEP 3	Substitute gas data and calculate unknown value.

MasteringChemistry

Tutorial: Introduction to the Ideal Gas Law

Self Study Activity: The Ideal Gas Law

Study Note

Identify the three known variables for the ideal gas law, and arrange the equation to solve for the unknown variable.

Example: Solve the ideal gas law for *P*.

$$PV = nRT \qquad P = \frac{nRT}{V}$$

◆ Learning Exercise 7.8A

Use the *ideal gas law* to solve for the unknown variable in each of the following:

a. What volume, in L, is occupied by 0.25 mole of nitrogen gas (N_2) at 0 °C and 1.50 atm?

b. What is the temperature (°C) of 0.500 mole of helium that occupies a volume of 15.0 L at a pressure of 1200 mmHg?

c. What is the pressure, in atm, of 1.0 mole of neon gas in a 5.0 L steel container at a temperature of 18 °C?

d. What is the pressure, in atm, of 8.0 g of oxygen gas (O_2) that has a volume of 245 mL at a temperature of 22 °C?

Answers **a.** 3.7 L **b.** 304 °C **c.** 4.8 atm **d.** 25 atm

◆ Learning Exercise 7.8B

Use the ideal gas law to determine the quantity of a reactant or product in each of the following chemical reactions:

a. How many grams of KNO_3 must decompose to produce 35.8 L of O_2 at 28 °C and 745 mmHg?

$$2KNO_3(s) \longrightarrow 2KNO_2(s) + O_2(g)$$

b. At a temperature of 325 °C and a pressure of 1.20 atm, how many liters of CO_2 can be produced when 50.0 g of propane (C_3H_8) reacts with oxygen gas?

$$C_3H_8(g) + 5O_2(g) \longrightarrow 3CO_2(g) + 4H_2O(g)$$

Propane

Answers **a.** 287 g of KNO_3 **b.** 139 L of CO_2

◆ Learning Exercise 7.8C

Use gas laws to determine the molar mass of a gas for each of the following:

a. A gas has a mass of 0.650 g and a volume of 560 mL at STP. What is the molar mass of the gas?

b. A sample of gas with a mass of 0.412 g, has a volume of 273 mL, and a pressure of 746 mmHg at 25 °C. What is the molar mass of the gas?

Answers **a.** 26.0 g/mole **b.** 44.0 g/mole

7.9 Partial Pressures (Dalton's Law)

- In a mixture of two or more gases, the total pressure is the sum of the partial pressures of the individual gases.

$$P_{total} = P_1 + P_2 + P_3 + \ldots$$

- The partial pressure of a gas in a mixture is the pressure it would exert if it were the only gas in the container.

Guide to Solving Partial Pressure	
STEP 1	Write the equation for the sum of partial pressures.
STEP 2	Solve for the unknown quantity.
STEP 3	Substitute known pressures and calculate the unknown.

MasteringChemistry

Tutorial: Mixture of Gases

◆ Learning Exercise 7.9A

Use *Dalton's law* to solve the following problems about gas mixtures:

a. What is the pressure, in mmHg, of a sample of gases containing oxygen gas (O_2) at 0.500 atm, nitrogen (N_2) at 132 torr, and helium at 224 mmHg?

b. What is the pressure, in atm, of a gas sample containing helium at 285 mmHg and oxygen gas (O_2) at 1.20 atm?

c. A gas sample containing nitrogen (N_2) and oxygen (O_2) has a pressure of 1500 mmHg. If the partial pressure of the nitrogen is 0.900 atm, what is the partial pressure (mmHg) of the oxygen gas in the mixture?

Answers **a.** 736 mmHg **b.** 1.58 atm **c.** 816 mmHg

◆ Learning Exercise 7.9B

Fill in the blanks by writing *I (increases)* or *D (decreases)* for a gas in a closed container.

	Pressure	Volume	Moles	Temperature
a.	________	Increases	Constant	Constant
b.	Increases	Constant	________	Constant
c.	Constant	Decreases	________	Constant
d.	________	Constant	Constant	Increases
e.	Constant	________	Constant	Decreases
f.	________	Constant	Increases	Constant

Answers **a.** D **b.** I **c.** D **d.** I **e.** D **f.** I

◆ Learning Exercise 7.9C

Complete the following table for typical blood gas values for partial pressures:

Gas	Alveoli	Oxygenated blood	Deoxygenated blood	Tissues
CO_2	________	________	________	________
O_2	________	________	________	________

Answers

CO_2	40 mmHg	40 mmHg	50 mmHg or greater	50 mmHg or greater
O_2	100 mmHg	100 mmHg	30 mmHg or less	30 mmHg or less

Checklist for Chapter 7

You are ready to take the practice test for Chapter 7. Be sure that you have accomplished the following learning goals for this chapter. If you are not sure, review the section listed at the end of the goal. Then apply your new skills and understanding to the practice test.

After studying Chapter 7, I can successfully:

_____ Describe the kinetic molecular theory of gases (7.1).

_____ Change the units of pressure from one to another (7.2).

_____ Use the pressure-volume relationship (Boyle's law) to determine the new pressure or volume of a fixed amount of gas at constant temperature (7.3).

_____ Use the temperature-volume relationship (Charles's law) to determine the new temperature or volume of a fixed amount of gas at a constant pressure (7.4).

_____ Use the temperature-pressure relationship (Gay-Lussac's law) to determine the new temperature or pressure of a certain amount of gas at a constant volume (7.5).

_____ Use the combined gas law to find the new pressure, volume, or temperature of a gas when changes in two of these properties are given (7.6).

_____ Describe the relationship between the amount of a gas and its volume and use this relationship in calculations (7.7).

_____ Determine the quantity of a reactant or product in a reaction involving a gas (7.7).

_____ Use the ideal gas law to solve for pressure, volume, temperature, or amount of a gas (7.8).

_____ Calculate the total pressure of a gas mixture from the partial pressures (7.9).

Practice Test for Chapter 7

For questions 1–5, answer using T (true) or F (false):

1. ____ The kinetic energy of a gas is related to its volume.

2. ____ The molecules of a gas are moving extremely fast.

3. ____ The collisions of gas molecules with the walls of their container create pressure.

4. ____ Gas molecules are close together and move in straight-line patterns.

5. ____ Gas molecules have no attractions between them.

6. When a gas is heated in a closed metal container, the

A. pressure increases
B. pressure decreases
C. volume increases
D. volume decreases
E. number of molecules increases

7. The pressure of a gas will increase when

A. the volume increases
B. the temperature decreases
C. more molecules of gas are added
D. molecules of gas are removed
E. none of these

8. If the temperature of a gas increases,

A. the pressure will decrease
B. the volume will increase
C. the volume will decrease
D. the number of molecules will increase
E. none of these

9. The relationship that the volume of a gas is inversely related to its pressure at constant temperature is known as

A. Boyle's law **B.** Charles's law **C.** Gay-Lussac's law
D. Dalton's law **E.** Avogadro's law

10. What is the pressure (atm) of a gas with a pressure of 1200 mmHg?

A. 0.63 atm **B.** 0.79 atm **C.** 1.2 atm
D. 1.6 atm **E.** 2.0 atm

11. A 6.00-L sample of oxygen has a pressure of 660 mmHg. When the volume is reduced to 2.00 liters at constant temperature, it will have a new pressure of

A. 1980 mmHg **B.** 1320 mmHg **C.** 330.mmHg
D. 220.mmHg **E.** 110 mmHg

12. A sample of nitrogen gas at 180 K has a pressure of 1.0 atm. When the temperature is increased to 360 K at constant volume, the new pressure will be

A. 0.50 atm **B.** 1.0 atm **C.** 1.5 atm
D. 2.0 atm **E.** 3.6 atm

13. If two gases have the same volume, temperature, and pressure, they also have the same

A. density **B.** number of molecules **C.** molar mass
D. speed **E.** size molecules

14. A gas sample with a volume of 4.00 L has a pressure of 750 mmHg and a temperature of 77 °C. What is its new volume at 277 °C and 250 mmHg?

A. 7.6 L **B.** 19 L **C.** 2.1 L
D. 0.00056 L **E.** 3.3 L

15. If the temperature of a gas does not change, but its volume doubles, its pressure will

A. double
B. triple
C. decrease to one-half the original pressure
D. decrease to one-fourth thc original pressure
E. not change

16. A sample of oxygen with a pressure of 400 mmHg contains 2.0 moles of gas and has a volume of 4.0 L. What will the new pressure be when the volume expands to 5.0 L, and 3.0 moles of helium gas are added while temperature is constant?

A. 160 mmHg **B.** 250 mmHg **C.** 800 mmHg
D. 1000 mmHg **E.** 1560 mmHg

17. A sample of 2.00 moles of gas initially at STP is converted to a volume of 5.0 L and a temperature of 27 °C. What is its new pressure in atm?

A. 0.12 atm **B.** 5.5 atm **C.** 7.5 atm
D. 8.9 atm **E.** 9.9 atm

18. The conditions for standard temperature and pressure (STP) are

A. 0 K, 1 atm **B.** 0 °C, 10 atm **C.** 25 °C, 1 atm
D. 273 K, 1 atm **E.** 273 K, 0.5 atm

19. The volume occupied by 1.50 moles of CH_4 at STP is

A. 44.8 L **B.** 33.6 L **C.** 22.4 L
D. 11.2 L **E.** 5.60 L

20. How many grams of oxygen gas (O_2) are present in 44.8 L of oxygen at STP?

A. 8.0 g **B.** 16.0 g **C.** 32.0 g
D. 48.0 g **E.** 64.0 g

21. What is the volume, in liters, of 0.50 moles of nitrogen gas (N_2) at 25 °C and 2.0 atm?

A. 0.51 L **B.** 1.0 L **C.** 4.2 L
D. 6.1 L **E.** 24 L

22. A gas mixture contains helium with a partial pressure of 0.80 atm, oxygen with a partial pressure of 450 mmHg, and nitrogen with a partial pressure of 230 mmHg. What is the total pressure in atm for the gas mixture?

A. 1.10 atm **B.** 1.39 atm **C.** 1.69 atm
D. 2.00 atm **E.** 8.00 atm

23. A mixture of oxygen and nitrogen has a total pressure of 840 mmHg. If the oxygen has a partial pressure of 510 mmHg, what is the partial pressure of the nitrogen?

A. 240 mmHg **B.** 330 mmHg **C.** 775 mmHg
D. 1040 mmHg **E.** 1350 mmHg

24. The exchange of gases between the alveoli, blood, and tissues of the body is a result of

A. pressure gradients
B. different molecular weights
C. shapes of molecules
D. altitude
E. all of these

25. Oxygen moves into the tissues from the blood because its partial pressure

A. in arterial blood is higher than in the tissues
B. in venous blood is higher than in the tissues
C. in arterial blood is lower than in the tissues
D. in venous blood is lower than in the tissues
E. is equal in the blood and in the tissues

26. A gas sample with a mass of 0.440 g has a volume of 0.224 L at STP. The gas has a molar mass of

A. 19.6 g/mole **B.** 22.4 g/mole **C.** 44.0 g/mole
D. 44.8 g/mole **E.** 50.9 g/mole

27. 2.50 g $KClO_3$ decomposes by the equation: $2\ KClO_3(s) \longrightarrow 2\ KCl(s) + 3\ O_2(g)$ What volume of O_2 is produced at 25 °C and a pressure of 750 mmHg?

A. 0.00998 L **B.** 0.759 L **C.** 0.0636 L
D. 0.506 L **E.** 1.32 L

Answers to the Practice Test

1. F	**2.** T	**3.** T	**4.** F	**5.** T
6. A	**7.** C	**8.** B	**9.** A	**10.** D
11. A	**12.** D	**13.** B	**14.** B	**15.** C
16. C	**17.** E	**18.** D	**19.** B	**20.** E
21. D	**22.** C	**23.** B	**24.** A	**25.** A
26. C	**27.** B			

8
Solutions

Study Goals

- Identify the solute and solvent in a solution.
- Describe hydrogen bonding in water.
- Describe electrolytes in a solution.
- Define solubility.
- Identify a salt as soluble or insoluble.
- Write an equation (molecular or ionic) to show the formation of an insoluble salt.
- Calculate the percent concentrations and molarity of a solution.
- Use the molarity of a solution in a chemical reaction to calculate the volume or quantity of a reactant or product.
- Describe the dilution of a solution.
- Distinguish between a solution, a colloid, and a suspension.
- Describe osmosis and dialysis.

Think About It

1. Why is salt used to preserve foods?

2. Why do raisins or dried prunes swell when placed in water?

3. Why are pickles made in a brine solution with a high salt concentration?

4. Why can't you drink seawater?

5. How do your kidneys remove toxic substances from the blood but retain the usable substances?

Key Terms

Match the following terms with the correct statement shown below:

a. solution **b.** concentration **c.** molarity
d. osmosis **e.** electrolyte

1. ____ A substance that dissociates into ions when it dissolves in water
2. ____ The flow of solvent through a semipermeable membrane into a solution with a higher solute concentration
3. ____ The amount of solute that is dissolved in a specified amount of solution
4. ____ The number of moles of solute in one liter of solution
5. ____ A mixture of at least two components called a solute and a solvent

Answers **1.** e **2.** d **3.** b **4.** c **5.** a

8.1 Solutions

- The partial positive charge (δ^+) of hydrogen and the partial negative charge (δ^-) of oxygen permitwater molecules to hydrogen bond with other water molecules.
- A polar solute is soluble in a polar solvent; a nonpolar solute is soluble in a nonpolar solvent; "like dissolves like".
- A solution is a homogeneous mixture that forms when a solute dissolves in a solvent.
- An ionic solute dissolves in water, a polar solvent, because the polar water molecules attract and pull the positive and negative ions into solution. In solution, water molecules surround the ions due to a process called hydration.

MasteringChemistry

Self Study Activity: Hydrogen Bonding

◆ Learning Exercise 8.1A

Indicate the solute and solvent in each of the following:	**Solute**	**Solvent**
a. 10 g of KCl dissolved in 100 g of water	____	____
b. Soda water: $CO_2(g)$ dissolved in water	____	____
c. An alloy composed of 80% Zn and 20% Cu	____	____

d. A mixture of O_2 (200 mmHg) and He (500 mmHg) __________ __________

e. A solution of 40 mL of CCl_4 and 2 mL of Br_2 __________ __________

Answers **a.** KCl; water **b.** CO_2; water **c.** Cu; Zn
d. oxygen; helium **e.** Br_2; CCl_4

◆ Learning Exercise 8.1B

Essay How does the polarity of the water molecule allow it to hydrogen bond?

Answer The O-H bonds in water molecules are polar because the hydrogen atoms are partially positive and the oxygen atoms are partially negative. Hydrogen bonding occurs because the partially positive hydrogen atoms in one water molecule are attracted to partially negative oxygen atoms of other water molecules.

◆ Learning Exercise 8.1C

Water is polar and hexane is nonpolar. In which solvent is each of the following soluble?

a. bromine, Br_2, nonpolar __________ **b.** HCl, polar __________

c. cholesterol, nonpolar __________ **d.** vitamin D, nonpolar __________

e. vitamin C, polar __________

Answers **a.** hexane **b.** water **c.** hexane **d.** hexane **e.** water

8.2 Electrolytes and Nonelectrolytes

- Electrolytes conduct an electrical current because they produce ions in aqueous solutions.
- Strong electrolytes are nearly completely ionized, whereas weak electrolytes are slightly ionized. Nonelectrolytes do not form ions in solution but dissolve as molecules.
- An equivalent is the amount of an electrolyte that carries 1 mole of electrical charge.
- There are 1, 2, or 3 equivalents per mole of a positive or negative ion depending on the charge.

◆ Learning Exercise 8.2A

Write an equation for the formation of an aqueous solution of each of the following strong electrolytes:

a. LiCl ______________________________

b. $Mg(NO_3)_2$ ______________________________

c. Na_3PO_4 ______________________________

d. K_2SO_4 ______________________

e. $MgCl_2$ ______________________

Answers

a. $LiCl(s) \xrightarrow{H_2O} Li^+(aq) + Cl^-(aq)$

b. $Mg(NO_3)_2(s) \xrightarrow{H_2O} Mg^{2+}(aq) + 2NO_3^-(aq)$

c. $Na_3PO_4(s) \xrightarrow{H_2O} 3Na^+(aq) + PO_4^{3-}(aq)$

d. $K_2SO_4(s) \xrightarrow{H_2O} 2K^+(aq) + SO_4^{2-}(aq)$

e. $MgCl_2(s) \xrightarrow{H_2O} Mg^{2+}(aq) + 2Cl^-(aq)$

◆ Learning Exercise 8.2B

Indicate whether an aqueous solution of each of the following contains mostly ions, molecules only, or mostly molecules with some ions. Write an equation for the formation of the solution.

a. glucose, $C_6H_{12}O_6$, a nonelectrolyte ______________________

b. NaOH, a strong electrolyte ______________________

c. K_2SO_4, a strong electrolyte ______________________

d. HF, a weak electrolyte ______________________

Answers

a. $C_6H_{12}O_6(s) \longrightarrow C_6H_{12}O_6(aq)$ molecules only
b. $NaOH(s) \longrightarrow Na^+(aq) + OH^-(aq)$ mostly ions
c. $K_2SO_4(s) \longrightarrow 2K^+(aq) + SO_4^{2-}(aq)$ mostly ions
d. $HF(g) + H_2O(l) \rightleftarrows H_3O^+(aq) + F^-(aq)$ mostly molecules and a few ions

◆ Learning Exercise 8.2C

Calculate the following:

a. Number of equivalents in 1 mole of Mg^{2+}

b. Number of equivalents in 2.5 moles of Cl^-

c. Number of equivalents in 2.0 moles of Ca^{2+}

Answers **a.** 2 Eq **b.** 2.5 Eq **c.** 4.0 Eq

8.3 Solubility

- The amount of solute that dissolves depends on the nature of the solute and solvent.
- Solubility describes the maximum amount of a solute that dissolves in 100 g of solvent at a given temperature.
- A saturated solution contains the maximum amount of dissolved solute at a certain temperature.
- An increase in temperature increases the solubility of most solids, but decreases the solubility of gases in water.
- The solubility rules describe the kinds of ionic combinations that are soluble and insoluble in water. If a salt contains Li^+, Na^+, K^+, NO_3^-, $HC_2H_3O^-$ or NH_4^+ ion, it is soluble in water. Most halides and sulfates are soluble.

MasteringChemistry

Self Study Activity: Solubility

Tutorial: Solubility

Case Study: Kidney Stones and Saturated Solutions

◆ Learning Exercise 8.3A

Identify each of the following as a saturated solution (S) or an unsaturated solution (U):

1. A sugar cube dissolves when added to a cup of coffee. ________

2. A KCl crystal added to a KCl solution does not change in size. ________

3. A layer of sugar forms in the bottom of a glass of iced tea. ________

4. The rate of crystal formation equals the rate of dissolving. ________

5. Upon heating, all the sugar dissolves. ________

Answers **1.** U **2.** S **3.** S **4.** S **5.** U

◆ Learning Exercise 8.3B

Use the $NaNO_3$ solubility chart given below for the following problems:

Solubility of $NaNO_3$

Temperature (°C)	g of $NaNO_3$/100 g of H_2O
40	100
60	120
80	150
100	200

a. How many grams of $NaNO_3$ will dissolve in 100 g of water at 40 °C?

b. How many grams of $NaNO_3$ will dissolve in 300 g of water at 60 °C?

c. A solution is prepared using 200 g of water and 350 g of $NaNO_3$ at 80 °C. Will any solute remain undissolved? If so, how much?

d. Will 150 g of $NaNO_3$ dissolve when added to 100 g of water at 100 °C?

Answers

a. 100 g
b. 360 g
c. 300 g of $NaNO_3$ will dissolve leaving 50 g of $NaNO_3$ that will not dissolve.
d. Yes, all 150 g of $NaNO_3$ will dissolve.

◆ Learning Exercise 8.3C

Predict whether each of the following salts are soluble (S) or insoluble (I) in water:

1. ______ NaCl　　**2.** ______ $AgNO_3$　　**3.** ______ $PbCl_2$

4. ______ Ag_2S　　**5.** ______ $BaSO_4$　　**6.** ______ Na_2CO_3

7. ______ K_2S　　**8.** ______ $MgCl_2$　　**9.** ______ BaS

Answers

1. S　**2.** S　**3.** I　**4.** I　**5.** I
6. S　**7.** S　**8.** S　**9.** I

◆ Learning Exercise 8.3D

Predict whether an insoluble salt forms in the following solutions of soluble salts are mixed. If so, write the formula of the solid.

1. $NaCl(aq)$ and $Pb(NO_3)_2(aq)$ ________________

2. $BaCl_2(aq)$ and $Na_2SO_4(aq)$ ________________

3. $K_3PO_4(aq)$ and $NaNO_3(aq)$ ________________

4. $Na_2S(aq)$ and $AgNO_3(aq)$ ________________

Answers　**1.** Yes; $PbCl_2$　**2.** Yes; $BaSO_4$　**3.** None　**4.** Yes; Ag_2S

◆ Learning Exercise 8.3E

For the mixtures that form insoluble salts in Learning Exercise 8.3D, write the ionic equation and the net ionic equation.

1.

2.

3.

4.

Answers

1. $2Na^+(aq) + 2Cl^-(aq) + Pb^{2+}(aq) + 2NO_3^-(aq) \longrightarrow 2Na^+(aq) + PbCl_2(s) + 2NO_3^-(aq)\ 2Cl^-(aq)$
$Pb^{2+}(aq) + 2Cl^- \longrightarrow PbCl_2(s)$

2. $Ba^{2+}(aq) + 2Cl^-(aq) + 2Na^+(aq) + SO_4^{2-}(aq) \longrightarrow BaSO_4(s) + 2Na^+(aq) + 2Cl^-(aq)$
$Ba^{2+}(aq) + SO_4^{2-} \longrightarrow BaSO_4(s)$

3. No insoluble salt forms.

4. $2Na^+(aq) + S^{2-}(aq) + 2Ag^+(aq) + 2NO_3^-(aq) \longrightarrow 2Na^+(aq) + 2NO_3^-(aq) + Ag_2S(s)$
$2Ag^+(aq) + S^{2-}(aq) \longrightarrow Ag_2S(s)$

8.4 Percent Concentration

- The concentration of a solution is the relationship between the amount of solute (g or mL) and the amount (g or mL) of solution.
- A mass percent (mass/mass) expresses the ratio of the mass of solute to the mass of solution multiplied by 100.

$$\text{Percent (m/m)} = \frac{\text{grams of solute}}{\text{grams of solution}} \times 100\%$$

- Percent concentrations can also be expressed as a mass/volume ratio.

$$\text{Percent (m/v)} = \frac{\text{grams of solute}}{\text{volume (mL) of solution}} \times 100\%$$

MasteringChemistry

Tutorial: Calculating Percent Concentration

Tutorial: Percent Concentration as a Conversion Factor

Study Note

Calculate mass percent concentration (m/m) as

$$\frac{\text{grams of solute}}{\text{grams of solution}} \times 100\%$$

Example: What is the mass percent (m/m) when 2.4 g of $NaHCO_3$ dissolves in 120 g of solution?

Solution: $\frac{2.4 \text{ g } NaHCO_3}{120 \text{ g solution}} \times 100\% = 2.0\% \text{ (m/m)}$

◆ Learning Exercise 8.4A

Determine the percent concentration for each of the following solutions:

a. The mass-mass percent (m/m) concentration for 18.0 g of NaCl in 90.0 g of solution.

b. The mass-volume percent (m/v) concentration for 5.0 g of KCl in 2.0 L of solution.

c. The mass-mass percent (m/m) concentration for 4.0 g of KOH in 50.0 g of solution.

d. The mass-volume percent (m/v) concentration for 0.25 kg of glucose in 5.0 L of solution.

Answers **a.** 20.0% **b.** 0.25% **c.** 8.0% **d.** 5.0%

Study Note

In solution problems, the percent concentration is useful as a conversion factor. The factor is obtained by rewriting the % as g of solute/100 g (or mL) of solution.

Example 1: How many grams of KI are needed to prepare 250 mL of a 4% (m/v) KI solution?

Solution:

$$250 \text{ mL solution} \times \underbrace{\frac{4 \text{ g KI}}{100 \text{ mL solution}}}_{\%\ (m/v)\ factor} = 10 \text{ g of KI}$$

Example 2: How many grams of a 25% (m/m) NaOH solution can be prepared from 75 g of NaOH?

Solution:

$$75 \text{ g NaOH} \times \underbrace{\frac{100 \text{ g NaOH solution}}{25 \text{ g NaOH}}}_{\%\ (m/m)\ factor\ (inverted)} = 300 \text{ g of NaOH solution}$$

◆ Learning Exercise 8.4B

Calculate the number of grams of solute needed to prepare each of the following solutions:

a. How many grams of glucose are needed to prepare 400 mL of a 10.0% (m/v) solution?

b. How many grams of lidocaine hydrochloride are needed to prepare 50.0 g of a 2.0% (m/m) solution?

c. How many grams of KCl are needed to prepare 0.80 L of a 0.15% (m/v) solution?

d. How many grams of NaCl are needed to prepare 250 mL of a 1.0% (m/v) solution?

Answers **a.** 40.0 g **b.** 1.0 g **c.** 1.2 g **d.** 2.5 g

◆ Learning Exercise 8.4C

Use percent-concentration factors to calculate the volume (mL) of each solution that contains the amount of solute stated in each problem.

a. 2.00 g of NaCl from a 1.00% (m/v) NaCl solution

b. 25.0 g of glucose from a 5.00% (m/v) glucose solution

c. 1.5 g of KCl from a 0.50% (m/v) KCl solution

d. 7.50 g of NaOH from a 15.0% (m/v) NaOH solution

Answers **a.** 200 mL **b.** 500 mL **c.** 300 mL (3.0×10^2 mL) **d.** 50.0 mL

8.5 Molarity and Dilution

- Molarity is a concentration term that describes the number of moles of solute dissolved in 1 L (1000 mL) of solution.

$$M = \frac{\text{moles of solute}}{\text{L solution}}$$

- *Dilution* is the process of mixing a solution with solvent to obtain a lower concentration.
- For dilutions, use the expression $C_1V_1 = C_2V_2$ or $M_1V_1 = M_2V_2$ and solve for the unknown value.
- The molarity and volume of a solution can be used to calculate the amount of a reactant or a product in a reaction.

MasteringChemistry
Tutorial: Dilution

◆ Learning Exercise 8.5A

Calculate the molarity of the following solutions:

a. 2.0 moles of HCl in 1.0 L of solution

b. 10.0 moles of glucose ($C_6H_{12}O_6$) in 2.0 L of solution

c. 80.0 g of NaOH in 4.0 L of solution (Hint: Find moles of NaOH.)

Answers **a.** 2.0 M HCl **b.** 5.0 M glucose **c.** 0.50 M NaOH

Study Note

Molarity can be used as a conversion factor to convert between the amount of solute and the volume of solution.

Example 1: How many grams of NaOH are in 0.20 L of a 4.0 M NaOH solution?

Solution: The concentration 4.0 M can be expressed as the conversion factors:

$$\frac{4.0 \text{ moles NaOH}}{1 \text{ L NaOH}} \quad \text{and} \quad \frac{1 \text{ L NaOH}}{4.0 \text{ moles NaOH}}$$

$$0.20 \cancel{\text{L NaOH}} \times \frac{4.0 \cancel{\text{moles NaOH}}}{1 \cancel{\text{L NaOH}}} \times \frac{40.0 \text{ g NaOH}}{1 \cancel{\text{mole NaOH}}} = 32 \text{ g of NaOH}$$

Example 2: How many mL of a 6 M HCl solution will provide 0.36 mole of HCl?

Solution: $$0.36 \cancel{\text{mole HCl}} \times \frac{1 \cancel{\text{L HCl}}}{6 \cancel{\text{moles HCl}}} \times \frac{1000 \text{ mL}}{1 \cancel{\text{L}}} = 60 \text{ mL of HCl solution}$$

◆ Learning Exercise 8.5B

Calculate the quantity of solute in the following solutions:

a. How many moles of HCl are in 1.50 L of a 2.50 M HCl solution?

b. How many moles of KOH are in 125 mL of a 2.40 M KOH solution?

c. How many grams of NaOH are needed to prepare 225 mL of a 3.00 M NaOH solution? (Hint: Find moles of NaOH.)

d. How many grams of NaCl are in 415 mL of a 1.30 M NaCl solution?

Answers **a.** 3.75 moles of HCl **b.** 0.300 mole of KOH
c. 27.0 g of NaOH **d.** 31.6 g of NaCl

◆ Learning Exercise 8.5C

Calculate the milliliters needed of each solution to obtain each of the following:

a. 0.200 mole of $Mg(OH)_2$ from a 2.50 M $Mg(OH)_2$ solution

b. 0.125 mole of glucose from a 5.00 M glucose solution

c. 0.250 mole of KI from a 4.00 M KI solution

d. 16.0 g of NaOH from a 3.20 M NaOH solution

Answers **a.** 80.0 mL **b.** 25.0 mL **c.** 62.5 mL **d.** 125 mL

◆ Learning Exercise 8.5D

Solve each of the following dilution problems (assume the volumes add):

a. What is the final concentration after 100 mL of a 5.0 M KCl solution is diluted with water to give a final volume of 200 mL?

b. What is the final concentration of the diluted solution if 5.0 mL of a 15% (m/v) KCl solution is diluted to 25 mL?

c. What is the final concentration after 250 mL of an 8% (m/v) NaOH is diluted with 750 mL of water?

d. 160 mL of water is added to 40 mL of an 1.0 M NaCl solution. What is the final concentration?

e. What volume of water must be added to 2.0 L of 12% (m/v) KCl to obtain a 4.0 % (m/v) KCl solution? What is the total volume of the solution?

f. What volume of 6.0 M HCl is needed to prepare 300. mL of 1.0 M HCl? How much water must be added?

Answers

a. 2.5 M **b.** 3.0% (m/v) **c.** 2% (m/v)
d. 0.20 M **e.** add 4.0 L of water; $V_2 = 6.0$ L **f.** $V_1 = 50.$ mL; add 250 mL of water

◆ Learning Exercise 8.5E

For the following reaction,
$2AgNO_3(aq) + H_2SO_4(aq) \longrightarrow Ag_2SO_4(s) + 2H_2O(l)$

a. How many milliliters of 1.5 M $AgNO_3$ will react with 40.0 mL of 1.0 M H_2SO_4?

b. How many grams of Ag_2SO_4 will be produced?

Answers **a.** 53 mL **b.** 12 g of Ag_2SO_4

◆ Learning Exercise 8.5F

Calculate the milliliters of 1.80 M KOH that react with 18.5 mL of 2.20 M HCl.

$HCl(aq) + KOH(aq) \longrightarrow KCl(aq) + H_2O(l)$

Answer 22.6 mL of KOH

8.6 Physical Properties of Solutions

- Colloids contain particles that do not settle out and pass through filters but not through semipermeable membranes.
- Suspensions are composed of large particles that settle out of solution.
- In the process of osmosis, water (solvent) moves through a semipermeable membrane from the solution that has a lower solute concentration to a solution where the solute concentration is higher.
- Osmotic pressure is the pressure that prevents the flow of water into a more concentrated solution.
- Particles in a solution lower the freezing point and elevate the boiling point of the solvent.
- Isotonic solutions have osmotic pressures equal to that of body fluids. A hypotonic solution has a lower osmotic pressure than body fluids; a hypertonic solution has a higher osmotic pressure.
- A red blood cell maintains its volume in an isotonic solution, but it swells (hemolysis) in a hypotonic solution and shrinks (crenation) in a hypertonic solution.
- In dialysis, water and small solute particles can pass through a dialyzing membrane, while larger particles are retained.

MasteringChemistry

Self Study Activity: Diffusion
Self Study Activity: Osmosis
Tutorial: Osmosis
Tutorial: Dialysis

◆ Learning Exercise 8.6A

Identify each of the following as a solution, colloid, or suspension:

1. ______ contains single atoms, ions, or small molecules

2. ______ settles out with gravity

3. ______ retained by filters

4. ______ cannot diffuse through a cellular membrane

5. ______ aggregates of atoms, molecules, or ions larger in size than solution particles

6. ______ large particles that are visible

Answers **1.** solution **2.** suspension **3.** suspension
4. colloid **5.** colloid **6.** suspension

◆ Learning Exercise 8.6B

Fill in the blanks:

In osmosis, the direction of solvent flow is from the (1) [higher/lower] solvent concentration to the (2) [higher/lower] solvent concentration. A semipermeable membrane separates 5% (m/v) and 10% (m/v) sucrose solutions. The (3) ______________% (m/v) solution has the greater osmotic pressure. Water will move from the (4) ______________% (m/v) solution into the (5) ____________% (m/v) solution. The compartment that contains the (6) ______________% (m/v) solution increases in volume.

Answers **(1)** higher **(2)** lower **(3)** 10 **(4)** 5 **(5)** 10 **(6)** 10

◆ Learning Exercise 8.6C

What occurs when 2% (A) and a 10% (B) starch solutions are separated by a semipermeable membrane?

Semipermeable membrane

2% starch A	10% starch B

a. Water will flow from side __________ to side __________.

b. The volume in compartment __________ will increase and decrease in compartment __________.

c. The final concentration of the solutions in both compartments will be___________.

Answers **a.** A, B **b.** B, A **c.** 6%

◆ Learning Exercise 8.6D

One mole of particles lowers the freezing point of 1000 g of water by 1.86 °C and raises the boiling point by 0.52 °C. For the following solutes each in 1000 g of water, indicate:

(1) the number of moles of particles

(2) the freezing point change and freezing point of the solution

(3) boiling point change and boiling point of the solution

Solute	Number of Moles of Particles	Freezing Point Change and Freezing Point	Boiling Point Change and Boiling Point
a. 1.00 mole of fructose (nonelectrolyte)			
b. 1.50 moles of KCl (strong electrolyte)			
c. 1.25 mole of $Ca(NO_3)_2$ (strong electrolyte)			

Answers

Solute	Number of Moles of Particles	Freezing Point Change and Freezing Point	Boiling Point Change and Boiling Point
a. 1.00 mole of fructose (nonelectrolyte)	1.00 mole	Decreases 1.86 °C; FP = −1.86 °C	Increases 0.52 °C; BP = 100.52 °C

b. 1.50 moles of KCl (strong electrolyte)	3.00 moles	Decreases 5.58 °C; FP = −5.58 °C	Increases 1.56 °C; BP = 101.56 °C
c. 1.25 moles of $Ca(NO_3)_2$ (strong electrolyte)	3.75 moles	Decreases 6.98 °C; FP = −6.98 °C	Increases 1.95 °C; BP = 101.95 °C

◆ Learning Exercise 8.6E

Fill in the blanks:

A (1) ________% (m/v) NaCl solution and a (2) ________% (m/v) glucose solution are isotonic to the body fluids. A red blood cell placed in these solutions does not change in volume because these solutions are (3) ________ tonic. When a red blood cell is placed in water, it undergoes (4) ________ because water is (5) ________ tonic. A 20% (m/v) glucose solution will cause a red blood cell to undergo (6) ________ because the 20% (m/v) glucose solution is (7) ________ tonic.

Answers **(1)** 0.9 **(2)** 5 **(3)** iso **(4)** hemolysis **(5)** hypo **(6)** crenation **(7)** hyper

◆ Learning Exercise 8.6F

Indicate whether the following solutions are

a. hypotonic **b.** hypertonic **c.** isotonic

1. _____ 5% (m/v)glucose **2.** _____ 3% (m/v) NaCl **3.** 2% (m/v) glucose

4. _____ water **5.** _____ 0.9% (m/v)NaCl **6.** 10% (m/v) glucose

Answers **1.** c **2.** b **3.** a **4.** a **5.** c **6.** b

◆ Learning Exercise 8.6G

Indicate whether the following solutions will cause a red blood cell to undergo

a. crenation **b.** hemolysis **c.** no change (stays the same)

1. ______ 10% (m/v) NaCl **2.** ______ 1% (m/v) glucose **3.** 5% (m/v) glucose

4. ______ 0.5% (m/v) NaCl **5.** ______ 10% (m/v) glucose **6.** water

Answers **1.** a **2.** b **3.** c **4.** b **5.** a **6.** b

◆ Learning Exercise 8.6H

A dialysis bag contains starch, glucose, NaCl, protein, and urea.

a. When the dialysis bag is placed in water, what components would you expect to dialyze through the bag? Why?

b. Which components will stay inside the dialysis bag? Why?

Answers **a.** Glucose, NaCl, urea; they are solution particles.
b. Starch, protein; colloids are retained by semipermeable membranes.

Checklist for Chapter 8

You are ready to take the Practice Test for Chapter 8. Be sure that you have accomplished the following learning goals for this chapter. If you are not sure, review the section listed at the end of the goal. Then apply your new skills and understanding to the Practice Test.

After studying Chapter 8, I can successfully:

_____ Describe hydrogen bonding in water (8.1).

_____ Identify the solute and solvent in a solution (8.1).

_____ Describe the process of dissolving an ionic solute in water (8.1).

_____ Identify the components in solutions of electrolytes and nonelectrolytes (8.2).

_____ Calculate the number of equivalents for an electrolyte (8.2).

_____ Identify a saturated and an unsaturated solution (8.3).

_____ Identify a salt as soluble or insoluble (8.3).

_____ Write a chemical equation (or ionic or net ionic equation) to show the formation of an insoluble salt (8.3).

_____ Describe the effects of temperature and nature of the solute on its solubility in a solvent (8.3).

_____ Calculate the percent concentration of a solute in a solution and use percent concentration to calculate the amount of solute or solution (8.4).

_____ the new volume or new concentration after a solution is diluted (8.4).

_____ Calculate the molarity of a solution (8.5).

_____ molarity as a conversion factor to calculate between the mole (or grams) of a solute and the volume of the solution (8.5).

_____ the molarity of a solution in a chemical reaction to calculate the volume or quantity of a reactant or product (8.5).

_____ Use the concentration of particles in a solution to calculate the freezing point or boiling point of the solution. (8.6).

_____ Identify a mixture as a solution, a colloid, or a suspension (8.6).

_____ Explain the processes of osmosis and dialysis (8.6).

Practice Test for Chapter 8

For questions 1–4, indicate if the following are more soluble in (A) water (polar solvent) or (B) benzene (nonpolar solvent):

1. _____ I_2 (*g*), nonpolar **2.** _____ NaBr(*s*), polar

3. _____ KI(*s*), polar **4.** _____ C_6H_{12} (*l*), nonpolar

5. When dissolved in water, $Ca(NO_3)_2$ dissociates into

A. $Ca^{2+}(aq) + (NO_3)_2^{2-}(aq)$

B. $Ca^{+}(aq) + NO_3^{-}(aq)$

C. $Ca^{2+}(aq) + 2NO_3^{-}(aq)$

D. $Ca^{2+}(aq) + 2N^{5+}(aq) + 2O_3^{6-}(aq)$

E. $CaNO_3^{+}(aq) + NO_3^{-}(aq)$

6. What is the number of equivalents in 2 moles of Mg^{2+}?

A. 0.50 Eq **B.** 1 Eq **C.** 1.5 Eq
D. 2 Eq **E.** 4 Eq

7. CH_3CH_2OH, ethyl alcohol, is a nonelectrolyte. When placed in water it

A. dissociates completely. **B.** dissociates partially. **C.** does not dissociate.
D. makes the solution acidic. **E.** makes the solution basic.

8. The solubility of NH_4Cl is 46 g in 100 g of water at 40 °C. How much NH_4Cl can dissolve in 500 g of water at 40 °C?

A. 9.2 g **B.** 46 g **C.** 100 g **D.** 180 g **E.** 230 g

For questions 9–12, indicate if each of the following are soluble(S) or not soluble(N) in water:

9. _____ NaCl **10.** _____ AgCl

11. _____ $BaSO_4$ **12.** _____ FeO

13. A solution containing 1.20 g of sucrose in 50.0 mL of solution has a percent concentration of

A. 0.600% (m/v) **B.** 1.20% (m/v) **C.** 2.40% (m/v) **D.** 30.0% (m/v) **E.** 41.6% (m/v)

14. The amount of lactose in 250 mL of a 3.0% (m/v) lactose solution of infant formula is

A. 0.15 g **B.** 1.2 g **C.** 6.0 g **D.** 7.5 g **E.** 30 g

15. The volume needed to obtain 0.40 g of glucose from a 5.0% (m/v)glucose solution is

A. 1.0 mL **B.** 2.0 mL **C.** 4.0 mL **D.** 5.0 mL **E.** 8.0 mL

16. The amount of NaCl needed to prepare 50.0 mL of a 4.00% (m/v)NaCl solution is

A. 20.0 g **B.** 15.0 g **C.** 10.0 g **D.** 4.00 g **E.** 2.00 g

17. A solution containing 6.0 g of NaCl in 1500 mL of solution has a mass-volume percent concentration of

A. 0.40% (m/v) **B.** 0.25% (m/v) **C.** 4.0% (m/v)
D. 0.90% (m/v) **E.** 2.5% (m/v)

For questions 18–22, indicate whether each statement describes a

A. solution **B.** colloid **C.** suspension

18. _____contains single atoms, ions, or small molecules of solute

19. _____ settles out upon standing

20. _____ can be separated by filtering

21. _____ can be separated by semipermeable membranes

22. _____ passes through semipermeable membranes

23. The separation of colloids from solution particles by use of a membrane is called

A. osmosis **B.** dispersion **C.** dialysis
D. hemolysis **E.** collosis

24. Any two solutions that have identical osmotic pressures are

A. hypotonic **B.** hypertonic **C.** isotonic
D. isotopic **E.** hyperactive

25. In osmosis, water flows

A. between solutions of equal concentrations
B. from higher solute concentrations to lower solute concentrations
C. from lower solute concentrations to higher solute concentrations
D. from colloids to solutions of equal concentrations
E. from lower solvent concentrations to higher solvent concentrations

26. A normal red blood cell will shrink when placed in a solution that is

A. isotonic **B.** hypotonic **C.** hypertonic
D. colloidal **E.** semitonic

27. A red blood cell undergoes hemolysis when placed in a solution that is

A. isotonic **B.** hypotonic **C.** hypertonic
D. colloidal **E.** semitonic

28. A solution that has the same osmotic pressure as body fluids is

A. 0.1% (m/v) NaCl **B.** 0.9% (m/v) NaCl **C.** 5% (m/v) NaCl
D. 10% (m/v) glucose **E.** 15% (m/v) glucose

29. Which of the following is hypertonic to red blood cells?

A. 0.5% (m/v)NaCl **B.** 0.9% (m/v) NaCl **C.** 1% (m/v) glucose
D. 5% (m/v)glucose **E.** 10% (m/v) glucose

30. Which of the following is hypotonic to red blood cells?

A. 2.0%(m/v) NaCl **B.** 0.9% (m/v) NaCl **C.** 1% (m/v) glucose
D. 5% (m/v)glucose **E.** 10% (m/v)glucose

For questions 31–35, select the correct term from the following:

A. isotonic **B.** hypertonic **C.** hypotonic **D.** osmosis **E.** dialysis

31. _____ A solution with a higher osmotic pressure than the blood

32. _____ A solution of 10% (m/v) NaCl surrounding a red blood cell

33. _____ A 1% (m/v) glucose solution

34. _____ The cleansing process of the artificial kidney

35. _____ The flow of water up the stem of a plant

36. In dialysis,

A. dissolved salts and small molecules are separated from colloids.
B. nothing but water passes through the membrane.
C. only ions pass through a membrane.
D. two kinds of colloids are separated.
E. colloids are separated from suspensions.

37. A dialyzing membrane

A. is a semipermeable membrane
B. allows only water and true solution particles to pass through
C. does not allow colloidal particles to pass through
D. all of the above
E. none of the above

38. Which substance will remain inside a dialysis bag?

A. water **B.** NaCl **C.** starch **D.** glucose **E.** Mg^{2+}

39. Waste removal in hemodialysis is based on

A. concentration gradients between the bloodstream and the dialysate
B. a pH difference between the bloodstream and the dialysate
C. use of an osmotic membrane
D. greater osmotic pressure in the bloodstream
E. renal compensation

40. If a solution contains 0.50 mole of $CaCl_2$ in 1000 g of water, what is the freezing point of the solution?

A. 0 °C **B.** 2.8 °C **C.** −2.8 °C **D.** 0.93 °C **E.** −0.93 °C

41. The amount, in grams, of NaOH needed to prepare 7.5 mL of a 5.0 M NaOH is

A. 1.5 g **B.** 3.8 g **C.** 6.7 g **D.** 15 g **E.** 38 g

For questions 42–44, consider a 20.0-mL sample of a solution that contains 2.0 g of NaOH.

42. The mass/volume percent concentration of the solution is

A. 1.0% (m/v) **B.** 4.0% (m/v) **C.** 5.0% (m/v)
D. 10.% (m/v) **E.** 20.% (m/v)

43. The number of moles of NaOH in the sample is

A. 0.050 mole **B.** 0.40 mole **C.** 1.0 mole
D. 2.5 moles **E.** 4.0 moles

44. The molarity of the sample is

A. 0.10 M **B.** 0.5 M **C.** 1.0 M
D. 1.5 M **E.** 2.5 M

45. What mass of Ag_2SO_4 is formed when 25.0 mL of 0.111 M $AgNO_3$ solution reacts?

$$2AgNO_3(aq) + H_2SO_4(aq) \longrightarrow Ag_2SO_4(s) + 2H_2O(l)$$

A. 0.866 g **B.** 1.74 g **C.** 866 g
D. 0.433 g **E.** 2.78 g

Answers to the Practice Test

1. B	**2.** A	**3.** A	**4.** B	**5.** C
6. E	**7.** C	**8.** E	**9.** S	**10.** N
11. N	**12.** N	**13.** C	**14.** D	**15.** E
16. E	**17.** A	**18.** A	**19.** C	**20.** C
21. B	**22.** A	**23.** C	**24.** C	**25.** C
26. C	**27.** B	**28.** B	**29.** E	**30.** C
31. B	**32.** B	**33.** C	**34.** E	**35.** D
36. A	**37.** D	**38.** C	**39.** A	**40.** C
41. A	**42.** D	**43.** A	**44.** E	**45.** D

9

Chemical Equilibrium

Study Goals

- Describe how temperature, concentration, and catalysts affect the rate of a reaction.
- Use the concept of reversible reactions to explain chemical equilibrium.
- Calculate the equilibrium constant for a reversible reaction using the concentrations of reactants and products at equilibrium.
- Use an equilibrium constant to predict the extent of reaction and to calculate equilibrium concentrations.
- Use Le Châtelier's principle to describe the changes made in equilibrium concentrations when reaction conditions change.
- Calculate the solubility product for a saturated solution; use the solubility product to calculate the molar ion concentrations.

Think About It

1. Why does a high temperature cook food faster than a low temperature?

2. Why do automobile engines now use a catalytic converter?

3. What does a small equilibrium constant indicate about the relative concentrations of reactants and products?

Key Terms

Match the following terms with the statements below:

a. activation energy   **b.** equilibrium   **c.** catalyst
d. equilibrium constant   **e.** collision theory   **f.** heterogeneous equilibrium

1. ____ a substance that lowers the activation energy and increases the rate of reaction

2. ____ equilibrium components are present in at least two different states

3. ____ the ratio of the concentrations of products to those of the reactants raised to exponents equal to their coefficients

4. ____ the energy required to convert reactants to products in a chemical reaction

5. ____ a reaction requires that reactants to collide with sufficient energy to form products

6. ____ the point at which the rate of the forward reaction is equal to the rate of the reverse reaction

Answers **1.** c **2.** f **3.** d **4.** a **5.** e **6.** b

9.1 Rates of Reactions

- The rate of a reaction is the speed at which products form.
- At higher temperatures, reaction rates increase because reactants move faster, collide more often, and produce more collisions with the required energy of activation.
- Increasing the concentrations of reactants or lowering the energy of activation by adding a catalyst increases the rate of a reaction.
- The reaction rate slows when the temperature or the concentrations of reactants is decreased.

MasteringChemistry

Self Study Activity: Factors That Affect Rate

◆ Learning Exercise 9.1A

Indicate the effect of each of the following on the rate of a chemical reaction:

increase (I)   decrease (D)   no effect (N)

1. ____ adding a catalyst

2. ____ running the reaction at a lower temperature

3. ____ doubling the concentrations of the reactants

4. ____ removing a catalyst

5. ____ running the experiment in a different laboratory

6. ____ increasing the temperature

7. ____ using a container with a different shape

8. ____ using lower concentrations of reactants

Answers **1.** I **2.** D **3.** I **4.** D **5.** N **6.** I **7.** N **8.** D

◆ Learning Exercise 9.1B

For the following reaction, $NO_2(g) + CO(g) \longrightarrow NO(g) + CO_2(g)$ indicate the effect of each of the following as:

increase (I) decrease (D) no effect (N)

1. ____ adding CO
2. ____ running the experiment on Wednesday
3. ____ removing NO_2
4. ____ adding a catalyst
5. ____ adding NO_2

Answers **1.** I **2.** N **3.** D **4.** I **5.** I

9.2 Chemical Equilibrium

- Chemical equilibrium is achieved when the rate of the forward reaction becomes equal to the rate of the reverse reaction.
- In a system at equilibrium, there is no change in the concentrations of reactants and products.
- At equilibrium, the concentrations of reactants typically different from the concentrations of products; they are not usually equal.

MasteringChemistry

Self Study Activity: Equilibrium

Tutorial: Chemical Equilibrium

◆ Learning Exercise 9.2

Indicate if each of the following indicates a system at equilibrium (E) or not (NE):

1. ____ The rate of the forward reaction is faster than the rate of the reverse reaction.
2. ____ There is no change in the concentrations of reactants and products.
3. ____ The rate of the forward reaction is equal to the rate of the reverse reaction.
4. ____ The concentrations of reactants are decreasing.
5. ____ The concentrations of products are increasing.

Answers **1.** NE **2.** E **3.** E **4.** NE **5.** NE

9.3 Equilibrium Constants

- The equilibrium constant expression for a system at equilibrium is the ratio of the concentrations of the products to the concentrations of the reactants with the concentration of each substance raised to a power equal to its coefficient in the balanced chemical equation.
- For the general equation, aA + bB ⇄ cC + dD, the equilibrium constant expression is written:

$$K_c = \frac{[C]^c\,[D]^d}{[A]^a\,[B]^b}$$

MasteringChemistry
Tutorial: Equilibrium Constant

◆ Learning Exercise 9.3A

Write the expression for the equilibrium constant (K_c) for each of the following reactions:

a. $2SO_3(g) \rightleftarrows 2SO_2(g) + O_2(g)$

b. $2NO(g) + Br_2(g) \rightleftarrows 2NOBr(g)$

c. $N_2(g) + 3H_2(g) \rightleftarrows 2NH_3(g)$

d. $2NO_2(g) \rightleftarrows N_2O_4(g)$

Answers

a. $K_c = \frac{[SO_2]^2[O_2]}{[SO_3]^2}$

b. $K_c = \frac{[NOBr]^2}{[NO]^2[Br_2]}$

c. $K_c = \frac{[NH_3]^2}{[N_2][H_2]^3}$

d. $K_c = \frac{[N_2O_4]}{[NO_2]^2}$

◆ Learning Exercise 9.3B

Write the expression for the equilibrium constant (K_c) for each of the following heterogeneous equilibria:

a. $H_2(g) + S(s) \rightleftarrows H_2S(g)$

b. $SiO_2(g) + 3C(s) \rightleftarrows SiC(s) + 2CO(g)$

c. $2PbS(s) + 3O_2(g) \rightleftarrows 2PbO(s) + 2SO_2(g)$

d. $SiH_4(g) + 2O_2(g) \rightleftarrows SiO(s) + 2H_2O(g)$

Answers

a. $K_c = \dfrac{[H_2S]}{[H_2]}$ **b.** $K_c = \dfrac{[CO]^2}{[SiO_2]}$

c. $K_c = \dfrac{[SO_2]^2}{[O_2]^3}$ **d.** $K_c = \dfrac{[H_2O]^2}{[SiH_4][O_2]^2}$

◆ Learning Exercise 9.3C

Calculate the K_c value for each of the following equilibrium concentrations:

a. $H_2(g) + I_2(g) \rightleftarrows 2HI(g)$

$[H_2] = 0.28$ M $[I_2] = 0.28$ M $[HI] = 2.0$ M

b. $2NO_2(g) \rightleftarrows N_2(g) + 2O_2(g)$

$[NO_2] = 0.60$ M $[N_2] = 0.010$ M $[O_2] = 0.020$ M

c. $N_2(g) + 3H_2(g) \rightleftarrows 2NH_3(g)$

$[N_2] = 0.50$ M $[H_2] = 0.20$ M $[NH_3] = 0.80$ M

Answers

a. $K_c = \dfrac{[HI]^2}{[H_2][I_2]} = \dfrac{[2.0]^2}{[0.28][0.28]} = 51$

b. $K_c = \dfrac{[N_2][O_2]^2}{[NO_2]} = \dfrac{[0.010][0.020]^2}{[0.60]^2} = 1.1\times10^{-5}$

c. $K_c = \dfrac{[NH_3]^2}{[N_2][H_2]^3} = \dfrac{[0.80]^2}{[0.50][0.20]^3} = 1.6\times10^2$

9.4 Using Equilibrium Constants

- A large K_c indicates that a reaction at equilibrium has more product than reactant; a small K_c indicates that a reaction at equilibrium has more reactant than product.
- The concentration of a component in an equilibrium mixture is calculated from the K_c and the concentrations of all the other components.

MasteringChemistry
Tutorial: Calculations Using the Equilibrium Constant

◆ Learning Exercise 9.4A

Consider the reaction $2NOBr(g) \rightleftarrows NO(g) + Br_2(g)$.

a. Write the expression for the equilibrium constant for the reaction.

b. If the equilibrium constant is 2×10^3, does the equilibrium mixture contain mostly reactants, mostly products, or both reactants and products? Explain.

Answers **a.** $K_c = \dfrac{[NO]^2[Br_2]}{[NOBr]^2}$

b. A large K_c (>1) means that the equilibrium mixture contains mostly products.

◆ Learning Exercise 9.4B

Consider the reaction $2HI(g) \rightleftarrows H_2(g) + I_2(g)$

a. Write the expression for the equilibrium constant for the reaction.

b. If the equilibrium constant is 1.6×10^{-2}, does the equilibrium mixture contain mostly reactants, mostly products, or both reactants and products? Explain.

Answers **a.** $K_c = \dfrac{[H_2][I_2]}{[2HI]^2}$

b. A small K_c (<1) means that the equilibrium mixture contains mostly reactants.

◆ Learning Exercise 9.4C

Calculate the concentration of the indicated component for each of the following equilibrium systems:

a. $PCl_5(g) \rightleftarrows PCl_3(g) + Cl_2(g)$ $K_c = 1.2 \times 10^{-2}$

$[PCl_5] = 2.50$ M $[PCl_3] = 0.50$ M $[Cl_2] = ?$

b. $CO(g) + H_2O(g) \rightleftarrows CO_2(g) + H_2(g)$ $K_c = 1.6$

$[CO] = 1.0$ M $[H_2O] = 0.80$ M $[CO_2] = ?$ $[H_2] = 1.2$ M

Answers

a. $K_c = \dfrac{[PCl_3][Cl_2]}{[PCl_5]}$ $[Cl_2] = \dfrac{K_c[PCl_5]}{[PCl_3]} = \dfrac{1.2\times10^{-2}[2.5]}{[0.50]} = 0.060\,M = 6.0\times10^{-2}\,M$

b. $K_c = \dfrac{[CO_2][H_2]}{[CO][H_2O]}$ $[CO_2] = \dfrac{K_c[CO][H_2O]}{[H_2]} = \dfrac{1.6[1.0][0.80]}{[1.2]} = 1.1\,M$

9.5 Changing Equilibrium Conditions: Le Châtelier's Principle

- A change in the concentration of a reactant or product, temperature, or volume, shifts the equilibrium in the direction to relieve the stress.

MasteringChemistry

Tutorial: Le Châtelier's Principle

◆ Learning Exercise 9.5A

Identify the effect of the each of the following on the equilibrium of the following reaction:

$N_2(g) + O_2(g) + 180\text{ kJ} \rightleftarrows 2NO(g)$

A. shift toward products **B.** shift toward reactants **C.** no change

1. ____adding $O_2(g)$ **2.** ____removing $N_2(g)$

3. ____removing $NO(g)$ **4.** ____adding heat

5. ____reducing the volume of the container **6.** ____increasing the volume

Answers **1.** A **2.** B **3.** A **4.** A **5.** C **6.** C

◆ Learning Exercise 9.5B

Identify the effect of the each change on the equilibrium of the following reaction:

$2NOBr(g) \rightleftarrows 2NO(g) + Br_2(g) + 81$ kcal

A. shift toward products **B.** shift toward reactants **C.** no change

1. ____adding $NO(g)$ **2.** ____removing $Br_2(g)$

3. ____removing $NOBr(g)$ **4.** ____adding heat

5. ____lowering the temperature **6.** ____increasing the volume

Answers **1.** B **2.** A **3.** B **4.** B **5.** A **6.** A

9.6 Equilibrium in Saturated Solutions

- In a saturated solution of a salt, the equilibrium expression is the *solubility product constant.*
- As in heterogeneous equilibrium, the concentration of the solid is constant and not included in the K_{sp} expression. For example, the K_{sp} of Ag_2CO_3 is: $K_{sp} = [Ag^+]^2[CO_3^{2-}]$

◆ Learning Exercise 9.6A

Write the equilibrium equation and K_{sp} expression for each of the following slightly soluble salts:

a. BaF_2

b. NiS

c. Ag_2CO_3

d. Ag_3PO_4

Answers

a. $BaF_2(s) \rightleftarrows Ba^{2+}(aq) + 2F^-(aq)$ $K_{sp} = [Ba^{2+}][F^-]^2$

b. $NiS(s) \rightleftarrows Ni^{2+}(aq) + S^{2-}(aq)$ $K_{sp} = [Ni^{2+}][S^{2-}]$

c. $Ag_2CO_3(s) \rightleftarrows 2Ag^+(aq) + CO_3^{2-}(aq)$ $K_{sp} = [Ag^+]^2[CO_3^{2-}]$

d. $Ag_3PO_4(s) \rightleftarrows 3Ag^+(aq) + PO_4^{3-}(aq)$ $K_{sp} = [Ag^+]^3[PO_4^{3-}]$

◆ Learning Exercise 9.6B

Calculate the K_{sp} value for each of the following saturated solutions:

a. CdS with $[Cd^{2+}] = [S^{2-}] = 3 \times 10^{-14}$ M

b. $AgIO_3$ with $[Ag^+] = [IO_3^-] = 1.7 \times 10^{-4}$ M

c. SrF_2 with $[Sr^{2+}] = 8.5 \times 10^{-4}$ M and $[F^-] = 1.7 \times 10^{-3}$ M

d. Ag_2SO_3 with $[Ag^+] = 3.2 \times 10^{-5}$ M and $[SO_3^{2-}] = 1.6 \times 10^{-5}$ M

Answers   **a.** $K_{sp} = 9 \times 10^{-28}$ **b.** $K_{sp} = 2.9 \times 10^{-8}$
c. $K_{sp} = 2.5 \times 10^{-9}$ **d.** $K_{sp} = 1.6 \times 10^{-14}$

◆ Learning Exercise 9.6C

Calculate the solubility (S) of each of the following salts in moles per liter:

a. NiS $K_{sp} = 4 \times 10^{-20}$

b. $CdCO_3$ $K_{sp} = 1 \times 10^{-12}$

c. CoS $K_{sp} = 5.0 \times 10^{-22}$

d. CuCN $K_{sp} = 3.5 \times 10^{-20}$

Answers

a. NiS $S = 2 \times 10^{-10}$ M **b.** $CdCO_3$ $S = 1 \times 10^{-6}$ M
c. CoS $S = 2.2 \times 10^{-11}$ M **d.** CuCN $S = 1.9 \times 10^{-10}$ M

Checklist for Chapter 9

You are ready to take the Practice Test for Chapter 9. Be sure that you have accomplished the following learning goals for this chapter. If you are not sure, review the section listed at the end of the goal. Then apply your new skills and understanding to the Practice Test.

After studying Chapter 9, I can successfully:

____ Describe the factors that increase or decrease the rate of a reaction (9.1).

____ Write the forward and reverse reactions of a reversible reaction (9.2).

____ Explain how equilibrium occurs when the rate of a forward reaction is equal to the rate of a reverse reaction (9.2).

____ Write the equilibrium constant expression for a reaction system at equilibrium (9.3).

____ Calculate the equilibrium constant from the equilibrium concentrations (9.3).

____ Use the equilibrium constant to determine whether a reaction favors the reactants or products (9.4).

____ Use the equilibrium constant to determine the equilibrium concentration of a component in the reaction (9.4).

____ Use Le Châtelier's principle to describe the shift in a system at equilibrium when stress is applied to the system (9.5).

____ Calculate the solubility product for a saturated salt solution (9.6).

____ Use the solubility product to calculate the molar ion concentrations of an slightly soluble salt (9.6).

Practice Test for Chapter 9

1. The number of molecular collisions increases when

A. more reactants are added
B. products are removed
C. the energy of collision is below the energy of activation
D. the reaction temperature is lowered
E. the reacting molecules have an incorrect orientation upon impact

2. The energy of activation is lowered when

A. more reactants are added
B. products are removed
C. a catalyst is used
D. the reaction temperature is lowered
E. the reaction temperature is raised

3. Food deteriorates more slowly in a refrigerator because

A. more reactants are added
B. products are removed
C. the energy of activation is higher
D. fewer collisions have the energy of activation
E. collisions they have the wrong orientation upon impact

4. A reaction reaches equilibrium when

A. the rate of the forward reaction is faster than the rate of the reverse reaction
B. the rate of the reverse reaction is faster than the rate of the forward reaction
C. the concentrations of reactants and products are changing
D. fewer collisions have the energy of activation
E. the rate of the forward reaction is equal to the rate of the reverse reaction

5. The equilibrium constant expression for the following reaction is

$2NOCl(g) \rightleftarrows 2NO(g) + Cl_2(g)$

A. $\frac{[NO][Cl_2]}{[NOCl]}$ **B.** $\frac{[NOCl_2]^2}{[NO]^2[Cl_2]}$ **C.** $\frac{[NOCl_2]}{[NO][Cl_2]}$

D. $\frac{[NO]^2Cl_2]}{[NOCl_2]}$ **E.** $\frac{[NO]^2[Cl_2]}{[NOCl]^2}$

6. The equilibrium constant expression for the following reaction is

$MgO(s) + CO_2(g) \rightleftarrows MgCO_3(s)$

A. $[CO_2]$ **B.** $\frac{[CO_2][MgCO_3]}{[MgO]}$ **C.** $\frac{[MgO]}{[CO_2][MgCO_3]}$

D. $\frac{1}{[CO_2]}$ **E.** $\frac{[CO_2]}{[MgO]}$

7. The equilibrium constant expression for the following reaction is

$2PbS(s) + 3O_2(g) \rightleftarrows 2PbO(s) + 2SO_2(g)$

A. $\frac{[PbO][SO_3]}{[PbS][O_2]}$ **B.** $\frac{[PbO]^2[SO_2]^2}{[PbS]^2[O_2]^3}$ **C.** $\frac{[SO_2]^2}{[O_2]^3}$

D. $\frac{[SO_2]}{[O_2]}$ **E.** $\frac{[O_2]^3}{[SO_2]^2}$

8. The equilibrium equation that has the following equilibrium constant expression

$\frac{[H_2S]^2}{[H_2]^2[S_2]}$

A. $H_2S(g) \rightleftarrows H_2(g) + S_2(g)$
B. $2H_2S(g) \rightleftarrows H_2(g) + S_2(g)$
C. $2H_2(g) + S_2(g) \rightleftarrows 2H_2S(g)$
D. $2H_2S(g) \rightleftarrows 2H_2(g)$
E. $2H_2(g) \rightleftarrows 2H_2S(g)$

9. The value of the equilibrium constant for the following equilibrium is

$COBr_2(g) \rightleftarrows CO(g) + Br_2(g)$

$[COBr_2] = 0.93$ M $[CO] = [Br_2] = 0.42$ M

A. 0.19 **B.** 0.39 **C.** 0.42 **D.** 2.2 **E.** 5.3

10. The value of the equilibrium constant for the following equilibrium is

$2NO(g) + O_2(g) \rightleftarrows 2NO_2(g)$

$[NO] = 2.7$ M $[O_2] = 1.0$ $[NO_2] = 3.0$ M

A. 0.81 **B.** 1.1 **C.** 1.2 **D.** 8.1 **E.** 9.0

11. Calculate the $[PCl_5]$ for the decomposition of PCl_5 that has a $K_c = 0.050$.

$PCl_5(g) \rightleftarrows PCl_3(g) + Cl_2(g)$

$[PCl_3] = [Cl_2] = 0.20$ M

A. 0.01 M **B.** 0.050 M **C.** 0.20 M
D. 0.40 M **E.** 0.80 M

12. The reaction that has a much greater concentration of products at equilibrium has a K_c value of

A. 1.6×10^{-15} **B.** 2×10^{-11} **C.** 1.2×10^{-5}
D. 3×10^{-3} **E.** 1.4×10^{5}

13. The reaction that has a much greater concentration of reactants at equilibrium has a K_c value of

A. 1.1×10^{-11} **B.** 2×10^{-2} **C.** 1.2×10^{2}
D. 2×10^{4} **E.** 1.3×10^{12}

14. The reaction that has about the same concentration of reactant and products at equilibrium has a K_c value of

A. 1.4×10^{-12} **B.** 2×10^{-8} **C.** 1.2
D. 3×10^{2} **E.** 1.3×10^{7}

For questions 15–19, indicate how each of the following affects the equilibrium of the reaction shown:

$PCl_5(g) + \text{heat} \rightleftarrows PCl_3(g) + Cl_2(g)$

A. shift toward products **B.** shift toward reactants **C.** no change

15. ____ add more Cl_2 **16.** ____ cool the reaction **17.** ____remove some PCl_3

18. ____add more PCl_5 **19.** ____ remove some PCl_5

For questions 20–24, indicate if each of the following shifts the equilibrium:

A. toward products **B.** toward reactants **C.** no change

$2NO(g) + O_2(g) \rightleftarrows 2NO_2(g) + \text{heat}$

20. ____ add more NO **21.** ____ increase temperature

22. ____ add a catalyst **23.** ____ add some O_2

24. ____ remove NO_2

25. The solubility product expression for the slightly soluble salt $Ca_3(PO_4)_2$ is:

A. $[Ca^{2+}][PO_4^{3-}]$ **B.** $[Ca^{2+}]_3[PO_4^{3-}]_2$ **C.** $[Ca^{2+}]^3[PO_4^{3-}]^2$

D. $[Ca^{2+}]^2[PO_4^{3-}]^3$ **E.** $\frac{[Ca^{2+}][PO_4^{3-}]}{[Ca_3(PO_4)_2]}$

26. The K_{sp} of CuI when a saturated solution has $[Cu^+] = 1 \times 10^{-6}$ M and $[I^-] = 1 \times 10^{-6}$ M is

A. 1×10^{-12} **B.** 1×10^{-6} **C.** 1
D. 2×10^{-6} **E.** 2×10^{-12}

27. What is the solubility of $SrCO_3$ if it has a K_{sp} of 5.6×10^{-10}?

A. 2.8×10^{-10} **B.** 2.8×10^{-5} **C.** 5.6×10^{-10}
D. 2.3×10^{-20} **E.** 2.4×10^{-5}

Answers to the Practice Test

1. A	**2.** C	**3.** D	**4.** E	**5.** E
6. D	**7.** C	**8.** C	**9.** A	**10.** C
11. E	**12.** E	**13.** A	**14.** C	**15.** B
16. B	**17.** A	**18.** A	**19.** B	**20.** A
21. B	**22.** C	**23.** A	**24.** A	**25.** C
26. A	**27.** E			

10
Acids and Bases

Study Goals

- Describe the characteristics of acids and bases.
- Identify conjugate acid–base pairs in Brønsted–Lowry acids and bases.
- Use the ion product of water to calculate [H_3O^+], [OH^-], and pH.
- Write balanced equations for reactions of an acid with metals, carbonates, and bases.
- Calculate the concentration of an acid solution from titration data.
- Predict if a salt solution will be acidic, basic, or neutral.
- Describe the function of a buffer.
- Calculate the pH of a buffer solution.

Think About It

1. Why do a lemon, grapefruit, and vinegar taste sour?

2. What do antacids do? What are some bases listed on the labels of antacids?

3. Why are some aspirin products buffered?

Key Terms

a. acid **b.** base **c.** pH **d.** neutralization **e.** buffer

1. ___ a substance that forms hydroxide ions (OH^-) in water and/or accepts protons (H^+)

2. ___ a reaction between an acid and a base to form a salt and water

3. ___ a substance that forms hydrogen ions (H^+) in water

4. ___ a mixture of a weak acid (or base) and its salt that maintains the pH of a solution

5. ___ a measure of the acidity (H_3O^+) of a solution

Answers **1.** b **2.** d **3.** a **4.** e **5.** c

10.1 Acids and Bases

- In water, an Arrhenius acid produces hydrogen ions (H^+), and an Arrhenius base produces OH^-.
- According to the Brønsted–Lowry theory, acids are proton (H^+) donors and bases are proton acceptors.
- Protons form hydronium ions, H_3O^+, in water when they bond to polar water molecules.
- According to the Brønsted–Lowry theory, acids donate protons (H^+) to bases.
- Conjugate acid–base pairs are molecules or ions linked by the loss and gain of one proton (H^+).

MasteringChemistry

Tutorial: Acid and Base Formulas

Tutorial: Naming Acids and Bases

◆ Learning Exercise 10.1A

Indicate if each of the following characteristics describe an (A) acid or (B) base:

1. _____ turns blue litmus red

2. _____ tastes sour

3. _____ contains more OH^- ions than H_3O^+ ions

4. _____ neutralizes bases

5. _____ tastes bitter

6. _____ turns red litmus blue

7. _____ contains more H_3O^+ ions than OH^- ions

8. _____ neutralizes acids

Answers **1.** A **2.** A **3.** B **4.** A
5. B **6.** B **7.** A **8.** B

◆ Learning Exercise 10.1B

Fill in the blanks with the formula or name of an acid or base:

1. HCl ______________________

2. ______________________ sodium hydroxide

3. ______________________ sulfurous acid

4. ______________________ nitric acid

5. $Ca(OH)_2$ ______________________

6. H_2CO_3 ______________________

7. $Al(OH)_3$ ____________________

8. ____________________ potassium hydroxide

9. $HClO_4$ ____________________

10. H_3PO_3 ____________________

Answers
1. hydrochloric acid **2.** NaOH **3.** H_2SO_3
4. HNO_3 **5.** calcium hydroxide **6.** carbonic acid
7. aluminum hydroxide **8.** KOH
9. perchloric acid **10.** phosphorous acid

MasteringChemistry

Tutorial: Identifying Conjugate Acid–Base Pairs

Study Note

Identify the conjugate acid–base pairs in the following equation:

$$HCl(aq) + H_2O(l) \longrightarrow H_3O^+(aq) + Cl^-(aq)$$

Solution: HCl (proton donor) and Cl^- (proton acceptor)
H_2O (proton acceptor) and H_3O^+ (proton donor)

◆ Learning Exercise 10.1C

Complete each of the following conjugate acid–base pairs:

Conjugate Acid	**Conjugate Base**
1. H_2O	______
2. HSO_4^-	______
3. ______	F^-
4. ______	CO_3^{2-}
5. HNO_3	______
6. NH_4^+	______
7. ______	HS^-
8. ______	$H_2PO_4^-$

Answers
1. OH^- **2.** SO_4^{2-} **3.** HF **4.** HCO_3^-
5. NO_3^- **6.** NH_3 **7.** H_2S **8.** H_3PO_4

◆ Learning Exercise 10.1D

Identify the conjugate acid–base pairs in each of the following reactions:

1. $HF(aq) + H_2O(l) \rightleftarrows H_3O^+(aq) + F^-(aq)$

2. $NH_4^+(aq) + SO_4^{2-}(aq) \rightleftarrows NH_3(aq) + HSO_4^-(aq)$

3. $NH_3(aq) + H_2O(l) \rightleftarrows NH_4^+(aq) + OH^-(aq)$

4. $HNO_3(aq) + OH^-(aq) \rightleftarrows H_2O(l) + NO_3^-(aq)$

Answers

1. HF/F^- and H_2O/H_3O^+ **2.** NH_4^+/NH_3 and SO_4^{2-}/HSO_4^-
3. NH_3/NH_4^+ and H_2O/OH^- **4.** HNO_3/NO_3^- and OH^-/H_2O

◆ Learning Exercise 10.1E

Write an equation with conjugate acid–base pairs starting with the following reactants:

1. HBr (acid) and CO_3^{2-} (base)

2. HSO_4^- (acid) and OH^- (base)

3. NH_4^+ (acid) and H_2O (base)

4. HCl (acid) and SO_4^{2-} (base)

Answers

1. $HBr(aq) + CO_3^{2-}(aq) \rightleftarrows HCO_3^-(aq) + Br^-(aq)$

2. $HSO_4^-(aq) + OH^-(aq) \rightleftarrows H_2O(l) + SO_4^{2-}(aq)$

3. $NH_4^+(aq) + H_2O(l) \rightleftarrows H_3O^+(aq) + NH_3(aq)$

4. $HCl(aq) + SO_4^{2-}(aq) \rightleftarrows Cl^-(aq) + HSO_4^-(aq)$

10.2 Strengths of Acids and Bases

- In aqueous solution, a strong acid donates nearly all of its protons to water, whereas a weak acid donates only a small percentage of protons to water.
- Most hydroxides of Groups 1A (1) and 2A (2) are strong bases, which dissociate nearly completely in water. In an aqueous ammonia solution, NH_3, which is a weak base, accepts only a small percentage of protons to form NH_4^+.
- An acid or a base with a large dissociation constant is more dissociated than an acid or base with a small dissociation constant.
- In the acid dissociation constant, the molar concentrations of the products are divided by the molar concentrations of the reactants.

$$\mathbf{HA}(aq) + H_2O(l) \rightleftarrows \mathbf{H_3O^+}(aq) + \mathbf{A^-}(aq)$$

$$K_a = K_c[H_2O] = \frac{[\mathbf{H_3O^+}][\mathbf{A^-}]}{[\mathbf{HA}]}$$

- Dissociation constants greater than 1 favor the products, whereas constants smaller than 1 favor reactants.

MasteringChemistry

Tutorial: Using Dissociation Constants

Study Note

Only six common acids are strong acids; other acids are considered weak acids.

HCl	HNO_3
HBr	H_2SO_4 (first H)
HI	$HClO_4$

Example: Is H_2S a strong or weak acid?
Solution: H_2S is a weak acid because it is not one of the six strong acids.

◆ Learning Exercise 10.2A

Identify each of the following as a strong or weak acid or base:

1. HNO_3 ________ **2.** H_2CO_3 ________ **3.** $H_2PO_4^-$ ________

4. NH_3 ________ **5.** LiOH ________ **6.** H_3BO_3 ________

7. $Ca(OH)_2$ ________ **8.** H_2SO_4 ________

Answers **1.** strong acid **2.** weak acid **3.** weak acid **4.** weak base
5. strong base **6.** weak acid **7.** strong base **8.** strong acid

◆ Learning Exercise 10.2B

Using Table 10.3, identify the stronger acid in each of the following pairs of acids:

1. HCl or H_2CO_3 ________ **2.** HNO_2 or HCN ________

3. H_2S or HBr ________ **4.** H_2SO_4 or HSO_4^- ________

5. HF or H_3PO_4 ________

Answers **1.** HCl **2.** HNO_2 **3.** HBr **4.** H_2SO_4 **5.** H_3PO_4

Study Note

In an acid–base reaction, the relative strengths of the two acids or two bases indicate whether the equilibrium position favors the reactants or products:

Example: Does the following reaction favor the reactants or products?

$$NO_3^-(aq) + H_2O(l) \rightleftarrows HNO_3(aq) + OH^-(aq)$$

Solution: The reactants contain the weaker base and acid (NO_3^- and H_2O), which make the equilibrium favor the reactants. This can be represented with a long arrow to the left.

$$NO_3^-(aq) + H_2O(l) \rightleftarrows HNO_3(aq) + OH^-(aq)$$

◆ Learning Exercise 10.2C

Indicate whether each of the following reactions favors the reactants or the products:

1. $HNO_3(aq) + H_2O(l) \rightleftarrows H_3O^+(aq) + NO_3^-(aq)$

2. $I^-(aq) + H_3O^+(aq) \rightleftarrows H_2O(l) + HI(aq)$

3. $NH_3(aq) + H_2O(l) \rightleftarrows NH_4^+(aq) + OH^-(aq)$

4. $HCl(aq) + CO_3^{2-}(aq) \rightleftarrows Cl^-(aq) + HCO_3^-(aq)$

Answers **1.** products **2.** reactants **3.** reactants **4.** products

◆ Learning Exercise 10.2D

Write the equation for the dissociation and the acid dissociation constant expression for the ionization of each of the following weak acids:

1. HCN

2. HNO_2

3. H_2CO_3 (first ionization only)

4. H_2S (first ionization only)

Answers **1.** $HCN(aq) + H_2O(l) \rightleftarrows H_3O^+(aq) + CN^-(aq)$

$$K_a = \frac{[H_3O^+][CN^-]}{[HCN]}$$

2. $HNO_2(aq) + H_2O(l) \rightleftarrows H_3O^+(aq) + NO_2^-(aq)$

$$K_a = \frac{[H_3O^+][NO_2^-]}{HNO_2}$$

3. $H_2CO_3(aq) + H_2O(l) \rightleftarrows H_3O^+(aq) + HCO_3^-(aq)$

$$K_a = \frac{[H_3O^+][HCO_3^-]}{[H_2CO_3]}$$

4. $H_2S(aq) + H_2O(l) \rightleftarrows H_3O^+(aq) + HS^-(aq)$

$$K_a = \frac{[H_3O^+][HS^-]}{[H_2S]}$$

◆ Learning Exercise 10.2E

For each of the following pairs of acid dissociation constants, indicate the constant of the weaker acid.

1. 5.2×10^{-5} or 3.8×10^{-3} ____________________

2. 3.0×10^{8} or 1.6×10^{-10} ____________________

3. 4.5×10^{-2} or 7.2×10^{-6} ________________

Answers **1.** 5.2×10^{-5} **2.** 1.6×10^{-10} **3.** 7.2×10^{-6}

10.3 Ionization of Water

- In pure water, a few water molecules transfer H^+ to other water molecules, producing small but equal amounts of $[H_3O^+]$ and $[OH^-] = 1 \times 10^{-7}$ mole/L.
$$H_2O(l) + H_2O(l) \rightleftarrows H_3O^+(aq) + OH^-(aq)$$
- K_w, the ion product constant of water, $[H_3O^+][OH^-] = [1.0 \times 10^{-7}][1.0 \times 10^{-7}] = 1.0 \times 10^{-14}$, applies to all aqueous solutions.
- In acidic solutions, the $[H_3O^+]$ is greater than the $[OH^-]$. In basic solutions, the $[OH^-]$ is greater than the $[H_3O^+]$.

MasteringChemistry
Tutorial: Ionization of Water

Study Note

Example: What is the $[H_3O^+]$ in a solution that has $[OH^-] = 2.0 \times 10^{-9}$ M?

Solution: $K_w = [H_3O^+][OH^-] = 1.0 \times 10^{-14}$

Rearrange for $[H_3O^+]$ and substitute $[OH^-] = 2.0 \times 10^{-9}$ M

$$[H_3O^+] = \frac{1.0\times10^{-14}}{[2.0\times10^{-9}]} = 5.0\times10^{-6} \text{ M}$$

Guide to Calculating $[H_3O^+]$ and $[OH^-]$ in Aqueous Solutions	
STEP 1	Write the K_w for water.
STEP 2	Solve the K_w for the unknown $[H_3O^+]$ or $[OH^-]$.
STEP 3	Substitute the known $[H_3O^+]$ or $[OH^-]$ and calculate unknown concentration.

◆ Learning Exercise 10.3A

Use the K_w to calculate the $[H_3O^+]$ when the $[OH^-]$ has each of the following values:

a. $[OH^-] = 1.0 \times 10^{-10}$ M $[H_3O^+] =$

b. $[OH^-] = 2.0 \times 10^{-5}$ M $[H_3O^+] =$

c. $[OH^-] = 4.5 \times 10^{-7}$ M $[H_3O^+] =$

d. $[OH^-] = 8.0 \times 10^{-4}$ M $[H_3O^+] =$

e. $[OH^-] = 5.5 \times 10^{-8}$ M $[H_3O^+] =$

Answers **a.** 1.0×10^{-4} M **b.** 5.0×10^{-10} M **c.** 2.2×10^{-8} M
d. 1.3×10^{-11} M **e.** 1.8×10^{-7} M

◆ Learning Exercise 10.3B

Use the K_w to determine the $[OH^-]$ when the $[H_3O^+]$ has each of the following values:

a. $[H_3O^+] = 1.0 \times 10^{-3}$ M $[OH^-] =$

b. $[H_3O^+] = 3.0 \times 10^{-10}$ M $[OH^-] =$

c. $[H_3O^+] = 4.0 \times 10^{-6}$ M $[OH^-] =$

d. $[H_3O^+] = 2.8 \times 10^{-13}$ M $[OH^-] =$

e. $[H_3O^+] = 8.6 \times 10^{-7}$ M $[OH^-] =$

Answers **a.** 1.0×10^{-11} M **b.** 3.3×10^{-5} M **c.** 2.5×10^{-9} M
d. 3.6×10^{-2} M **e.** 1.2×10^{-8} M

10.4 The pH Scale

- The pH scale is a range of numbers from 0 to 14 related to the $[H_3O^+]$ of the solution.
- A neutral solution has a pH of exactly 7. In acidic solutions, the pH is below 7.0, and in basic solutions the pH is above 7.0.
- The pH is the negative logarithm of the hydronium ion concentration: $pH = -\log [H_3O^+]$

MasteringChemistry

Case Study: Hyperventilation and Blood pH

Self Study Activity: The pH Scale

Tutorial: Logarithms

Tutorial: The pH Scale

◆ Learning Exercise 10.4A

State whether the following pH values are acidic, basic or neutral:

1. __________ plasma, pH = 7.4 **2.** __________ soft drink, pH = 2.8

3. __________ maple syrup, pH = 6.8 **4.** __________ beans, pH = 5.0

5. __________ tomatoes, pH = 4.2 **6.** __________ lemon juice, pH = 2.2

7. __________ saliva, pH = 7.0 **8.** __________ eggs, pH = 7.8

9. __________ lime juice, pH = 12.4 **10.** __________ strawberries, pH = 3.0

Answers **1.** basic **2.** acidic **3.** acidic **4.** acidic **5.** acidic
6. acidic **7.** neutral **8.** basic **9.** basic **10.** acidic

Guide to Calculating pH of an Aqueous Solution	
STEP 1	Enter the $[H_3O^+]$ value.
STEP 2	Press the *log* key and then the *change sign* key.
STEP 3	Adjust the number of digits to the right of the decimal point to equal the SFs in the coefficient.

◆ Learning Exercise 10.4B

Calculate the pH of each of the following solutions:

a. $[H_3O^+] = 1.0 \times 10^{-6}$ M ______ **b.** $[OH^-] = 1 \times 10^{-12}$ M ______
c. $[H_3O^+] = 1 \times 10^{-3}$ M ______ **d.** $[OH^-] = 1 \times 10^{-5}$ M ______
e. $[H_3O^+] = 3.4 \times 10^{-8}$ M ______ **f.** $[OH^-] = 7.8 \times 10^{-2}$ M ______

Answers **a.** 6.00 **b.** 2.0 **c.** 3.0
d. 9.0 **e.** 7.47 **f.** 12.89

◆ Learning Exercise 10.4C

Calculate the pH of each of the following solutions.

a. $[H_3O^+] = 1.0 \times 10^{-3}$ M

b. $[OH^-] = 1.9 \times 10^{-6}$ M

c. $[H_3O^+] = 1 \times 10^{-8}$ M

d. $[OH^-] = 1 \times 10^{-10}$ M

Answers **a.** 3.00 **b.** 8.28 **c.** 8.0 **d.** 4.0

◆ Learning Exercise 10.4D

Complete the following table:

	$[H_3O^+]$	$[OH^-]$	pH
a.	______	1×10^{-13} M	____
b.	______	______	8.0
c.	1×10^{-11} M	______	____
d.	______	______	7.80
e.	______	______	4.25
f.	2.0×10^{-10} M	______	____

Answers

	$[H_3O^+]$	$[OH^-]$	pH
a.	1×10^{-1} M	1×10^{-13} M	1.0
b.	1×10^{-8} M	1×10^{-6} M	8.0
c.	1×10^{-11} M	1×10^{-3} M	11.0
d.	1.6×10^{-8} M	6.3×10^{-7} M	7.80
e.	5.6×10^{-5} M	1.8×10^{-10} M	4.25
f.	2.0×10^{-10} M	5.0×10^{-5} M	9.70

10.5 Reactions of Acids and Bases

- Acids react with many metals to yield hydrogen gas (H_2) and the salt of the metal.
- Acids react with carbonates and bicarbonates to yield CO_2, H_2O, and the salt of the metal.
- Acids neutralize bases in a reaction that produces water and a salt.
- The net ionic equation for any neutralization is $H^+(aq) + OH^-(aq) \longrightarrow H_2O(l)$.
- In a balanced neutralization equation, an equal number of moles of H^+ and OH^- must react.
- The concentration of an acid can be determined by titration.

MasteringChemistry
Self Study Activity: Reactions of Acids and Bases

◆ Learning Exercise 10.5A

Complete and balance each of the following reactions of acids:

1. ___ $Zn(s)$ + ___ $HCl(aq) \longrightarrow$ ___ $ZnCl_2(aq)$ + ____________

2. ___ $HCl(aq)$ + ___ $NaHCO_3(aq) \longrightarrow$ ___ $CO_2(g)$ + ___ $H_2O(l)$ + ___ $NaCl(aq)$

3. ___ $HCl(aq)$ + ___ $Li_2CO_3(aq) \longrightarrow$ ________ + _________ + _______

4. ___ $Al(s)$ + ___ $H_2SO_4(aq) \longrightarrow$ ___ $Al_2(SO_4)_3(aq)$ + ____________

Answers

1. $Zn(s) + 2HCl(aq) \longrightarrow ZnCl_2(aq) + H_2(g)$
2. $HCl(aq) + NaHCO_3 \longrightarrow CO_2(g) + H_2O(l) + NaCl(aq)$
3. $2HCl(aq) + Li_2CO_3(aq) \longrightarrow CO_2(g) + H_2O(l) + 2LiCl(aq)$
4. $2Al(s) + 3H_2SO_4(aq) \longrightarrow Al_2(SO_4)_3(aq) + 3H_2(g)$

Guide to Balancing an Equation for Neutralization	
STEP 1	Write the chemical formulas of the reactants and products.
STEP 2	Balance the H^+ in the acid with the OH^- in the base.
STEP 3	Balance the H_2O with the H^+ and the OH^-.
STEP 4	Write the formula of the salt from the remaining ions.

◆ Learning Exercise 10.5B

Balance each of the following neutralization reactions:

1. $NaOH(aq) + H_2SO_4(aq) \longrightarrow Na_2SO_4(aq) + H_2O(l)$

2. $Mg(OH)_2(s) + HCl(aq) \longrightarrow MgCl_2(aq) + H_2O(l)$

3. $Al(OH)_3(s) + HNO_3(aq) \longrightarrow Al(NO_3)_3(aq) + H_2O(l)$

4. $Ca(OH)_2(s) + H_3PO_4(aq) \longrightarrow Ca_3(PO_4)_2(s) + H_2O(l)$

Answers

1. $2NaOH(aq) + H_2SO_4(aq) \longrightarrow Na_2SO_4(aq) + 2H_2O(l)$
2. $Mg(OH)_2(s) + 2HCl(aq) \longrightarrow MgCl_2(aq) + 2H_2O(l)$

3. $Al(OH)_3(s)$ + $3HNO_3(aq)$ ⟶ $Al(NO_3)_3(aq)$ + $3H_2O(l)$
4. $3Ca(OH)_2(s)$ + $2H_3PO_4(aq)$ ⟶ $Ca_3(PO_4)_2(s)$ + $6H_2O(l)$

◆ Learning Exercise 10.5C

Complete each of the following neutralization reactions and then balance:

a. $KOH(aq)$ + ____ $H_3PO_4(aq)$ ⟶ ____________ + ___ $H_2O(l)$

b. $NaOH(aq)$ + ____________ ⟶ ____ $Na_2SO_4(aq)$ + ____________

c. ____________ + ____________ ⟶ ____ $AlCl_3(aq)$ + ____________

d. ____________ + ____________ ⟶ ____ $Fe_2(SO_4)_3(aq)$ + ____________

Answers

a. $3KOH(aq)$ + $H_3PO_4(aq)$ ⟶ $K_3PO_4(aq)$ + $3H_2O(l)$
b. $2NaOH(aq)$ + $H_2SO_4(aq)$ ⟶ $Na_2SO_4(aq)$ + $2H_2O(l)$
c. $Al(OH)_3(s)$ + $3HCl(aq)$ ⟶ $AlCl_3(aq)$ + $3H_2O(l)$
d. $2Fe(OH)_3(s)$ + $3H_2SO_4(aq)$ ⟶ $Fe_2(SO_4)_3(aq)$ + $6H_2O(l)$

Guide to Calculations for an Acid–Base Titration	
STEP 1	State the given and needed quantities and/or concentrations.
STEP 2	Write a plan to calculate molarity or volume.
STEP 3	State the equalities and conversion factors including concentration.
STEP 4	Set up problem to calculate needed quantity.

◆ Learning Exercise 10.5D

a. A 5.00-mL sample of HCl is placed in a flask. In the titration, 15.0 mL of 0.200 M NaOH is required for neutralization. What is the molarity of the HCl in the sample?

$HCl(aq) + NaOH(aq) \longrightarrow NaCl(aq) + H_2O(l)$

b. How many milliliters of 0.200 M NaOH are required to completely neutralize 8.50 mL of 0.500 M H_2SO_4?

$H_2SO_4(aq) + 2NaOH(aq) \longrightarrow Na_2SO_4(aq) + 2H_2O(l)$

c. A 10.0–mL sample of H_3PO_4 is placed in a flask. If the titration required 42.0 mL of 0.100 M NaOH, what is the molarity of the H_3PO_4?

$$H_3PO_4(aq) + 3NaOH(aq) \longrightarrow Na_3PO_4(aq) + 3H_2O(l)$$

d. A 24.6–mL sample of HCl reacts with 33.0 mL of 0.222 M NaOH solution. What is the molarity of the HCl solution?

e. A 15.7–mL sample of H_2SO_4 reacts with 27.7 mL of 0.187 M KOH solution. What is the molarity of the H_2SO_4 solution?

Answers **a.** 0.600 M HCl **b.** 42.5 mL **c.** 0.140 M H_3PO_4
d. 0.298 M HCl **e.** 0.165 M H_2SO_4

10.6 Acid–Base Properties of Salt Solutions

- Salts of strong acids and strong bases produce neutral aqueous solutions.
- Salts of weak acids and strong bases form basic aqueous solutions.
- Salts of strong acids and weak bases form acidic aqueous solutions.

MasteringChemistry

Tutorial: Salts of Weak Acids and Bases

Study Note

Use the cation and anion of a salt to determine the acidity of its aqueous solution.

Example: Will the salt Na_2CO_3 form an acidic, basic, or neutral aqueous solution?

Solution: A salt of a strong base (NaOH) and a weak acid (HCO_3^-) will remove H^+ from water to produce a basic solution:

$$CO_3^{2-}(aq) + H_2O(l) \longrightarrow HCO_3^-(aq) + OH^-(aq)$$

◆ Learning Exercise 10.6A

Identify solutions of each of the following salts as acidic, basic, or neutral:

1. NaBr __________ **2.** KNO_2 __________

3. NH_4Cl __________ **4.** Li_2SO_4 __________

5. KF __________

Answers **1.** neutral **2.** basic **3.** acidic **4.** basic **5.** basic

◆ Learning Exercise 10.6B

Determine if each of the following salts dissolved in water forms a solution that is acidic, basic, or neutral. If acidic or basic, write an equation for the reaction:

	Acidic, basic, or neutral	**Equation**
1. NaCN	__________	__________
2. LiBr	__________	__________
3. NH_4NO_3	__________	__________
4. Na_2S	__________	__________
5. $BaCl_2$	__________	__________

Answers

1. NaCN	basic	$CN^-(aq) + H_2O(l) \longrightarrow HCN(aq) + OH^-(aq)$
2. LiBr	neutral	
3. NH_4NO_3	acidic	$NH_4^+(aq) + H_2O(l) \longrightarrow NH_3(aq) + H_3O^+(aq)$
4. Na_2S	basic	$S^{2-}(aq) + H_2O(l) \longrightarrow HS^-(aq) + OH^-(aq)$
5. $BaCl_2$	neutral	

10.7 Buffers

- A buffer solution resists a change in pH when small amounts of acid or base are added.
- A buffer contains either (1) a weak acid and its salt, or (2) a weak base and its salt. The weak acid picks up excess OH^-, and the anion of the salt picks up excess H_3O^+.
- The pH of a buffer can be calculated by rearranging the K_a for $[H_3O^+]$.

MasteringChemistry

Self Study Activity: pH and Buffers

Tutorial: Preparing Buffer Solutions

Tutorial: Calculating the pH of a Buffer

◆ Learning Exercise 10.7A

State whether each of the following represents a buffer system or not:

a. $HCl + NaCl$ **b.** K_2SO_4 **c.** H_2CO_3 **d.** $H_2CO_3 + NaHCO_3$

Answers
a. No. A strong acid is not a buffer.
b. No. A salt alone cannot act as a buffer.
c. No. A weak acid alone cannot act as a buffer.
d. Yes. A weak acid and its salt act as a buffer system.

Guide to Calculating pH of a Buffer	
STEP 1	Write the K_a expression.
STEP 2	Rearrange the K_a for $[H_3O^+]$.
STEP 3	Substitute in the [HA] and $[A^-]$ values.
STEP 4	Use $[H_3O^+]$ to calculate pH.

Study Note

Rearranging the K_a for an acid HA to solve for $[H_3O^+]$ gives the following expression:

$$[H_3O^+] = K_a \times \frac{[HA]}{[A^-]}$$

Using the $[H_3O^+]$, calculate the pH of the buffer.

◆ Learning Exercise 10.7B

The K_a for acetic acid $HC_2H_3O_2$ is 1.8×10^{-5}.

a. What is the pH of a buffer that contains 1.0 M $HC_2H_3O_2$ and 1.0 M $NaC_2H_3O_2$?

b. What is the pH of a buffer made from 0.10 M $HC_2H_3O_2$ and 0.10 M $NaC_2H_3O_2$?

c. What is the pH of a buffer made from 0.10 M $HC_2H_3O_2$ and 1.0 M $NaC_2H_3O_2$?

Answers

a. $[H_3O^+] = 1.8 \times 10^{-5} \times \dfrac{[1.0]}{[1.0]} = 1.8 \times 10^{-5}\,M$ $pH = -\log[1.8 \times 10^{-5}] = 4.74$

b. $[H_3O^+] = 1.8 \times 10^{-5} \times \dfrac{[0.1]}{[0.1]} = 1.8 \times 10^{-5}\,M$ $pH = -\log[1.8 \times 10^{-5}] = 4.74$

c. $[H_3O^+] = 1.8 \times 10^{-5} \times \dfrac{[0.1]}{[1.0]} = 1.8 \times 10^{-6}\,M$ $pH = -\log[1.8 \times 10^{-6}] = 5.74$

Checklist for Chapter 10

You are ready to take the Practice Test for Chapter 10. Be sure that you have accomplished the following learning goals for this chapter. If you are not sure, review the section listed at the end of the goal. Then apply your new skills and understanding to the Practice Test.

After studying Chapter 10, I can successfully:

____ Describe the properties of Arrhenius acids and bases and write their names (10.1).

____ Describe the Brønsted–Lowry concept of acids and bases; write conjugate acid–base pairs for an acid–base reaction (10.1).

____ Write equations for the ionization of strong and weak acids and bases (10.2).

____ Use the ion product constant of water to calculate $[H_3O^+]$ and $[OH^-]$ (10.3).

____ Calculate pH from the $[H_3O^+]$ of a solution (10.4).

____ Write a balanced equation for the reactions of acids with metals, carbonates, and bases (10.5).

____ Calculate the concentration of an acid from titration data (10.5).

____ Determine if a salt dissolved in water forms a solution that is acidic, basic, or neutral (10.6).

____ Describe the role of buffers in maintaining the pH of a solution (10.7).

____ Calculate the pH of a buffer solution (10.7).

Practice Test for Chapter 10

1. An acid is a compound which when placed in water yields this characteristic ion:

A. H_3O^+ **B.** OH^- **C.** Na^+ **D.** Cl^- **E.** CO_3^{2-}

2. $MgCl_2$ would be classified as a(n)

A. acid **B.** base **C.** salt **D.** buffer **E.** nonelectrolyte

3. $Mg(OH)_2$ would be classified as a

A. weak acid **B.** strong base **C.** salt **D.** buffer **E.** nonelectrolyte

4. In the K_w expression for pure H_2O, the $[H_3O^+]$ has the value

A. 1×10^{-7} M **B.** 1×10^{-1} M **C.** 1×10^{-14} M
D. 1×10^{-6} M **E.** 1×10^{-12} M

5. Of the following pH values, which is the most acidic?

A. 8.0 **B.** 5.5 **C.** 1.5
D. 3.2 **E.** 9.0

6. Of the following pH values, which is the most basic?

A. 10.0 **B.** 4.0 **C.** 2.2 **D.** 11.5 **E.** 9.0

For questions 7 through 9, consider a solution with $[H_3O^+] = 1 \times 10^{-11}$ M.

7. The pH of the solution is

A. 1.0 **B.** 2.0 **C.** 3.0 **D.** 11.0 **E.** 14.0

8. The hydroxide ion concentration is

A. 1×10^{-1} M **B.** 1×10^{-3} M **C.** 1×10^{-4} M
D. 1×10^{-7} M **E.** 1×10^{-11} M

9. The solution is

A. acidic **B.** basic **C.** neutral **D.** a buffer **E.** neutralized

For questions 10 through 12, consider a solution with $[OH^-] = 1 \times 10^{-5}$ M.

10. The hydrogen ion concentration of the solution is

A. 1×10^{-5} M **B.** 1×10^{-7} M **C.** 1×10^{-9} M
D. 1×10^{-10} M **E.** 1×10^{-14} M

11. The pH of the solution is

A. 2.0 **B.** 5.0 **C.** 9.0 **D.** 11 **E.** 14

12. The solution is

A. acidic **B.** basic **C.** neutral
D. a buffer **E.** neutralized

13. Acetic acid is a weak acid because

A. it forms a dilute acid solution **B.** it is isotonic **C.** it is less than 50% ionized in water
D. it is a nonpolar molecule **E.** it can form a buffer

14. A weak base when added to water

A. makes the solution slightly basic **B.** does not affect the pH **C.** dissociates completely
D. does not dissociate **E.** makes the solution slightly acidic

15. Which of the following is an equation for neutralization?

A. $CaCO_3(s) \longrightarrow CaO(s) + CO_2(g)$
B. $Na_2SO_4(s) \longrightarrow 2Na^+(aq) + SO_4^{2-}(aq)$
C. $H_2SO_4(aq) + 2NaOH(aq) \longrightarrow Na_2SO_4(aq) + 2H_2O(l)$
D. $Na_2O(s) + SO_3(g) \longrightarrow Na_2SO_4(aq)$
E. $H_2CO_3(aq) \longrightarrow CO_2(g) + H_2O(l)$

16. What is the name given to components in the body that keep blood pH within its normal 7.35 to 7.45 range?

A. nutrients **B.** buffers **C.** metabolites **D.** regufluids **E.** neutralizers

17. What is true of a typical buffer system?

A. It maintains a pH of 7.0.
B. It contains a weak base.
C. It contains a salt.
D. It contains a strong acid and its salt.
E. It maintains the pH of a solution.

18. Which of the following would act as a buffer system?

A. HCl **B.** Na_2CO_3 **C.** $NaOH + NaNO_3$ **D.** NH_4OH **E.** $NaHCO_3 + H_2CO_3$

19. Which of the following pairs is a conjugate acid–base pair?

A. HCl/HNO_3 **B.** HNO_2/NO_2^- **C.** NaOH/KOH
D. HSO_4^-/HCO_3^- **E.** Cl^-/F^-

20. The conjugate base of HSO_4^- is

A. SO_4^{2-} **B.** H_2SO_4 **C.** HS^- **D.** H_2S **E.** SO_3^{2-}

21. In which of the following reactions does H_2O act as an acid?

A. $H_3PO_4(aq) + H_2O(l) \longrightarrow H_3O^+(aq) + H_2PO_4^-(aq)$
B. $H_2SO_4(aq) + H_2O(l) \longrightarrow H_3O^+(aq) + HSO_4^-(aq)$
C. $H_2O(l) + HS^-(aq) \longrightarrow H_3O^+(aq) + S^{2-}(aq)$
D. $NaOH(aq) + HCl(aq) \longrightarrow NaCl(aq) + H_2O(l)$
E. $NH_3(g) + H_2O(l) \longrightarrow NH_4^+(aq) + OH^-(aq)$

22. If 23.7 mL of HCl reacts with 19.6 mL of 0.179 M NaOH, what is its molarity?

A. 6.76 M **B.** 0.216 M **C.** 0.148 M
D. 0.163 M **E.** 0.333 M

For questions 23 through 25, determine if each salt when dissolved in water will make an acidic (A), basic (B), or neutral (N) solution.

23. NaCl

24. KF

25. NH_4Cl

26. What is the molarity of a 10.0-mL sample of HCl that is neutralized by 15.0 mL of 2.0 M NaOH?

A. 0.50 M HCl **B.** 1.0 M HCl **C.** 1.5 M HCl **D.** 2.0 M HCl **E.** 3.0 M HCl

27. How many moles of H_2SO_4 will be completely neutralized by 6.0 moles of NaOH?

A. 1.0 **B.** 2.0 **C.** 3.0 **D.** 6.0 **E.** 11

28. Which of the following acids has the smallest K_a value?

A. HNO_3 **B.** H_2SO_4 **C.** HCl **D.** H_2CO_3 **E.** HBr

29. Using the following K_a values, identify the strongest acid in the group.

A. 7.5×10^{-3} **B.** 1.8×10^{-5} **C.** 4.5×10^{8}
D. 4.9×10^{-10} **E.** 3.2×10^{4}

30. A buffer is made with 1.0 M HF and 1.0 M NaF. If HF has a K_a of 7.2×10^{-4}, what is the pH of the buffer?

A. 3.14 **B.** 4.00 **C.** 4.14 **D.** 4.72 **E.** 7.20

Answers to the Practice Test

1. A	**2.** C	**3.** B	**4.** A	**5.** C
6. D	**7.** D	**8.** B	**9.** B	**10.** C
11. C	**12.** B	**13.** C	**14.** A	**15.** C
16. B	**17.** E	**18.** E	**19.** B	**20.** A
21. E	**22.** C	**23.** N	**24.** B	**25.** A
26. E	**27.** C	**28.** D	**29.** C	**30.** A

11

Introduction to Organic Chemistry: Alkanes

Study Goals

- Identify the number of bonds for carbon and other atoms in organic compounds.
- Describe the tetrahedral shape of carbon with single bonds in organic compounds.
- Draw expanded and condensed structural formulas for alkanes.
- Write the IUPAC names for alkanes and cycloalkanes.
- Describe the physical properties of alkanes.
- Write equations for the combustion of alkanes.
- Describe the properties such as density, boiling point, and solubility that are characteristic of organic compounds.
- Identify the functional groups in organic compounds.

Think About It

1. What is the meaning of the term "organic"?

2. What two elements are found in all organic compounds?

3. In some salad dressings, why is there a layer of vegetable oil floating on the vinegar and water layer?

Key Terms

1. Match the statements shown below with the following key terms:

a. alkene
b. isomers
c. hydrocarbon
d. alcohol
e. functional group
f. alkane
g. condensed structural formula
h. main chain
i. combustion
j. cycloalkane

1. ____ an atom or group of atoms that influences the chemical reactions of an organic compound

2. ____ a class of organic compounds with one or more hydroxyl (—OH) group

3. ____ a type of hydrocarbon with one or more carbon–carbon double bond
4. ____ an organic compound consisting of only carbon and hydrogen atoms
5. ____ compounds having the same molecular formula but a different arrangement of atoms
6. ____ a hydrocarbon that contains only carbon–carbon single bonds
7. ____ an alkane that exists as a cyclic structure
8. ____ the chemical reaction of an alkane and oxygen that yields CO_2, H_2O, and heat
9. ____ the type of formula that shows the arrangement of the carbon atoms grouped with their attached H atoms
10. ____ the longest continuous chain of carbon atoms in a condensed structural formula

Answers	**1.** e	**2.** d	**3.** a	**4.** c	**5.** b
	6. f	**7.** j	**8.** i	**9.** g	**10.** h

11.1 Organic Compounds

- Organic compounds are compounds of carbon and hydrogen that have covalent bonds, have low melting and boiling points, burn vigorously in air, are nonelectrolytes, and are usually more soluble in nonpolar solvents than in water.
- Each carbon in an alkane has four bonds arranged so that the bonded atoms are in the corners of a tetrahedron.

> ***MasteringChemistry***
>
> **Self Study Activity: Introduction to Organic Molecules**

◆ Learning Exercise 11.1A

Identify each the following as typical of organic (O) or inorganic (I) compounds:

1. ____ has covalent bonds
2. ____ has a low boiling point
3. ____ burns in air
4. ____ is soluble in water
5. ____ has a high melting point
6. ____ is soluble in a nonpolar solvent
7. ____ has ionic bonds
8. ____ has a long carbon chain
9. ____ contains carbon
10. ____ is not combustible
11. ____ has a formula of Na_2SO_4
12. ____ has a formula of $CH_3—CH_2—CH_3$

Answers	**1.** O	**2.** O	**3.** O	**4.** I	**5.** I	**6.** O
	7. I	**8.** O	**9.** O	**10.** I	**11.** I	**12.** O

◆ Learning Exercise 11.1B

1. What is the name of the three-dimensional shape of methane shown above?

2. Draw the expanded structural formula (two-dimensional) for methane.

Answers **1.** tetrahedron

2.
```
   H
   |
H—C—H
   |
   H
```

11.2 Alkanes

- In an IUPAC name, the prefix indicates the number of carbon atoms, and the suffix describes the family of the compound. For example, in the name *propane,* the prefix *prop* indicates a chain of three carbon atoms and the ending *ane* indicates single bonds (alkane). The names of the first six alkanes follow:

Name	Number of Carbon Atoms	Condensed Structural Formula
Methane	1	CH_4
Ethane	2	$CH_3—CH_3$
Propane	3	$CH_3—CH_2—CH_3$
Butane	4	$CH_3—CH_2—CH_2—CH_3$
Pentane	5	$CH_3—CH_2—CH_2—CH_2—CH_3$
Hexane	6	$CH_3—CH_2—CH_2—CH_2—CH_2—CH_3$

- An expanded structural formula shows a separate line to each bonded atom; a condensed structural formula depicts each carbon atom and its attached hydrogen atoms as a group. A molecular formula gives the total number of each kind of atom.

Expanded Structural Formula	**Condensed Structural Formula**	**Molecular Formula**
$\begin{array}{ccccccccc} & & H & & H & & H & & \\ & & \vert & & \vert & & \vert & & \\ H & - & C & - & C & - & C & - & H \\ & & \vert & & \vert & & \vert & & \\ & & H & & H & & H & & \end{array}$	$CH_3{-}CH_2{-}CH_3$	C_3H_8

◆ Learning Exercise 11.2A

Indicate if each of the following is a molecular formula (M), an expanded structural formula (E), or a condensed structural formula (C):

1. ____ $CH_3{-}CH_3$

2. ____ C_5H_{12}

3. ____ $CH_3{-}CH_2{-}CH_3$

4. ____ $\begin{array}{ccccccccc} & & H & & H & & H & & \\ & & | & & | & & | & & \\ H & - & C & - & C & - & C & - & H \\ & & | & & | & & | & & \\ & & H & & H & & H & & \end{array}$

5. ____ $\begin{array}{ccccccc} & & CH_3 & & & & \\ & & | & & & & \\ CH_3 & - & CH & - & CH_2 & - & CH_3 \end{array}$

6. ____ C_8H_{18}

Answers **1.** C **2.** M **3.** C **4.** E **5.** C **6.** M

◆ Learning Exercise 11.2B

Draw the condensed structural formula for each of the following expanded structural formulas:

1. $\begin{array}{ccccccc} & & H & & H & & \\ & & | & & | & & \\ H & - & C & - & C & - & H \\ & & | & & | & & \\ & & H & & H & & \end{array}$

2. $\begin{array}{ccccccccc} & & H & & H & & H & & \\ & & | & & | & & | & & \\ H & - & C & - & C & - & C & - & H \\ & & | & & | & & | & & \\ & & H & & H & & H & & \end{array}$

3. $\begin{array}{ccccccccccc} & & H & & H & & H & & H & & \\ & & | & & | & & | & & | & & \\ H & - & C & - & C & - & C & - & C & - & H \\ & & | & & | & & | & & | & & \\ & & H & & H & & H & & H & & \end{array}$

4. $\begin{array}{ccccccccccc} & & & & H & & & & & & \\ & & & & | & & & & & & \\ & & & & H{-}C{-}H & & & & & & \\ & & H & & | & & H & & H & & \\ & & | & & | & & | & & | & & \\ H & - & C & - & C & - & C & - & C & - & H \\ & & | & & | & & | & & | & & \\ & & H & & H & & | & & H & & \\ & & & & & & H{-}C{-}H & & & & \\ & & & & & & | & & & & \\ & & & & & & H & & & & \end{array}$

Answers

1. $CH_3{-}CH_3$

2. $CH_3{-}CH_2{-}CH_3$

3. $CH_3{-}CH_2{-}CH_2{-}CH_3$

4. $\begin{array}{ccccccc} & & CH_3 & & & & \\ & & | & & & & \\ CH_3 & - & CH & - & CH & - & CH_3 \\ & & & & | & & \\ & & & & CH_3 & & \end{array}$

◆ Learning Exercise 11.2C

Draw the condensed structural formula and give the name for the straight-chain alkane of each of the following molecular formulas:

1. C_2H_6 ______________________________

2. C_3H_8 ______________________________

3. C_4H_{10} ______________________________

4. C_5H_{12} ______________________________

5. C_6H_{14} ______________________________

Answers

1. $CH_3—CH_3$, ethane
2. $CH_3—CH_2—CH_3$, propane
3. $CH_3—CH_2—CH_2—CH_3$, butane
4. $CH_3—CH_2—CH_2—CH_2—CH_3$, pentane
5. $CH_3—CH_2—CH_2—CH_2—CH_2—CH_3$, hexane

MasteringChemistry

Tutorial: Naming Cycloalkanes

◆ Learning Exercise 11.2D

Give the IUPAC name for each of the following cycloalkanes:

1. 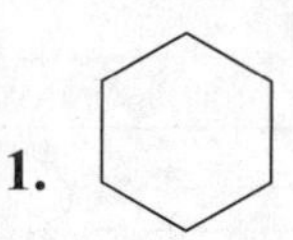 **2.** 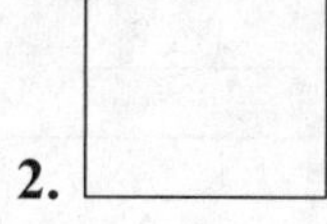 **3.** 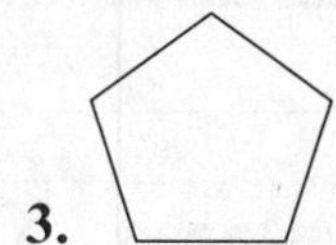 **4.** 

Answers **1.** cyclohexane **2.** cyclobutane **3.** cyclopentane **4.** cyclopropane

◆ Learning Exercise 11.2E

Draw the line-bond formula for each of the following alkanes:

1. butane ______________________________

2. pentane ______________________________

3. hexane ______________________________

4. octane ______________________________

Answers

1.  2. 
3. 4.

11.3 Alkanes with Substituents

- The IUPAC system is a set of rules used to name organic compounds in a systematic manner.
- Each substituent is numbered and listed alphabetically in front of the name of the longest chain.
- Carbon groups that are substituents are named as alkyl groups or alkyl substituents. An alkyl group is named by replacing the *ane* of the alkane name with *yl.* For example, CH_3—is named as methyl (from CH_4 methane), and CH_3—CH_2—is named as an ethyl group (from CH_3—CH_3 ethane).
- Structural isomers have the same molecular formula but differ in the sequence of atoms in each of their condensed structural formulas.
- In a haloalkane, a halogen atom, —F, —Cl, —Br, or —I, replaces a hydrogen atom in an alkane.
- A halogen atom is named as a substituent (fluoro, chloro, bromo, iodo) attached to the alkane chain.

MasteringChemistry

Tutorial: Naming Alkanes with Substituents

Study Note

Example: Write the IUPAC name for the following compound:

$$\begin{array}{c} \quad\quad\quad\quad\quad\quad CH_3 \\ \quad\quad\quad\quad\quad\quad | \\ CH_3—CH_2—CH—CH_3 \end{array}$$

Solution: The four-carbon chain butane is numbered from the end nearer the side group, which places the *methyl* substituent on carbon 2: *2-methylbutane.*

Guide to Naming Alkanes

STEP 1	Write the alkane name of the longest continuous chain of carbon atoms.
STEP 2	Number the carbon atoms starting from the end nearest a substituent.
STEP 3	Give the location and name of each substituent in alphabetical order as a prefix to the name of the longest chain.

◆ Learning Exercise 11.3A

Give the IUPAC name for each of the following compounds:

$$\begin{array}{c} CH_3 \\ | \\ CH_3—CH—CH_3 \end{array}$$

1. $CH_3—CH(CH_3)—CH_3$ ________________________________

$$\begin{array}{c} CH_3 \quad\quad\quad\quad CH_3 \\ | \quad\quad\quad\quad\quad | \\ CH_3—CH—CH_2—CH—CH_2—CH_3 \end{array}$$

2. $CH_3—CH(CH_3)—CH_2—CH(CH_3)—CH_2—CH_3$ ________________________________

$$\begin{array}{l} \quad\;\; CH_3 \qquad\qquad\qquad\quad\; CH_3 \\ \quad\;\; | \qquad\qquad\qquad\qquad\;\; | \\ \textbf{3. } CH_3-CH-CH_2-CH_2-CH-CH_2-CH_3 \end{array}$$ ________________________________

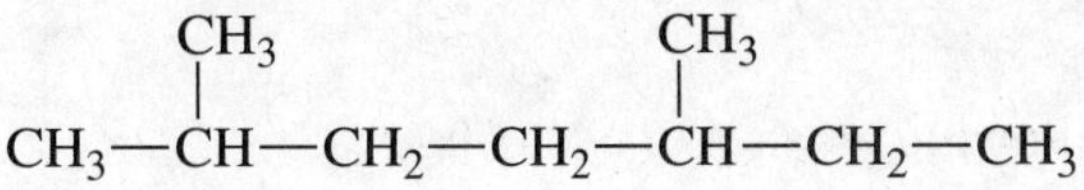

$$\begin{array}{l} \quad\;\; CH_3 \\ \quad\;\; | \\ \textbf{4. } CH_3-C-CH_2-CH_3 \\ \quad\;\; | \\ \quad\;\; CH_3 \end{array}$$ ________________________________

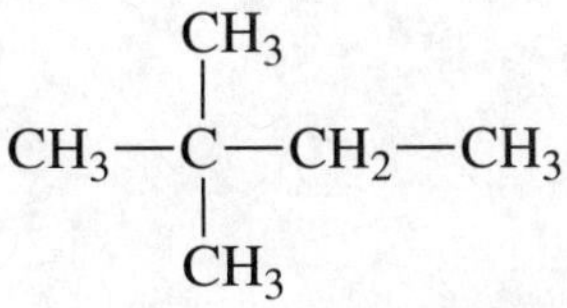

Answers **1.** 2-methylpropane **2.** 2,4-dimethylhexane **3.** 2,5-dimethylheptane
4. 2,2-dimethylbutane

MasteringChemistry
Tutorial: Drawing Haloalkanes and Branched Alkanes

Guide to Drawing Alkane Formulas	
STEP 1	Draw the main chain of carbon atoms.
STEP 2	Number the chain and place the substituents on the carbon atoms indicated by the numbers.
STEP 3	Add the correct number of hydrogen atoms to give four bonds to each C atom.

◆ Learning Exercise 11.3B

Draw the condensed structural formula for each of the following compounds:

1. hexane

2. methane

3. 2,4-dimethylpentane

4. propane

Answers **1.** $CH_3-CH_2-CH_2-CH_2-CH_2-CH_3$ **2.** CH_4

$$\begin{array}{l} \qquad\quad CH_3 \qquad\quad CH_3 \\ \qquad\quad | \qquad\qquad\;\; | \\ \textbf{3. } CH_3-CH-CH_2-CH-CH_3 \end{array}$$

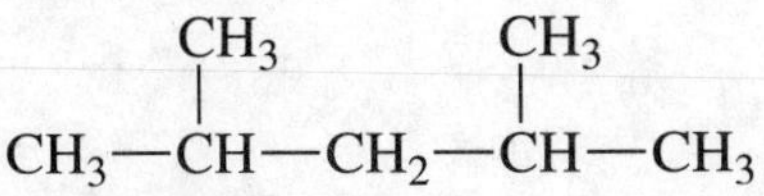

4. $CH_3-CH_2-CH_3$

◆ Learning Exercise 11.3C

Draw the condensed structural formula for each of the following alkanes or cycloalkanes:

1. pentane

2. 2-methylpentane

3. 4-ethyl-2-methylhexane

4. 2,2,4-trimethylhexane

5. 1,2-dichlorocyclobutane

6. methylcyclohexane

Answers

1. $CH_3-CH_2-CH_2-CH_2-CH_3$

2. 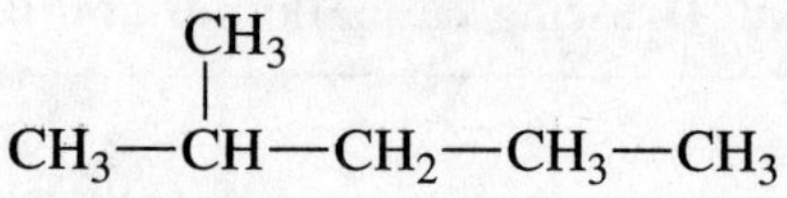 $CH_3-\underset{}{\overset{CH_3}{\overset{|}{C}H}}-CH_2-CH_3-CH_3$

3. $CH_3-\overset{CH_3}{\overset{|}{C}H}-CH_2-\overset{CH_2-CH_3}{\overset{|}{C}H}-CH_2-CH_3$

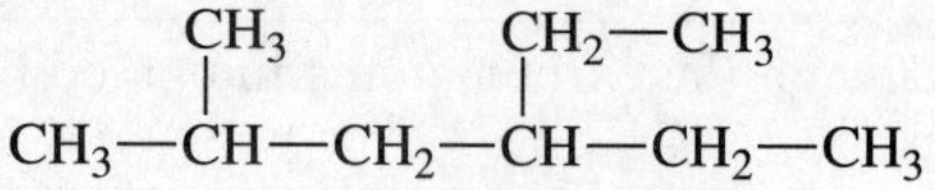

4. 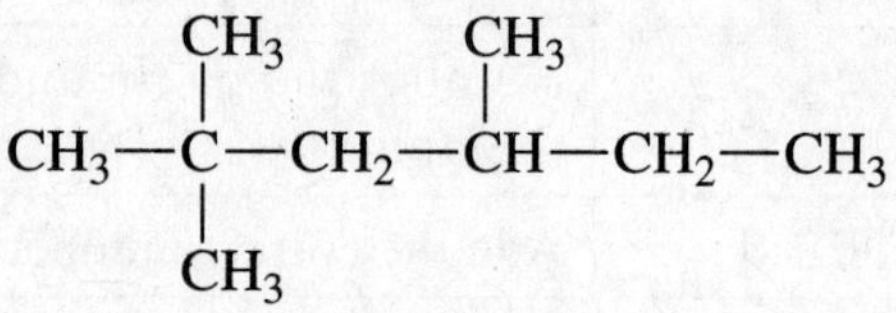 $CH_3-\underset{\underset{CH_3}{|}}{\overset{CH_3}{\overset{|}{C}}}-CH_2-\overset{CH_3}{\overset{|}{C}H}-CH_2-CH_3$

5. 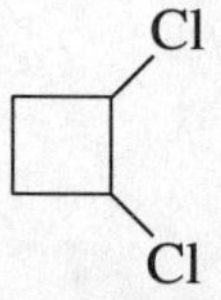 Cl, Cl (cyclobutane ring with Cl on adjacent carbons)

6. 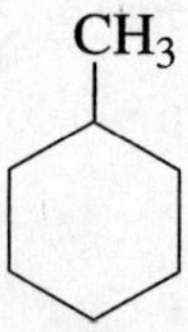 CH_3 (cyclohexane ring with CH_3)

◆ Learning Exercise 11.3D

Give the IUPAC (and common) name for the following:

1. CH_3-CH_2-Br

2. 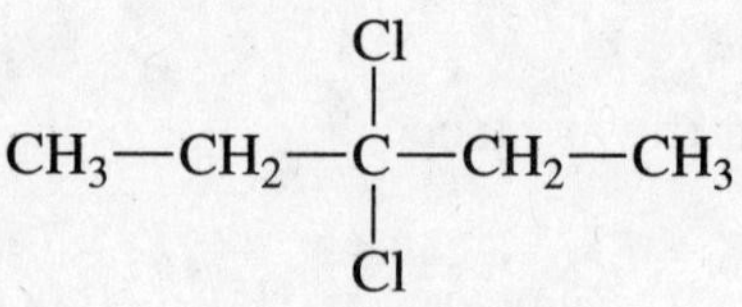 $CH_3-CH_2-\underset{\underset{Cl}{|}}{\overset{Cl}{\overset{|}{C}}}-CH_2-CH_3$

3. $CH_3-CH_2-\overset{Cl}{\overset{|}{C}H}-CH_2-\overset{Br}{\overset{|}{C}H}-CH_3$

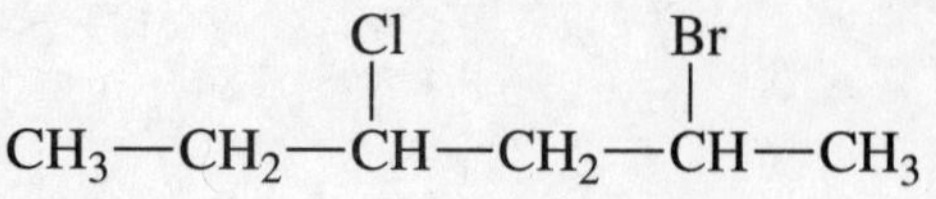

4. 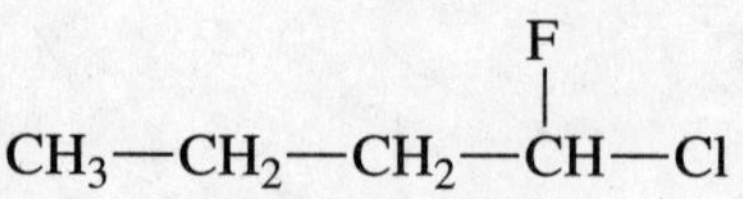 $CH_3-CH_2-CH_2-\overset{F}{\overset{|}{C}H}-Cl$

5.  Br (cyclopropane ring with Br)

Answers

1. bromoethane (ethyl bromide)
2. 3,3-dichloropentane
3. 2-bromo-4-chlorohexane
4. 1-chloro-1-fluorobutane
5. bromocyclopropane

◆ Learning Exercise 11.3E

Draw the condensed structural formula for each of the following haloalkanes:

1. ethyl chloride

2. bromomethane

3. 3-bromo-1-chloropentane

4. 1,1-dichlorohexane

5. 2,2,3-trichlorobutane

6. 2,4-dibromo-2,4-dichloropentane

Answers

1. CH_3-CH_2-Cl

2. CH_3-Br

3. $Cl-CH_2-CH_2-\overset{\displaystyle Br}{\overset{|}{C}}H-CH_2-CH_3$

4. $Cl-\overset{\displaystyle Cl}{\overset{|}{C}}H-CH_2-CH_2-CH_2-CH_2-CH_3$

5. $CH_3-\underset{\displaystyle Cl}{\underset{|}{\overset{\displaystyle Cl}{\overset{|}{C}}}}-\overset{\displaystyle Cl}{\overset{|}{C}}H-CH_3$

6. $CH_3-\underset{\displaystyle Cl}{\underset{|}{\overset{\displaystyle Br}{\overset{|}{C}}}}-CH_2-\underset{\displaystyle Cl}{\underset{|}{\overset{\displaystyle Br}{\overset{|}{C}}}}-CH_3$

MasteringChemistry

Self Study Activity: Isomers: Diversity in Molecules

◆ Learning Exercise 11.3F

Write the condensed structural formula for the four isomers that have the molecular formula of C_3H_9N.

Answers

$$CH_3-\underset{|}{\overset{CH_3}{N}}-CH_3 \qquad CH_3-CH_2-CH_2-NH_2$$

$$CH_3-\overset{H}{\underset{}{N}}-CH_2-CH_3 \qquad CH_3-\overset{NH_2}{CH}-CH_3$$

11.4 Properties of Alkanes

- Alkanes are less dense than water, and mostly unreactive, except that they burn vigorously.
- Alkanes are nonpolar, insoluble in water, and have low boiling points.
- Alkanes are found in natural gas, gasoline, and diesel fuels.
- In combustion, an alkane at a high temperature reacts rapidly with oxygen to produce carbon dioxide, water, and a great amount of heat.

MasteringChemistry

Tutorial: Writing Balanced Equations for the Combustion of Alkanes

Case Study: Hazardous Materials

Study Note

Example: Write the equation for the combustion of methane.
Solution: Write the molecular formulas for the following reactants: methane (CH_4) and oxygen (O_2). Write the products CO_2 and H_2O and balance the equation.

$$CH_4(g) + O_2(g) \rightarrow CO_2(g) + H_2O(g) + \text{heat}$$
$$CH_4(g) + 2O_2(g) \rightarrow CO_2(g) + 2H_2O(g) + \text{heat (balanced)}$$

◆ Learning Exercise 11.4A

Write a balanced equation for the complete combustion of the following:

1. propane ______________________________

2. hexane ______________________________

3. pentane ______________________________

4. cyclobutane ______________________________

Answers

1. $C_3H_8(g) + 5O_2(g) \rightarrow 3CO_2(g) + 4H_2O(g) + \text{heat}$
2. $2C_6H_{14}(g) + 19O_2(g) \rightarrow 12CO_2(g) + 14H_2O\,(g) + \text{heat}$
3. $C_5H_{12}(g) + 8O_2(g) \rightarrow 5CO_2(g) + 6H_2O(g) + \text{heat}$
4. $C_4H_8(g) + 6O_2(g) \rightarrow 4CO_2\,(g) + 4H_2O(g) + \text{heat}$

◆ Learning Exercise 11.4B

Indicate which property in each of the following pairs is more likely to be a property of hexane:

a. density is 0.66 g/mL or 1.66 g/mL ____________

b. solid or liquid at room temperature ____________

c. soluble or insoluble in water ____________

d. flammable or nonflammable in oxygen ____________

e. melting point is 95 °C or –95 °C ____________

Answers **a.** 0.66 g/mL **b.** liquid **c.** insoluble
d. flammable **e.** –95 °C

11.5 Functional Groups

- Organic compounds are classified by *functional groups*, which are atoms or groups of atoms where specific chemical reactions occur.
- Alkenes are hydrocarbons that contain one or more double bonds (C=C); alkynes contain a triple bond (C≡C). Aromatic compounds contain a benzene ring.
- Alcohols contain a hydroxyl (—OH) group; ethers have an oxygen atom (—O—) between two alkyl or aromatic group.
- Aldehydes contain a carbonyl group (C=O) bonded to at least one H atom; ketones contain the carbonyl group bonded to two alkyl or aromatic groups.
- Carboxylic acids have a carboxyl group attached to hydrogen (—COOH); esters contain the carboxyl group attached to an alkyl or aromatic group.
- Amines are derived from ammonia (NH_3) in which alkyl or aromatic groups replace one or more of the H atoms of NH_3.
- Amides have a carbonyl group attached to nitrogen from NH_3 or amines.

MasteringChemistry

Tutorial: Identifying Functional Groups

Tutorial: Drawing Organic Compounds with Functional Groups

Self Study Activity: Functional Groups

◆ Learning Exercise 11.5A

Classify the organic compounds shown below according to their functional groups:

a. alkane **b.** alkene **c.** alcohol **d.** ether **e.** aldehyde

1. ____ $CH_3{-}CH_2{-}CH{=}CH_2$

2. ____ $CH_3{-}CH_2{-}CH_3$

3. ____ $CH_3{-}CH_2{-}\overset{\overset{\displaystyle O}{\|}}{C}{-}H$

4. ____ $CH_3{-}CH_2{-}CH_2{-}OH$

5. ____ $CH_3{-}CH_2{-}O{-}CH_2{-}CH_3$

6. ____ $CH_3{-}CH_2{-}CH_2{-}CH_3$

Answers **1.** b **2.** a **3.** e **4.** c **5.** d **6.** a

◆ Learning Exercise 11.5B

Classify the following compounds according to their functional groups:

a. alcohol **b.** aldehyde **c.** ketone **d.** ether **e.** amine

1. _____ $CH_3{-}CH_2{-}CH_2{-}\overset{\overset{\displaystyle O}{\|}}{C}{-}H$

2. _____ $CH_3{-}CH_2{-}CH_2{-}NH_2$

3. _____ $CH_3{-}CH_2{-}\overset{\overset{\displaystyle O}{\|}}{C}{-}CH_2{-}CH_3$

4. _____ $CH_3{-}CH_2{-}O{-}CH_3$

5. _____ $CH_3{-}\overset{\overset{\displaystyle O}{\|}}{C}{-}CH_2{-}CH_3$

6. _____ $CH_3{-}\overset{\overset{\displaystyle O}{\|}}{C}{-}H$

7. _____ $CH_3{-}CH_2{-}\overset{\overset{\displaystyle NH_2}{|}}{CH}{-}CH_3$

8. _____ $CH_3{-}CH_2{-}\overset{\overset{\displaystyle OH}{|}}{CH}{-}CH_3$

Answers **1.** b **2.** e **3.** c **4.** d **5.** c **6.** b **7.** e **8.** a

◆ Learning Exercise 11.5C

Draw the condensed structural formula for each of the following:

1. a two-carbon alcohol	**2.** a three-carbon ketone
3. a three-carbon aldehyde	**4.** a three-carbon alkene
5. an amine with two methyl groups	**6.** an ether with two ethyl groups

Answers

1. $CH_3—CH_2—OH$

2. $CH_3—\overset{\overset{\large O}{\|}}{C}—CH_3$

3. $CH_3—CH_2—\overset{\overset{\large O}{\|}}{C}—H$

4. $CH_3—CH{=}CH_2$

5. $CH_3—\overset{\overset{\large H}{|}}{N}—CH_3$

6. $CH_3—CH_2—O—CH_2—CH_3$

Checklist for Chapter 11

You are ready to take the Practice Test for Chapter 11. Be sure that you have accomplished the following learning goals for this chapter. If you are not sure, review the section listed at the end of the goal. Then apply your new skills and understanding to the Practice Test.

After studying Chapter 11, I can successfully:

_____ Identify properties as characteristic of organic or inorganic compounds (11.1).

_____ Identify the number of bonds for carbon (11.1).

_____ Describe the tetrahedral shape of carbon in carbon compounds (11.1).

_____ Draw the expanded structural formula and the condensed structural formula for an alkane (11.2).

_____ Use the IUPAC system to write the names for alkanes and cycloalkanes (11.2).

_____ Use the IUPAC system to write the names for alkanes with substituents (11.3).

_____ Draw the condensed structural formulas of alkanes from the name (11.3).

_____ Describe some physical properties of alkanes (11.4).

_____ Write and balance equations for the combustion of alkanes (11.4).

_____ Identify the functional groups in organic compounds (11.5).

Practice Test for Chapter 11

For questions 1 through 8, indicate whether the following characteristic are typical of organic (O) compounds or inorganic (I) compounds.

1. ____ higher melting points

2. ____ fewer compounds

3. ____ covalent bonds

4. ____ soluble in water

5. ____ ionic bonds

6. ____ combustible

7. ____ low boiling points

8. ____ soluble in nonpolar solvents

For questions 9 through 13, match the name of each alkane with its following condensed structural formulas:

A. methane **B.** ethane **C.** propane **D.** pentane **E.** heptane

9. ____ $CH_3—CH_2—CH_3$

10. ____ $CH_3—CH_2—CH_2—CH_2—CH_2—CH_2—CH_3$

11. ____ CH_4

12. ____ $CH_3—CH_2—CH_2—CH_2—CH_3$

13. ____ $CH_3—CH_3$

For questions 14 through 17, match the name of each hydrocarbon with one of the condensed structural formulas below:

A. butane
B. methylcyclohexane
C. cyclopropane
D. 3,5-dimethylhexane
E. 2,4-dimethylhexane

14. ____ $CH_3—CH_2—CH_2—CH_3$

15. ____
```
        CH3          CH3
        |            |
CH3—CH—CH2—CH—CH2—CH3
```

16. ____ (cyclopropane ring)

17. ____ (cyclohexane ring with CH_3)

For questions 18 through 20, match the structural formula with the correct name:

A. methylcyclopentane
B. cyclobutane
C. cyclohexane
D. ethylcyclopentane

18. ____ (cyclohexane)

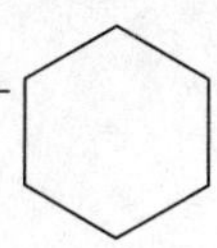

19. ____ (cyclopentane with CH_3)

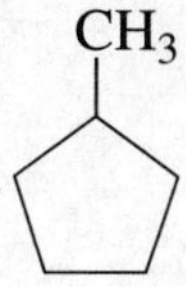

20. ____ (cyclopentane with $CH_2—CH_3$)

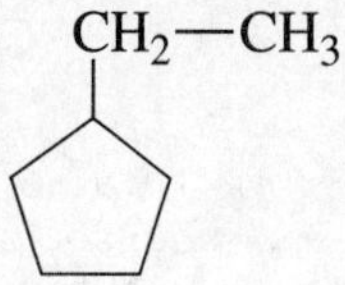

For questions 21 through 23, match the name of each of the following compounds with its correct condensed structural formula:

A. 2,4-dichloropentane
B. chlorocyclopentane
C. 1,2-dichloropentane
D. 4,5-dichloropentane

21. ____ $CH_3—CH_2—CH_2—CH(Cl)—CH_2—Cl$

22. ____ (cyclopentane with Cl)

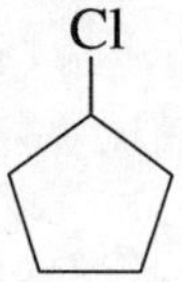

23. ____ $CH_3—CH(Cl)—CH_2—CH(Cl)—CH_3$

24. The correctly balanced equation for the complete combustion of ethane is

A. $C_2H_6(g) + O_2(g) \rightarrow 2CO(g) + 3H_2O(g)$
B. $C_2H_6(g) + O_2(g) \rightarrow CO_2(g) + H_2O(g)$
C. $C_2H_6(g) + 2O_2(g) \rightarrow 2CO_2(g) + 3H_2O(g)$
D. $2C_2H_6(g) + 7O_2(g) \rightarrow 4CO_2(g) + 6H_2O(g)$
E. $2C_2H_6(g) + 4O_2(g) \rightarrow 4CO_2(g) + 6H_2O(g)$

For questions 25 through 33, match the name of each type of organic compound with one of the condensed structural formulas below:

A. alkane
B. alkene
C. alcohol
D. aldehyde
E. ketone
F. ether
G. amine
H. amide

25. ____ $CH_3—CH_2—C(=O)—NH_2$

26. ____ $CH_3—CH_2—C(=O)—CH_3$

27. ____ $CH_3—CH_2—CH_2—OH$

28. ____ $CH_3—CH_2—CH(CH_3)—CH_3$

29. ____ $CH_3—CH_2—O—CH_3$

30. ____ $CH_3—CH(NH_2)—CH_2—CH_3$

31. ____ $CH_3—C(=O)—H$

32. ____ $CH_3—CH_2—CH{=}CH_2$

33. ____ $CH_3—CH_2—CH(OH)—CH_3$

For questions 34 through 38, indicate whether the pairs of compounds are isomers (I), the same compound (S), or different compounds (D).

34. ____ $CH_3—CH_2—CH_2—CH_3$ and $CH_2(CH_3)—CH_2—CH_3$

35. ____ $CH_3—CH_2—OH$ and $CH_3—O—CH_3$

36. ____ $CH_3—CH_2—NH_2$ and $CH_3—N(H)—CH_2—CH_3$

37. ____ $CH_3—CH_2—C(=O)—OH$ and $CH_3—C(=O)—O—CH_3$

38. ____ $CH_3—CH_2—CH_2—CH_3$ and $CH_3—C{\equiv}C—CH_3$

Answers to the Practice Test

1. I	**2.** I	**3.** O	**4.** I	**5.** I
6. O	**7.** O	**8.** O	**9.** C	**10.** E
11. A	**12.** D	**13.** B	**14.** A	**15.** E
16. C	**17.** B	**18.** C	**19.** A	**20.** D
21. C	**22.** B	**23.** A	**24.** D	**25.** H
26. E	**27.** C	**28.** A	**29.** F	**30.** G
31. D	**32.** B	**33.** C	**34.** S	**35.** I
36. D	**37.** I	**38.** D		

12

Alkenes, Alkynes, and Aromatic Compounds

Study Goals

- Classify unsaturated compounds as alkenes, cycloalkenes, and alkynes.
- Write IUPAC and common names for alkenes and alkynes.
- Draw condensed structural formulas and names for cis–trans isomers of alkenes.
- Write equations for halogenation, hydration, hydrohalogenation, and hydrogenation of alkenes and alkynes.
- Describe the formation of a polymer from alkene monomers.
- Describe the bonding in benzene.
- Draw condensed structural formulas and give the names of aromatic compounds.
- Describe the physical and chemical properties of aromatic compounds.

Think About It

1. The label on a bottle of vegetable oil says the oil is unsaturated. What does this mean?

2. What are polymers?

3. A margarine is partially hydrogenated. What does that mean?

Key Terms

Match the statements shown below with the following key terms:

a. alkene **b.** hydrogenation **c.** alkyne **d.** hydration **e.** polymer

1. ____ A long-chain molecule formed by linking many small molecules

2. ____ The addition of H_2 to a carbon–carbon double bond

3. ____ An unsaturated hydrocarbon containing a carbon–carbon double bond

4. ____ The addition of H_2O to a carbon–carbon double bond

5. ____ A compound that contains a carbon–carbon triple bond

Answers **1.** e **2.** b **3.** a **4.** d **5.** c

12.1 Alkenes and Alkynes

- Alkenes are unsaturated hydrocarbons that contain one or more carbon–carbon double bond.
- In alkenes, the three groups bonded to each carbon in the double bond are planar and arranged at angles of 120°.
- Alkynes are unsaturated hydrocarbons that contain a carbon–carbon triple bond.
- The atoms bonded to a carbon–carbon triple bond are linear.
- The IUPAC names of alkenes are derived by changing the *ane* ending of the parent alkane to *ene*. For example, the IUPAC name of $H_2C{=}CH_2$ is ethene. It has a common name of ethylene. In alkenes, the longest carbon chain containing the double bond is numbered from the end nearer the double bond. In cycloalkenes with substituents, the double bond carbons are given positions of 1 and 2, and the ring is numbered to give the next lower numbers to the substituents.

$CH_3{-}CH{=}CH_2$ — Propene (propylene)

$CH_2{=}CH{-}CH_2{-}CH_3$ — 1-Butene

$CH_3{-}CH{=}\overset{\overset{\large CH_3}{|}}{C}{-}CH_3$ — 2-Methylbutene

- The IUPAC names of alkynes are derived by changing the *ane* ending of the parent alkane to *yne*. In alkynes, the longest carbon chain containing the double bond is numbered from the end nearer the triple bond.

$HC{\equiv}CH$ — Ethyne

$CH_3{-}C{\equiv}CH$ — Propyne

$CH_3{-}CH_2{-}C{\equiv}CH$ — 1-Butyne

◆ Learning Exercise 12.1A

Classify the following condensed structural formulas as alkane, alkene, cycloalkene, or alkyne:

1. ____ $CH_3{-}CH_2{-}CH_3$

2. ____ [skeletal structure]

3. ____ $CH_3{-}C{\equiv}C{-}CH_3$

4. ____ $CH_3{-}CH_2{-}CH{=}\overset{\overset{\large CH_3}{|}}{C}{-}CH_2{-}CH_3$

Answers **1.** alkane **2.** alkene **3.** alkyne **4.** alkene

MasteringChemistry

Tutorial: Naming Alkenes and Alkynes

Guide to Naming Alkenes and Alkynes	
STEP 1	Name the longest carbon chain with a double or triple bond.
STEP 2	Number the carbon chain starting from the end nearer a double or triple bond.
STEP 3	Give the location and name of any substituents in alphabetical order as a prefix to the name.

◆ Learning Exercise 12.1B

Write the IUPAC name for each of the following alkenes:

1. $CH_3-CH=CH_2$

2. $CH_3-CH=CH-CH_3$

3. 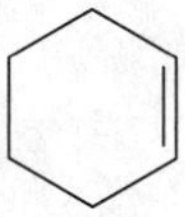 (cyclohexene ring structure)

4. 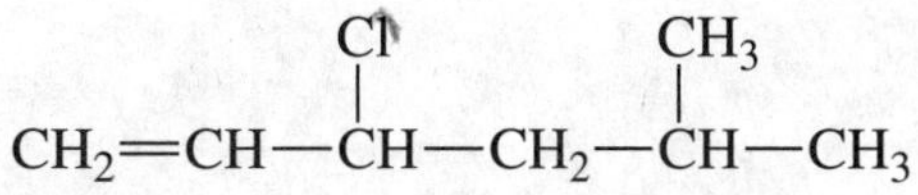 $CH_2=CH-CH(Cl)-CH_2-CH(CH_3)-CH_3$

5. 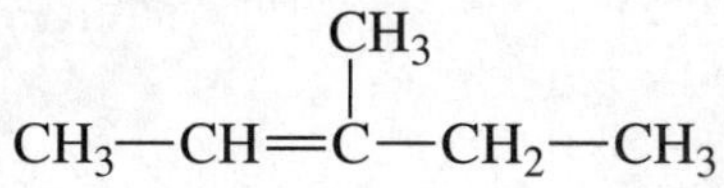 $CH_3-CH=C(CH_3)-CH_2-CH_3$

6. 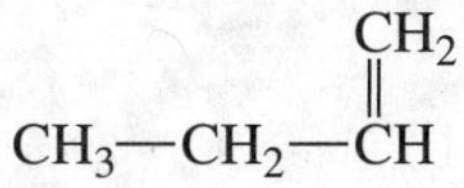 $CH_3-CH_2-CH=CH_2$

Answers **1.** propene **2.** 2-butene **3.** cyclohexene **4.** 3-chloro-5-methyl-1-hexene **5.** 3-methyl-2-pentene **6.** 1-butene

◆ Learning Exercise 12.1C

Write the IUPAC name of each of the following alkynes:

1. $HC\equiv CH$

2. $CH_3-C\equiv CH$

3. $CH_3-CH_2-C\equiv CH$

4. 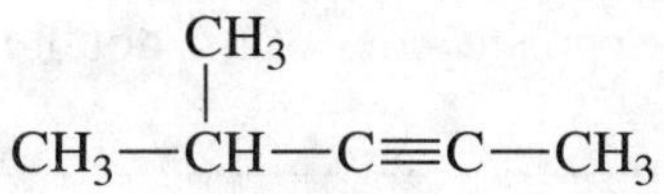 $CH_3-CH(CH_3)-C\equiv C-CH_3$

Answers **1.** ethyne **2.** propyne **3.** 1-butyne **4.** 4-methyl-2-pentyne

MasteringChemistry

Tutorial: Drawing Alkenes and Alkynes

◆ Learning Exercise 12.1D

Draw the condensed structural formula for each of the following:

1. 2-pentyne

2. 2-chloro-2-butene

3. 3-bromo-2-methyl-2-pentene

4. 3-methylcyclohexene

Answers

1. $CH_3—C≡C—CH_2—CH_3$

2. 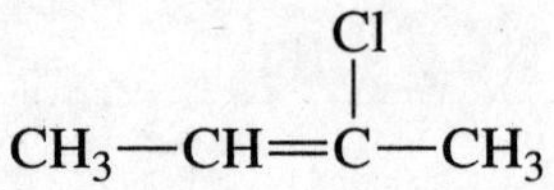 $CH_3—CH=C(Cl)—CH_3$ (Cl on the C of the double bond)

3. $CH_3—C(CH_3)=C(Br)—CH_2—CH_3$ (Br above C-3, CH_3 below C-2)

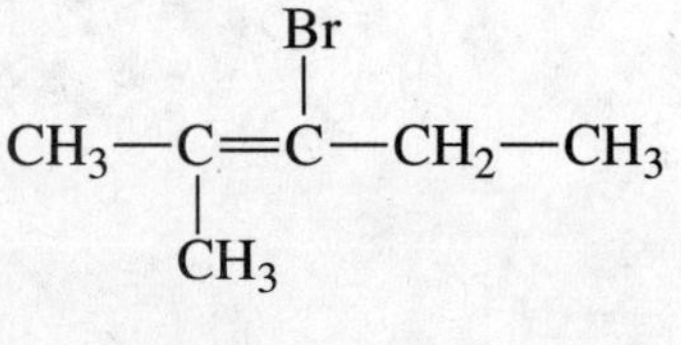

4. 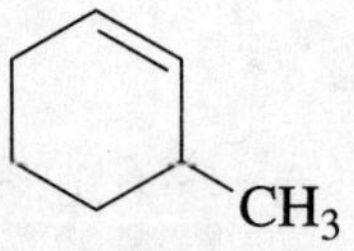 cyclohexene ring with CH_3

12.2 Cis–Trans Isomers

- Cis–trans isomers are possible for alkenes because there is not rotation around the rigid double bond.
- In the cis isomer, groups are attached on the same side of the double bond, whereas in the trans isomer, they are attached on the opposite sides of the double bond.

MasteringChemistry

Self Study Activity: Geometric Isomers

Tutorial: Cis–Trans Isomers

◆ Learning Exercise 12.2A

Draw the condensed structural formulas of the cis and trans isomers of 2,3-dibromo-2-butene and name each.

Answers In the cis–isomer, the bromine atoms are attached on the same side of the double bond; in the trans-isomer, they are on opposite sides.

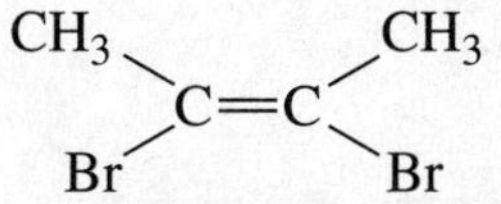

$$\begin{array}{c} CH_3 \qquad CH_3 \\ C{=}C \\ Br \qquad Br \end{array} \qquad \begin{array}{c} CH_3 \qquad Br \\ C{=}C \\ Br \qquad CH_3 \end{array}$$

cis-2,3-Dibromo-2-butene 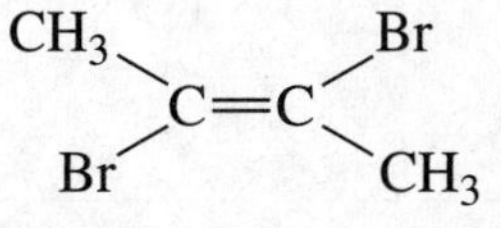 *trans*-2,3-Dibromo-2-butene

◆ Learning Exercise 12.2B

Name the following alkenes using the cis–trans prefix where isomers are possible:

1. 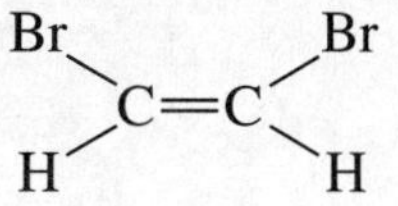 $\begin{array}{c} Br \qquad Br \\ C{=}C \\ H \qquad H \end{array}$

2. 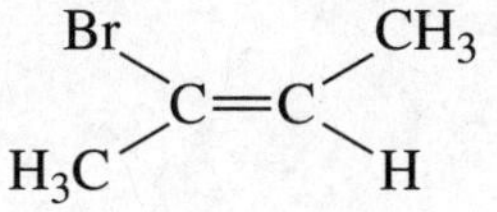 $\begin{array}{c} Br \qquad CH_3 \\ C{=}C \\ H_3C \qquad H \end{array}$

3. $\begin{array}{c} Cl \qquad H \\ C{=}C \\ H_3C \qquad H \end{array}$

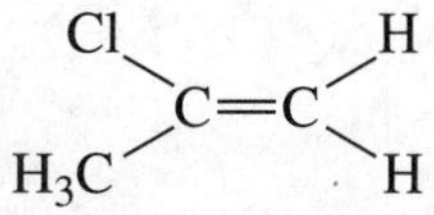

4. 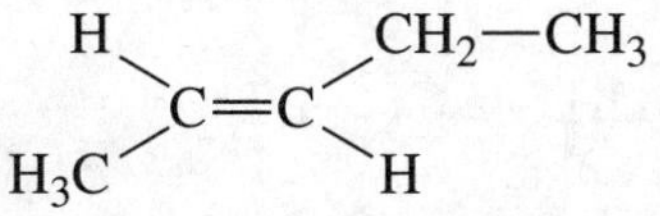 $\begin{array}{c} H \qquad CH_2{-}CH_3 \\ C{=}C \\ H_3C \qquad H \end{array}$

Answers

1. *cis*-1,2-dibromoethene **2.** *trans*-2-bromo-2-butene
3. 2-chloropropene (not a cis–trans isomer) **4.** *trans*-2-pentene

12.3 Addition Reactions

- The addition of small molecules to the double bond is a characteristic reaction of alkenes.
- Hydrogenation adds hydrogen atoms to the double bond of an alkene or the triple bond of an alkyne to yield an alkane.

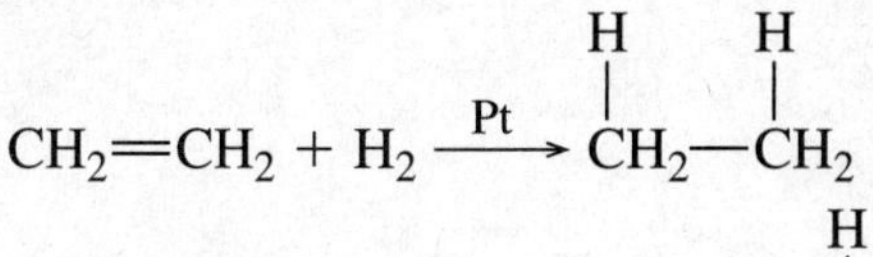

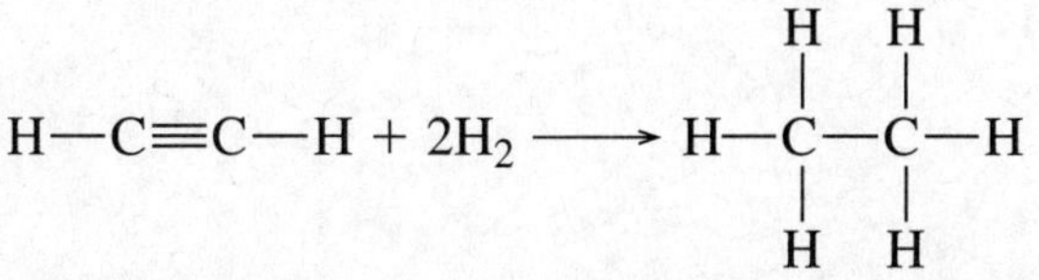

$$CH_2{=}CH_2 + H_2 \xrightarrow{Pt} \begin{array}{cc} H & H \\ | & | \\ CH_2 & {-}CH_2 \end{array}$$

$$H{-}C{\equiv}C{-}H + 2H_2 \longrightarrow H{-}\begin{array}{c} H \\ | \\ C \\ | \\ H \end{array}{-}\begin{array}{c} H \\ | \\ C \\ | \\ H \end{array}{-}H$$

- Halogenation adds bromine or chlorine atoms to produce dihaloalkanes.

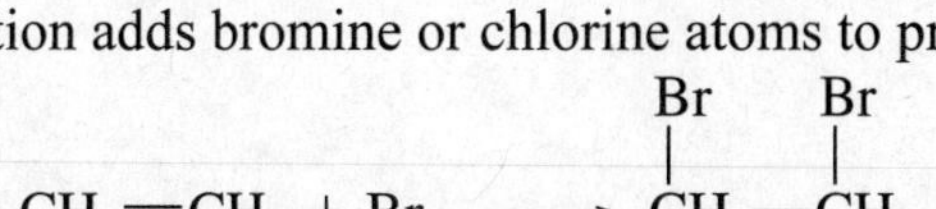

$$CH_2{=}CH_2 + Br_2 \longrightarrow \begin{array}{cc} Br & Br \\ | & | \\ CH_2 & {-}CH_2 \end{array}$$

- Hydrohalogenation adds hydrogen halides, and hydration adds water to a double bond.

$$CH_2{=}CH_2 + HCl \longrightarrow \underset{\displaystyle CH_2}{\overset{\displaystyle H}{|}}{-}\underset{\displaystyle CH_2}{\overset{\displaystyle Cl}{|}}$$

$$CH_2{=}CH_2 + HOH \xrightarrow{H^+} \underset{\displaystyle CH_2}{\overset{\displaystyle H}{|}}{-}\underset{\displaystyle CH_2}{\overset{\displaystyle OH}{|}}$$

- According to Markovnikov's rule, the H from the reactant (HX or HOH) bonds to the carbon in the double bond that has the greater number of hydrogen atoms.

MasteringChemistry
Tutorial: Addition Reactions

◆ Learning Exercise 12.3A

Draw the condensed structural formulas of the products of the following addition reactions:

1. $CH_3{-}CH_2{-}CH{=}CH_2 + H_2 \xrightarrow{Pt}$

2. [cyclopentene] $+ H_2 \xrightarrow{Pt}$

3. $CH_3{-}CH{=}CH{-}CH_2{-}CH_3 + Cl_2 \longrightarrow$

4. $CH_3{-}C{\equiv}CH + 2H_2 \xrightarrow{Pt}$

5. $CH_3{-}CH{=}CH{-}CH_3 + Br_2 \longrightarrow$

Answers

1. $CH_3{-}CH_2{-}CH_2{-}CH_3$

2. [cyclopentane]

3. $CH_3{-}\underset{\displaystyle CH}{\overset{\displaystyle Cl}{|}}{-}\underset{\displaystyle CH}{\overset{\displaystyle Cl}{|}}{-}CH_2{-}CH_3$

4. $CH_3{-}CH_2{-}CH_3$

5. $CH_3{-}\underset{\displaystyle CH}{\overset{\displaystyle Br}{|}}{-}\underset{\displaystyle CH}{\overset{\displaystyle Br}{|}}{-}CH_3$

◆ Learning Exercise 12.3B

1. $CH_3{-}CH{=}CH{-}CH_3 + HCl \longrightarrow$

2. 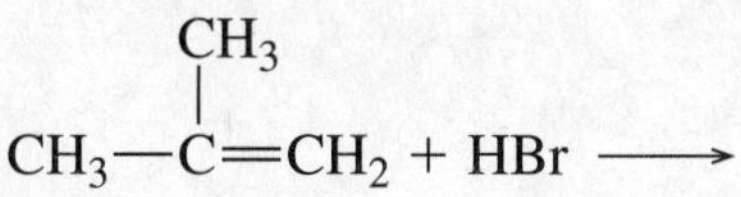 $CH_3-\overset{\overset{\displaystyle CH_3}{|}}{C}=CH_2 + HBr \longrightarrow$

3. $CH_3-CH=CH_2 + HOH \xrightarrow{H^+}$

4. 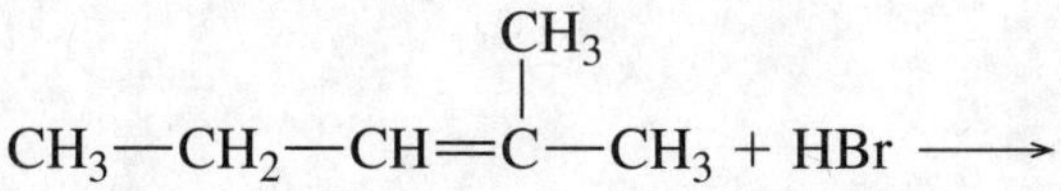 $CH_3-CH_2-CH=\overset{\overset{\displaystyle CH_3}{|}}{C}-CH_3 + HBr \longrightarrow$

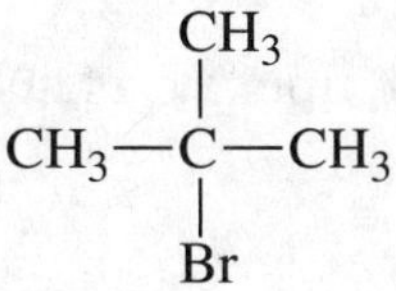

5. 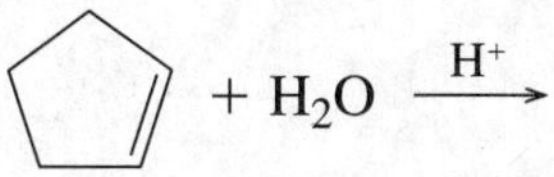 cyclopentene $+ H_2O \xrightarrow{H^+}$

Answers

1. 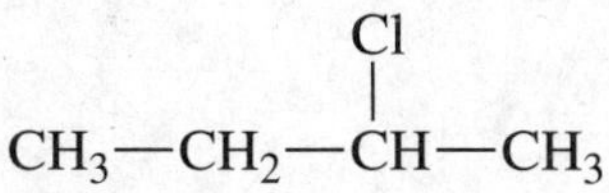 $CH_3-CH_2-\overset{\overset{\displaystyle Cl}{|}}{CH}-CH_3$

2. $CH_3-\underset{\underset{\displaystyle Br}{|}}{\overset{\overset{\displaystyle CH_3}{|}}{C}}-CH_3$

3. $CH_3-\overset{\overset{\displaystyle OH}{|}}{CH}-CH_3$

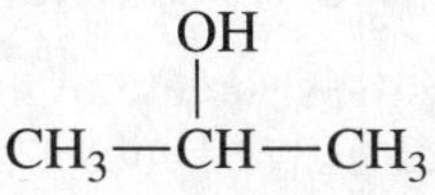

4. 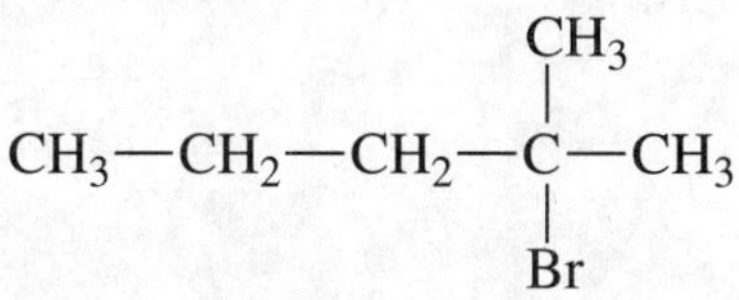 $CH_3-CH_2-CH_2-\underset{\underset{\displaystyle Br}{|}}{\overset{\overset{\displaystyle CH_3}{|}}{C}}-CH_3$

5. 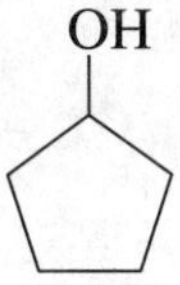 cyclopentanol (OH on cyclopentane ring)

12.4 Polymers of Alkenes

- Polymers are large molecules prepared from the bonding of many small units called *monomers.*
- Many synthetic polymers are made from small alkene monomers.

> ***MasteringChemistry***
>
> **Self Study Activity: Polymers**
>
> **Tutorial: Polymers**

◆ Learning Check 12.4A

Draw the condensed structural formula of the alkene monomer that would be used for each of the following polymers:

1. 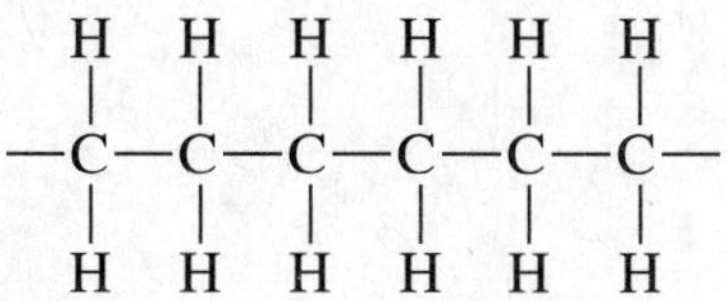 $-\underset{\underset{\displaystyle H}{|}}{\overset{\overset{\displaystyle H}{|}}{C}}-\underset{\underset{\displaystyle H}{|}}{\overset{\overset{\displaystyle H}{|}}{C}}-\underset{\underset{\displaystyle H}{|}}{\overset{\overset{\displaystyle H}{|}}{C}}-\underset{\underset{\displaystyle H}{|}}{\overset{\overset{\displaystyle H}{|}}{C}}-\underset{\underset{\displaystyle H}{|}}{\overset{\overset{\displaystyle H}{|}}{C}}-\underset{\underset{\displaystyle H}{|}}{\overset{\overset{\displaystyle H}{|}}{C}}-$

2.

$$\begin{array}{cccccccccccccc} & \mathrm{H} & & \mathrm{CH_3} & & \mathrm{H} & & \mathrm{CH_3} & & \mathrm{H} & & \mathrm{CH_3} & \\ & | & & | & & | & & | & & | & & | & \\ - & \mathrm{C} & - & \mathrm{C} & - & \mathrm{C} & - & \mathrm{C} & - & \mathrm{C} & - & \mathrm{C} & - \\ & | & & | & & | & & | & & | & & | & \\ & \mathrm{H} & & \mathrm{H} & & \mathrm{H} & & \mathrm{H} & & \mathrm{H} & & \mathrm{H} & \end{array}$$

3.

$$\begin{array}{cccccccccccccc} & \mathrm{F} & & \mathrm{F} & & \mathrm{F} & & \mathrm{F} & & \mathrm{F} & & \mathrm{F} & \\ & | & & | & & | & & | & & | & & | & \\ - & \mathrm{C} & - & \mathrm{C} & - & \mathrm{C} & - & \mathrm{C} & - & \mathrm{C} & - & \mathrm{C} & - \\ & | & & | & & | & & | & & | & & | & \\ & \mathrm{F} & & \mathrm{F} & & \mathrm{F} & & \mathrm{F} & & \mathrm{F} & & \mathrm{F} & \end{array}$$

Answers **1.** $H_2C{=}CH_2$ **2.** $\begin{array}{c} \qquad\quad \mathrm{CH_3} \\ \qquad\quad | \\ \mathrm{H_2C{=}CH} \end{array}$ **3.** $F_2C{=}CF_2$

◆ Learning Check 12.4B

Draw the structure of the polymer formed from the addition of three monomers of 1, 1-difluoroethene.

Answer

$$\begin{array}{cccccccccccccc} & \mathrm{F} & & \mathrm{H} & & \mathrm{F} & & \mathrm{H} & & \mathrm{F} & & \mathrm{H} & \\ & | & & | & & | & & | & & | & & | & \\ - & \mathrm{C} & - & \mathrm{C} & - & \mathrm{C} & - & \mathrm{C} & - & \mathrm{C} & - & \mathrm{C} & - \\ & | & & | & & | & & | & & | & & | & \\ & \mathrm{F} & & \mathrm{H} & & \mathrm{F} & & \mathrm{H} & & \mathrm{F} & & \mathrm{H} & \end{array}$$

12.5 Aromatic Compounds

- Most aromatic compounds contain benzene, a cyclic structure containing six CH units. The structure of benzene is represented as a hexagon with a circle in the center.
- The names of many aromatic compounds use the parent name benzene, although many common names were retained as IUPAC names, such as toluene, phenol, and aniline. The position of two substituents on the ring is often shown by the prefixes *ortho* (1,2-), *meta* (1,3-), and *para* (1,4-).
- Aromatic compounds have higher melting and boiling points than cycloalkanes.
- Aromatic compounds undergo substitution reactions of halogenation, nitration, and sulfonation.

MasteringChemistry
Tutorial: Naming Aromatic Compounds

◆ Learning Exercise 12.5A

Write the IUPAC (and common) name for each of the following:

1.

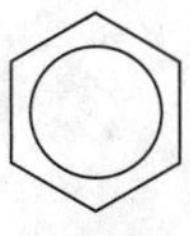

2. 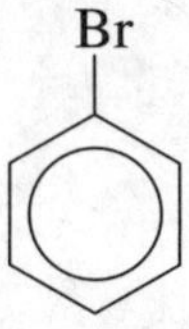 Br

3. CH_3

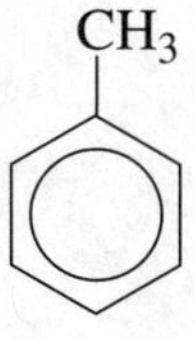

4. 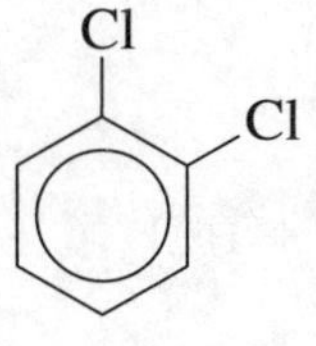 Cl, Cl

5. 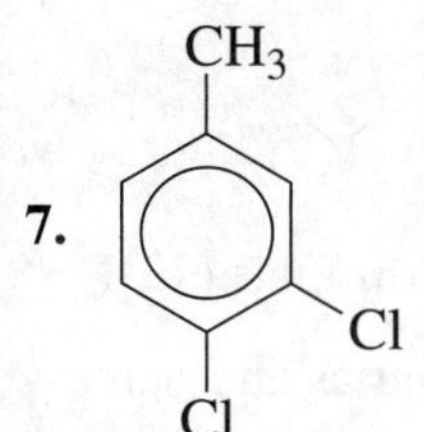

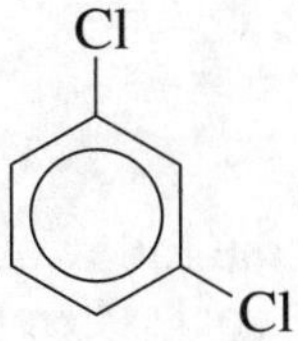

6. 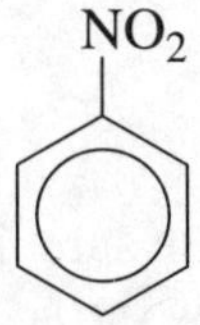 NO_2

7. CH_3, Cl, Cl

8. 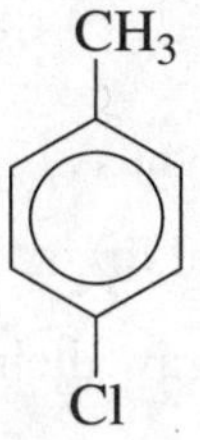 CH_3, Cl

Answers **1.** benzene **2.** bromobenzene **3.** methylbenzene; toluene
4. 1,2-dichlorobenzene; *o*-dichlorobenzene **5.** 1,3-dichlorobenzene; *m*-dichlorobenzene
6. nitrobenzene **7.** 3,4-dichlorotoluene **8.** 4-chlorotoluene; *p*-chlorotoluene

MasteringChemistry

Tutorial: Substitution Reactions of Aromatic Compounds

◆ Learning Exercise 12.5B

Draw the condensed structural formula of the missing reactant, catalyst, or product(s) for each of the following reactions:

1. Benzene and $Br_2 \xrightarrow{FeBr_3}$

2. Benzene and $SO_3 \xrightarrow{H_2SO_4}$

3. Benzene and $HNO_3 \xrightarrow{H_2SO_4}$

4. 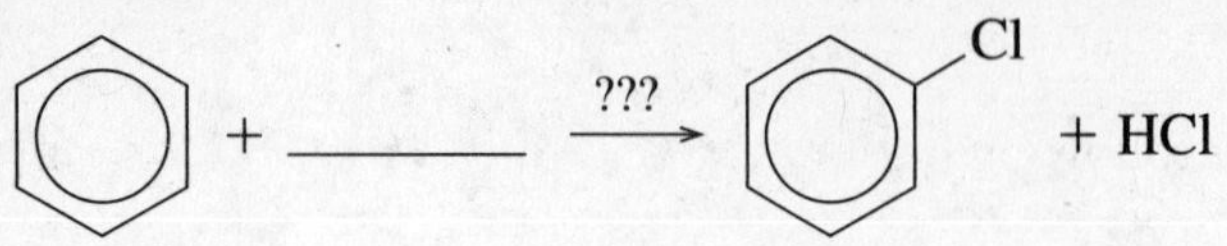 Benzene + ______ $\xrightarrow{???}$ chlorobenzene (Cl) + HCl

Answers

1. 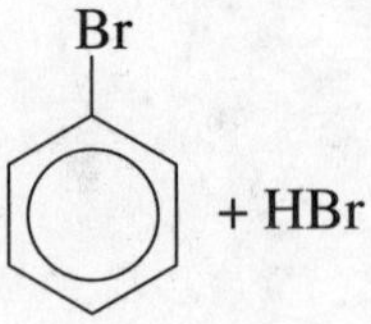 bromobenzene (Br) + HBr
2.  benzenesulfonic acid (SO_3H)
3. 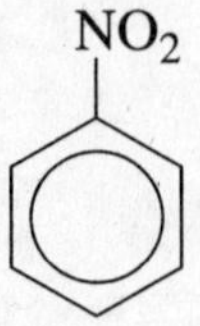 nitrobenzene (NO_2) + H_2O
4. 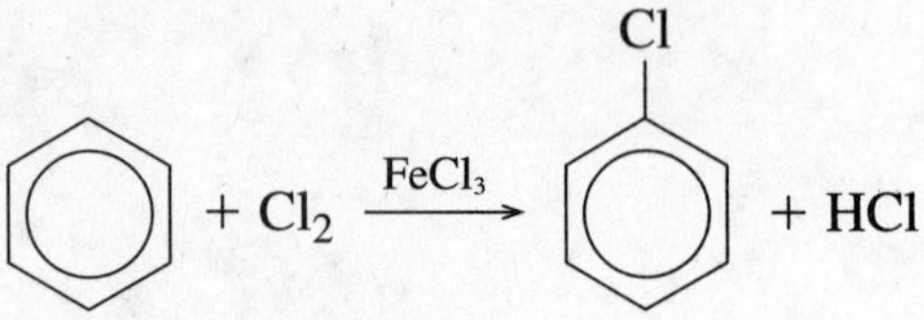 Benzene + Cl_2 $\xrightarrow{FeCl_3}$ chlorobenzene (Cl) + HCl

Checklist for Chapter 12

You are ready to take the Practice Test for Chapter 12. Be sure that you have accomplished the following learning goals for this chapter. If you are not sure, review the section listed at the end of the goal. Then apply your new skills and understanding to the Practice Test.

After studying Chapter 12, I can successfully:

_____ Identify the structural features of alkenes and alkynes (12.1).

_____ Name alkenes and alkynes using IUPAC rules and draw their condensed structural formulas (12.1).

_____ Identify alkenes that exist as cis–trans isomers; draw their condensed structural formulas and names (12.2).

_____ Draw the condensed structural formulas and give the names for the products of the addition of hydrogen, halogens, hydrogen halides, and water to alkenes, applying Markovnikov's rule when necessary (12.3).

_____ Describe the process of forming polymers from alkene monomers (12.4).

_____ Give the names and draw the condensed structural formulas for compounds that contain a benzene ring (12.5).

_____ Draw the structures of the products of substitution reactions of benzene (12.5).

Practice Test for Chapter 12

For questions 1 through 4, refer to the following compounds (A) and (B):

(A) $H_2C{=}CH{-}CH_3$

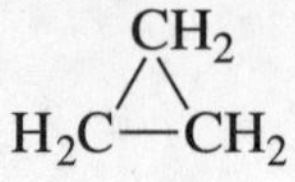

(B) cyclopropane: CH_2 bonded to $H_2C{-}CH_2$ (three-membered ring)

1. These compounds are
   A. aromatic B. alkanes C. isomers D. alkenes E. cycloalkanes

2. Compound (A) is a(n)
   A. alkane B. alkene C. cycloalkane D. alkyne E. aromatic

3. Compound (B) is named

A. propane **B.** propylene **C.** cyclobutane **D.** cyclopropane **E.** cyclopropene

4. Compound (A) is named

A. propane **B.** propene **C.** 2-propene **D.** propyne **E.** 1-butene

In questions 5 through 8, match each name with its condensed structural formula:

A. cyclopentene **B.** methylpropene
C. cyclohexene **D.** ethene **E.** 3-methylcyclopentene

5. $CH_2{=}CH_2$

6. $CH_3{-}\overset{\overset{\displaystyle CH_3}{|}}{C}{=}CH_2$

7. 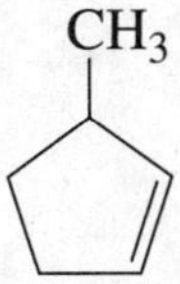 (cyclopentene ring with CH_3 substituent)

8. 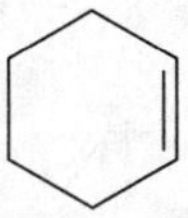 (cyclohexene ring)

9. The cis isomer of 2-butene is

A. $CH_2{=}CH{-}CH_2{-}CH_3$ **B.** $CH_3{-}CH{=}CH{-}CH_3$

C. 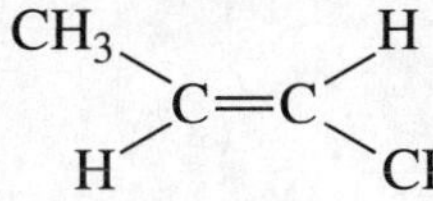 $\overset{CH_3}{\underset{H}{}}C{=}C\overset{H}{\underset{CH_3}{}}$ **D.** 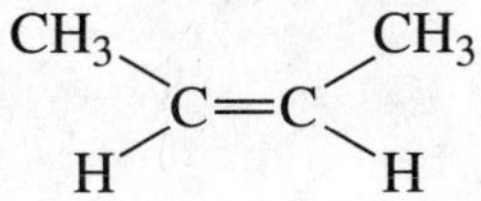 $\overset{CH_3}{\underset{H}{}}C{=}C\overset{CH_3}{\underset{H}{}}$ **E.** $\overset{\overset{\displaystyle CH_3}{|}}{CH}{=}\overset{\overset{\displaystyle CH_3}{|}}{CH}$

10. The name of this compound is

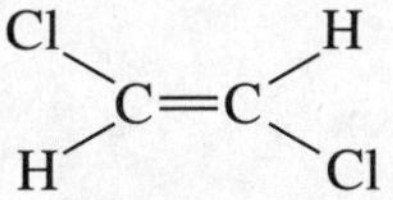

$\overset{Cl}{\underset{H}{}}C{=}C\overset{H}{\underset{Cl}{}}$

A. dichloroethene **B.** *cis*-1,2-dichloroethene
C. *trans*-1,2-dichloroethene **D.** *cis*-chloroethene
E. *trans*-chloroethene

11. Hydrogenation of $CH_3{-}CH{=}CH_2$ gives

A. $3CO_2 + 6H_2$ **B.** $CH_3{-}CH_2{-}CH_3$ **C.** $CH_2{=}CH{-}CH_3$
D. no reaction **E.** $CH_3{-}CH_2{-}CH_2{-}CH_3$

12. Choose the product of the following reaction: $CH_3{-}CH{=}CH_2 + HBr \rightarrow$

A. $CH_3{-}CH_2{-}CH_2{-}Br$ **B.** no reaction **C.** $CH_3{-}CH_2{-}CH_3$

D. $CH_3{-}\overset{\overset{\displaystyle Br}{|}}{CH}{-}CH_2{-}CH_2{-}Br$ **E.** $CH_3{-}\overset{\overset{\displaystyle Br}{|}}{CH}{-}CH_3$

13. Addition of bromine (Br_2) to ethene gives

A. $CH_3{-}CH_2{-}Br$ **B.** $Br{-}CH_2{-}CH_2{-}Br$ **C.** $CH_3{-}CH{-}Br_2$
D. $CH_3{-}CH_3$ **E.** no reaction

14. Hydration of 2-butene gives

A. $CH_3—CH_2—CH_2—CH_3$ **B.** $CH_3—CH_2—CH_2—CH_2—OH$

C. $CH_3—CH(OH)—CH_2—CH_3$ **D.** 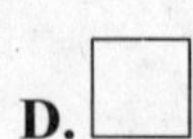 **E.** 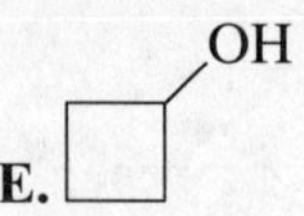

15. What is the common name for the compound 1,3-dichlorobenzene?

A. *m*-dichlorobenzene **B.** *o*-dichlorobenzene
C. *p*-dichlorobenzene **D.** *x*-dichlorobenzene
E. *z*-dichlorobenzene

16. What is the common name of methylbenzene?

A. aniline **B.** phenol **C.** toluene
D. xylene **E.** toluidine

17. What is the IUPAC name of $CH_3—CH_2—C{\equiv}CH$?

A. methylacetylene **B.** propyne **C.** propylene
D. 4-butyne **E.** 1-butyne

18. What is the product when cyclopentene reacts with Cl_2?

A. chlorocyclopentene **B.** 1,1-dichlorocyclopentane
C. 1,2-dichlorocyclopentane **D.** 1,3-dichlorocyclopentane
E. no reaction

19. The reaction $CH_2{=}CH_2 + Cl_2 \rightarrow Cl—CH_2—CH_2—Cl$ is called

A. hydrogenation **B.** halogenation **C.** hydrohalogenation
D. hydration **E.** combustion

20. The reaction in question 19 is

A. a hydration reaction **B.** an oxidation reaction **C.** a substitution reaction
D. an addition reaction **E.** a reduction reaction

21. The following reaction is called:

$$CH_3—CH{=}CH_2 + H_2O \xrightarrow{H^+} CH_3—\underset{}{\overset{OH}{\overset{|}{C}H}}—CH_3$$

A. hydrogenation **B.** halogenation **C.** hydrohalogenation
D. hydration **E.** combustion

For questions 22 through 25, match the name of the family with one of the compounds below:

A. alkane **B.** alkene **C.** alkyne **D.** cycloalkene

22. $CH_3—CH{=}CH_2$

23. 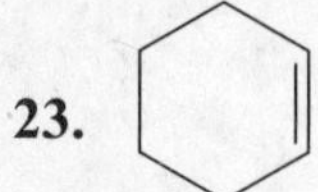

24. $CH_3-CH_2-\underset{\displaystyle CH_3}{\overset{|}{CH}}-CH_2-CH_3$ (with CH_3 on the middle CH)

25. $CH_3-CH_2-C\equiv CH$

For questions 26 through 30, match the name of each of the following aromatic compounds with the correct structure.

A. 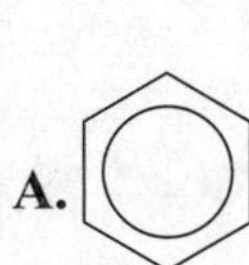

B. CH_3

C. CH_3 CH_3

D. Cl

E. CH_3 Cl

26. ______ chlorobenzene

27. ______ benzene

28. ______ toluene

29. ______ *p*-chlorotoluene

30. ______ 1,3-dimethylbenzene

Answers to the Practice Test

1. C	**2.** B	**3.** D	**4.** B	**5.** D
6. B	**7.** E	**8.** C	**9.** D	**10.** C
11. B	**12.** E	**13.** B	**14.** C	**15.** A
16. C	**17.** E	**18.** C	**19.** B	**20.** D
21. D	**22.** B	**23.** D	**24.** A	**25.** C
26. D	**27.** A	**28.** B	**29.** E	**30.** C

13
Alcohols, Phenols, Thiols, and Ethers

Study Goals

- Classify alcohols as primary, secondary, or tertiary.
- Name and draw the condensed structural formulas for alcohols, phenols, and thiols.
- Identify the uses of some alcohols and phenols.
- Name and draw the condensed structural formulas for ethers.
- Describe the solubility in water and boiling points of alcohols, phenols, and ethers.
- Write equations for combustion, dehydration, and oxidation of alcohols.

Think About It

1. What are the functional groups of alcohols, phenols, ethers, and thiols?

2. Phenol is sometimes used in mouthwashes. Why does it form a solution with water?

3. What reaction of ethanol takes place when you make a fondue dish or a flaming dessert?

Key Terms

Match the following terms with the statements shown below:

a. primary alcohol	**b.** thiol	**c.** ether
d. phenol	**e.** tertiary alcohol	

1. ____ An organic compound with one alkyl group bonded to the carbon with the —OH group

2. ____ An organic compound that contains an —SH group

3. ____ An organic compound that contains an oxygen atom —O— attached to two alkyl groups

4. ____ An organic compound with three alkyl groups bonded to the carbon with the —OH group

5. ____ An organic compound that contains a benzene ring bonded to a hydroxyl group

Answers **1.** a **2.** b **3.** c **4.** e **5.** d

13.1 Alcohols, Phenols, and Thiols

- Alcohols are classified according to the number of alkyl groups attached to the carbon bonded to the —OH group. Phenols have a hydroxyl group attached to an aromatic ring. Thiols have an —SH functional group.
- In a primary alcohol, there is one alkyl group attached to the carbon atom bonded to the —OH. In a secondary alcohol, there are two alkyl groups, and in a tertiary alcohol, there are three alkyl groups attached to the carbon atom with the —OH functional group.
- In the IUPAC system, alcohols are named by replacing the *ane* of the alkane name with *ol.* The location of the —OH group is given by numbering the carbon chain. Simple alcohols are generally named by their common names with the alkyl name preceding the term *alcohol.* For example, CH_3—OH is methyl alcohol, and CH_3—CH_2—OH is ethyl alcohol.

  CH_3—OH
Methanol
(methyl alcohol)

  CH_3—CH_2—OH
Ethanol
(ethyl alcohol)

  CH_3—CH_2—CH_2—OH
1-Propanol
(propyl alcohol)
- To name a thiol, give the alkane name of the chain, followed by *thiol.*

  CH_3—SH
Methanethiol

  CH_3—CH_2—SH
Ethanethiol

Study Note

Example Identify each of the following as a primary, secondary, or tertiary alcohol:

Solution Determine the number of alkyl groups attached to the hydroxyl carbon atom.

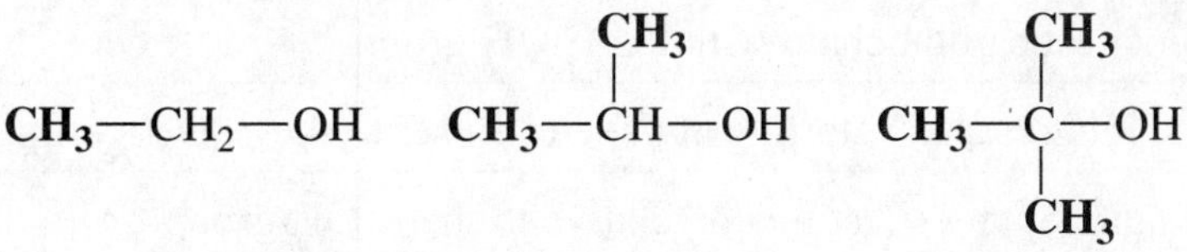

$$CH_3-CH_2-OH \qquad CH_3-\overset{\displaystyle CH_3}{\overset{|}{CH}}-OH \qquad CH_3-\overset{\displaystyle CH_3}{\overset{|}{\underset{\underset{\displaystyle CH_3}{|}}{C}}}-OH$$

Primary (1°) Secondary (2°) Tertiary (3°)

◆ Learning Exercise 13.1A

Classify each of the following alcohols as primary (1°), secondary (2°), or tertiary (3°):

1. CH_3—CH_2—OH ____________

2. 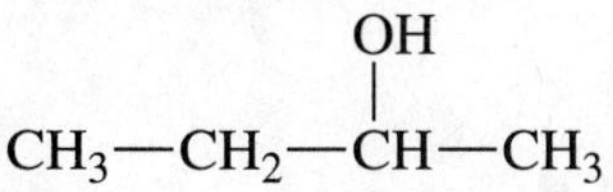 $CH_3-CH_2-\overset{\displaystyle OH}{\overset{|}{CH}}-CH_3$ ____________

3. $CH_3-\overset{\overset{OH}{|}}{\underset{\underset{CH_3}{|}}{C}}-CH_2-CH_3$ ________________

4. $CH_3-\overset{\overset{CH_3}{|}}{\underset{\underset{CH_3}{|}}{C}}-CH_2-CH_2-OH$ ________________

5. $CH_3-\overset{\overset{CH_3}{|}}{\underset{\underset{CH_3}{|}}{C}}-CH_2-OH$ ________________

6. OH (cyclopentane ring with OH) ________________

Answers **1.** primary (1°) **2.** secondary (2°) **3.** tertiary (3°)
4. tertiary (3°) **5.** primary (1°) **6.** secondary (2°)

> ***MasteringChemistry***
>
> **Self Study Activity: Alcohols and Thiols**
>
> **Tutorial: Naming Alcohols, Phenols, and Thiols**
>
> **Tutorial: Drawing Alcohols, Phenols, and Thiols**

Guide to Naming Alcohols	
STEP 1	Name the longest carbon chain with the —OH group.
STEP 2	Number the longest chain starting at the end closer to the —OH group.
STEP 3	Name and number any substituents relative to the —OH group.
STEP 4	Name a cyclic alcohol as a cycloalkanol.

◆ Learning Exercise 13.1B

Give the correct IUPAC and common name (if any) for each of the following compounds:

1. CH_3-CH_2-OH

2. $CH_3-CH_2-CH_2-OH$

3. $CH_3-\overset{\overset{OH}{|}}{CH}-CH_2-CH_2-CH_3$

4. $CH_3-CH_2-\overset{\overset{CH_3}{|}}{CH}-\overset{\overset{OH}{|}}{CH}-CH_3$

5. 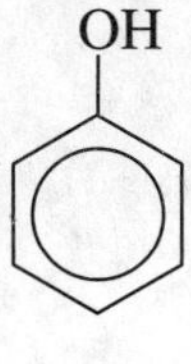 OH (benzene ring with OH)

6. 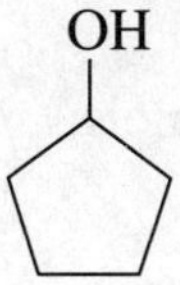 OH (cyclopentane ring with OH)

Answers

1. ethanol (ethyl alcohol) **2.** 1-propanol (propyl alcohol)
3. 2-pentanol **4.** 3-methyl-2-pentanol
5. phenol **6.** cyclopentanol

◆ Learning Exercise 13.1C

Draw the correct condensed structural formula for each of the following compounds:

1. 2-butanol **2.** 2-chloro-1-propanol

3. 2,4-dimethyl-1-pentanol **4.** cyclohexanol

5. 3-methylcyclopentanol **6.** *o*-chlorophenol

Answers

1. 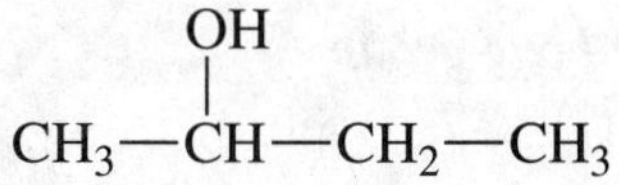 $CH_3-\underset{}{\overset{OH}{\overset{|}{CH}}}-CH_2-CH_3$

2. $CH_3-\overset{Cl}{\overset{|}{CH}}-CH_2-OH$

3. $CH_3-\overset{CH_3}{\overset{|}{CH}}-CH_2-\overset{CH_3}{\overset{|}{CH}}-CH_2-OH$

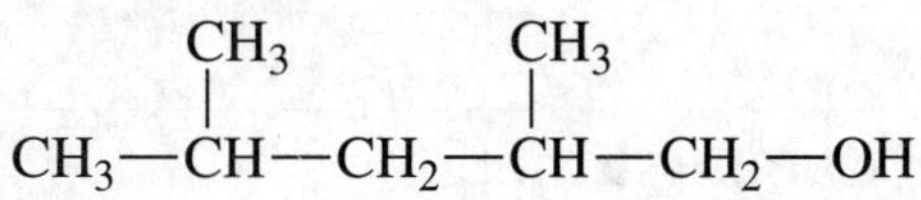

4. 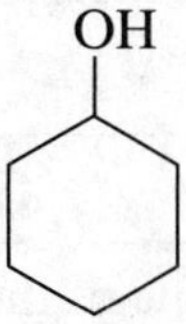 OH (cyclohexane ring with OH)

5. 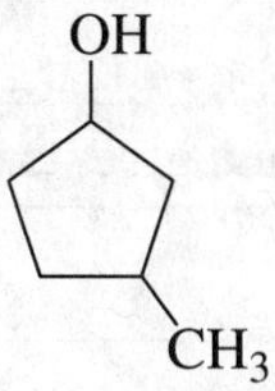 OH (cyclopentane ring with OH and CH_3)

6. 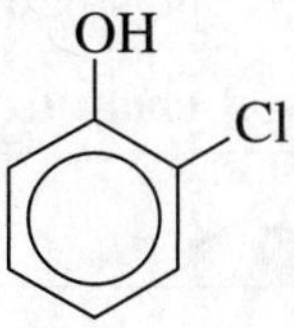 OH, Cl (benzene ring with OH and Cl on adjacent carbons)

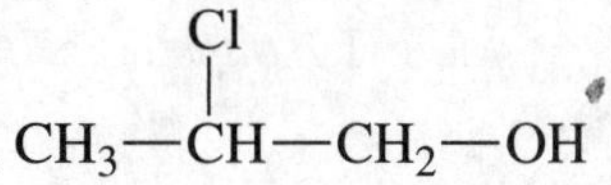

◆ Learning Exercise 13.1D

Give the correct IUPAC name for the following thiols:

1. $CH_3—CH_2—SH$ ____________

2. $CH_3—CH_2—CH_2—SH$ ____________

3. $CH_3—CH_2—CH(SH)—CH_3$ ____________

4. Cyclobutane ring with SH ____________

Answers

1. ethanethiol **2.** 1-propanethiol
3. 2-butanethiol **4.** cyclobutanethiol

13.2 Ethers

- In ethers, an oxygen atom is connected by single bonds to two alkyl or aromatic groups.
- In the IUPAC name, the smaller alkyl group and the oxygen are named as an *alkoxy group* attached to the longer alkane chain, which is numbered to give the location of the alkoxy group. In the common names of ethers, the alkyl groups are listed alphabetically followed by the name *ether.*

Study Note

Example Write the common and IUPAC names for $CH_3—CH_2—O—CH_3$.

Solution The common name lists the alkyl groups alphabetically before the name *ether.* Using the IUPAC system, the smaller alkyl group and the oxygen are named as a substituent *methoxy* attached to the two-carbon chain ethane.

Ethyl group *Methyl group*
$CH_3—CH_2—O—CH_3$
Common: ethyl methyl ether

Ethane *Methoxy group*
$CH_3—CH_2—O—CH_3$
IUPAC: methoxyethane

Guide to Naming Ethers	
STEP 1	Write the alkane name of the longer carbon chain.
STEP 2	Name the oxygen and smaller alkyl group as an *alkoxy group.*
STEP 3	Number the longer chain from the end nearer the alkoxy group and give its location.

MasteringChemistry

Tutorial: Naming Ethers

◆ Learning Exercise 13.2A

Write an IUPAC and common name for each of the following:

1. $CH_3—O—CH_3$

2. $CH_3—CH_2—O—CH_2—CH_3$

3. $CH_3—CH_2—CH_2—CH_2—O—CH_3$

4. $CH_3—O—CH_2—CH_3$

5.

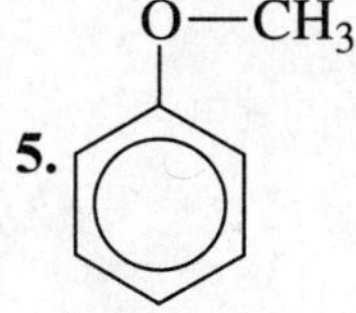

Answers

1. methoxymethane; (di)methyl ether
2. ethoxyethane; (di)ethyl ether
3. 1-methoxybutane; butyl methyl ether
4. methoxyethane; ethyl methyl ether
5. methoxybenzene; methyl phenyl ether

MasteringChemistry

Tutorial: Drawing Ethers

◆ Learning Exercise 13.2B

Draw the condensed structural formula for each of the following ethers:

1. ethyl propyl ether

2. 2-methoxypropane

3. dipropyl ether

4. 3-ethoxypentane

Answers

1. $CH_3—CH_2—O—CH_2—CH_2—CH_3$

2. $CH_3—CH(O—CH_3)—CH_3$ (O—CH_3 attached to the CH)

3. $CH_3—CH_2—CH_2—O—CH_2—CH_2—CH_3$

4. $CH_3—CH_2—CH(O—CH_2—CH_3)—CH_2—CH_3$

◆ Learning Exercise 13.2C

Identify each of the following heterocyclic structures as a furan, pyran, or dioxane:

1.  O

2. 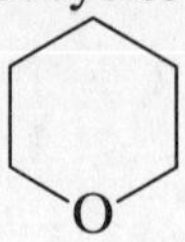 O

3. 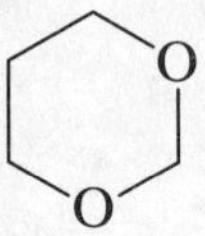 O O

4. 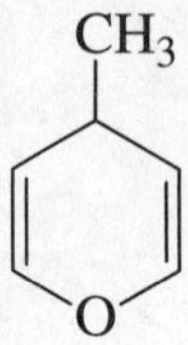 CH_3 O

Answers **1.** furan **2.** pyran **3.** dioxane **4.** pyran

◆ Learning Exercise 13.2D

Identify each of the following pairs of compounds as isomers (I), the same compound (S), or different (D) compounds:

1. CH_3-O-CH_3 and CH_3-CH_2-OH ______

OH

2. $CH_3-O-CH_2-CH_3$ and $CH_3-CH-CH_3$ ______

CH_3 OH

3. $CH_3-CH-OH$ and $CH_3-CH-CH_3$ ______

4. $CH_3-CH_2-O-CH_3$ and $CH_3-CH_2-CH_2-CH_2-OH$ ______

Answers
1. isomers (I) of C_2H_6O
2. isomers (I) of C_2H_6O
3. same (S) compound (2-propanol)
4. different (D) compounds

13.3 Physical Properties of Alcohols, Phenols, and Ethers

- The polar —OH group gives alcohols higher boiling points than alkanes and ethers of similar mass.
- Alcohols with one to four carbons are soluble in water because the —OH group forms hydrogen bonds with water molecules.
- Phenol is soluble in water and acts as a weak acid.
- Because ethers are less polar than alcohols, they have boiling points similar to alkanes. Ethers are soluble in water due to hydrogen bonding. Ethers are widely used as solvents but can be dangerous to use because their vapors are highly flammable.

MasteringChemistry

Tutorial: Physical Properties of Alcohols and Ethers

◆ Learning Exercise 13.3A

Which compound in each pair is more soluble in water?

1. ____ $CH_3—CH_3$ or $CH_3—CH_2—OH$

2. ____ $CH_3—CH_2—CH_2—OH$ or $CH_3—CH_2—CH_2—CH_2—CH_2—OH$

3. ____ $CH_3—CH_2—CH_2—CH_3$ or $CH_3—CH_2—CH_2—CH_2—OH$

4. ____ benzene or phenol

5. ____ $CH_3—CH_2—O—CH_2—CH_3$ or $CH_3—CH_2—CH_2—CH_2—OH$

6. ____ methoxymethane or methoxypentane

Answers
1. $CH_3—CH_2—OH$
2. $CH_3—CH_2—CH_2—OH$
3. $CH_3—CH_2—CH_2—CH_2—OH$
4. phenol
5. $CH_3—CH_2—CH_2—CH_2—OH$
6. methoxymethane

◆ Learning Exercise 13.3B

Select the compound in each pair with the higher boiling point.

1. $CH_3—CH_2—CH_3$ or $CH_3—CH_2—OH$

2. 2-butanol or 2-hexanol

3. $CH_3—O—CH_2—CH_3$ or $CH_3—CH_2—CH_2—OH$

4. $CH_3—CH_2—CH_2—OH$ or $CH_3—CH_2—CH_2—CH_3$

Answers
1. $CH_3—CH_2—OH$
2. 2-hexanol
3. $CH_3—CH_2—CH_2—OH$
4. $CH_3—CH_2—CH_2—OH$

13.4 Reactions of Alcohols and Thiols

- At high temperatures, an alcohol dehydrates in the presence of an acid to yield an alkene and water.

$$CH_3—CH_2—OH \xrightarrow[\text{Heat}]{H^+} H_2C{=}CH_2 + H_2O$$

- Ethers are produced from primary alcohols in the presence of acid and at lower temperatures than needed for dehydration.

$$CH_3—OH + HO—CH_3 \xrightarrow[\text{Heat}]{H^+} CH_3—O—CH_3 + H_2O$$

- Using an oxidizing agent [O], primary alcohols oxidize to aldehydes, which usually oxidize further to carboxylic acids. Secondary alcohols are oxidized to ketones, but tertiary alcohols do not oxidize.

$$CH_3{-}CH_2{-}OH \xrightarrow{[O]} CH_3{-}\overset{\overset{\displaystyle O}{\|}}{C}{-}H + H_2O$$

1° Alcohol → Aldehyde

$$CH_3{-}\overset{\overset{\displaystyle OH}{|}}{CH}{-}CH_3 \xrightarrow{[O]} CH_3{-}\overset{\overset{\displaystyle O}{\|}}{C}{-}CH_3 + H_2O$$

2° Alcohol → Ketone

- Thiols undergo oxidation and lose hydrogen from the —SH group to form disulfides.

MasteringChemistry

Case Study: Alcohol Toxicity

Tutorial: Dehydration and Oxidation of Alcohols

Tutorial: Oxidation of Thiols

Study Note

When a secondary alcohol is dehydrated, two products may be formed. According to Saytzeff's rule, the major product will be the alkene formed by removing the hydrogen atom from the carbon with the smaller number of hydrogen atoms.

◆ Learning Exercise 13.4A

Draw the condensed structural formula of the product expected from dehydration of each of the following reactants:

1. $CH_3{-}CH_2{-}CH_2{-}CH_2{-}OH \xrightarrow{H^+,\ heat}$

2. Cyclohexanol (cyclohexane ring with OH) $\xrightarrow{H^+,\ heat}$

3. $CH_3{-}\overset{\overset{\displaystyle OH}{|}}{CH}{-}CH_3 \xrightarrow{H^+,\ heat}$

4. $CH_3{-}CH_2{-}\overset{\overset{\displaystyle OH}{|}}{CH}{-}CH_2{-}CH_3 \xrightarrow{H^+,\ heat}$

Answers

1. $CH_3—CH_2—CH{=}CH_2$
2. 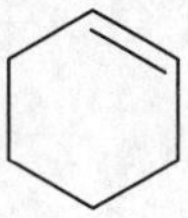
3. $CH_3—CH{=}CH_2$
4. $CH_3—CH_2—CH{=}CH—CH_3$

◆ Learning Exercise 13.4B

Draw the condensed structural formula of the major product expected from dehydration of each of the following:

1. $CH_3—\underset{}{\overset{OH}{\overset{|}{C}H}}—CH_2—CH_3 \xrightarrow{H^+,\ heat}$
2. $CH_3—CH_2—\overset{OH}{\overset{|}{C}H}—\overset{CH_3}{\overset{|}{C}H}—CH_3 \xrightarrow{H^+,\ heat}$
3. OH, CH_3 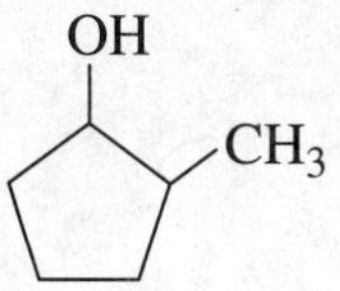 $\xrightarrow{H^+,\ heat}$

Answers

1. $CH_3—CH{=}CH—CH_3$
2. $CH_3—CH_2—CH{=}\overset{CH_3}{\overset{|}{C}}—CH_3$
3. CH_3

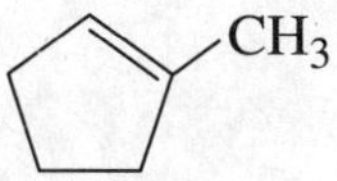

◆ Learning Exercise 13.4C

Draw the condensed structural formula of the ether formed in each of the following reactions:

1. $CH_3—CH_2—OH + HO—CH_2—CH_3 \xrightarrow{H^+,\ heat}$
2. $CH_3—OH + HO—CH_3 \xrightarrow{H^+,\ heat}$

Answers 1. $CH_3—CH_2—O—CH_2—CH_3$ 2. $CH_3—O—CH_3$

◆ Learning Exercise 13.4D

Draw the condensed structural formula of the aldehyde or ketone expected in the oxidation reaction of each of the following:

1. $CH_3—CH_2—CH_2—CH_2—OH \xrightarrow{[O]}$

2. 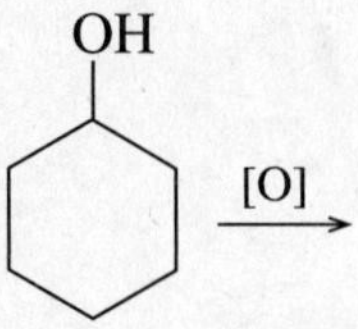 cyclohexanol (cyclohexane ring with OH) $\xrightarrow{[O]}$

3. $CH_3—\underset{}{\overset{OH}{\overset{|}{C}H}}—CH_3 \xrightarrow{[O]}$

4. $CH_3—CH_2—\overset{OH}{\overset{|}{C}H}—CH_2—CH_3 \xrightarrow{[O]}$

Answers

1. $CH_3—CH_2—CH_2—\overset{O}{\overset{\|}{C}}—H$

2. 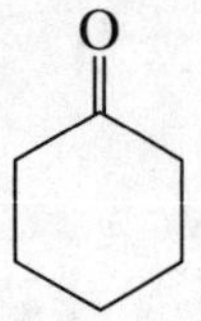 cyclohexanone (cyclohexane ring with =O)

3. $CH_3—\overset{O}{\overset{\|}{C}}—CH_3$

4. $CH_3—CH_2—\overset{O}{\overset{\|}{C}}—CH_2—CH_3$

Checklist for Chapter 13

You are ready to take the Practice Test for Chapter 13. Be sure that you have accomplished the following learning goals for this chapter. If you are not sure, review the section listed at the end of the goal. Then apply your new skills and understanding to the Practice Test.

After studying Chapter 13, I can successfully:

______ Classify an alcohol as primary, secondary, or tertiary (13.1).

______ Give the IUPAC or common name of an alcohol, phenol, or thiol; draw the condensed structural formula from the name (13.1).

______ Write the IUPAC or common name of an ether; draw the condensed structural formula from the name (13.2).

______ Describe the solubility of alcohols, phenols, and ethers in water; compare their boiling points (13.3).

______ Write the products of alcohols that undergo dehydration, ether formation, and oxidation (13.4).

Practice Test for Chapter 13

For questions 1 through 5, match the names of the following compounds with their condensed structural structures:

A. 1-propanol **B.** cyclobutanol **C.** 2-propanol
D. ethyl methyl ether **E.** diethyl ether

1. $CH_3-\underset{}{\overset{OH}{\overset{|}{C}H}}-CH_3$

2. $CH_3-CH_2-CH_2-OH$

3. $CH_3-O-CH_2-CH_3$

4. 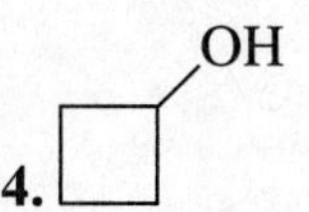

5. $CH_3-CH_2-O-CH_2-CH_3$

6. The compound $CH_3-\overset{O}{\overset{\|}{C}}-CH_3$ is formed by the oxidation of

A. 2-propanol **B.** propane **C.** 1-propanol
D. dimethyl ether **E.** methyl ethyl ketone

7. Why are short-chain alcohols water soluble?

A. They are nonpolar. **B.** They can hydrogen bond. **C.** They are organic.
D. They are bases. **E.** They are acids.

8. Phenol is

A. the alcohol of benzene **B.** the aldehyde of benzene **C.** the phenyl group of benzene
D. the ketone of benzene **E.** cyclohexanol

9. $CH_3-CH_2-OH + HO-CH_2-CH_3 \xrightarrow{H^+}$ [ ] $+ H_2O$

A. an alkane **B.** an aldehyde **C.** a ketone
D. an ether **E.** a phenol

10. The dehydration of cyclohexanol gives

A. cyclohexane **B.** cyclohexene **C.** cyclohexyne
D. benzene **E.** phenol

11. The condensed structural formula of ethanethiol is

A. CH_3-SH **B.** CH_3-CH_2-OH **C.** CH_3-CH_2-SH
D. $CH_3-CH_2-S-CH_3$ **E.** CH_3-S-OH

In questions 12 through 16, classify each alcohol as:

A. primary (1°) **B.** secondary (2°) **C.** tertiary (3°)

12. $CH_3—CH_2—CH_2—OH$

13. 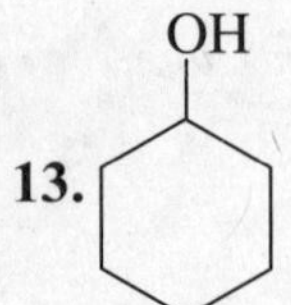

14. CH_3 OH (cyclopentane ring)

15.

$$\begin{array}{c} \text{OH} \\ | \\ CH_3—C—CH_2—CH_2—CH_3 \\ | \\ CH_3 \end{array}$$

16.

$$\begin{array}{c} \text{OH} \\ | \\ CH_3—CH—CH_2—CH_2—CH_2—CH_3 \end{array}$$

Complete questions 17 through 20 by indicating one of the products (A–E) formed in each of the following reactions:

A. primary alcohol **B.** secondary alcohol **C.** aldehyde
D. ketone **E.** carboxylic acid

17. _____ oxidation of a primary alcohol

18. _____ oxidation of a secondary alcohol

19. _____ oxidation of an aldehyde

20. _____ hydration of 1-propene

21. The major product from the dehydration of 2-methylcyclobutanol is:

A. cyclobutene **B.** 1-methylcyclobutene **C.** 2-methylcyclobutene
D. 3-methylcyclobutene **E.** 1-methylcyclobutane

Answers to the Practice Test

1. C	**2.** A	**3.** D	**4.** B	**5.** E
6. A	**7.** B	**8.** A	**9.** D	**10.** B
11. C	**12.** A	**13.** B	**14.** C	**15.** C
16. B	**17.** C, E	**18.** D	**19.** E	**20.** B
21. B				

14

Aldehydes, Ketones, and Chiral Molecules

Study Goals

- Name and draw the condensed structural formulas for aldehydes and ketones.
- Describe some important aldehydes and ketones.
- Write equations for the oxidation of aldehydes and for the reduction of aldehydes and ketones.
- Identify the chiral carbon atoms in organic molecules.
- Draw the condensed structural formulas of hemiacetals and acetals produced from the addition of alcohols to aldehydes and ketones.

Think About It

1. What are the functional groups of an aldehyde and ketone?

2. How is an alcohol changed to an aldehyde or ketone?

3. How are hemiacetals and acetals formed?

4. When are mirror images not superimposable?

Key Terms

Match the following terms with the statements shown below:

a. chiral carbon **b.** hemiacetal **c.** Fischer projection **d.** aldehyde **e.** ketone

1. ____ an organic compound with a carbonyl group attached to two alkyl or aromatic groups
2. ____ a carbon that is bonded to four different groups
3. ____ the product that forms when an alcohol adds to an aldehyde or a ketone

4. ____ a system for drawing chiral molecules that uses horizontal lines for bonds coming forward and vertical lines for bonds going back with the chiral atom at the center

5. ____ an organic compound that contains a carbonyl group and a hydrogen atom at the end of the carbon chain

Answers **1.** e **2.** a **3.** b **4.** c **5.** d

14.1 Aldehydes and Ketones

- In an aldehyde, the carbonyl group appears at the end of a carbon chain attached to at least one hydrogen atom.
- In a ketone, the carbonyl group occurs between carbon groups and has no hydrogens attached to it.
- In the IUPAC system, aldehydes and ketones are named by replacing the *e* in the longest chain containing the carbonyl group with *al* for aldehydes and *one* for ketones. The location of the carbonyl group in a ketone is given if there are more than four carbon atoms in the chain.

$CH_3-\overset{\large O \atop \Vert}{C}-H$ Ethanal (acetaldehyde)

$CH_3-\overset{\large O \atop \Vert}{C}-CH_3$ Propanone (dimethyl ketone)

MasteringChemistry

Self Study Activity: Aldehydes and Ketones

Tutorial: Aldehyde or Ketone?

Tutorial: Naming Aldehydes and Ketones

◆ Learning Exercise 14.1A

Classify each of the following compounds:

a. alcohol **b.** aldehyde **c.** ketone **d.** ether **e.** thiol

______ **1.** $CH_3-CH_2-CH_2-\overset{\large O \atop \Vert}{C}-H$

______ **2.** $CH_3-CH_2-CH_2-OH$

______ **3.** $CH_3-CH_2-\overset{\large O \atop \Vert}{C}-CH_2-CH_3$

______ **4.** $CH_3-CH_2-O-CH_3$

______ **5.** $CH_3-\overset{\large O \atop \Vert}{C}-CH_2-CH_3$

______ **6.** $CH_3-\overset{\large O \atop \Vert}{C}-H$

______ **7.** $CH_3-CH_2-\overset{SH \atop |}{CH}-CH_3$

______ **8.** $CH_3-CH_2-\overset{OH \atop |}{CH}-CH_3$

Answers	**1.** b	**2.** a	**3.** c	**4.** d
	5. c	**6.** b	**7.** e	**8.** a

◆ Learning Exercise 14.1B

Indicate whether the compounds in each of the following pairs are isomers (I), the same compound (S), or different compounds (D):

1. ______ $CH_3-CH_2-\overset{\overset{O}{\|}}{C}-H$ and $CH_3-\overset{\overset{O}{\|}}{C}-CH_3$

2. ______ and

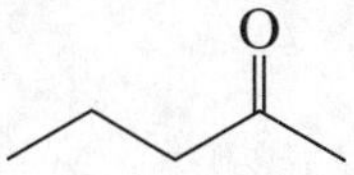

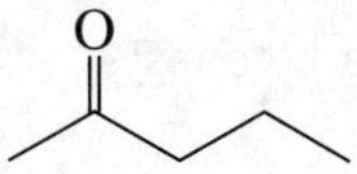

3. ______ $CH_3-\overset{\overset{O}{\|}}{C}-CH_2-CH_3$ and $CH_3-\overset{\overset{O}{\|}}{C}-CH_2-CH_2-CH_3$

Answers	**1.** I	**2.** S	**3.** D

Guide to Naming Aldehydes	
STEP 1	Name the longest carbon chain by replacing the *e* in the alkane name with *al.*
STEP 2	Name and number the substituents by counting the carbonyl group as carbon 1.

◆ Learning Exercise 14.1C

Write the IUPAC (or common) name for each of the following aldehydes:

1. $CH_3-\overset{\overset{O}{\|}}{C}-H$

2. $CH_3-CH_2-CH_2-CH_2-\overset{\overset{O}{\|}}{C}-H$

3. $CH_3-CH_2-\overset{\overset{CH_3}{|}}{CH}-CH_2-CH_2-\overset{\overset{O}{\|}}{C}-H$

4. 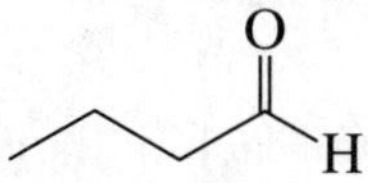 H

5. $H-\overset{\overset{O}{\|}}{C}-H$

Answers	**1.** ethanal; acetaldehyde	**2.** pentanal	**3.** 4-methylhexanal
	4. butanal; butyraldehyde	**5.** methanal; formaldehyde	

Guide to Naming Ketones	
STEP 1	Name the longest carbon chain containing the carbonyl group by replacing the *e* in the corresponding alkane name with *one*.
STEP 2	Number the main chain starting from the end nearer the carbonyl group.
STEP 3	Name and number any substituents and include its location in the carbon chain.
STEP 4	For cyclic ketones, the prefix *cyclo* is used in front of the ketone name.

◆ Learning Exercise 14.1D

Write the IUPAC (or common) name for each of the following ketones:

1. $CH_3-\overset{\overset{\displaystyle O}{\|}}{C}-CH_3$

2. 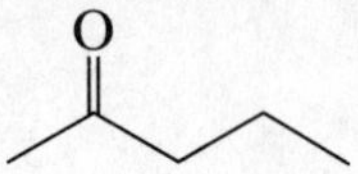 (skeletal structure: 2-pentanone)

3. $CH_3-CH_2-\overset{\overset{\displaystyle O}{\|}}{C}-CH_2-CH_3$

4. 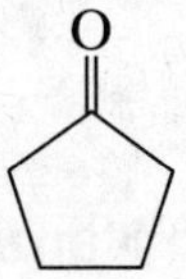 (skeletal structure: cyclopentanone)

5. 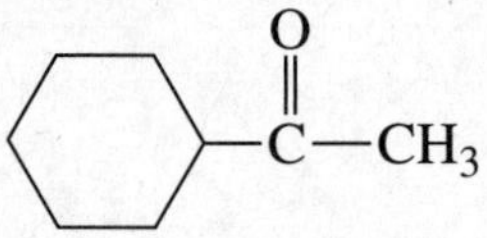 (cyclohexane ring)$-\overset{\overset{\displaystyle O}{\|}}{C}-CH_3$

Answers
1. propanone; dimethyl ketone, acetone
2. 2-pentanone; methyl propyl ketone
3. 3-pentanone; diethyl ketone
4. cyclopentanone
5. cyclohexyl methyl ketone

◆ Learning Exercise 14.1E

Draw the condensed structural formulas for each of the following:

1. ethanal

2. butyraldehyde

3. 2-chloropropanal

4. ethyl methyl ketone

5. 3-hexanone

6. benzaldehyde

Answers
1. $CH_3-\overset{\overset{\displaystyle O}{\|}}{C}-H$
2. $CH_3-CH_2-CH_2-\overset{\overset{\displaystyle O}{\|}}{C}-H$

3. $CH_3—CH(Cl)—C(=O)—H$ **4.** $CH_3—CH_2—C(=O)—CH_3$

5. $CH_3—CH_2—C(=O)—CH_2—CH_2—CH_3$ **6.** 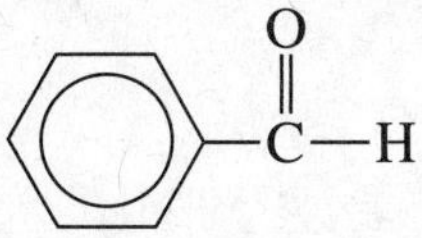 $C_6H_5—C(=O)—H$

14.2 Physical Properties of Aldehydes and Ketones

- The polarity of the carbonyl group makes aldehydes and ketones of one to four carbon atoms soluble in water.

MasteringChemistry
Tutorial: Properties of Aldehydes and Ketones

◆ Learning Exercise 14.2A

Indicate the compound with the highest boiling point in each of the following groups of compounds:

1. $CH_3—CH_2—C(=O)—H$, $CH_3—CH_2—CH_2—OH$, or $CH_3—C(=O)—CH_3$

2. acetaldehyde or propionaldehyde

3. propanone or butanone

4. methylcyclohexane or cyclohexanone

Answers **1.** $CH_3—CH_2—CH_2—OH$ **2.** propionaldehyde
3. butanone **4.** cyclohexanone

◆ Learning Exercise 14.2B

Indicate whether each of the following compounds is soluble (S) or not soluble (NS) in water:

1. _____ 3-hexanone **2.** _____ propanal **3.** _____ acetaldehyde
4. _____ butanal **5.** _____ cyclohexanone

Answers **1.** NS **2.** S **3.** S **4.** S **5.** NS

14.3 Oxidation and Reduction of Aldehydes and Ketones

- Using an oxidizing agent, primary alcohols oxidize to aldehydes, which usually oxidize further to carboxylic acids. Secondary alcohols are oxidized to ketones, but tertiary alcohols do not oxidize.

$$CH_3-CH_2-OH \xrightarrow{[O]} CH_3-\overset{\overset{\Large O}{\|}}{C}-H + H_2O$$

1° Alcohol → Aldehyde

$$CH_3-\underset{}{\overset{\overset{\large OH}{|}}{CH}}-CH_3 \xrightarrow{[O]} CH_3-\overset{\overset{\Large O}{\|}}{C}-CH_3 + H_2O$$

2° Alcohol → Ketone

- Aldehydes and ketones are reduced when hydrogen is added in the presence of a metal catalyst to produce primary or secondary alcohols.

MasteringChemistry
Tutorial: Oxidation-Reduction Reactions of Aldehydes and Ketones

◆ Learning Exercise 14.3A

Draw the condensed structural formula of the alcohol that oxidized to give each of the following compounds:

1. $CH_3-\overset{\overset{O}{\|}}{C}-CH_2-CH_3$

2. cyclohexanone (cyclohexane ring with =O)

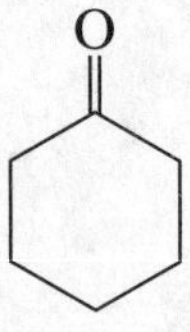

3. $CH_3-CH_2-\overset{\overset{O}{\|}}{C}-H$

Answers **1.** $CH_3-\overset{\overset{OH}{|}}{CH}-CH_2-CH_3$ **2.** cyclohexanol (cyclohexane ring with —OH) **3.** $CH_3-CH_2-CH_2-OH$

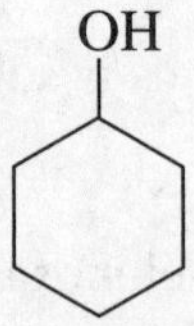

◆ Learning Exercise 14.3B

Indicate the compound in each of the following pairs that will oxidize:

1. propanal or propanone ____________

2. butane or butanal ____________

3. ethane or acetaldehyde ____________

Answers **1.** propanal **2.** butanal **3.** acetaldehyde

◆ Learning Exercise 14.3C

Draw the condensed structural formulas for the reduction products from each of the following:

1. $CH_3-\overset{\overset{\large O}{\|}}{C}-CH_3 + H_2 \xrightarrow{Pt}$

2. $CH_3-CH_2-\overset{\overset{\large O}{\|}}{C}-H + H_2 \xrightarrow{Pt}$

3. $CH_3-\overset{\overset{\large O}{\|}}{C}-H + H_2 \xrightarrow{Pt}$

4. 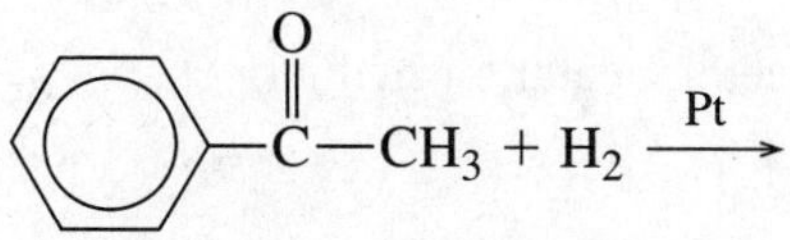 $C_6H_5-\overset{\overset{\large O}{\|}}{C}-CH_3 + H_2 \xrightarrow{Pt}$ (benzene ring attached to C)

5. cyclopentane ring bearing CH_3 and, on the adjacent carbon, $\overset{\overset{\large O}{\|}}{C}-H$ $+ H_2 \xrightarrow{Pt}$

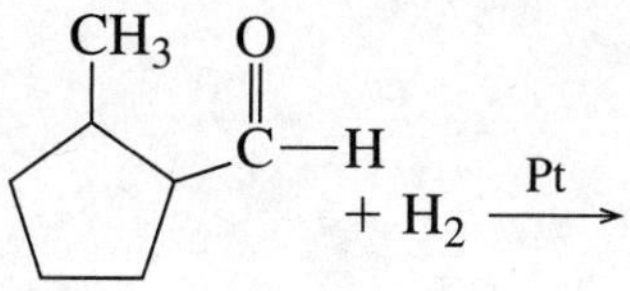

Answers

1. $CH_3-\overset{\overset{\large OH}{|}}{CH}-CH_3$

2. $CH_3-CH_2-CH_2-OH$

3. CH_3-CH_2-OH

4. 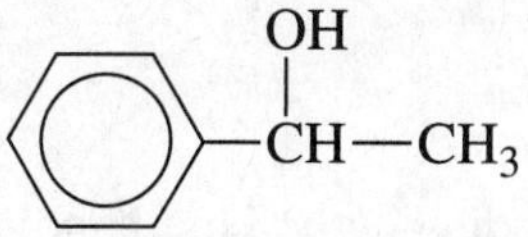 $C_6H_5-\overset{\overset{\large OH}{|}}{CH}-CH_3$ (benzene ring attached to CH)

5. cyclopentane ring bearing CH_3 and, on the adjacent carbon, CH_2OH

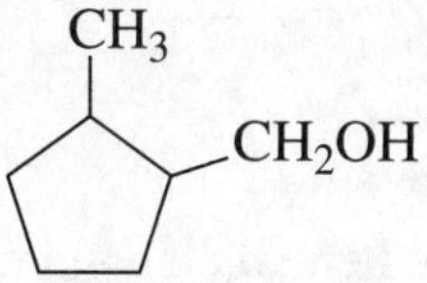

14.4 Addition Reactions of Aldehydes and Ketones

- Alcohols add to the carbonyl group of aldehyde and ketones.
- Hemiacetals form when one alcohol adds to aldehydes or ketones.
- Acetals form when a second alcohol molecule adds to hemiacetals.

MasteringChemistry
Tutorial: Addition of Polar Molecules to a Carbonyl Group
Tutorial: Formation of Acetals
Tutorial: Cyclic Hemiacetals

◆ Learning Exercise 14.4A

Match the statements shown below with the following types of compounds:

a. hemiacetal **b.** acetal

1. _____ the product from the addition of one alcohol to an aldehyde

2. _____ the product from the addition of one alcohol to a ketone

3. _____ a compound that contains two ether groups

4. _____ a compound that consists of one ether group, an alcohol group, and two alkyl groups

Answers **1.** a **2.** a **3.** b **4.** a

◆ Learning Exercise 14.4B

Identify each of the following condensed structural formulas as a hemiacetal, acetal, or neither:

1. $CH_3—O—CH_2—OH$

2. 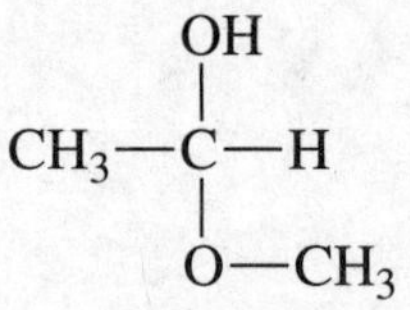 $CH_3—C(OH)(O—CH_3)—H$ (OH above C; $O—CH_3$ below C)

3. $CH_3—C(O—CH_2—CH_3)_2—CH_3$ ($O—CH_2—CH_3$ above and below C)

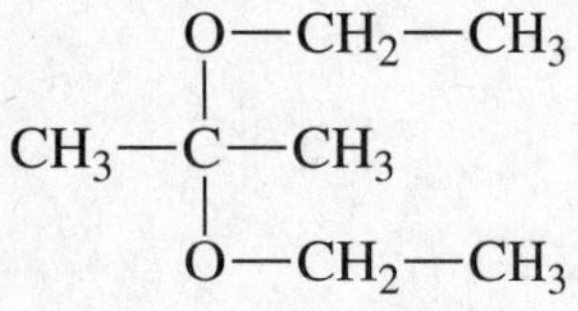

4. 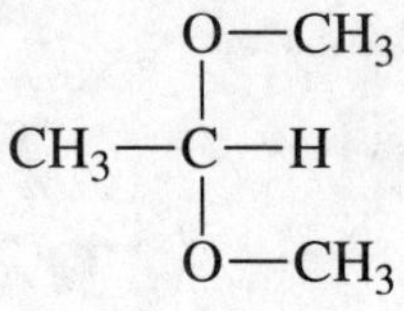 $CH_3—C(O—CH_3)_2—H$ ($O—CH_3$ above and below C)

Answers **1.** hemiacetal **2.** hemiacetal **3.** acetal **4.** acetal

◆ Learning Exercise 14.4C

Draw the condensed structural formula of the hemiacetal and acetal products when methanol adds to propanone.

Answer

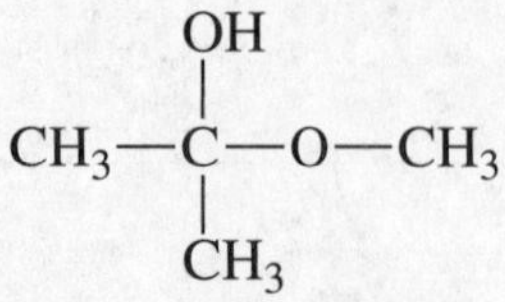

$CH_3—C(OH)(CH_3)—O—CH_3$ (OH above C; CH_3 below C)
Hemiacetal

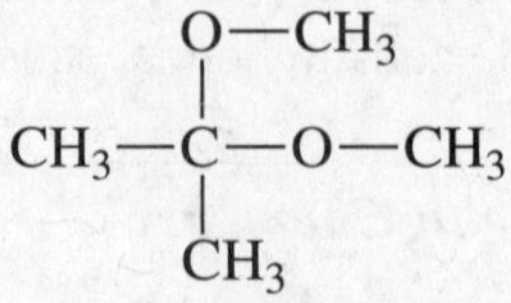

$CH_3—C(O—CH_3)(CH_3)—O—CH_3$ ($O—CH_3$ above C; CH_3 below C)
Acetal

14.5 Chiral Molecules

- Chiral molecules have mirror images that cannot be superimposed.
- In a chiral molecule, there is one or more carbon atoms attached to four different atoms or groups.
- The mirror images of a chiral molecule represent two different molecules called enantiomers.
- In a Fischer projection (straight chain), the prefixes D and L are used to distinguish between the mirror images. In D-glyceraldehyde, the —OH is on the right of the chiral carbon; it is on the left in L-glyceraldehyde.

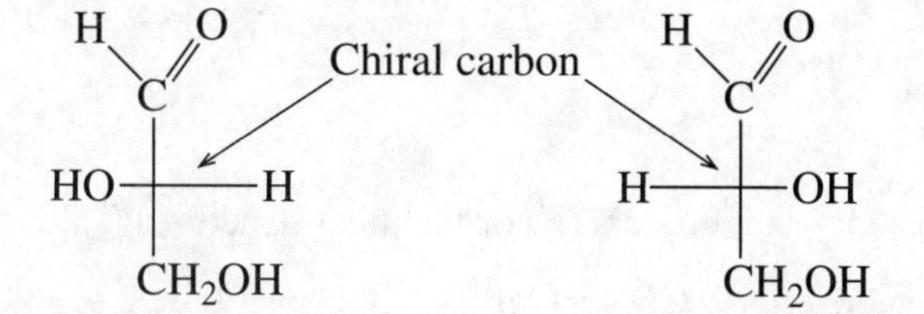

```
 H   O                            H   O
  \ //      Chiral carbon          \ //
   C     ______/      \_____        C
   |    /                    \      |
HO—+—H                        H—+—OH
   |                                |
 CH2OH                            CH2OH
L-Glyceraldehyde            D-Glyceraldehyde
```

MasteringChemistry

Tutorial: Chiral Carbon Atoms

◆ Learning Exercise 14.5A

Indicate whether each of the following objects would be chiral or not chiral:

1. a piece of plain computer paper ______ **2.** a glove ______

3. a baseball cap ______ **4.** a volleyball net ______

5. a left foot ______

Answers **1.** not chiral **2.** chiral **3.** not chiral
4. not chiral **5.** chiral

◆ Learning Exercise 14.5B

State whether each of the following molecules is chiral or not chiral:

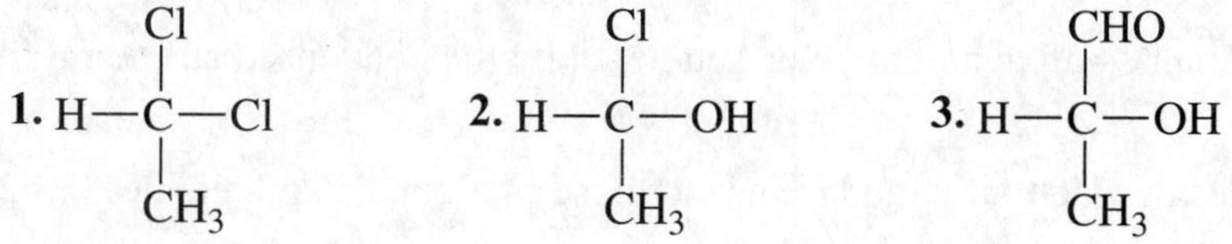

```
        Cl                  Cl                  CHO
        |                   |                   |
1. H—C—Cl           2. H—C—OH           3. H—C—OH
        |                   |                   |
       CH3                 CH3                 CH3

   ______              ______              ______
```

Answers **1.** not chiral **2.** chiral **3.** chiral

◆ Learning Exercise 14.5C

Identify each of the following as a feature characteristic of a chiral compound or not chiral:

1. the central atom is attached to two identical groups ____________

2. contains a carbon attached to four different groups ____________

3. has identical mirror images ____________

Answers **1.** not chiral **2.** chiral **3.** not chiral

◆ Learning Exercise 14.5D

Indicate whether each pair of Fischer projections represents enantiomers (E) or identical structures (I).

1. HO—C(COOH)(CH$_2$OH)—H and H—C(COOH)(CH$_2$OH)—OH

(top: COOH; left: HO; right: H; bottom: CH_2OH) and (top: COOH; left: H; right: OH; bottom: CH_2OH)

2. (top: CH_2—OH; left: Cl; right: H; bottom: CH_3) and (top: CH_2—OH; left: Cl; right: H; bottom: CH_3)

3. (top: CHO; left: Cl; right: Br; bottom: CH_3) and (top: CHO; left: Br; right: Cl; bottom: CH_3)

4. (top: COOH; left: H; right: OH; bottom: COOH) and (top: COOH; left: HO; right: H; bottom: COOH)

Answers **1.** E **2.** I **3.** E **4.**I

Checklist for Chapter 14

You are ready to take the practice test for Chapter 14. Be sure that you have accomplished the following learning goals for this chapter. If you are not sure, review the section listed at the end of the goal. Then apply your new skills and understanding to the Practice Test.

After studying Chapter 14, I can successfully:

____ Identify condensed structural formulas as aldehydes or ketones (14.1).

____ Give the IUPAC and common names of an aldehyde or ketone; draw the condensed structural formula from the name (14.1).

____ Compare the physical properties of aldehydes and ketones to those of alcohols and alkanes (14.2).

____ Draw the condensed structural formulas for reactants and products of the oxidation of alcohols or reduction of aldehydes and ketones (14.3).

____ Draw the condensed structural formulas of the hemiacetals and acetals that form when alcohols add to aldehyde or ketones (14.4).

____ Identify a molecule as chiral or not chiral; draw the D- and L-Fischer projections (14.5).

Practice Test for Chapter 14

For questions 1 through 5, match each of the following compounds with the names given:

A. dimethyl ether **B.** acetaldehyde **C.** methanal
D. dimethyl ketone **E.** propanal

1. ______ $H-\overset{\overset{\displaystyle O}{\|}}{C}-H$ **2.** ______ CH_3-O-CH_3

3. ______ $CH_3-\overset{\overset{\displaystyle O}{\|}}{C}-CH_3$ **4.** ______ $CH_3-\overset{\overset{\displaystyle O}{\|}}{C}-H$

5. ______ 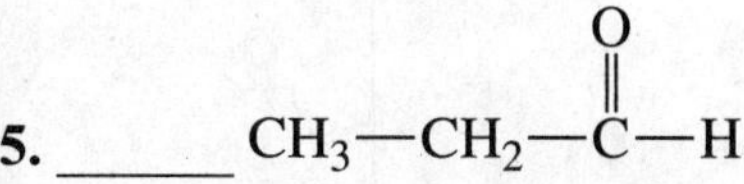

6. The compound with the highest boiling point is

A. $CH_3-CH_2-CH_2-CH_3$ **B.** $CH_3-CH_2-CH_2-OH$

C. $CH_3-\overset{\overset{\displaystyle O}{\|}}{C}-CH_3$ **D.** $CH_3-CH_2-\overset{\overset{\displaystyle O}{\|}}{C}-H$

E. $CH_3-CH_2-O-CH_3$

For questions 7 through 11, indicate the product (A–E) formed in each of the following reactions:

A. primary alcohol **B.** secondary alcohol **C.** aldehyde
D. ketone **E.** carboxylic acid

7. ______ oxidation of a primary alcohol **8.** ______ oxidation of a secondary alcohol

9. ______ oxidation of an aldehyde **10.** ______ reduction of a ketone

11. ______ reduction of an aldehyde

12. Benedict's reagent will oxidize

A. $CH_3-\overset{\overset{\displaystyle O}{\|}}{C}-CH_3$ **B.** $CH_3-\overset{\overset{\displaystyle OH}{|}}{CH}-CH_2-OH$

C. $CH_3-\overset{\overset{\displaystyle O}{\|}}{C}-CH_2-OH$ **D.** $CH_3-\overset{\overset{\displaystyle OH}{|}}{CH}-\overset{\overset{\displaystyle O}{\|}}{C}-H$

E. $CH_3-\overset{\overset{\displaystyle OH}{|}}{CH}-\overset{\overset{\displaystyle O}{\|}}{C}-OH$

13. In the Tollens' test

A. an aldehyde is oxidized and Ag^+ is reduced
B. an aldehyde is reduced and Ag^+ is oxidized
C. a ketone is oxidized and Ag^+ is reduced
D. a ketone is reduced and Ag^+ is oxidized
E. all of these

For questions 14 through 17, match the name with one of the following condensed structural formulas:

14. alcohol **15.** ether **16.** hemiacetal **17.** acetal

A. 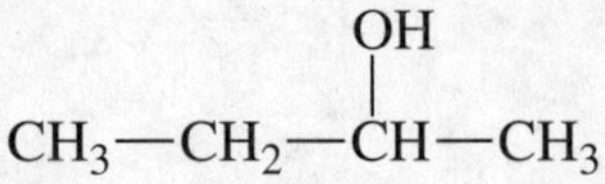 $CH_3-CH_2-CH(OH)-CH_3$

B. 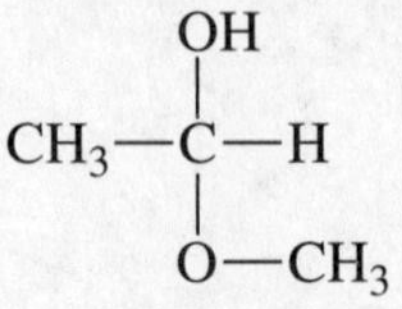 $CH_3-C(OH)(H)-O-CH_3$

C. $CH_3-C(O-CH_2-CH_3)_2-CH_3$

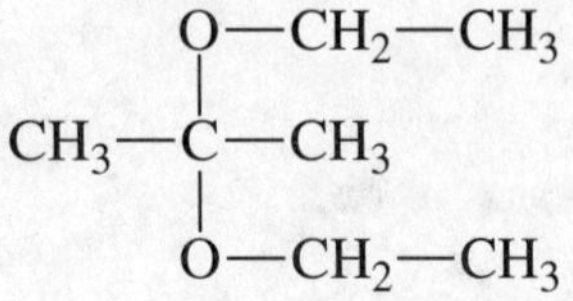

D. 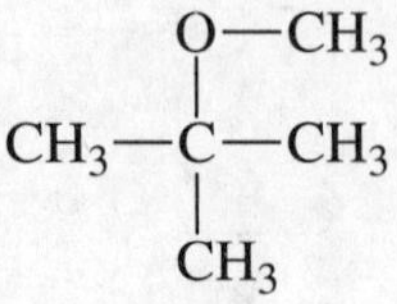 $CH_3-C(O-CH_3)(CH_3)-CH_3$

18. The condensed structural formula for 4-bromo-3-methylcyclohexanone is

A. 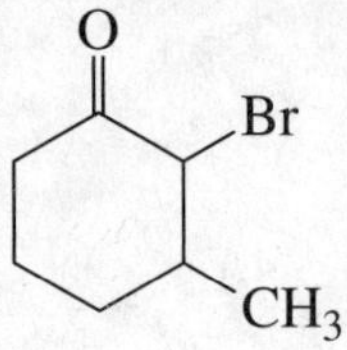 O Br CH_3

B. 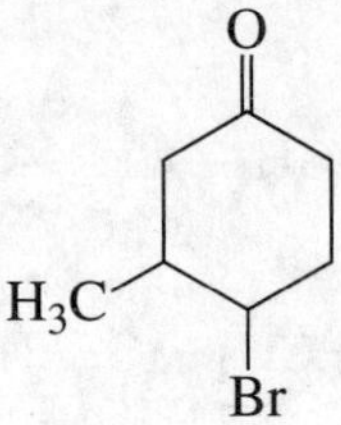 O H_3C Br

C. 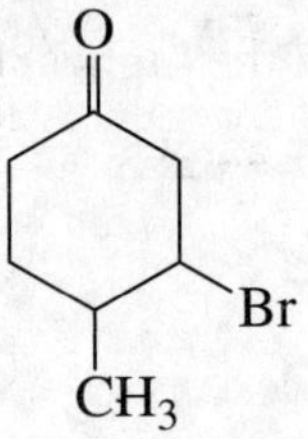 O Br CH_3

D. 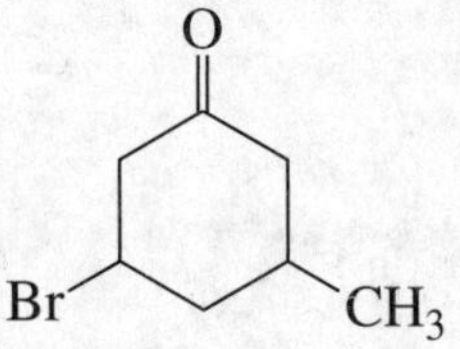 O Br CH_3

E. 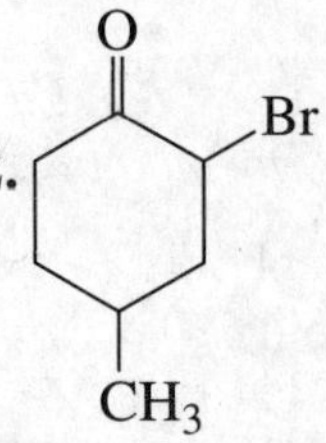 O Br CH_3

19. The name of the following compound is:

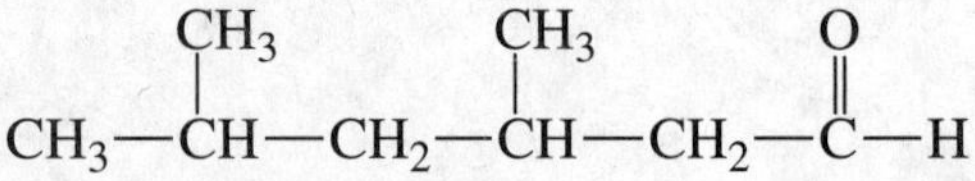

$$CH_3-\underset{CH_3}{CH}-CH_2-\underset{CH_3}{CH}-CH_2-\overset{O}{\overset{\|}{C}}-H$$

A. 3,5-dimethyl-1-hexanal
B. 2,4-dimethyl-6-hexanal
C. 3,5-dimethylhexanal
D. 1-aldo-3,5-dimethylhexane
E. 2,4-dimethylhexanal

20. The reaction of an alcohol with an aldehyde is called a(n)

A. elimination
B. addition
C. substitution
D. hydrolysis
E. oxidation

For questions 21 through 25, identify each of the following pairs of Fischer projections as enantiomers (E), identical (I), or different (D) compounds:

21. 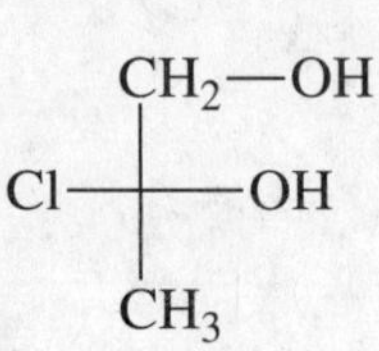 Fischer projection: top CH_2-OH, left Cl, right OH, bottom CH_3 and Fischer projection: top CH_2-OH, left HO, right Cl, bottom CH_3

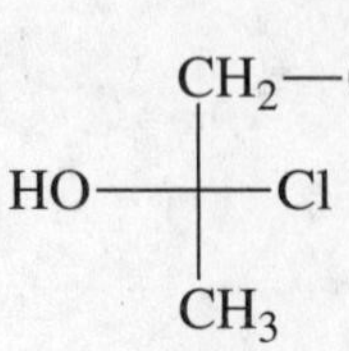

22. 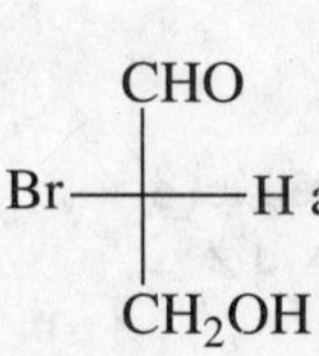 Fischer projection: top CHO, left Br, right H, bottom CH_2OH and Fischer projection: top CHO, left H, right Br, bottom CH_2OH

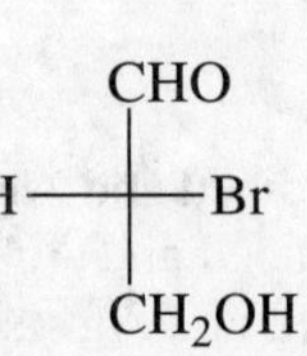

23. 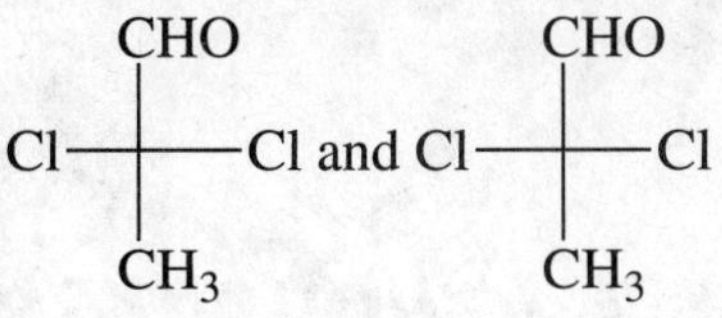 Fischer projections: $Cl-C(CHO)(CH_3)-Cl$ and $Cl-C(CHO)(CH_3)-Cl$

CHO above, Cl—|—Cl, CH_3 below; and CHO above, Cl—|—Cl, CH_3 below

24. 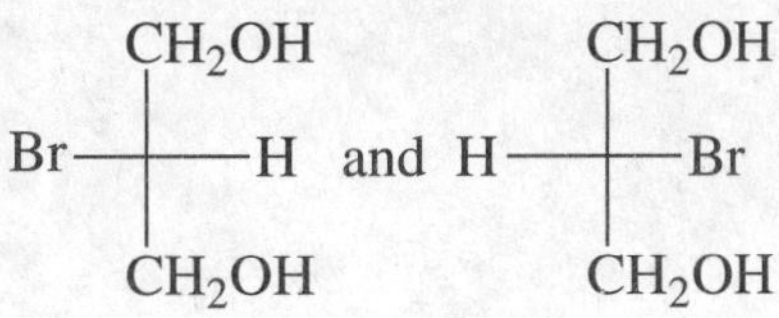 CH_2OH above, Br—|—H, CH_2OH below; and CH_2OH above, H—|—Br, CH_2OH below

25. 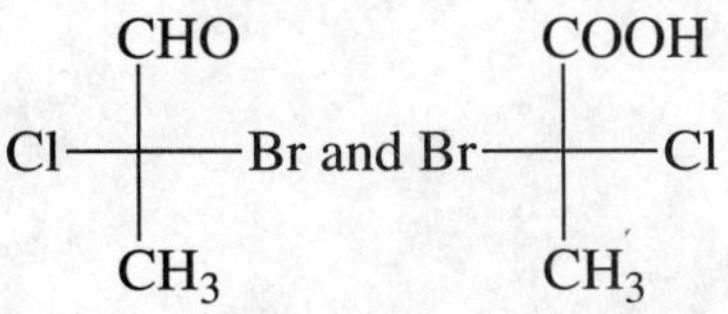 CHO above, Cl—|—Br, CH_3 below; and COOH above, Br—|—Cl, CH_3 below

Answers to the Practice Test

1. C	**2.** A	**3.** D	**4.** B	**5.** E
6. B	**7.** C, E	**8.** D	**9.** E	**10.** B
11. A	**12.** D	**13.** A	**14.** A	**15.** D
16. B	**17.** C	**18.** B	**19.** C	**20.** B
21. E	**22.** E	**23.** I	**24.** I	**25.** D

15

Carbohydrates

Study Goals

- Identify the common carbohydrates in the diet.
- Distinguish between monosaccharides, disaccharides, and polysaccharides.
- Identify the chiral carbons in a carbohydrate.
- Label the Fischer projection for a monosaccharide as the D- or L-isomer.
- Draw Haworth structures for monosaccharides.
- Describe the structural units and bonds in disaccharides and polysaccharides.

Think About It

1. What are some foods you eat that contain carbohydrates?

2. What elements are found in carbohydrates?

3. What carbohydrates are present in table sugar, milk, and wood?

4. What is meant by a "high-fiber" diet?

Key Terms

Match the following key terms with the descriptions on the following page.

a. carbohydrate **b.** glucose **c.** disaccharide
d. Haworth structure **e.** cellulose

1. ____ a simple or complex sugar composed of a carbon chain with an aldehyde or ketone group and several hydroxyl groups
2. ____ a cyclic structure that represents the closed chain form of a monosaccharide
3. ____ an unbranched polysaccharide that cannot be digested by humans
4. ____ an aldohexose that is the most prevalent monosaccharide in the diet
5. ____ a carbohydrate that contains two monosaccharides linked by a glycosidic bond

Answers **1.** a **2.** d **3.** e **4.** b **5.** c

15.1 Carbohydrates

- Carbohydrates are classified as monosaccharides (simple sugars), disaccharides (two monosaccharide units), and polysaccharides (many monosaccharide units).
- In a chiral molecule, there is one or more carbon atom attached to four different atoms or groups.
- Monosaccharides are polyhydroxy aldehydes (aldoses) or ketones (ketoses).
- Monosaccharides are classified by the number of carbon atoms as *trioses*, *tetroses*, *pentoses*, or *hexoses*.

MasteringChemistry

Self Study Activity: Carbohydrates

Tutorial: Types of Carbohydrates

Self Study Activity: Forms of Carbohydrates

Tutorial: Carbonyls in Carbohydrates

◆ Learning Exercise 15.1A

Complete and balance the equations for the photosynthesis of

1. Glucose: ________ + ________ $\rightarrow C_6H_{12}O_6$ + ________

2. Ribose: ________ + ________ $\rightarrow C_5H_{10}O_5$ + ________

Answers

1. $6CO_2 + 6H_2O \rightarrow C_6H_{12}O_6 + 6O_2$

2. $5CO_2 + 5H_2O \rightarrow C_5H_{10}O_5 + 5O_2$

◆ Learning Exercise 15.1B

Indicate the number of monosaccharide units (1, 2, or many) in each of the following carbohydrates:

1. sucrose, a disaccharide ________ **2.** cellulose, a polysaccharide ________

3. glucose, a monosaccharide ________ **4.** amylose, a polysaccharide ________

5. maltose, a disaccharide ________

Answers **1.** two **2.** many **3.** one **4.** many **5.** two

◆ Learning Exercise 15.1C

Identify the following monosaccharides as aldotrioses, ketotrioses, tetroses, pentoses, or hexoses:

1.
$$\begin{array}{c} CH_2OH \\ | \\ C{=}O \\ | \\ CH_2OH \end{array}$$

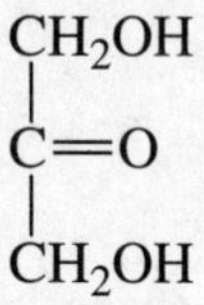

2.
$$\begin{array}{rcl} & \overset{H\diagdown\;\diagup\!\!\!/ O}{C} & \\ & | & \\ H- & C & -OH \\ & | & \\ H- & C & -OH \\ & | & \\ HO- & C & -H \\ & | & \\ & CH_2OH & \end{array}$$

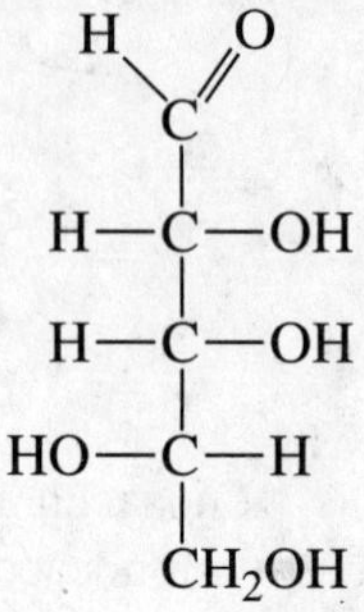

3.
$$\begin{array}{rcl} & CH_2OH & \\ & | & \\ & C{=}O & \\ & | & \\ HO- & C & -H \\ & | & \\ HO- & C & -H \\ & | & \\ H- & C & -OH \\ & | & \\ & CH_2OH & \end{array}$$

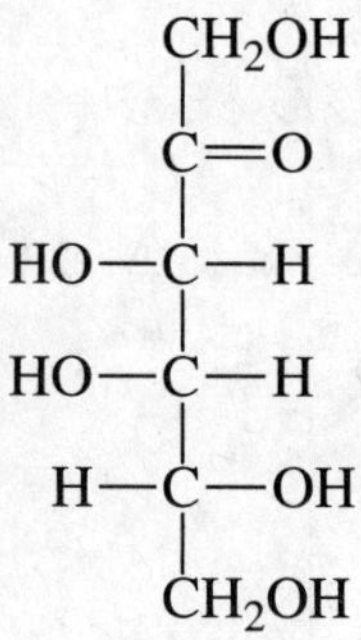

4.
$$\begin{array}{rcl} & \overset{H\diagdown\;\diagup\!\!\!/ O}{C} & \\ & | & \\ H- & C & -OH \\ & | & \\ HO- & C & -H \\ & | & \\ H- & C & -OH \\ & | & \\ H- & C & -OH \\ & | & \\ & CH_2OH & \end{array}$$

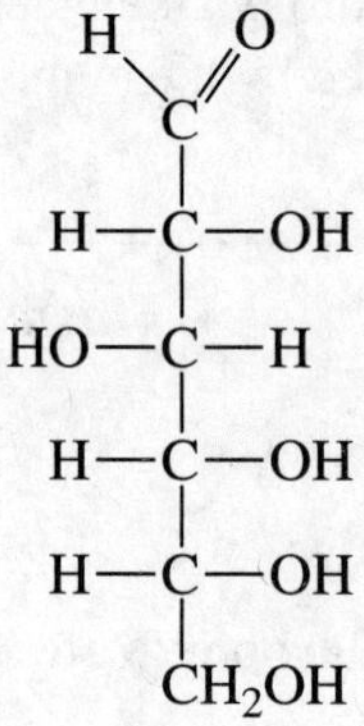

5.
$$\begin{array}{rcl} & \overset{H\diagdown\;\diagup\!\!\!/ O}{C} & \\ & | & \\ H- & C & -OH \\ & | & \\ H- & C & -OH \\ & | & \\ & CH_2OH & \end{array}$$

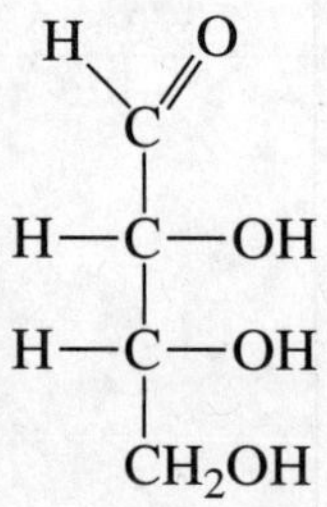

1. ________________ **2.** ________________ **3.** ________________

4. ________________ **5.** ________________

Answers **1.** ketotriose **2.** aldopentose **3.** ketohexose
4. aldohexose **5.** aldotetrose

15.2 Fischer Projections of Monosaccharides

- In a Fischer projection, the carbon chain is written vertically, with the most oxidized carbon (usually an aldehyde or ketone) at the top.

- In the Fischer projection of a monosaccharide, the chiral —OH *farthest* from the carbonyl group (C═O) is written on the left side in the L isomer and on the right side in the D isomer.
- The carbon atom in the $-CH_2OH$ group at the bottom of the Fischer projection is not chiral because it does not have four different groups bonded to it.
- Important monosaccharides are the aldopentose ribose, the aldohexoses glucose and galactose and the ketohexose fructose.

MasteringChemistry

Self Study Activity: Forms of Carbohydrates

Tutorial: Identifying Chiral Carbons in Monosaccharides

Tutorial: Drawing Fischer Projections of Monosaccharides

Tutorial: Identifying D and L Sugars

◆ Learning Exercise 15.2A

Identify each of the following Fischer projections of sugars as the D or L isomer:

CH_2OH
═O
1. HO—H
H—OH
CH_2OH

____ Xylulose

CHO
H—OH
H—OH
2. HO—H
HO—H
CH_2OH

____ Mannose

CHO
3. HO—H
H—OH
CH_2OH

____ Threose

CH_2OH
═O
4. HO—H
HO—H
CH_2OH

____ Ribulose

Answers **1.** D–Xylulose **2.** L–Mannose **3.** D–Threose **4.** L–Rribulose

◆ Learning Exercise 15.2B

Draw the mirror image of each of the sugars in Learning Exercise 15.2A and give the D or L name.

1. **2.** **3.** **4.**

Answers

1.

CH_2OH
=O
H—OH
HO—H
CH_2OH
L-Xylulose

2.

CHO
HO—H
HO—H
H—OH
H—OH
CH_2OH
D-Mannose

3.

CHO
H—OH
HO—H
CH_2OH
L-Threose

4.

CH_2OH
=O
H—OH
H—OH
CH_2OH
D-Ribulose

◆ Learning Exercise 15.2C

Identify the monosaccharide (glucose, fructose, or galactose) that fits each of the following descriptions:

1. a building block in cellulose __________

2. also known as fruit sugar __________

3. accumulates in the disease known as *galactosemia* __________

4. the most common monosaccharide __________

5. the sweetest monosaccharide __________

Answers **1.** glucose **2.** fructose **3.** galactose **4.** glucose **5.** fructose

◆ Learning Exercise 15.2D

Draw the open-chain structure for each of the following monosaccharides:

D–glucose L–galactose D–fructose

Answers

```
       O                  O
       ‖                  ‖
       C—H                C—H              CH2OH
       |                  |                  |
   H—C—OH             H—C—OH               C=O
       |                  |                  |
  HO—C—H            HO—C—H             HO—C—H
       |                  |                  |
   H—C—OH            HO—C—H              H—C—OH
       |                  |                  |
   H—C—OH             H—C—OH              H—C—OH
       |                  |                  |
     CH2OH              CH2OH              CH2OH
   D-Glucose         D-Galactose        D-Fructose
```

15.3 Haworth Structures of Monosaccharides

- The Haworth structure is a cyclic representation of the most stable form of monosaccharides, which has five or six atoms. The cyclic structure forms by a reaction between an —OH on carbon 5 of hexoses and the carbonyl group of the same molecule.
- The formation of a new hydroxyl group on carbon 1 (or 2 in fructose) gives α and β forms of the cyclic monosaccharide. Because the molecule opens and closes continuously in solution, both the α and β forms are present.

MasteringChemistry
Self Study Activity: Forms of Carbohydrates
Tutorial: Drawing Cyclic Sugars

Guide to Drawing Haworth Structures	
STEP 1	Turn the open chain structure clockwise 90 °.
STEP 2	Fold the chain into a hexagon and bond the O on carbon 5 to carbon 1 of the carbonyl group.
STEP 3	Draw the new –OH group on carbon 1 down to give the α anomer or up to give the β anomer.

◆ Learning Exercise 15.3

Draw the α anomer of the Haworth structure for each of the following:

1. D-glucose **2.** D-galactose **3.** D-fructose

Answers

1.

CH_2—OH
H O H
H
OH H
OH OH
H OH

2.

CH_2—OH
OH O H
H
OH H
H OH
H OH

3.

HO—CH_2 O CH_2—OH
H OH
H OH
OH H

15.4 Chemical Properties of Monosaccharides

- Monosaccharides contain functional groups that undergo oxidation or reduction.
- Monosaccharides are called *reducing sugars* because the aldehyde group (also available in ketoses) is oxidized by a metal ion such as Cu^{2+} in Benedict's solution, which is reduced.
- Monosaccharides are also reduced to give sugar alcohols.

MasteringChemistry
Case Study: Diabetes and Blood Glucose

◆ Learning Exercise 15.4

What changes occur when a reducing sugar reacts with Benedict's reagent?

Answers The carbonyl group of the reducing sugar is oxidized to a carboxylic acid group; the Cu^{2+} ion in Benedict's reagent is reduced to Cu^{+}, which forms a brick-red solid of Cu_2O.

15.5 Disaccharides

- Disaccharides are two monosaccharide units joined together by a glycosidic bond:

$$\text{monosaccharide }(1) + \text{monosaccharide }(2) \rightarrow \text{disaccharide} + H_2O$$

- In the most common disaccharides, maltose, lactose, and sucrose, there is at least one glucose unit.
- In the disaccharide maltose, two glucose units are linked by an α-1,4 bond. The α-1,4 indicates that the —OH on carbon 1 of alpha-D-glucose is bonded to carbon 4 of the other glucose molecule.
- When a disaccharide is hydrolyzed by water, the products are a glucose unit and one other monosaccharide.

$$\text{Maltose} + H_2O \rightarrow \text{glucose} + \text{glucose}$$

$$\text{Lactose} + H_2O \rightarrow \text{glucose} + \text{galactose}$$

$$\text{Sucrose} + H_2O \rightarrow \text{glucose} + \text{fructose}$$

◆ Learning Exercise 15.5

a. What is a glycosidic bond?

b. For the following disaccharides, state (a) the monosaccharide units, (b) the type of glycosidic bond, and (c) the name of the disaccharide:

1.

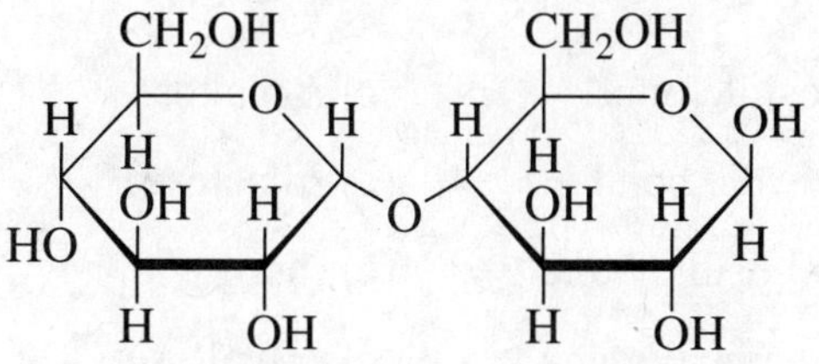

CH_2OH CH_2OH
H O H H O OH
H H
OH H O OH H
HO H
H OH H OH

2.

$CH_2—OH$
$CH_2—OH$ H O H
O H
OH H O OH H
H OH
OH H H
H H OH
H OH

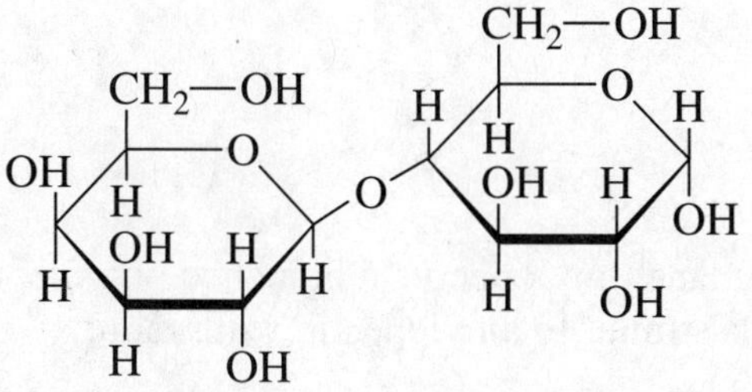

	a. Monosaccharide(s)	**b.** Type of glycosidic bond	**c.** Name of disaccharide
1.			
2.			

3.

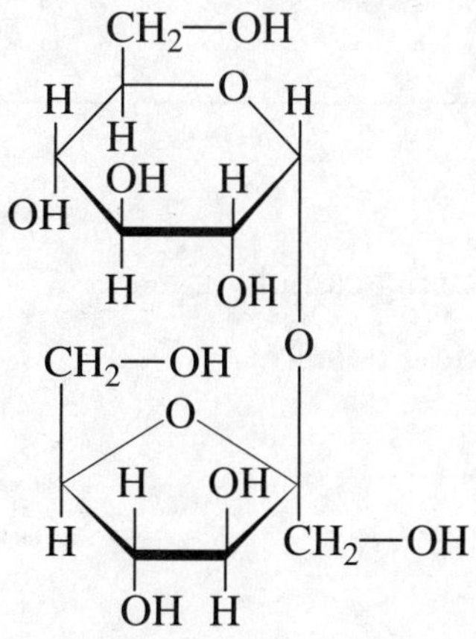

$CH_2—OH$
H O H
H
OH H
OH
H OH
$CH_2—OH$ O
O
H OH
H $CH_2—OH$
OH H

4.

CH_2OH CH_2OH
H O H H O H
H H
OH H O OH H
HO OH
H OH H OH

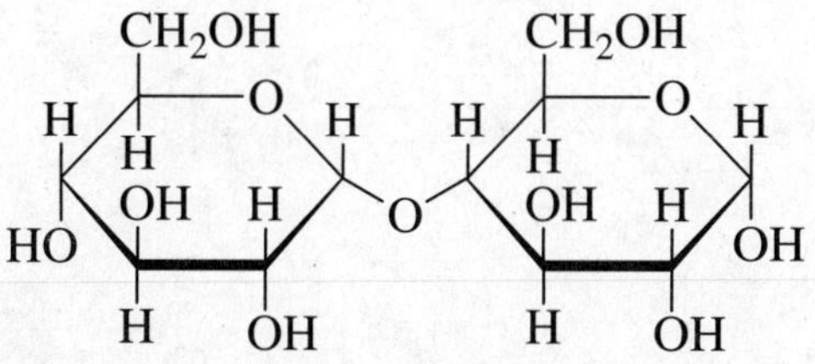

	a. Monosaccharide units	**b.** Type of glycosidic bond	**c.** Name of disaccharide
3.			
4.			

Answers **a.** A glycosidic bond forms between the —OH of a sugar and the —OH of another compound, usually another sugar.

b. 1. (a) two glucose units **(b)** α-1,4-glycosidic bond **(c)** β-maltose

2. (a) galactose + glucose **(b)** β-1,4-glycosidic bond **(c)** α-lactose

3. (a) fructose + glucose **(b)** α, β-1,2 glycosidic bond **(c)** sucrose

4. (a) two glucose units **(b)** α-1,4-glycosidic bond **(c)** α-maltose

15.6 Polysaccharides

- Polysaccharides are polymers of monosaccharide units.
- Starches consist of amylose, an unbranched chain of glucose, and amylopectin, a branched polymer of glucose. Glycogen, the storage form of glucose in animals, is similar to amylopectin, with more branching.
- Cellulose is also a polymer of glucose, but in cellulose the glycosidic bonds are β bonds rather than α bonds as in the starches. Humans can digest starches to obtain energy but not cellulose. However, cellulose is important as a source of fiber in our diets.

MasteringChemistry

Self Study Activity: Forms of Carbohydrates

Self Study Activity: Polymers

◆ Learning Exercise 15.6

List the monosaccharides and describe the glycosidic bonds in each of the following carbohydrates:

	Monosaccharides	Type(s) of glycosidic bonds
1. amylose	______________	______________
2. amylopectin	______________	______________
3. glycogen	______________	______________
4. Cellulose	______________	______________

Answers

1. glucose; α-1,4-glycosidic bonds
2. glucose; α-1,4- and α-1,6-glycosidic bonds
3. glucose; α-1,4- and α-1,6-glycosidic bonds
4. glucose; β-1,4-glycosidic bonds

Checklist for Chapter 15

You are ready to take the Practice Test for Chapter 15. Be sure that you have accomplished the following learning goals for this chapter. If you are not sure, review the section listed at the end of the goal. Then apply your new skills and understanding to the practice test.

After studying Chapter 15, I can successfully:

____ Classify carbohydrates as monosaccharides, disaccharides, and polysaccharides (15.1).

____ Classify a monosaccharide as aldose or ketose and indicate the number of carbon atoms (15.1).

____ Draw and identify D– and L– Fischer projections for carbohydrate molecules (15.2).

____ Draw the open-chain structures for D–glucose, D–galactose, and D–fructose (15.2).

____ Draw or identify the cyclic structures of monosaccharides (15.3).

____ Describe some chemical properties of carbohydrates (15.4).

____ Describe the monosaccharide units and linkages in disaccharides (15.5).

____ Describe the structural features of amylose, amylopectin, glycogen, and cellulose (15.6).

Practice Test for Chapter 15

1. The requirements for photosynthesis are

A. sun
B. sun and water
C. water and carbon dioxide
D. sun, water, and carbon dioxide
E. carbon dioxide and sun

2. What are the products of photosynthesis?

A. carbohydrates
B. carbohydrates and oxygen
C. carbon dioxide and oxygen
D. carbohydrates and carbon dioxide
E. water and oxygen

3. The name "carbohydrate" came from the fact that

A. carbohydrates are hydrates of water
B. carbohydrates contain hydrogen and oxygen in a 2:1 ratio
C. carbohydrates contain a great quantity of water
D. all plants produce carbohydrates
E. carbon and hydrogen atoms are abundant in carbohydrates.

4. What functional groups are in the open-chain forms of monosaccharides?

A. hydroxyl groups
B. aldehyde groups
C. ketone groups
D. hydroxyl and aldehyde or ketone groups
E. hydroxyl and ether groups

5. What is the classification of the following sugar?

$$\begin{array}{l} CH_2OH \\ | \\ C{=}O \\ | \\ CH_2OH \end{array}$$

A. aldotriose **B.** ketotriose **C.** aldotetrose **D.** ketotetrose **E.** ketopentose

For questions 6 through 10, refer to the following monosaccharide:

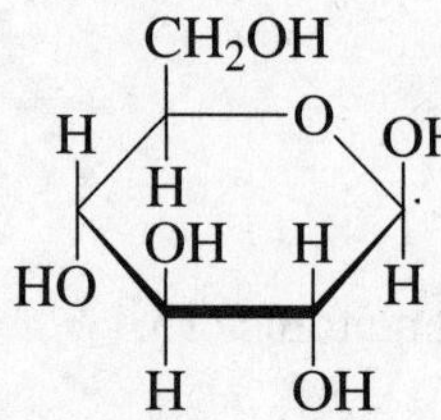

6. It is the cyclic structure of a(n)

A. aldotriose **B.** ketopentose **C.** aldopentose **D.** aldohexose **E.** aldoheptose

7. This is a Haworth structure of

A. fructose **B.** glucose **C.** ribose **D.** glyceraldehyde **E.** galactose

8. It is at least one of the products of the complete hydrolysis of

A. maltose **B.** sucrose **C.** lactose **D.** glycogen **E.** all of these

9. A Benedict's test with this sugar would

A. be positive
B. be negative
C. produce a blue precipitate
D. give no color change
E. produce a silver mirror

10. It is the monosaccharide unit used to build polymers of

A. amylose **B.** amylopectin **C.** cellulose **D.** glycogen **E.** all of these

For questions 11 through 15, identify each carbohydrate described as one of the following:

A. maltose **B.** sucrose **C.** cellulose **D.** amylopectin **E.** glycogen

11. ____ a disaccharide that is not a reducing sugar

12. ____ a disaccharide that occurs as a breakdown product of amylose

13. ____ a carbohydrate that is produced as a storage form of energy in plants

14. ____ the storage form of energy in humans

15. ____ a carbohydrate that is used for structural purposes by plants

For questions 16 through 20, select an answer from the following:

A. amylose **B.** cellulose **C.** glycogen **D.** lactose **E.** sucrose

16. ____ a polysaccharide composed of many glucose units linked by α-1,4-glycosidic bonds

17. ____ a sugar containing both glucose and galactose

18. ____ a sugar composed of glucose units joined by both α-1,4- and α-1,6-glycosidic bonds

19. ____ a disaccharide that is a reducing sugar

20. ____ a carbohydrate composed of glucose units joined by β-1,4-glycosidic bonds

For questions 21 through 25, select an answer from the following:

A. glucose **B.** lactose **C.** sucrose **D.** maltose

21. ____ a sugar composed of glucose and fructose

22. ____ also called table sugar

23. ____ found in milk and milk products

24. ____ gives sorbitol upon reduction

25. ____ gives galactose upon hydrolysis

Answers to the Practice Test

1. D	**2.** B	**3.** B	**4.** D	**5.** B
6. D	**7.** B	**8.** E	**9.** A	**10.** E
11. B	**12.** A	**13.** D	**14.** E	**15.** C
16. A	**17.** D	**18.** C	**19.** D	**20.** B
21. C	**22.** C	**23.** B	**24.** A	**25.** B

16

Carboxylic Acids and Esters

Study Goals

- Name and draw condensed structural formulas of carboxylic acids and esters.
- Describe the boiling points and solubility of carboxylic acids.
- Write equations for the ionization of carboxylic acids in water.
- Write equations for the esterification, hydrolysis, and saponification of esters.

Think About It

1. Why do vinegar and citrus juices taste sour?

2. What type of compound gives flowers and fruits their pleasant aromas?

Key Terms

Match the key term with the correct statement shown below.

a. carboxylic acid　**b.** saponification　**c.** esterification
d. hydrolysis　**e.** ester

1. ____ An organic compound containing the carboxyl group (—COOH)
2. ____ A reaction of a carboxylic acid and an alcohol in the presence of an acid catalyst
3. ____ A type of organic compound that produces pleasant aromas in flowers and fruits
4. ____ The hydrolysis of an ester with a strong base producing a salt of the carboxylic acid and an alcohol
5. ____ The splitting of a molecule such as an ester by the addition of water in the presence of an acid

Answers　**1.** a　**2.** c　**3.** e　**4.** b　**5.** d

16.1 Carboxylic Acids

- In the IUPAC system, a carboxylic acid is named by replacing the *ane* ending of the carbon chain that contains the carboxyl group with *oic acid.* Simple acids usually are named by the common naming system using the prefixes **form** (1C), **acet** (2C), **propion** (3C), or **butyr** (4C), followed by ***ic acid***.

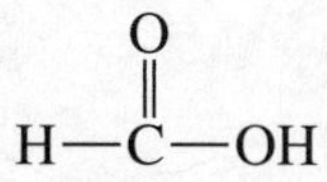

$$H-\overset{\overset{\large O}{\|}}{C}-OH \qquad CH_3-\overset{\overset{\large O}{\|}}{C}-OH \qquad CH_3-CH_2-CH_2-\overset{\overset{\large O}{\|}}{C}-OH$$

Methanoic acid (formic acid) — Ethanoic acid (acetic acid) — Butanoic acid (butyric acid)

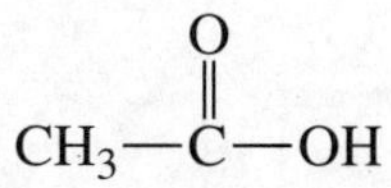

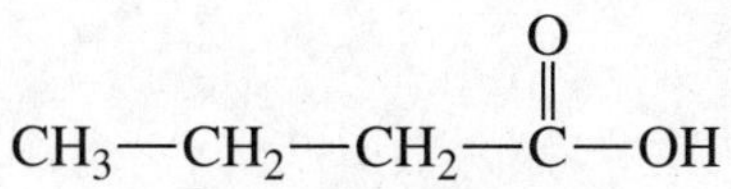

- A carboxylic acid can be prepared by the oxidation of a primary alcohol or an aldehyde.

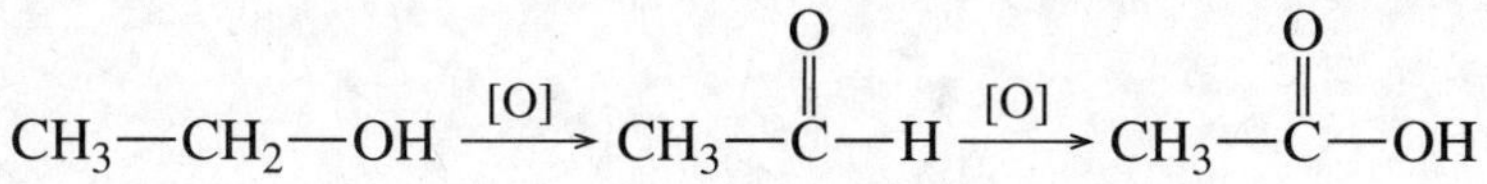

$$CH_3-CH_2-OH \xrightarrow{[O]} CH_3-\overset{\overset{\large O}{\|}}{C}-H \xrightarrow{[O]} CH_3-\overset{\overset{\large O}{\|}}{C}-OH$$

MasteringChemistry

Self Study Activity: Carboxylic Acids

Tutorial: Naming and Drawing Carboxylic Acids

Guide to Naming Carboxylic Acids	
STEP 1	Identify the longest carbon chain containing the carboxyl group and replace the *e* in the alkane name with *oic acid.*
STEP 2	Give the location and names of any substituents on the carbon chain.

◆ Learning Exercise 16.1A

Give the IUPAC and common names for each of the following carboxylic acids:

1. 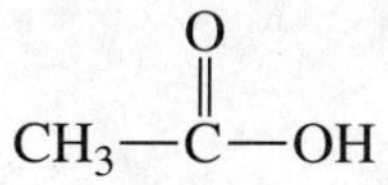 $CH_3-\overset{\overset{\large O}{\|}}{C}-OH$

2. $CH_3-\overset{\overset{\large OH}{|}}{CH}-\overset{\overset{\large O}{\|}}{C}-OH$

3. $CH_3-\overset{\overset{\large CH_3}{|}}{CH}-CH_2-\overset{\overset{\large O}{\|}}{C}-OH$

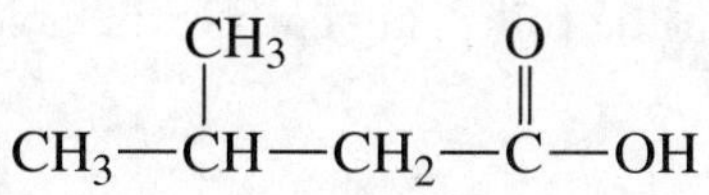

4. 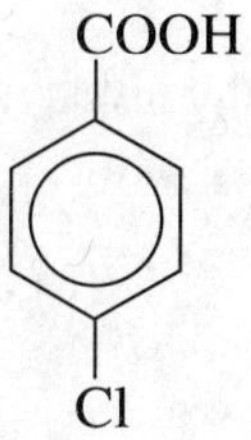 (benzene ring with COOH at top and Cl at bottom)

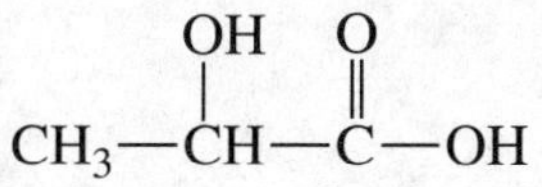

Answers

1. ethanoic acid (acetic acid)
2. 2-hydroxypropanoic acid (α-hydroxypropionic acid)
3. 3-methylbutanoic acid (β-methylbutyric acid)
4. 4-chlorobenzoic acid (*p*-chlorobenzoic acid)

◆ Learning Exercise 16.1B

Draw the condensed structural formulas for each of the following carboxylic acids:

1. acetic acid

2. 2-ketobutanoic acid

3. benzoic acid

4. *β*-hydroxypropionic acid

5. formic acid

6. 3-methylpentanoic acid

Answers

1. $CH_3-\overset{\overset{\displaystyle O}{\|}}{C}-OH$

2. $CH_3-CH_2-\overset{\overset{\displaystyle O}{\|}}{C}-\overset{\overset{\displaystyle O}{\|}}{C}-OH$

3. 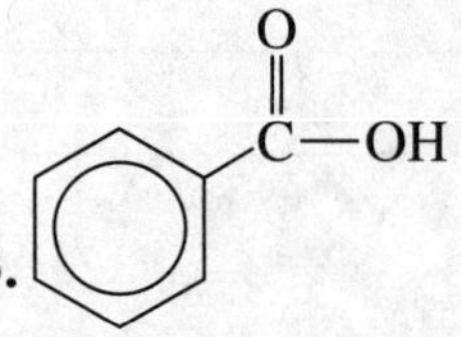 $C_6H_5-\overset{\overset{\displaystyle O}{\|}}{C}-OH$ (benzene ring bearing the carboxyl group)

4. $HO-CH_2-CH_2-\overset{\overset{\displaystyle O}{\|}}{C}-OH$

5. $H-\overset{\overset{\displaystyle O}{\|}}{C}-OH$

6. $CH_3-CH_2-\overset{\overset{\displaystyle CH_3}{|}}{CH}-CH_2-\overset{\overset{\displaystyle O}{\|}}{C}-OH$

◆ Learning Exercise 16.1C

Draw the condensed structural formula of the aldehyde that produces each of the following carboxylic acids by oxidation:

1. propanoic acid

2. *β*-methylbutyric acid

Answers

1. $CH_3-CH_2-\overset{\overset{\displaystyle O}{\|}}{C}-H$

2. $CH_3-\overset{\overset{\displaystyle CH_3}{|}}{CH}-CH_2-\overset{\overset{\displaystyle O}{\|}}{C}-H$

16.2 Properties of Carboxylic Acids

- Carboxylic acids have higher boiling points than other polar compounds such as alcohols.
- Because they have two polar groups, two carboxylic acids form a dimer, which contains two sets of hydrogen bonds.
- Carboxylic acids with one to four carbon atoms are very soluble in water.
- As weak acids, carboxylic acids ionize slightly in water to form acidic solutions of H_3O^+ and a carboxylate ion.
- When bases neutralize carboxylic acids, the products are carboxylic acid salts and water.

MasteringChemistry

Tutorial: Properties of Carboxylic Acids

◆ Learning Exercise 16.2A

Indicate whether each of the following carboxylic acids is soluble in water:

1. _______ hexanoic acid **2.** _______ acetic acid **3.** _______ propanoic acid

4. _______ benzoic acid **5.** _______ formic acid **6.** _______ octanoic acid

Answers **1.** no **2.** yes **3.** yes **4.** no **5.** yes **6.** no

◆ Learning Exercise 16.2B

Identify the compound in each pair that has the higher boiling point.

1. acetic acid or butyric acid **2.** propanoic acid or 2-propanol

3. propanoic acid or propanone **4.** acetic acid or acetaldehyde

Answers **1.** butyric acid **2.** propanoic acid
3. propanoic acid **4.** acetic acid

◆ Learning Exercise 16.2C

Draw the structural formulas of the products from the ionization of each of the following carboxylic acids in water:

1. $CH_3—CH_2—\overset{\overset{\large O}{\|}}{C}—OH + H_2O \rightleftarrows$

2. benzoic acid + $H_2O \rightleftarrows$

Answers 1. $CH_3—CH_2—\overset{\overset{\large O}{\|}}{C}—O^- + H_3O^+$ 2. 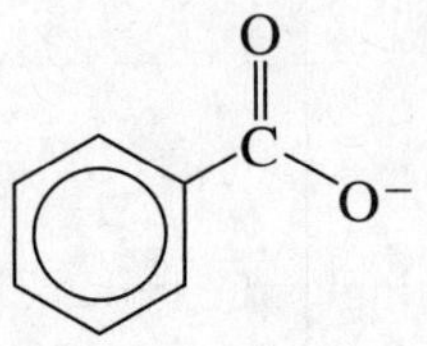 $C_6H_5—\overset{\overset{\large O}{\|}}{C}—O^-$ + H_3O^+

◆ Learning Exercise 16.2D

Draw the condensed structural formulas and write the names for the products from each of the following reactions:

1. $CH_3—CH_2—\overset{\overset{\large O}{\|}}{C}—OH + NaOH \longrightarrow$

2. formic acid + KOH →

Answers 1. $CH_3—CH_2—\overset{\overset{\large O}{\|}}{C}—O^-Na^+ + H_2O$
Sodium propanoate
(sodium propionate)

2. $H—\overset{\overset{\large O}{\|}}{C}—O^-K^+ + H_2O$
Potassium methanoate
(potassium formate)

16.3 Esters

- In the presence of a strong acid, carboxylic acids react with alcohols to produce esters and water.

MasteringChemistry
Tutorial: Formation of Esters from Carboxylic Acids
Tutorial: Writing Esterification Equations

◆ Learning Exercise 16.3

Draw the condensed structural formulas of the products of each of the following reactions:

1. $CH_3-\overset{\overset{O}{\|}}{C}-OH + CH_3-OH \overset{H^+}{\rightleftharpoons}$

2. $H-\overset{\overset{O}{\|}}{C}-OH + CH_3-CH_2-OH \overset{H^+}{\rightleftharpoons}$

3. 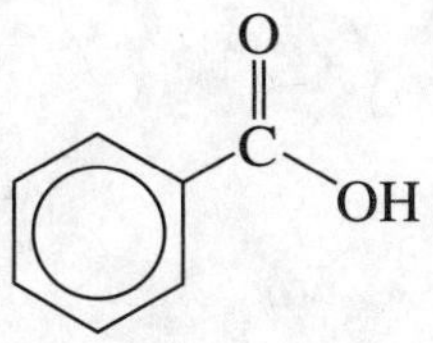 $C_6H_5-\overset{\overset{O}{\|}}{C}-OH + HO-CH_3 \overset{H^+}{\rightleftharpoons}$

4. Propanoic acid and ethanol $\overset{H^+}{\rightleftharpoons}$

Answers

1. $CH_3-\overset{\overset{O}{\|}}{C}-O-CH_3 + H_2O$

2. $H-\overset{\overset{O}{\|}}{C}-O-CH_2-CH_3 + H_2O$

3. $C_6H_5-\overset{\overset{O}{\|}}{C}-O-CH_3 + H_2O$

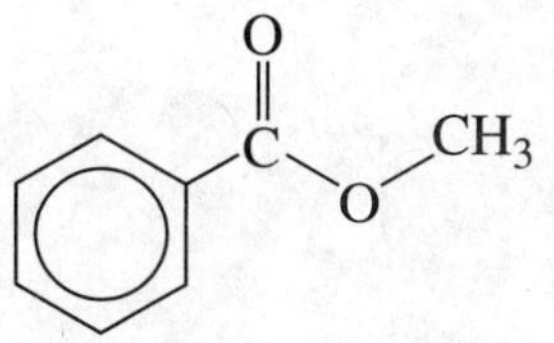

4. $CH_3-CH_2-\overset{\overset{O}{\|}}{C}-O-CH_2-CH_3 + H_2O$

16.4 Naming Esters

- The names of esters consist of two words, one from the alcohol and the other from the carboxylic acid, with the *ic acid* ending replaced by *ate.*

$CH_3-\overset{\overset{O}{\|}}{C}-O-CH_3$ methyl ethanoate (IUPAC) or methyl acetate (common)

Guide to Naming Esters	
STEP 1	Write the name of the carbon chain from the alcohol named as an *alkyl*.
STEP 2	Change the *ic acid* part of the carboxylic acid name to *ate*.

MasteringChemistry

Tutorial: Naming Esters

◆ Learning Exercise 16.4A

Name each of the following esters:

1. $CH_3-\overset{O}{\overset{\|}{C}}-O-CH_2-CH_3$

2. $CH_3-CH_2-CH_2-\overset{O}{\overset{\|}{C}}-O-CH_3$

3. $CH_3-CH_2-\overset{O}{\overset{\|}{C}}-O-CH_2-\overset{OH}{\overset{|}{C}H}-CH_3$

4. 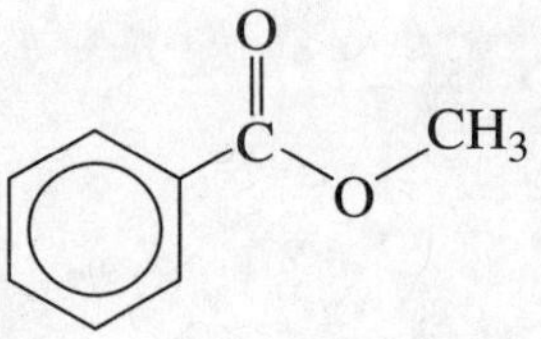 $C_6H_5-\overset{O}{\overset{\|}{C}}-O-CH_3$

Answers **1.** ethyl ethanoate (ethyl acetate)
2. methyl butanoate (methyl butyrate)
3. 2-hydroxypropyl propanoate (2-hydroxypropyl propionate)
4. methyl benzoate

◆ Learning Exercise 16.4B

Draw the condensed structural formulas for each of the following esters:

1. propyl acetate

2. ethyl butyrate

3. ethyl propanoate

4. ethyl benzoate

Answers: **1.** $CH_3{-}\overset{\overset{\Large O}{\|}}{C}{-}O{-}CH_2{-}CH_2{-}CH_3$ **2.** $CH_3{-}CH_2{-}CH_2{-}\overset{\overset{\Large O}{\|}}{C}{-}O{-}CH_2{-}CH_3$

3. $CH_3{-}CH_2{-}\overset{\overset{\Large O}{\|}}{C}{-}O{-}CH_2{-}CH_3$ **4.** 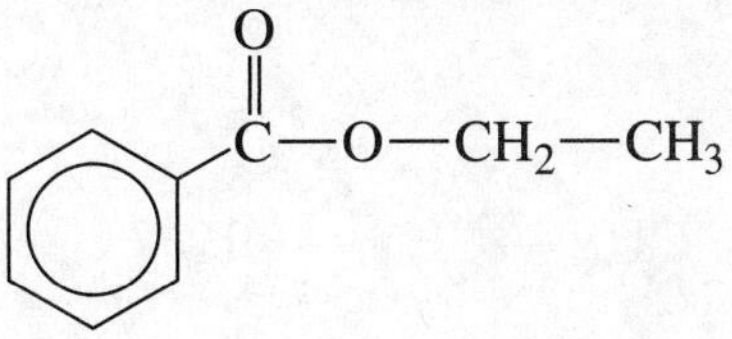 $C_6H_5{-}\overset{\overset{\Large O}{\|}}{C}{-}O{-}CH_2{-}CH_3$

16.5 Properties of Esters

- Esters have higher boiling points than alkanes but lower than alcohols and carboxylic acids of similar mass.
- In hydrolysis, esters are split apart by a reaction with water. When the catalyst is an acid, the products are a carboxylic acid salt and an alcohol.

$$CH_3{-}\overset{\overset{O}{\|}}{C}{-}O{-}CH_3 + H_2O \overset{H^+}{\rightleftharpoons} CH_3{-}\overset{\overset{O}{\|}}{C}{-}OH + HO{-}CH_3$$

Methyl ethanoate (methyl acetate) — Ethanoic acid (acetic acid) — Methanol (methyl alcohol)

- Saponification is the hydrolysis of an ester in the presence of a base, which produces a carboxylate salt and an alcohol.

$$CH_3{-}\overset{\overset{O}{\|}}{C}{-}O{-}CH_3 + NaOH \longrightarrow CH_3{-}\overset{\overset{O}{\|}}{C}{-}O^-Na^+ + HO{-}CH_3$$

Methyl ethanoate (methyl acetate) — Sodium ethanoate (sodium acetate) — Methanol (methyl alcohol)

- In saponification, long-chain fatty acids from fats react with strong bases to produce salts of the fatty acids, which are soaps.

MasteringChemistry

Tutorial: Hydrolysis of Esters

◆ Learning Exercise 16.5A

Identify the compound with the higher boiling point in each of the following pairs of compounds:

1. $CH_3{-}CH_2{-}OH$ or $H{-}\overset{\overset{O}{\|}}{C}{-}O{-}CH_3$

2. $CH_3{-}\overset{\overset{O}{\|}}{C}{-}O{-}CH_3$ or $CH_3{-}\overset{\overset{OH}{|}}{CH}{-}CH_2{-}CH_3$

3. $CH_3—\overset{\overset{\displaystyle O}{\|}}{C}—O—CH_3$ or $CH_3—CH_2—CH_2—CH_2—CH_3$

Answers 1. $CH_3—CH_2—OH$ 2. $CH_3—\overset{\overset{\displaystyle OH}{|}}{CH}—CH_2—CH_3$

3. $CH_3—\overset{\overset{\displaystyle O}{\|}}{C}—O—CH_3$

◆ Learning Exercise 16.5B

Draw the condensed structural formulas for the products of hydrolysis or saponification for each of the following esters:

1. $CH_3—CH_2—CH_2—\overset{\overset{\displaystyle O}{\|}}{C}—O—CH_3 + H_2O \overset{H^+}{\rightleftharpoons}$

2. $CH_3—\overset{\overset{\displaystyle O}{\|}}{C}—O—CH_3 + NaOH \longrightarrow$

3. $C_6H_5—\overset{\overset{\displaystyle O}{\|}}{C}—O—CH_2—CH_3 + KOH \longrightarrow$

4. $C_6H_5—\overset{\overset{\displaystyle O}{\|}}{C}—O—CH_2—CH_2—CH_3 + H_2O \overset{H^+}{\rightleftharpoons}$

Answers 1. $CH_3—CH_2—CH_2—\overset{\overset{\displaystyle O}{\|}}{C}—OH + HO—CH_3$

2. $CH_3—\overset{\overset{\displaystyle O}{\|}}{C}—O^-Na^+ + CH_3—OH$

3. $C_6H_5-\overset{O}{\overset{\|}{C}}-O^-K^+ + HO-CH_2-CH_3$

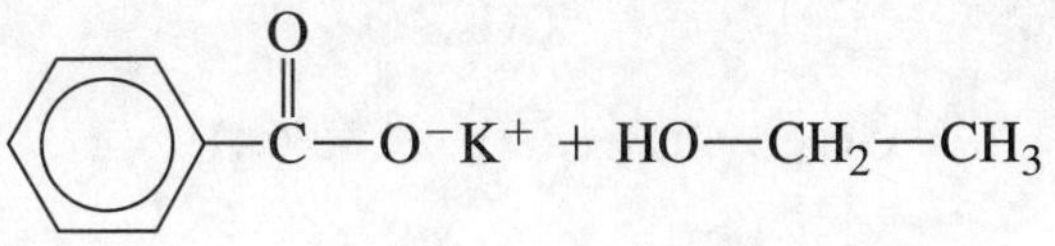

4. 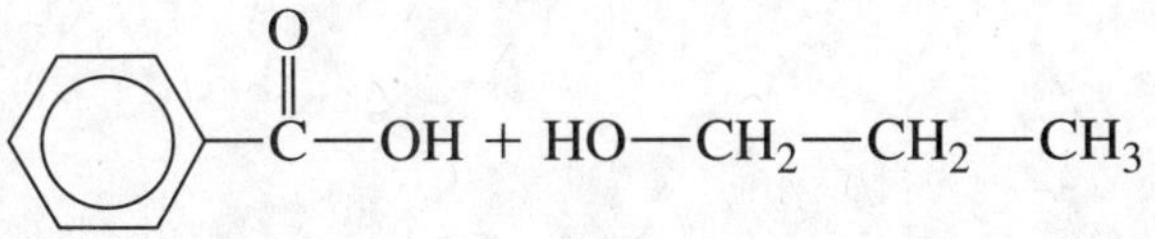 $C_6H_5-\overset{O}{\overset{\|}{C}}-OH + HO-CH_2-CH_2-CH_3$

Checklist for Chapter 16

You are ready to take the Practice Test for Chapter 16. Be sure that you have accomplished the following learning goals for this chapter. If you are not sure, review the section listed at the end of the goal. Then apply your new skills and understanding to the practice test.

After studying Chapter 16, I can successfully:

_____ Write the IUPAC and common names and draw condensed structural formulas of carboxylic acids (16.1).

_____ Describe the solubility and ionization of carboxylic acids in water (16.2).

_____ Describe the behavior of carboxylic acids as weak acids and draw the condensed structural formulas for the products of neutralization (16.2).

_____ Write equations for the preparation of esters (16.3).

_____ Write the IUPAC or common names and draw the condensed structural formulas of esters (16.4).

_____ Write equations for the hydrolysis and saponification of esters (16.5).

Practice Test for Chapter 16

For questions 1 through 5, match each condensed structural formula to its functional group.

A. alcohol **B.** aldehyde **C.** carboxylic acid **D.** ester **E.** ketone

1. ____ $CH_3-\underset{}{\overset{CH_3}{\overset{|}{C}H}}-CH_2-OH$

2. ____ $CH_3-CH_2-\overset{O}{\overset{\|}{C}}-H$

3. ____ $CH_3-\overset{O}{\overset{\|}{C}}-CH_2-CH_3$

4. ____ $CH_3-CH_2-\overset{O}{\overset{\|}{C}}-OH$

5. ____ $CH_3-\overset{O}{\overset{\|}{C}}-O-CH_3$

For questions 6 through 10, match the names of the compounds with their condensed structural formulas.

A. $CH_3-\overset{O}{\overset{\|}{C}}-O-CH_2-CH_3$

B. $CH_3-CH_2-CH_2-\overset{O}{\overset{\|}{C}}-O^-Na^+$

C. $CH_3-\overset{\overset{\large O}{\|}}{C}-O^-Na^+$

D. $CH_3-CH_2-\underset{}{\overset{\overset{\large CH_3}{|}}{CH}}-\overset{\overset{\large O}{\|}}{C}-OH$

E. $CH_3-CH_2-\overset{\overset{\large O}{\|}}{C}-O-CH_3$

6. _____ α-methylbutyric acid

7. _____ methyl propanoate

8. _____ sodium butanoate

9. _____ ethyl acetate

10. _____ sodium acetate

11. An aldehyde can be oxidized to give a(n)

A. alcohol **B.** ketone **C.** carboxylic acid **D.** ester **E.** no reaction

12. What is the product when a carboxylic acid reacts with sodium hydroxide?

A. carboxylic acid salt **B.** alcohol **C.** ester
D. aldehyde **E.** no reaction

13. Carboxylic acids are water soluble due to their

A. nonpolar nature **B.** ionic bonds **C.** ability to lower pH
D. ability to hydrogen bond **E.** high melting points

For questions 14 through 17, refer to the following reactions:

A. $CH_3-\overset{\overset{\large O}{\|}}{C}-OH + CH_3-OH \overset{H^+}{\rightleftharpoons} CH_3-\overset{\overset{\large O}{\|}}{C}-O-CH_3 + H_2O$

B. $CH_3-\overset{\overset{\large O}{\|}}{C}-OH + NaOH \longrightarrow CH_3-\overset{\overset{\large O}{\|}}{C}-O^-Na^+ + H_2O$

C. $CH_3-\overset{\overset{\large O}{\|}}{C}-O-CH_3 + H_2O \overset{H^+}{\rightleftharpoons} CH_3-\overset{\overset{\large O}{\|}}{C}-OH + CH_3-OH$

D. $CH_3-\overset{\overset{\large O}{\|}}{C}-O-CH_3 + NaOH \longrightarrow CH_3-\overset{\overset{\large O}{\|}}{C}-O^-Na^+ + CH_3-OH$

14. _____ is an ester hydrolysis

15. _____ is a neutralization

16. _____ is a saponification

17. _____ is an esterification

18. What is the name of the organic product in the following reaction?

$$CH_3-\overset{\overset{\large O}{\|}}{C}-OH + CH_3-OH \overset{H^+}{\rightleftharpoons} CH_3-\overset{\overset{\large O}{\|}}{C}-O-CH_3 + H_2O$$

A. methyl acetate **B.** acetic acid **C.** methyl alcohol
D. acetaldehyde **E.** ethyl methanoate

19. The compound with the highest boiling point is

A. formic acid **B.** acetic acid **C.** propanol
D. propanoic acid **E.** ethyl acetate

20. The ester produced from the reaction of 1-butanol and propanoic acid is

A. butyl propanoate **B.** butyl propanone **C.** propyl butyrate
D. propyl butanone **E.** heptanoate

21. The reaction of methyl acetate with NaOH produces

A. ethanol and formic acid
B. ethanol and sodium formate
C. ethanol and sodium ethanoate
D. methanol and acetic acid
E. methanol and sodium acetate

22. Identify the carboxylic acid and alcohol needed to produce

$$CH_3-CH_2-CH_2-\overset{\overset{\large O}{\|}}{C}-O-CH_2-CH_3$$

A. propanoic acid and ethanol **B.** acetic acid and 1-pentanol
C. acetic acid and 1-butanol **D.** butanoic acid and ethanol
E. hexanoic acid and methanol

23. When butanal is oxidized, the product is

A. butanone **B.** 1-butanol **C.** 2-butanol
D. butanoic acid **E.** butane

24. The name of $CH_3-CH_2-\overset{\overset{\large O}{\|}}{C}-O-CH_2-CH_3$ is

A. ethyl acetate **B.** ethyl ethanoate **C.** ethyl propanoate
D. propyl ethanoate **E.** ethyl butyrate

25. Soaps are

A. long-chain fatty acids **B.** fatty acid salts
C. esters of acetic acid **D.** alcohols with 10 carbon atoms
E. aromatic compounds

26. In a hydrolysis reaction

A. an acid reacts with an alcohol
B. an ester reacts with NaOH
C. an ester reacts with H_2O
D. an acid neutralizes a base
E. water is added to an alkene

27. Esters

A. have pleasant odors
B. can undergo hydrolysis
C. are formed from alcohols and carboxylic acids
D. have a lower boiling point than the corresponding acid
E. all of the above

28. The products of the following reaction are:

$$H-\overset{\overset{\large O}{\|}}{C}-OH + H_2O \xrightarrow{H^+}$$

A. $H-\overset{\overset{O}{\|}}{C}-O^- + H_3O^+$

B. $H-\overset{\overset{O}{\|}}{C}-\overset{+}{O}H_2 + OH^-$

C. $H-\overset{\overset{O}{\|}}{C}-O-CH_3$

D. $CH_3-\overset{\overset{O}{\|}}{C}-OH$

E. $H-\overset{\overset{O}{\|}}{C}-O^-Na^+ + H_2O$

29. The name of the following compound is:

(benzene ring with $\overset{\overset{O}{\|}}{C}-OH$ and Cl)

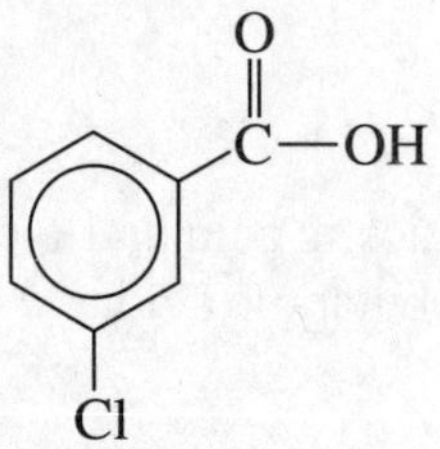

A. *p*-chlorobenzoic acid
B. chlorobenzoic acid
C. *m*-chlorobenzoic acid
D. 4-chlorobenzoic acid
E. benzoic acid chloride

30. The name of the following compound is:

(benzene ring with $\overset{\overset{O}{\|}}{C}-O^-Na^+$)

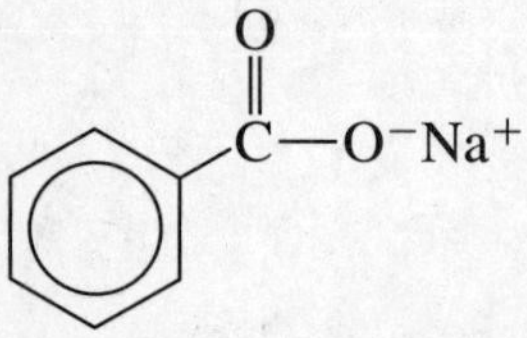

A. benzene sodium
B. sodium benzoate
C. *o*-benzoic acid
D. sodium benzene carboxylate
E. benzoic acid

Answers to the Practice Test

1. A	**2.** B	**3.** E	**4.** C	**5.** D
6. D	**7.** E	**8.** B	**9.** A	**10.** C
11. C	**12.** A	**13.** D	**14.** C	**15.** B
16. D	**17.** A	**18.** A	**19.** D	**20.** A
21. E	**22.** D	**23.** D	**24.** C	**25.** B
26. C	**27.** E	**28.** A	**29.** C	**30.** B

17
Lipids

Study Goals

- Describe the properties and types of lipids.
- Draw the condensed structural formulas of triacylglycerols obtained from glycerol and fatty acids.
- Draw the condensed structural formula of the product from hydrogenation, hydrolysis, and saponification of triacylglycerols.
- Distinguish between phospholipids, glycolipids, and sphingolipids.
- Describe steroids and their role in bile salts, vitamins, and hormones.
- Describe the lipid bilayer in a cell.

Think About It

1. What are fats used for in the body?

2. What foods are high in fat?

3. What oils are used to produce margarines?

4. What kind of lipid is cholesterol?

Key Terms

Match each of the following key terms with the correct statement shown below:

a. lipid **b.** fatty acid **c.** triacylglycerol
d. saponification **e.** glycerophospholipid **f.** steroid

1. ____ a lipid consisting of glycerol bonded to two fatty acids and a phosphoryl group attached to an amino alcohol

2. ____ a type of compound that is not soluble in water, but in nonpolar solvents

3. ____ the hydrolysis of a triacylglycerol with a strong base producing salts called soaps and glycerol

4. ____ a lipid consisting of glycerol bonded to three fatty acids

5. ____ a lipid composed of a multicyclic ring system

6. ____ a long-chain carboxylic acid found in triacylglycerols

Answers **1.** e **2.** a **3.** d **4.** c **5.** f **6.** b

17.1 Lipids

- Lipids are nonpolar compounds that are not soluble in water.
- Classes of lipids include waxes, triacylglycerols, glycerophospholipids, sphingolipids, glycosphingolipids, and steroids.

MasteringChemistry

Tutorial: Classes of Lipids

◆ Learning Exercise 17.1

Match one of the classes of lipids with the composition of lipids below:

a. wax **b.** triacylglycerol **c.** glycerophospholipid
d. sphingolipid **e.** glycosphingolipid **f.** steroid

1. ____ a fused structure of four cycloalkanes

2. ____ a long chain alcohol and a fatty acid

3. ____ glycerol and three fatty acids

4. ____ glycerol, two fatty acids, phosphate, and choline

5. ____ sphingosine, fatty acid, and galactose

6. ____ sphingosine, fatty acid, phosphate, and choline

Answers **1.** f **2.** a **3.** b **4.** c **5.** e **6.** d

17.2 Fatty Acids

- Fatty acids are unbranched carboxylic acids that typically contain an even number (12–20) of carbon atoms.
- Fatty acids may be saturated, monounsaturated with one double bond, or polyunsaturated with two or more carbon–carbon double bonds. The double bonds in naturally occurring unsaturated fatty acids are almost always cis.

MasteringChemistry
Tutorial: Structures and Properties of Fatty Acids
Self Study Activity: Fats

◆ Learning Exercise 17.2A

Draw the condensed structural formulas of each of the following fatty acids:

A. linoleic acid

B. stearic acid

C. oleic acid

Answers

A. Linoleic acid $CH_3{-}(CH_2)_4{-}CH{=}CH{-}CH_2{-}CH{=}CH{-}(CH_2)_7{-}\overset{\overset{\displaystyle O}{\|}}{C}{-}OH$

B. Stearic acid $CH_3{-}(CH_2)_{16}{-}\overset{\overset{\displaystyle O}{\|}}{C}{-}OH$

C. Oleic acid $CH_3{-}(CH_2)_7{-}CH{=}CH{-}(CH_2)_7{-}\overset{\overset{\displaystyle O}{\|}}{C}{-}OH$

◆ Learning Exercise 17.2B

For each of the fatty acids in Learning Exercise 17.2 A, identify which one:

1. _______ is the most saturated

2. _______ is the most unsaturated

3. _______ has the lowest melting point

4. _______ has the highest melting point

5. _______ is found in vegetables

6. _______ is from animal sources

Answers **1.** B **2.** A **3.** A **4.** B **5.** A, C **6.** B

◆ Learning Exercise 17.2C

For the following questions, refer to the line-bond formula for oleic acid:

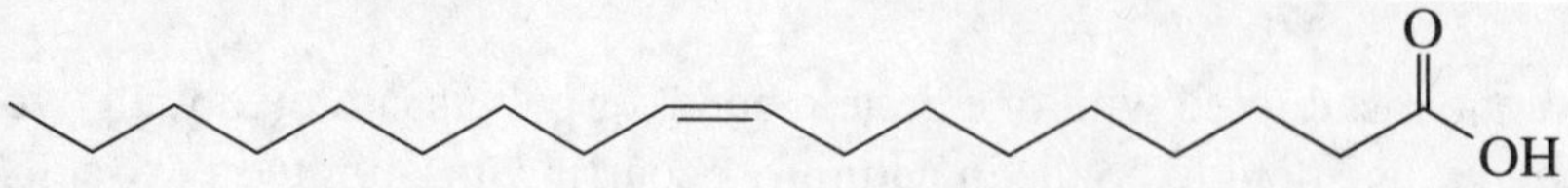

1. Why is the compound an acid?

2. Is it a saturated or unsaturated compound? Why?

3. Is the double bond cis or trans?

4. Is it likely to be a solid or a liquid at room temperature?

5. Why is it not soluble in water?

Answers
1. contains a carboxylic acid group
2. unsaturated; double bond
3. cis
4. liquid
5. it has a long hydrocarbon chain

17.3 Waxes, Fats, and Oils

- A wax is an ester of a long-chain saturated fatty acid and a long-chain alcohol.
- The triacylglycerols in fats and oils are esters of glycerol with three long-chain fatty acids.
- Fats from animal sources contain more saturated fatty acids and have higher melting points than fats found in most vegetable oils.

MasteringChemistry

Tutorial: Triacylglycerols

◆ Learning Exercise 17.3A

Draw the condensed structural formula of the wax formed by the reaction of palmitic acid, CH3— $(CH_2)_{14}$—COOH, and cetyl alcohol, CH_3— $(CH_2)_{14}$—CH_2—OH.

Answer $CH_3-(CH_2)_{14}-\overset{\overset{\displaystyle O}{\|}}{C}-O-CH_2-(CH_2)_{14}-CH_3$

◆ Learning Exercise 17.3B

Draw the condensed structural formula and name of the triacylglycerol formed from the following:

1. glycerol and three palmitic acid molecules, $CH_3—(CH_2)_{14}—COOH$

2. glycerol and three myristic acid molecules, $CH_3—(CH_2)_{12}—COOH$

Answers

1.

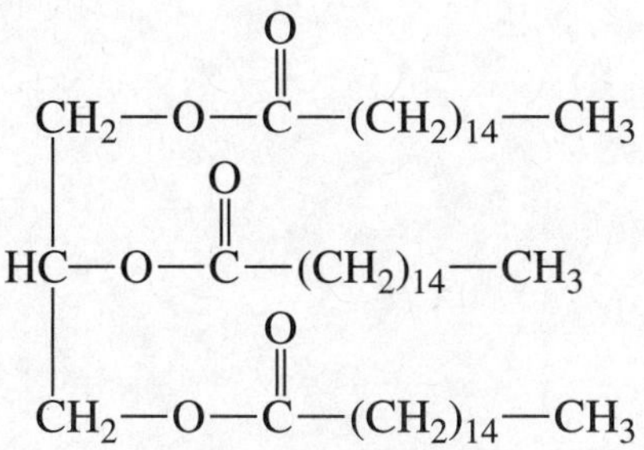

$$\begin{array}{l} CH_2—O—\overset{\displaystyle O}{\overset{\|}{C}}—(CH_2)_{14}—CH_3 \\ | \\ HC—O—\overset{\displaystyle O}{\overset{\|}{C}}—(CH_2)_{14}—CH_3 \\ | \\ CH_2—O—\overset{\displaystyle O}{\overset{\|}{C}}—(CH_2)_{14}—CH_3 \end{array}$$

Glyceryl tripalmitate
(tripalmitin)

2.

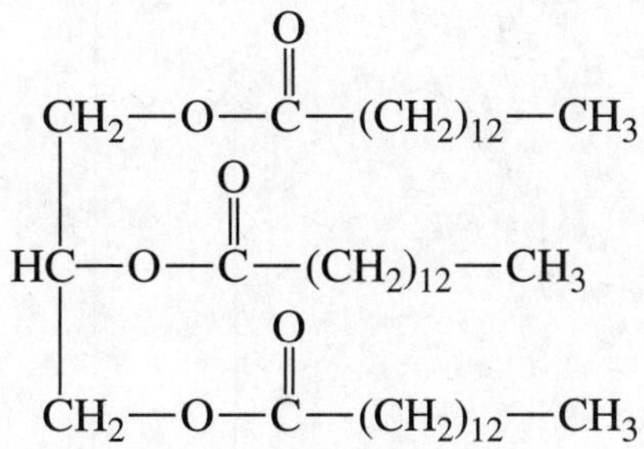

$$\begin{array}{l} CH_2—O—\overset{\displaystyle O}{\overset{\|}{C}}—(CH_2)_{12}—CH_3 \\ | \\ HC—O—\overset{\displaystyle O}{\overset{\|}{C}}—(CH_2)_{12}—CH_3 \\ | \\ CH_2—O—\overset{\displaystyle O}{\overset{\|}{C}}—(CH_2)_{12}—CH_3 \end{array}$$

Glyceryl trimyristate
(trimyristin)

◆ Learning Exercise 17.3C

Draw the structural formulas of the following triacylglycerols:

1. glyceryl tristearate (tristearin)

2. glyceryl trioleate (triolein)

Answers

1.

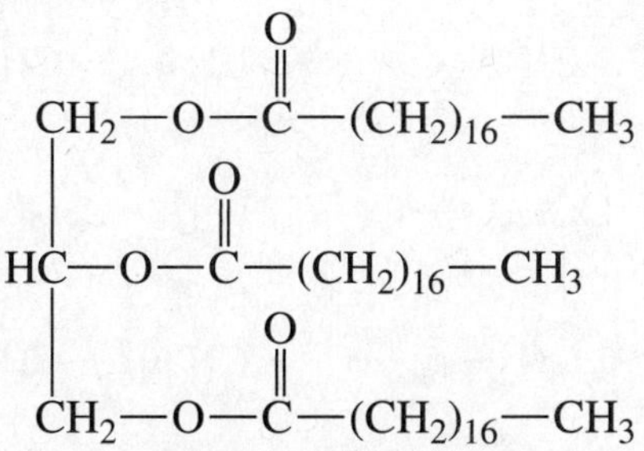

$$\begin{array}{l} CH_2—O—\overset{\displaystyle O}{\overset{\|}{C}}—(CH_2)_{16}—CH_3 \\ | \\ HC—O—\overset{\displaystyle O}{\overset{\|}{C}}—(CH_2)_{16}—CH_3 \\ | \\ CH_2—O—\overset{\displaystyle O}{\overset{\|}{C}}—(CH_2)_{16}—CH_3 \end{array}$$

Glyceryl tristearate
(tristearin)

2.

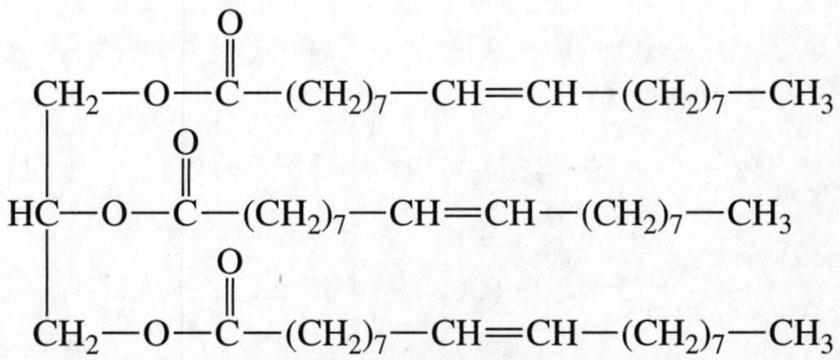

$$\begin{array}{l} CH_2—O—\overset{\displaystyle O}{\overset{\|}{C}}—(CH_2)_7—CH{=}CH—(CH_2)_7—CH_3 \\ | \\ HC—O—\overset{\displaystyle O}{\overset{\|}{C}}—(CH_2)_7—CH{=}CH—(CH_2)_7—CH_3 \\ | \\ CH_2—O—\overset{\displaystyle O}{\overset{\|}{C}}—(CH_2)_7—CH{=}CH—(CH_2)_7—CH_3 \end{array}$$

Glyceryl trioleate
(triolein)

17.4 Chemical Properties of Triacylglycerols

- The hydrogenation of unsaturated fatty acids converts carbon–carbon double bonds to carbon–carbon single bonds.
- The oxidation of unsaturated fatty acids produces short-chain fatty acids with disagreeable odors.
- The hydrolysis of the ester bonds in fats or oils produces glycerol and fatty acids.
- In saponification, a fat heated with a strong base produces glycerol and the salts of the fatty acids (soaps). The dual polarity of soap permits its solubility in both water and oil.

MasteringChemistry
Tutorial: Hydrolysis and Hydrogenation of Triacylglycerols

◆ Learning Exercise 17.4

Write the equations for the following reactions of glyceryl trioleate (triolein):

1. hydrogenation with a nickel catalyst

2. acid hydrolysis with HCl

3. saponification with NaOH

Answers

1.

$$\begin{array}{l} CH_2-O-\overset{O}{\overset{\|}{C}}-(CH_2)_7-CH{=}CH-(CH_2)_7-CH_3 \\ |\\ HC-O-\overset{O}{\overset{\|}{C}}-(CH_2)_7-CH{=}CH-(CH_2)_7-CH_3 \\ | \\ CH_2-O-\overset{O}{\overset{\|}{C}}-(CH_2)_7-CH{=}CH-(CH_2)_7-CH_3 \end{array} + 3H_2 \xrightarrow{Ni} \begin{array}{l} CH_2-O-\overset{O}{\overset{\|}{C}}-(CH_2)_{16}-CH_3 \\ | \\ HC-O-\overset{O}{\overset{\|}{C}}-(CH_2)_{16}-CH_3 \\ | \\ CH_2-O-\overset{O}{\overset{\|}{C}}-(CH_2)_{16}-CH_3 \end{array}$$

2.
$$\begin{array}{l} CH_2{-}O{-}\overset{\overset{\displaystyle O}{\|}}{C}{-}(CH_2)_7{-}CH{=}CH{-}(CH_2)_7{-}CH_3 \\ |\\ HC{-}O{-}\overset{\overset{\displaystyle O}{\|}}{C}{-}(CH_2)_7{-}CH{=}CH{-}(CH_2)_7{-}CH_3 \\ | \\ CH_2{-}O{-}\overset{\overset{\displaystyle O}{\|}}{C}{-}(CH_2)_7{-}CH{=}CH{-}(CH_2)_7{-}CH_3 \end{array} + 3H_2O \xrightarrow{H^+} \begin{array}{l} CH_2{-}OH \\ | \\ HC{-}OH \\ | \\ CH_2{-}OH \end{array}$$

$$+ 3\ HO{-}\overset{\overset{\displaystyle O}{\|}}{C}{-}(CH_2)_7{-}CH{=}CH{-}(CH_2)_7{-}CH_3$$

3.
$$\begin{array}{l} CH_2{-}O{-}\overset{\overset{\displaystyle O}{\|}}{C}{-}(CH_2)_7{-}CH{=}CH{-}(CH_2)_7{-}CH_3 \\ |\\ HC{-}O{-}\overset{\overset{\displaystyle O}{\|}}{C}{-}(CH_2)_7{-}CH{=}CH{-}(CH_2)_7{-}CH_3 \\ | \\ CH_2{-}O{-}\overset{\overset{\displaystyle O}{\|}}{C}{-}(CH_2)_7{-}CH{=}CH{-}(CH_2)_7{-}CH_3 \end{array} + 3NaOH \longrightarrow \begin{array}{l} CH_2{-}OH \\ | \\ HC{-}OH \\ | \\ CH_2{-}OH \end{array}$$

$$+ 3\ Na^{+}\,{}^{-}O{-}\overset{\overset{\displaystyle O}{\|}}{C}{-}(CH_2)_7{-}CH{=}CH{-}(CH_2)_7{-}CH_3$$

17.5 Glycerolphospholipids

- Glycerophospholipids are esters of glycerol with two fatty acids and a phosphate group attached to an amino alcohol.
- The fatty acids are a nonpolar region, whereas the phosphoric acid group and the ionized amino alcohol make up a polar region.

MasteringChemistry

Tutorial: The Split Personality of Glycerophospholipids

◆ Learning Exercise 17.5A

Draw the condensed structural formula of a glycerophospholipid that is formed from two molecules of palmitic acid and serine, an amino alcohol:

$$CH_3{-}(CH_2)_{14}{-}\overset{\overset{\displaystyle O}{\|}}{C}OH \qquad HO{-}CH_2{-}\overset{\overset{\displaystyle \overset{+}{N}H_3}{|}}{C}H{-}\overset{\overset{\displaystyle O}{\|}}{C}{-}O^-$$

Palmitic acid — Serine

Answer

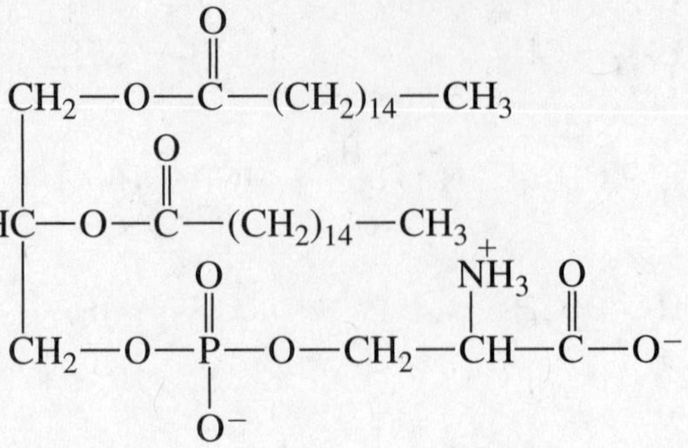

$$\begin{array}{l} CH_2-O-\overset{O}{\overset{\|}{C}}-(CH_2)_{14}-CH_3 \\ | \\ HC-O-\overset{O}{\overset{\|}{C}}-(CH_2)_{14}-CH_3 \\ | \qquad\qquad\qquad\qquad\qquad\quad \overset{+}{N}H_3 \quad O \\ | \qquad\qquad\qquad\qquad\qquad\qquad | \qquad \| \\ CH_2-O-\overset{O}{\overset{\|}{P}}-O-CH_2-CH-C-O^- \\ \qquad\qquad\quad | \\ \qquad\qquad\quad O^- \end{array}$$

◆ Learning Exercise 17.5B

Use the following glycerophospholipid to answer parts A to F and 1 to 3:

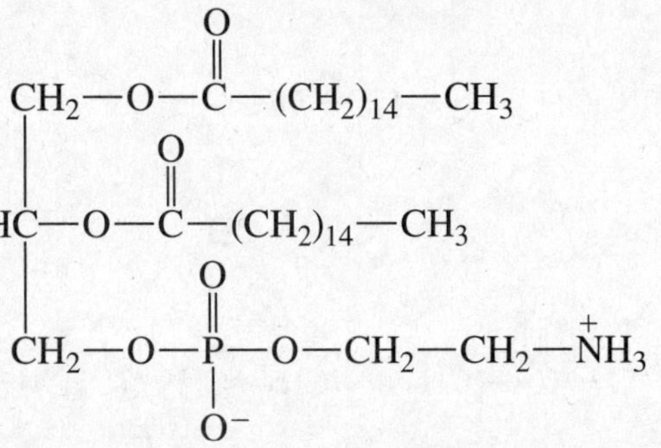

$$\begin{array}{l} CH_2-O-\overset{O}{\overset{\|}{C}}-(CH_2)_{14}-CH_3 \\ | \\ HC-O-\overset{O}{\overset{\|}{C}}-(CH_2)_{14}-CH_3 \\ | \\ CH_2-O-\overset{O}{\overset{\|}{P}}-O-CH_2-CH_2-\overset{+}{N}H_3 \\ \qquad\qquad\quad | \\ \qquad\qquad\quad O^- \end{array}$$

On the above condensed structural formula, indicate the

A. two fatty acids
B. part from the glycerol molecule
C. phosphate section
D. amino alcohol group
E. nonpolar region
F. polar region

1. What is the name of the amino alcohol group? ____________

2. What is the name of the glycerophospholipid? ____________

3. Why is a glycerophospholipid more soluble in water than most lipids? ____________

Answers

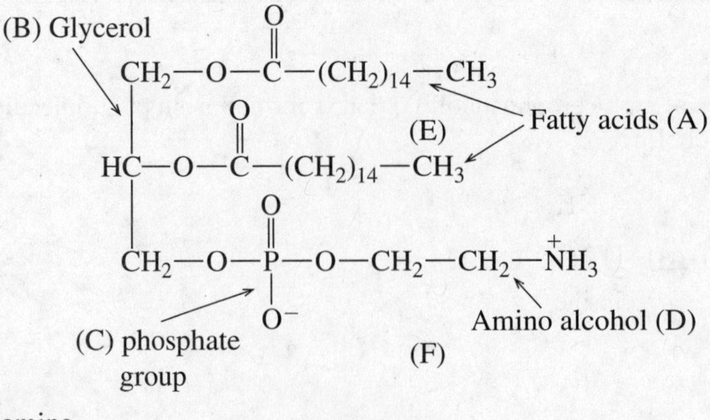

(B) Glycerol

$$\begin{array}{l} CH_2-O-\overset{O}{\overset{\|}{C}}-(CH_2)_{14}-CH_3 \\ | \\ HC-O-\overset{O}{\overset{\|}{C}}-(CH_2)_{14}-CH_3 \\ | \\ CH_2-O-\overset{O}{\overset{\|}{P}}-O-CH_2-CH_2-\overset{+}{N}H_3 \\ \qquad\qquad\quad | \\ \qquad\qquad\quad O^- \end{array}$$

Fatty acids (A)
(E)
Amino alcohol (D)
(C) phosphate group
(F)

1. ethanolamine
2. cephaline (ethanolamine glycerophospholipid)
3. The polar portion of the glycerophospholipid is attracted to water, which makes it more soluble in water than other lipids.

17.6 Sphingolipids

- In sphingolipids, the long-chain alcohol sphingosine forms an ester bond with one fatty acid and the phosphate-amino alcohol group.
- In glycosphingolipids, sphingosine is bonded to a fatty acid and one or more monosaccharides.

MasteringChemistry
Self Study Activity: Phospholipids

◆ Learning Exercise 17.6

Match one of the following classes of lipids with the composition listed below:

a. glycerophospholipid **b.** sphingolipid **c.** cerebroside **d.** ganglioside

1. ______ contains sphingosine, a fatty acid and two or more monosaccharides

2. ______ contains sphingosine, a fatty acid, phosphate and an amino alcohol

3. ______ contains sphingosine, a fatty acid, and one monosaccharide

4. ______ contains glycerol, two fatty acids, phosphate, and an amino alcohol

Answers **1.** d **2.** b **3.** c **4.** a

17.7 Steroids: Cholesterol, Bile Salts, and Steroid Hormones

- Steroids are lipids containing the steroid nucleus, which is a fused structure of four rings.
- Steroids include cholesterol, bile salts, and vitamin D.
- The steroid hormones are closely related in structure to cholesterol and depend on cholesterol for their synthesis.
- The sex hormones such as estrogen and testosterone are responsible for sexual characteristics and reproduction.
- The adrenal corticosteroids include aldosterone, which regulates water balance, and cortisone, which regulates glucose levels in the blood.

MasteringChemistry
Tutorial: Cholesterol

◆ Learning Exercise 17.7A

1. Draw the structure of the steroid nucleus. **2.** Draw the structure of cholesterol.

Answers

1.

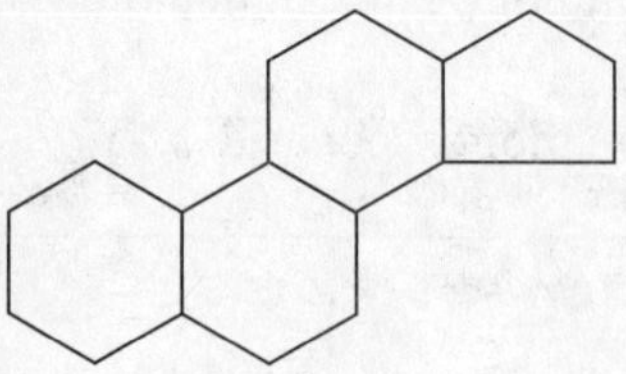

2.

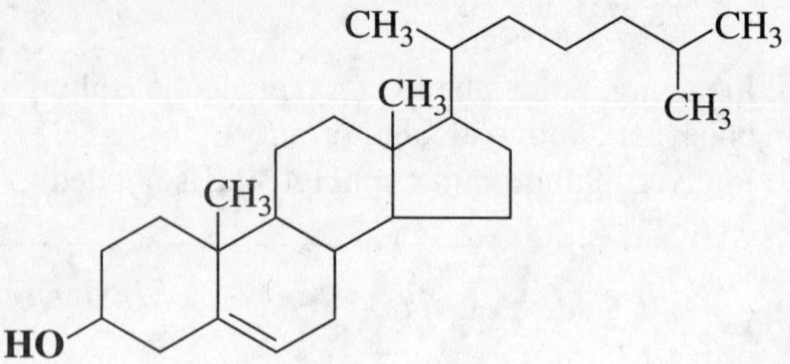

HO, CH_3, CH_3, CH_3, CH_3, CH_3

◆ Learning Exercise 17.7B

Match each of the following compounds with the statements below:

a. estrogen **b.** testosterone **c.** cortisone **d.** aldosterone **e.** bile salts

1. _______ increases the blood level of glucose

2. _______ increases the reabsorption of Na^+ by the kidneys

3. _______ stimulates the development of secondary sex characteristics in females

4. _______ stimulates the retention of water by the kidneys

5. _______ stimulates the secondary sex characteristics in males

6. _______ secreted by the gallbladder into the small intestine to emulsify fats in the diet

Answers **1.** c **2.** d **3.** a **4.** d **5.** b **6.** e

17.8 Cell Membranes

- Cell membranes surround all of our cells and separate the cellular contents from the external aqueous environment.
- A cell membrane is a lipid bilayer composed of two rows of phospholipids such that the nonpolar hydrocarbon tails are in the center and the polar sections are aligned along the outside.
- The center portion of the lipid bilayer consists of nonpolar chains of the fatty acids, with the polar heads at the outer and inner surfaces.
- Molecules of cholesterol, proteins, glycolipids, and glycoproteins are embedded in the lipid bilayer.

MasteringChemistry

Self Study Activity: Membrane Structure

Self Study Activity: Diffusion

Self Study Activity: Osmosis

Self Study Activity: Active Transport

◆ Learning Exercise 17.8

a. What is the function of the lipid bilayer in cell membranes?

b. What type of lipid makes up the lipid bilayer?

c. What is the general arrangement of the lipids in a lipid bilayer?

d. What are the functions of the proteins embedded in the lipid bilayer?

Answers

a. The lipid bilayer separates the contents of a cell from the surrounding aqueous environment.
b. The lipid bilayer is primarily composed of glycerophospholipids.
c. The nonpolar hydrocarbon tails are in the center of the bilayer, whereas the polar sections are aligned along the outside of the bilayer.
d. Some proteins provide channels for electrolytes and water to flow in and out of the cell. Other proteins act as receptors for chemicals such as hormones and neurotransmitters.

Checklist for Chapter 17

You are ready to take the Practice Test for Chapter 17. Be sure that you have accomplished the following learning goals for this chapter. If you are not sure, review the section listed at the end of the goal. Then apply your new skills and understanding to the Practice Test.

After studying Chapter 17, I can successfully:

_____ Describe the classes of lipids (17.1).

_____ Identify a fatty acid as saturated or unsaturated (17.2).

_____ Write the structural formula of a wax or triacylglycerol produced by the reaction of a fatty acid and an alcohol or glycerol (17.3).

_____ Draw the condensed structural formula of the product from the reaction of a triacylglycerol with hydrogen, an acid or base, or an oxidizing agent (17.4).

_____ Describe the components of glycerophospholipids (17.5).

_____ Describe the components of sphingolipids and glycosphingolipids (17.6).

_____ Describe the structure of a steroid and cholesterol (17.7).

_____ Describe the composition and function of the lipid bilayer in cell membranes (17.8).

Practice Test for Chapter 17

1. An ester of a fatty acid is called a

A. carbohydrate **B.** lipid **C.** protein **D.** oxyacid **E.** soap

2. A fatty acid that is unsaturated is usually

A. from animal sources and liquid at room temperature
B. from animal sources and solid at room temperature
C. from vegetable sources and liquid at room temperature
D. from vegetable sources and solid at room temperature
E. from both vegetable and animal sources and solid at room temperature

3. The following condensed structural formula is a:

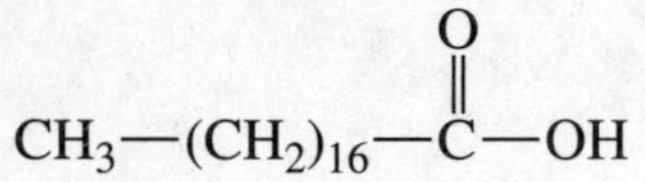

$$CH_3{-}(CH_2)_{16}{-}\overset{\overset{\displaystyle O}{\|}}{C}{-}OH$$

A. unsaturated fatty acid **B.** saturated fatty acid **C.** wax
D. triacylglycerol **E.** sphingolipid

For questions 4 through 7, consider the following compound:

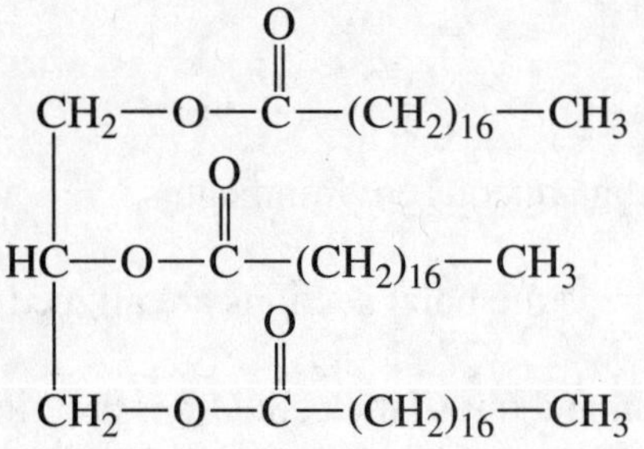

$$\begin{array}{l} CH_2{-}O{-}\overset{\overset{\displaystyle O}{\|}}{C}{-}(CH_2)_{16}{-}CH_3 \\ | \\ HC{-}O{-}\overset{\overset{\displaystyle O}{\|}}{C}{-}(CH_2)_{16}{-}CH_3 \\ | \\ CH_2{-}O{-}\overset{\overset{\displaystyle O}{\|}}{C}{-}(CH_2)_{16}{-}CH_3 \end{array}$$

4. This compound belongs to the family called

A. wax **B.** triacylglycerol **C.** glycerophospholipid
D. sphingolipid **E.** steroid

5. The molecule shown above was formed by

A. sterification **B.** hydrolysis (acid) **C.** saponification
D. emulsification **E.** oxidation

6. If this molecule were reacted with strong base such as NaOH, the products would be

A. glycerol and fatty acids **B.** glycerol and water
C. glycerol and soap **D.** an ester and salts of fatty acids
E. an ester and fatty acids

7. The compound would be expected to be

A. saturated and a solid at room temperature
B. saturated and a liquid at room temperature
C. unsaturated and a solid at room temperature
D. unsaturated and a liquid at room temperature
E. supersaturated and a liquid at room temperature

8. Which are found in glycerophospholipids?

A. fatty acids **B.** glycerol **C.** a nitrogen compound
D. phosphate **E.** all of these

For questions 9 and 10, consider the following reaction:

Triacylglycerol + 3NaOH → 3 sodium salts of fatty acids + glycerol

9. The reaction of a triacylglycerol with a strong base such as NaOH is called

A. esterification **B.** lipogenesis **C.** hydrolysis
D. saponification **E.** β–oxidation

10. What is another name for the sodium salts of the fatty acids?

A. margarines **B.** fat substitutes **C.** soaps **D.** perfumes **E.** vitamins

For questions 11 through 16, consider the following phosphoglyceride:

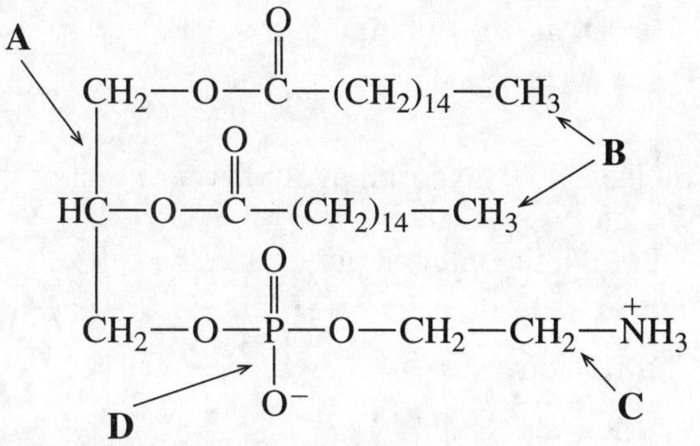

$$\begin{array}{l} \text{A} \rightarrow CH_2-O-\overset{\overset{O}{\|}}{C}-(CH_2)_{14}-CH_3 \\ \quad\;\;| \qquad\qquad\qquad\qquad\qquad\qquad\qquad \leftarrow \text{B} \\ \quad HC-O-\overset{\overset{O}{\|}}{C}-(CH_2)_{14}-CH_3 \\ \quad\;\;| \\ \quad CH_2-O-\underset{\underset{O^-}{|}}{\overset{\overset{O}{\|}}{P}}-O-CH_2-CH_2-\overset{+}{N}H_3 \\ \qquad\quad \text{D} \nearrow \qquad\qquad\qquad\qquad\qquad\quad \nwarrow \text{C} \end{array}$$

Match the labels with the following:

11. ______ the glycerol portion **12.** ______ the phosphate portion **13.** ______ the amino alcohol

14. ______ the polar region **15.** ______ the nonpolar region

16. This compound belongs in the family called

A. choline **B.** cephalin **C.** sphingomyelin **D.** glycolipid **E.** cerebroside

For questions 17 through 20, classify the following lipids as:

A. wax **B.** triacylglycerol **C.** glycerophospholipid **D.** steroid **E.** fatty acid

17. ______ cholesterol

18. ______ $CH_3-(CH_2)_{14}-\overset{\overset{O}{\|}}{C}-OH$

19. ______ $CH_3-(CH_2)_{14}-\overset{\overset{O}{\|}}{C}-O-(CH_2)_{30}-CH_3$

20. ______ an ester of glycerol with three palmitic acid molecules

For questions 21 through 25, select answers from the following:

A. testosterone **B.** estrogen **C.** prednisone **D.** cortisone **E.** aldosterone

21. ______ stimulates the female sexual characteristics

22. ______ increases the retention of water by the kidneys

23. ______ stimulates the male sexual characteristics

24. ______ increases the blood glucose level

25. ______ used medically to reduce inflammation and treat asthma

26. The following compound is a

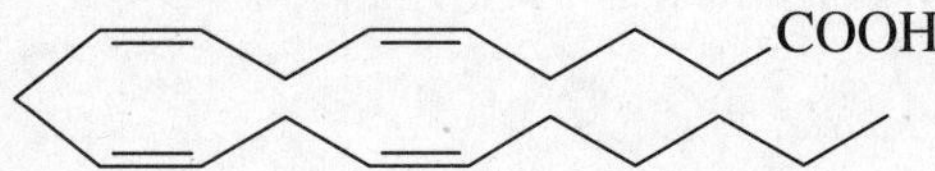

A. cholesterol **B.** sphingosine **C.** fatty acid **D.** glycerosphingolipid **E.** steroid

27. The lipid bilayer of a cell is composed of

A. cholesterol **B.** glycerophospholipids **C.** proteins **D.** glycosphingolipids **E.** all of these

28. The type of transport that allows chloride ions to move through the integral proteins in the cell membrane is

A. passive transport **B.** active transport **C.** diffusion
D. facilitated transport **E.** all of these

29. The movement of small molecules through a cell membrane from a higher concentration to a lower concentration is

A. passive transport **B.** active transport **C.** diffusion
D. facilitated transport **E.** A and C

30. The type of lipoprotein that transports cholesterol to the liver for elimination is called

A. chylomicron **B.** high-density lipoprotein **C.** low-density lipoprotein
D. very-low-density lipoprotein **E.** all of these

Answers to the Practice Test

1. B	**2.** C	**3.** B	**4.** B	**5.** A
6. C	**7.** A	**8.** E	**9.** D	**10.** C
11. A	**12.** D	**13.** C	**14.** C, D	**15.** B
16. B	**17.** D	**18.** E	**19.** A	**20.** B
21. B	**22.** E	**23.** A	**24.** D	**25.** C
26. C	**27.** E	**28.** D	**29.** E	**30.** B

18

Amines and Amides

Study Goals

- Name and draw condensed structural formulas of amines and amides.
- Describe the ionization of amines in water.
- Describe the boiling points of amines and amides compared with alkanes and alcohols.
- Describe the solubility of amines and amides in water.
- Describe the properties of amine salts.
- Write equations for the neutralization and amidation of amines.
- Describe the acid and base hydrolysis of amides.

Think About It

1. Fish smell "fishy," but lemon juice removes the "fishy" odor. Why?

2. What functional groups are often found in tranquilizers and hallucinogens?

Key Terms

Match the key term with the correct statement shown below.

a. heterocyclic amine **b.** amidation **c.** amine **d.** amide **e.** alkaloid

1. ____ A nitrogen-containing compound that is active physiologically

2. ____ A cyclic organic compound that contains one or more nitrogen atoms

3. ____ The reaction of a carboxylic acid and an amine

4. ____ The hydrolysis of this compound produces a carboxylic acid and an amine

5. ____ An organic compound that contains an amino group

Answers **1.** e **2.** a **3.** b **4.** d **5.** c

18.1 Amines

- Amines are derivative of ammonia (NH_3), in which alkyl or aromatic groups replace one or more hydrogen atoms.
- Amines are classified as primary, secondary, or tertiary when the nitrogen atom is bonded to one, two, or three alkyl or aromatic groups.

$$CH_3{-}NH_2 \qquad CH_3{-}\overset{\displaystyle CH_3}{\overset{|}{N}}{-}H \qquad CH_3{-}\overset{\displaystyle CH_3}{\overset{|}{N}}{-}CH_3$$

primary (1°) secondary (2°) 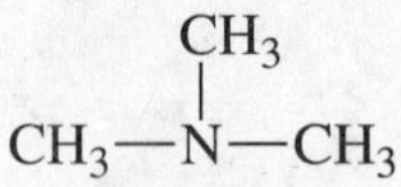 tertiary (3°)

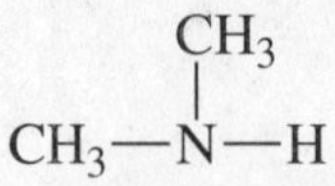

- Amines are usually named by common names in which the names of the alkyl groups are listed alphabetically preceding the suffix *amine*.
- In the IUPAC system, the *e* of the alkane name of the longest chain bonded to the N atom is replaced by *amine*. Alkyl groups attached to the *N* atom are named with the prefix *N*-.
- When another functional group takes priority, $-NH_2$ is named as an amino substituent.
- The amine of benzene is named aniline.

$CH_3{-}NH_2$	$CH_3{-}NH{-}CH_3$	$CH_3{-}\overset{\displaystyle CH_3}{\overset{|}{N}}{-}CH_3$	$C_6H_5{-}NH_2$
IUPAC: methanamine	*N*-methylmethanamine	*N,N*,-dimethylmethanamine	aniline
Common: methylamine	dimethylamine	trimethylamine	

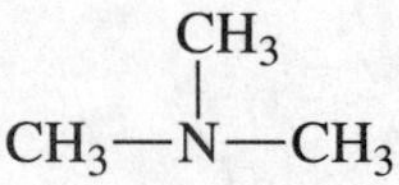

- Many amines, which are prevalent in synthetic and naturally occurring compounds, have physiological activity.

> ***MasteringChemistry***
>
> **Self Study Activity: Amine and Amide Functional Groups**

◆ Learning Exercise 18.1A

Classify each of the following as a primary (1°), secondary (2°), or tertiary (3°) amine:

1. _____ $CH_3{-}\overset{\displaystyle H}{\overset{|}{N}}{-}CH_2CH_3$

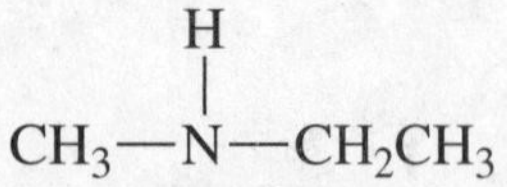

2. _____ (cyclohexane ring with NH_2)

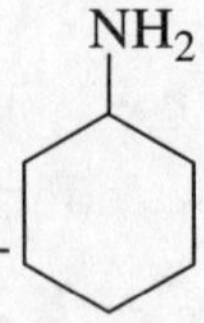

3. _____ $CH_3{-}\overset{\displaystyle NH_2}{\overset{|}{CH}}{-}\overset{\displaystyle O}{\overset{\|}{C}}{-}OH$

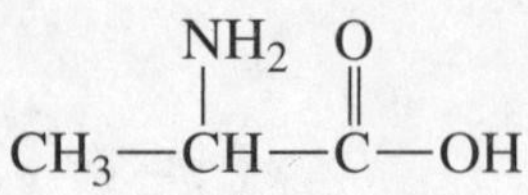

4. _____ $CH_3{-}CH_2{-}\overset{\displaystyle CH_3}{\overset{|}{N}}{-}CH_3$

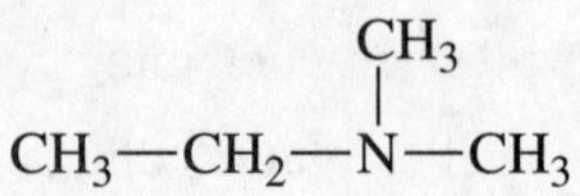

5. _____ $CH_3{-}CH_2{-}CH_2{-}CH_2{-}\overset{\displaystyle H}{\overset{|}{N}}{-}CH_2{-}CH_3$

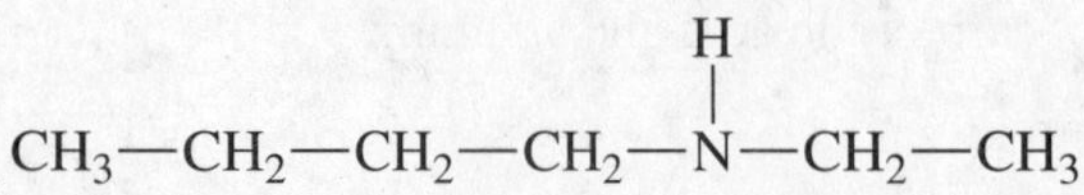

6. _____ (benzene ring with NH_2 and CH_3)

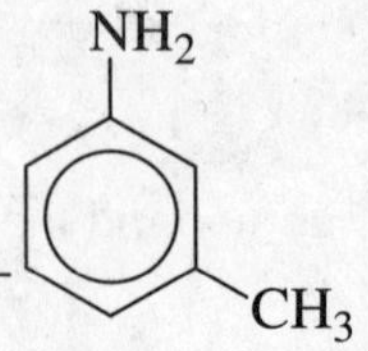

Answers **1.** 2° **2.** 1° **3.** 1° **4.** 3° **5.** 2° **6.** 1°

Guide to IUPAC Naming of Amines	
STEP 1	Name the longest carbon chain bonded to the N atom by replacing the *e* with *amine.*
STEP 2	Number the carbon chain to show the position of the amino group and other substituents.
STEP 3	In secondary and tertiary amines, use the prefix *N*-, to name groups attached to the *N* atom.

◆ Learning Exercise 18.1B

Name each of the amines in problem 18.1A.

1. ______________________ **2.** ______________________

3. ______________________ **4.** ______________________

5. ______________________ **6.** ______________________

Answers

1. ethylmethylamine; *N*-methylethanamine
2. cyclohexanamine
3. 2-aminopropanoic acid; *β*-aminopropionic acid
4. ethyldimethylamine; *N,N*-dimethylethanamine
5. butylethylamine; *N*-ethyl-1-butanamine
6. 3-methylaniline; *m*-methylaniline

MasteringChemistry

Tutorial: Know What Amine?

Tutorial: Drawing Amines

◆ Learning Exercise 18.1C

Draw the condensed structural formulas of the following amines:

1. 2-propanamine

2. *N*-ethyl-*N*-methyl-1-aminobutane

3. 3-bromoaniline

4. *N*-methylaniline

Answers

$$\begin{array}{c} NH_2 \\ | \\ CH_3-CH-CH_3 \end{array}$$
1.

$$\begin{array}{c} \quad\quad\quad\quad CH_3 \\ \quad\quad\quad\quad | \\ CH_3-CH_2-N-CH_2-CH_2-CH_2-CH_3 \end{array}$$
2.

3. (benzene ring with NH_2 and Br, meta)

4. (benzene ring with $NHCH_3$)

18.2 Properties of Amines

- The N—H bonds in primary and secondary amines form hydrogen bonds.
- Amines have higher boiling points than hydrocarbons but lower than alcohols of similar mass because the N atom is not as electronegative as the O atom in alcohols.
- Hydrogen bonding makes amines with one to six carbon atoms soluble in water.
- In water, amines act as weak bases by accepting protons from water to produce ammonium and hydroxide ions.
- $CH_3—NH_2 + H_2O \rightleftarrows CH_3—NH_3^+ + OH^-$
  Methylamine *Methylammonium ion* *Hydroxide ion*
- Strong acids neutralize amines to yield ammonium salts.
- $CH_3—NH_2 + HCl \longrightarrow CH_3—NH_3^+ + Cl^-$
  Methylamine *Methylammonium chloride*
- When a carboxylic acid reacts with ammonia or an amine, an amide is produced.

$$CH_3—\overset{O}{\overset{\|}{C}}—OH + NH_3 \xrightarrow{\text{Heat}} CH_3—\overset{O}{\overset{\|}{C}}—NH_2 + H_2O$$

$$CH_3—\overset{O}{\overset{\|}{C}}—OH + NH_2—CH_3 \xrightarrow{\text{Heat}} CH_3—\overset{O}{\overset{\|}{C}}—NH—CH_3 + H_2O$$

MasteringChemistry

Self Study Activity: Amines as Bases

Tutorial: Reactions of Amines

Case Study: Death by Chocolate?

◆ Learning Exercise 18.2A

Indicate the compound in each pair that has the higher boiling point.

1. $CH_3—NH_2$ or $CH_3—OH$ ____________
2. $CH_3—CH_2—CH_3$ or $CH_3—CH_2—NH_2$ ____________
3. $CH_3—CH_2—NH_2$ or $CH_3—CH_2—CH_2—NH_2$ ____________
4. $CH_3—\overset{H}{\overset{|}{N}}—CH_3$ ____________

Answers

1. $CH_3—OH$
2. $CH_3—CH_2—NH_2$
3. $CH_3—CH_2—CH_2—NH_2$
4. $CH_3—CH_2—NH_2$

◆ Learning Exercise 18.2B

Draw the products of the following reactions:

1. $CH_3—CH_2—NH_2 + H_2O \rightleftharpoons$

2. $CH_3—CH_2—CH_2—NH_2 + HCl \longrightarrow$

3. $CH_3—CH_2—NH—CH_3 + HCl \longrightarrow$

4. 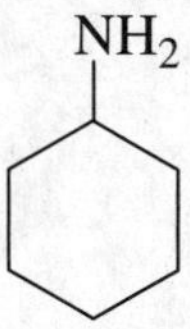 (cyclohexane ring with NH_2) $+ HBr \rightarrow$

5. 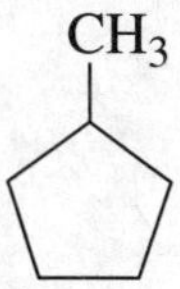 (cyclopentane ring with CH_3) $+ H_2O \leftrightarrows$

6. $CH_3—CH_2—NH_3^+\ Cl^- + NaOH \longrightarrow$

Answers

1. $CH_3—CH_2—NH_3^+ + OH^-$

2. $CH_3—CH_2—CH_2—NH_3^+\ Cl^-$

3. $CH_3—CH_2—\overset{+}{N}H_2—CH_3Cl^-$

4. 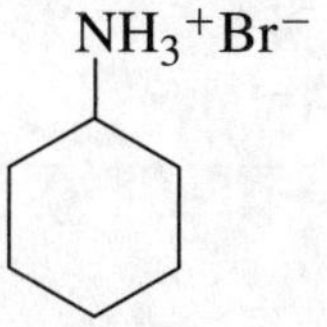 (cyclohexane ring with $NH_3^+Br^-$)

5. 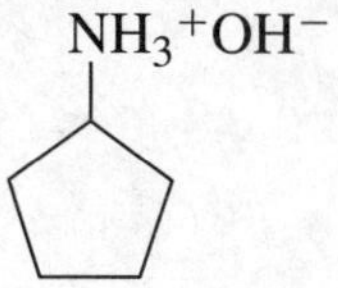 (cyclopentane ring with $NH_3^+OH^-$)

6. $CH_3—CH_2—NH_2 + NaCl + H_2O$

◆ Learning Exercise 18.2C

Draw the condensed structural formulas of the amides formed in each of the following reactions:

1. $CH_3—CH_2—\overset{\overset{\displaystyle O}{\|}}{C}—OH + NH_3 \xrightarrow{\text{heat}}$

2. 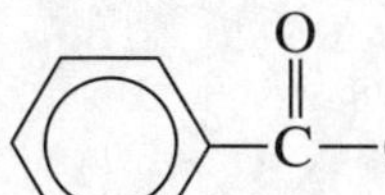 (benzene ring)$—\overset{\overset{\displaystyle O}{\|}}{C}—OH + CH_3—NH_3 \xrightarrow{\text{heat}}$

3. $CH_3—\overset{\overset{\displaystyle O}{\|}}{C}—OH + \overset{\overset{\displaystyle CH_3}{|}}{N}H—CH_3 \xrightarrow{\text{heat}}$

Answers

1. $CH_3-CH_2-\overset{\overset{\large O}{\|}}{C}-NH_2$

2. $C_6H_5-\overset{\overset{\large O}{\|}}{C}-NH-CH_3$

3. $CH_3-\overset{\overset{\large O}{\|}}{C}-\overset{\overset{\large CH_3}{|}}{N}-CH_3$

18.3 Heterocyclic Amines and Alkaloids

- A heterocyclic amine is a cyclic compound containing one or more nitrogen atoms in the ring.
- Most heterocyclic amines contain five or six atoms in the ring.
- An alkaloid is a physiologically active amine obtained from plants.

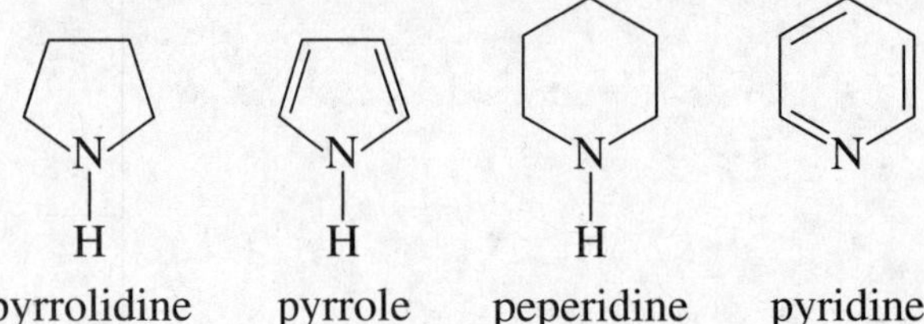

MasteringChemistry
Tutorial: Identifying Types of Heterocyclic Amines

◆ Learning Exercise 18.3

Match each of the following heterocyclic structures with the correct name:

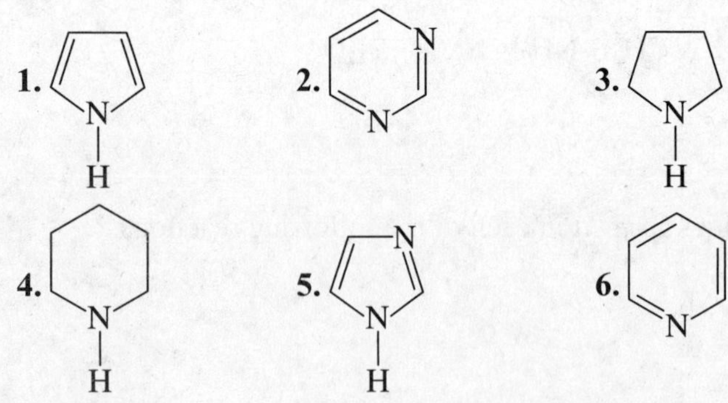

1. _____ pyrrolidine	**2.** _____ imidazole	**3.** _____ pyridine
4. _____ pyrrole	**5.** _____ pyrimidine	**6.** _____ piperidine

Answers **1.** c **2.** e **3.** f **4.** a **5.** b **6.** d

18.4 Amides

- Amides are derivatives of carboxylic acids in which an amino group replaces the —OH group in the acid.
- Amides are named by replacing the *ic acid* or *oic acid* ending with *amide.* When an alkyl group is attached to the *N* atom, it is listed as *N*-alkyl.

$CH_3—\overset{\overset{\large O}{\|}}{C}—NH_2$ Ethanamide (acetamide)

$CH_3—\overset{\overset{\large O}{\|}}{C}—NH—CH_3$ *N*-Methylethanamide; (*N*-methylacetamide)

MasteringChemistry
Tutorial: Amidation Reactions

Guide to Naming of Amides	
STEP 1	Identify the corresponding carboxylic acid using its common or IUPAC name.
STEP 2	For the amide name, replace the *oic* or *ic acid* with *amide.*
STEP 3	Name any substituents on *N* using the prefix *N*- before each name.

◆ Learning Exercise 18.4A

Name the following amides:

1. $CH_3—CH_2—\overset{\overset{\large O}{\|}}{C}—NH_2$ ____________

2. 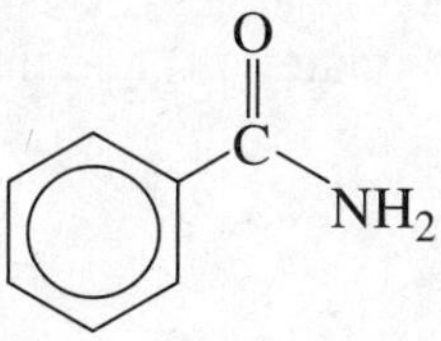 $C_6H_5—\overset{\overset{\large O}{\|}}{C}—NH_2$ (benzene ring) ____________

3. $CH_3—CH_2—CH_2—CH_2—\overset{\overset{\large O}{\|}}{C}—NH—CH_3$ ____________

4. $CH_3—\overset{\overset{\large O}{\|}}{C}—NH—CH_2—CH_3$ ____________

5. 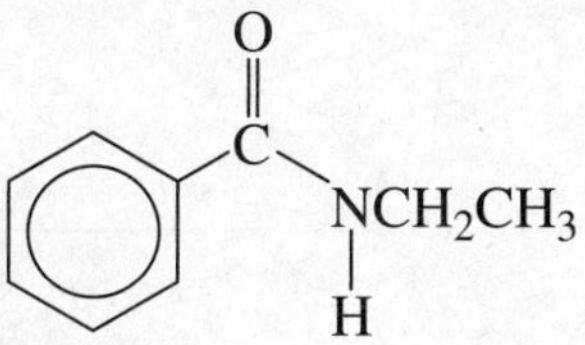 $C_6H_5—\overset{\overset{\large O}{\|}}{C}—\underset{\underset{\large H}{|}}{N}CH_2CH_3$ (benzene ring) ____________

Answers **1.** propanamide (propionamide) **2.** benzamide **3.** *N*-methylpentanamide **4.** *N*-ethylethanamide (*N*-ethylacetamide) **5.** *N*-ethylbenzamide

◆ Learning Exercise 18.4B

Draw the condensed structural formulas for each of the following amides:

1. butanamide

2. *N*-methylbutanamide

3. *N*-methyl-3-chloropentanamide

4. benzamide

Answers

1. $CH_3—CH_2—\overset{\overset{\displaystyle O}{\|}}{C}—NH_2$

2. $CH_3—CH_2—CH_2—\overset{\overset{\displaystyle O}{\|}}{C}—NH—CH_3$

3. $CH_3—CH_2—\overset{\overset{\displaystyle Cl}{|}}{C}H—CH_2—\overset{\overset{\displaystyle O}{\|}}{C}—\overset{\overset{\displaystyle CH_3}{|}}{N}—H$

4. 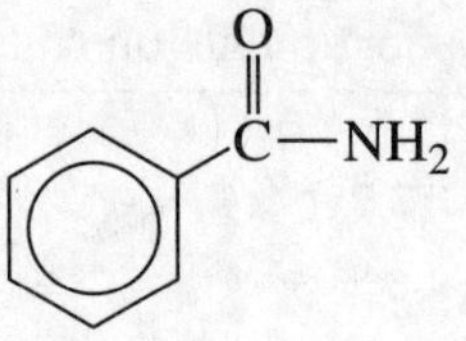 $C_6H_5—\overset{\overset{\displaystyle O}{\|}}{C}—NH_2$ (benzene ring)

18.5 Hydrolysis of Amines

- Amides undergo acid and base hydrolysis to produce the carboxylic acid (or carboxylate salt) and the amine (or amine salt).

$$CH_3—\overset{\overset{\displaystyle O}{\|}}{C}—NH_2 + HCl + H_2O \rightarrow CH_3—\overset{\overset{\displaystyle O}{\|}}{C}—OH + NH_4{}^+Cl^-$$

$$CH_3—\overset{\overset{\displaystyle O}{\|}}{C}—NH_2 + NaOH \rightarrow CH_3—\overset{\overset{\displaystyle O}{\|}}{C}—O^-Na^+ + NH_3$$

MasteringChemistry

Tutorial: Hydrolysis of Amides

◆ Learning Exercise18.5

Draw the condensed structural formulas for the hydrolysis of each of the following with HCl and NaOH:

1. $CH_3{-}CH_2{-}\overset{\overset{\displaystyle O}{\|}}{C}{-}NH_2$

2. $CH_3{-}\overset{\overset{\displaystyle O}{\|}}{C}{-}NH{-}CH_2{-}CH_3$

Answers

1. (HCl)$CH_3{-}CH_2{-}\overset{\overset{\displaystyle O}{\|}}{C}{-}OH + NH_4^+Cl^-$ (NaOH)$CH_3{-}CH_2{-}\overset{\overset{\displaystyle O}{\|}}{C}{-}O^-Na^+ + NH_3$

2. (HCl)$CH_3{-}\overset{\overset{\displaystyle O}{\|}}{C}{-}OH + \overset{+}{N}H_3{-}CH_2{-}CH_3Cl^-$ (NaOH)$CH_3{-}\overset{\overset{\displaystyle O}{\|}}{C}{-}O^-Na^+ + NH_2{-}CH_2{-}CH_3$

Checklist for Chapter 18

You are ready to take the Practice Test for Chapter 18. Be sure that you have accomplished the following learning goals for this chapter. If you are not sure, review the section listed at the end of the goal. Then apply your new skills and understanding to the Practice Test.

After studying Chapter 18, I can successfully:

______ Classify amines as primary, secondary, or tertiary (18.1).

______ Write the IUPAC and common names of amines and draw their condensed structural formulas (18.1).

______ Compare the boiling points and solubility of amines to alkanes and alcohols of similar mass (18.2).

______ Write equations for the ionization and neutralization of amines (18.2).

______ Identify heterocyclic amines (18.3).

______ Write the IUPAC and common names of amides and draw their condensed structural formulas (18.4).

______ Write equations for the acidic and basic hydrolysis of amines (18.5).

Practice Test

Classify the amines in questions 1 through 6 as:

A. primary amine **B.** secondary amine **C.** tertiary amine

1. _____ $CH_3-CH(CH_3)-NH_2$

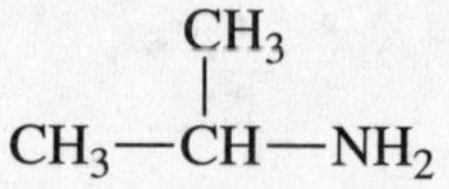

2. _____ $CH_3-CH_2-N(CH_3)-CH_3$

3. _____ $CH_3-CH_2-CH(NH_2)-CH_2-CH_3$

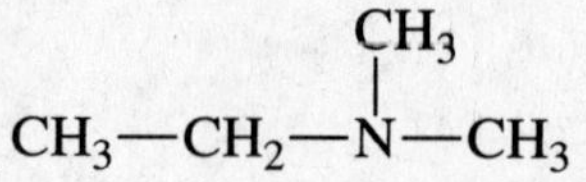

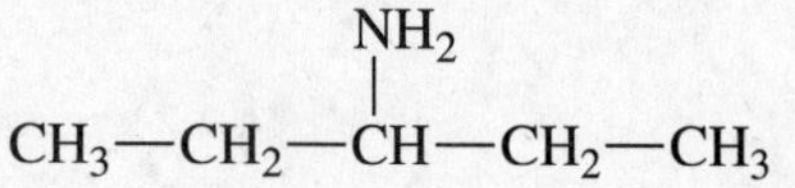

4. _____ $CH_3-N(H)-CH_2-CH_3$

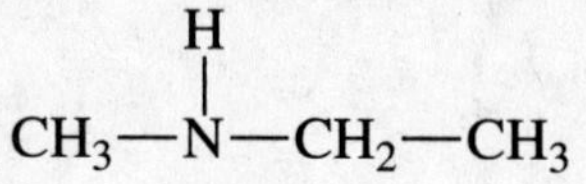

5. _____ $CH_3-CH(CH_3)-CH_2-NH-CH(CH_3)-CH_3$

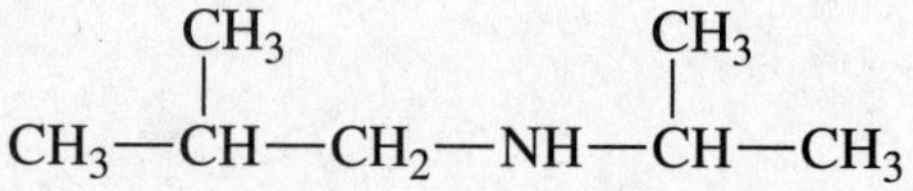

6. _____ $CH_3-C(CH_3)_2-CH_2-NH_2$

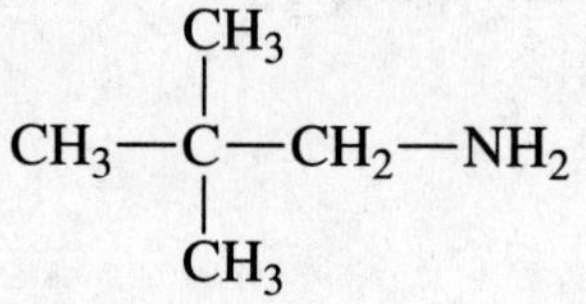

Match the amines and amides in questions 7 through 11 with the following names:

A. ethyldimethylamine **B.** butanamide **C.** *N*-methylacetamide
D. benzamide **E.** *N*-ethylbutyramide

7. 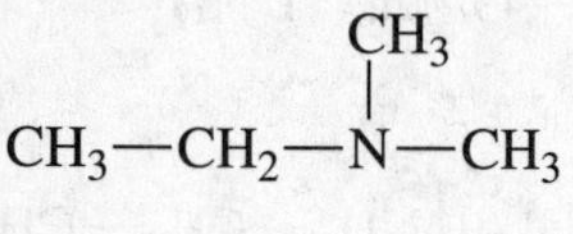 $CH_3-CH_2-N(CH_3)-CH_3$

8. 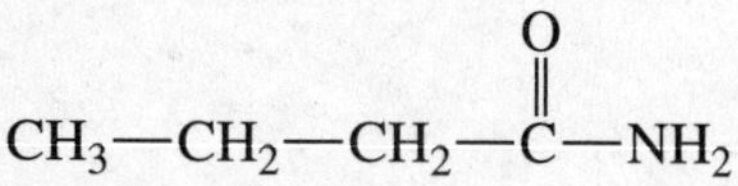 $CH_3-CH_2-CH_2-\overset{O}{\overset{\|}{C}}-NH_2$

9. 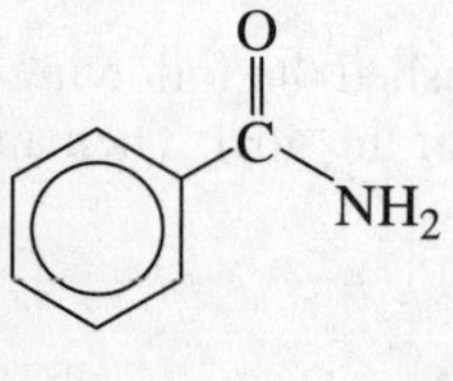 $C_6H_5-\overset{O}{\overset{\|}{C}}-NH_2$

10. 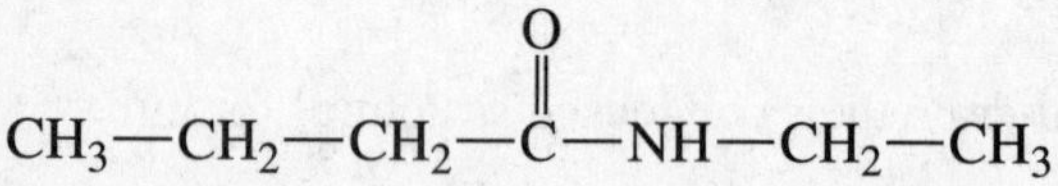 $CH_3-CH_2-CH_2-\overset{O}{\overset{\|}{C}}-NH-CH_2-CH_3$

11. 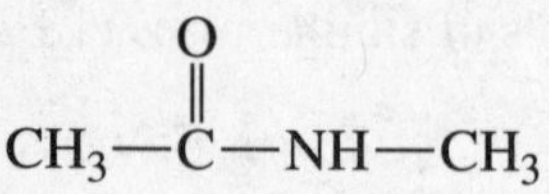 $CH_3-\overset{O}{\overset{\|}{C}}-NH-CH_3$

In questions 12 through 15, identify the compound with the higher boiling point.

12. A. $CH_3-CH_2-NH_2$ or **B.** CH_3-CH_2-OH

13. A. $CH_3-NH-CH_3$ or **B.** $CH_3-CH_2-NH_2$

14. A. $CH_3-CH_2-CH_2-CH_3$ or **B.** $CH_3-CH_2-CH_2-NH_2$

15. A. $CH_3—CH_2—CH_2—OH$ or **B.** $CH_3—CH_2—CH_2—NH_2$

For questions 16 through 19, identify the product as A to D:

16. ______ ionization of 1-propanamine in water

17. ______ hydrolysis of propanamide

18. ______ reaction of ethanamine and hydrochloric acid

19. ______ amidation of acetic acid

A. $CH_3—CH_2—\overset{\overset{\large O}{\|}}{C}—OH + NH_3$

B. $CH_3—CH_2—NH_3^+ \, Cl^-$

C. $CH_3—CH_2—CH_2—NH_3^+ + OH^-$

D. $CH_3—\overset{\overset{\large O}{\|}}{C}—NH_2$

20. Amines used in drugs are converted to their amine salt because the salt is

A. a solid at room temperature **B.** soluble in water **C.** odorless
D. soluble in body fluids **E.** all of these

21. Piperidine is a heterocyclic amine that

A. has a ring of six atoms
B. has a ring of five atoms
C. contains two nitrogen atoms in a ring
D. has one nitrogen atom in an aromatic ring system
E. has two nitrogen atoms in an aromatic ring system

22. Alkaloids are

A. physiologically active nitrogen-containing compounds
B. produced by plants
C. used in anesthetics, in antidepressants, and as stimulants
D. often habit forming
E. all of these

For questions 23 to 26, match each of the following alkaloids (A to E) with their sources):

A. caffeine **B.** nicotine **C.** morphine **D.** quinine

23. a painkiller from the oriental poppy plant

24. obtained from the bark of the cinchona tree and used in the treatment of malaria

25. a stimulant obtained from the leaves of tobacco plants

26. a stimulant obtained from coffee beans and tea leaves

Answers to the Practice Test

1. A	**2.** C	**3.** A	**4.** B	**5.** B
6. A	**7.** A	**8.** B	**9.** D	**10.** E
11. C	**12.** B	**13.** B	**14.** B	**15.** A
16. C	**17.** A	**18.** B	**19.** D	**20.** E
21. A	**22.** E	**23.** C	**24.** D	**25.** B
26. A				

19

Amino Acids and Proteins

Study Goals

- Classify proteins by their functions in the body.
- Draw the ionized condensed structural formulas of amino acids.
- Draw the zwitterion forms of amino acids at the isoelectric point and at pH levels above and below the isoelectric point.
- Write the ionized condensed structural formulas of dipeptides and tripeptides.
- Identify the structural levels of proteins as primary, secondary, tertiary, or quaternary.
- Describe the effects of denaturation on the structure of proteins.

Think About It

1. What are some uses of protein in the body?

2. What are the units that make up a protein?

3. How do you obtain protein in your diet?

Key Terms

Match the following key terms with the correct statement shown below:

a. amino acid **b.** peptide bond **c.** denaturation **d.** primary structure **e.** isoelectric point

1. ____ The order of amino acids in a protein

2. ____ The pH at which an amino acid has a net charge of zero

3. ____ The bond that connects amino acids in peptides and proteins

4. ____ The loss of secondary and tertiary protein structure caused by agents such as heat and acid

5. ____ The building block of proteins

Answers **1.** d **2.** e **3.** b **4.** c **5.** a

19.1 Proteins and Amino Acids

- Some proteins are enzymes or hormones, while others are important in structure, transport, protection, storage, and contraction of muscles.
- A group of 20 amino acids provides the molecular building blocks of proteins.
- In an ionized amino acid, a central (alpha) carbon is usually attached to an $—NH_3^+$ group, a carboxylate group ($—COO^-$), a hydrogen atom (—H) and a side chain or *R* group, which is unique for each amino acid.
- Each specific *R* group determines if an amino acid is nonpolar, polar (neutral), acidic, or basic. Nonpolar amino acids contain hydrocarbon side chains, whereas polar amino acids contain electronegative atoms such as oxygen (—OH) or sulfur (—SH). Acidic side chains contain a carboxylate group ($—COO^-$), and basic side chains contain an ammonium group ($—NH_3^+$).

MasteringChemistry

Tutorial: Proteins Building Blocks

Tutorial: Proteins 'R' Us

Self Study Activity: Functions of Proteins

◆ Learning Exercise 19.1A

Match one of the following functions of a protein with the examples below:

a. structural **b.** contractile **c.** storage **d.** transport
e. hormone **f.** enzyme **g.** protection

1. ____ hemoglobin, carries oxygen in blood
2. ____ amylase, hydrolyzes starch
3. ____ egg albumin, a protein in egg white
4. ____ vasopressin, regulates blood pressure
5. ____ collagen, makes up connective tissue
6. ____ immunoglobulin
7. ____ keratin, a major protein of hair
8. ____ lipoprotein, carries lipids in blood

Answers **1.** d **2.** f **3.** c **4.** e **5.** a **6.** g **7.** a **8.** d

◆ Learning Exercise 19.1B

Using the appropriate *R* group, complete the structural formula of each of the following amino acids. Indicate whether the amino acid would be nonpolar polar (neutral), acidic, or basic.

glycine (*R* = —H)

1. $H_3\overset{+}{N}—\overset{\square}{\underset{H}{C}}—\overset{O}{\overset{\|}{C}}—O^-$

alanine (*R* = $—CH_3$)

2. $H_3\overset{+}{N}—\overset{\square}{\underset{H}{C}}—\overset{O}{\overset{\|}{C}}—O^-$

serine ($R = -CH_2-OH$)

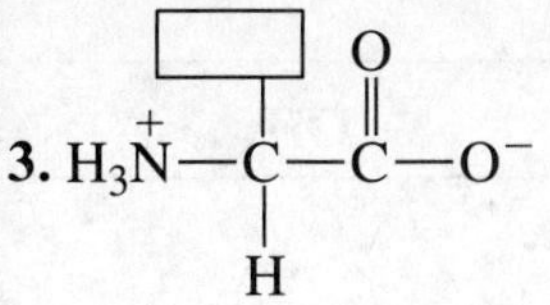

$$\mathbf{3.}\ H_3\overset{+}{N}-\overset{\boxed{}}{\underset{H}{C}}-\overset{O}{\overset{\|}{C}}-O^-$$

aspartic acid ($R = -CH_2-\overset{O}{\overset{\|}{C}}-OH$)

$$\mathbf{4.}\ H_3\overset{+}{N}-\overset{\boxed{}}{\underset{H}{C}}-\overset{O}{\overset{\|}{C}}-O^-$$

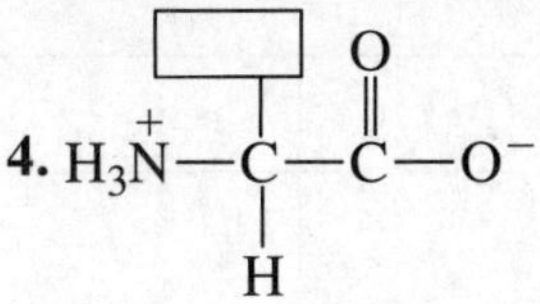

Answers

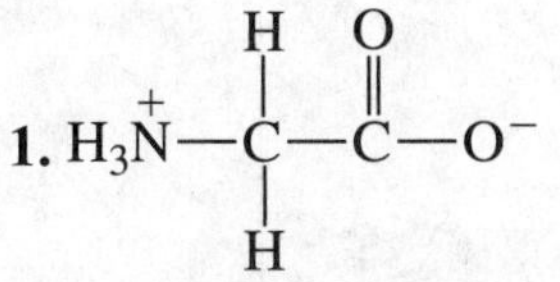

$$\mathbf{1.}\ H_3\overset{+}{N}-\overset{H}{\underset{H}{C}}-\overset{O}{\overset{\|}{C}}-O^-$$

nonpolar

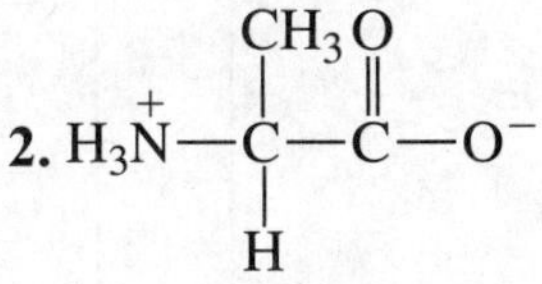

$$\mathbf{2.}\ H_3\overset{+}{N}-\overset{CH_3}{\underset{H}{C}}-\overset{O}{\overset{\|}{C}}-O^-$$

nonpolar

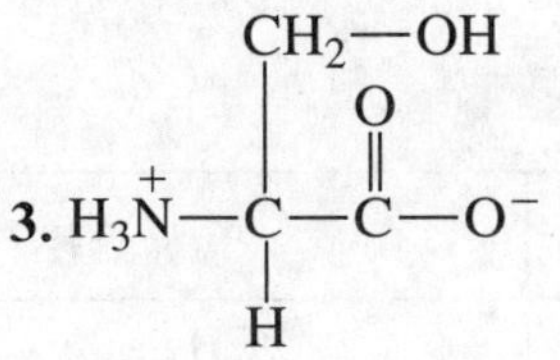

$$\mathbf{3.}\ H_3\overset{+}{N}-\overset{CH_2-OH}{\underset{H}{C}}-\overset{O}{\overset{\|}{C}}-O^-$$

polar

$$\mathbf{4.}\ H_3\overset{+}{N}-\overset{CH_2-\overset{O}{\overset{\|}{C}}-O^-}{\underset{H}{C}}-\overset{O}{\overset{\|}{C}}-O^-$$

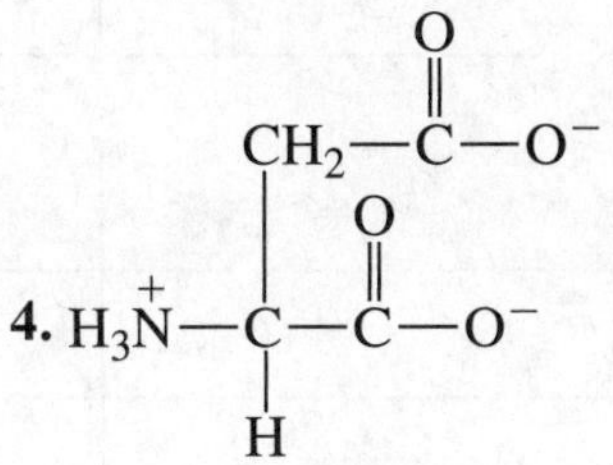

acidic

19.2 Amino Acids as Zwitterions

- Amino acids exist as zwitterions, which have an overall charge of zero at the isoelectric point (pI).
- A zwitterion has an overall positive charge at pH levels below its pI and an overall negative charge at pH levels higher than its pI.

MasteringChemistry

Tutorial: pH, pI, and Amino Acid Ionization

Study Note

Example: Glycine has an isoelectric point at a pH of 6.0. Draw the ionized structural formulas of glycine at its isoelectric point (pI) and at pH levels above and below its isoelectric point.

Solution: In a solution with a pH less than the pI, glycine has an overall positive charge. In a solution with a pH greater than the pI, glycine has an overall negative charge.

$$\underset{\textit{below pI}}{H_3\overset{+}{N}-CH_2-COOH} \xleftarrow{H^+} \underset{\textit{zwitterion of glycine}}{H_3\overset{+}{N}-CH_2-COO^-} \xrightarrow{OH^-} \underset{\text{above } \textit{pI}}{H_2N-CH_2-COO^-}$$

◆ Learning Exercise 19.2

Draw the ionized structural formulas of the amino acids under each of the following conditions:

Amino acid	Zwitterion (pI)	H^+	OH^-
1. Alanine	**1a.**	**1b.**	**1c.**
2. Serine	**2a.**	**2b.**	**2c.**

Answers

Zwitterion (pI)	H^+	OH^-
1a. $H_3\overset{+}{N}—\underset{}{\overset{CH_3}{\overset{\vert}{C}}}H—COO^-$	**1b.** $H_3\overset{+}{N}—\overset{CH_3}{\overset{\vert}{C}}H—COOH$	**1c.** $H_2N—\overset{CH_3}{\overset{\vert}{C}}H—COO^-$
2a. $H_3\overset{+}{N}—\overset{CH_2—OH}{\overset{\vert}{C}}H—COO^-$	**2b.** $H_3\overset{+}{N}—\overset{CH_2—OH}{\overset{\vert}{C}}H—COOH$	**2c.** $H_2N—\overset{CH_2—OH}{\overset{\vert}{C}}H—COO^-$

19.3 Formation of Peptides

- A peptide bond is an amide bond between the carboxylate group ($-COO^-$) of one amino acid and the ammonium group ($-NH_3^+$) of the next amino acid.

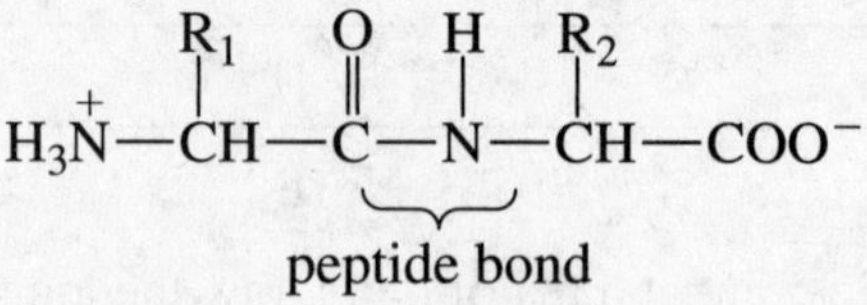

$$H_3\overset{+}{N}—\overset{R_1}{\overset{\vert}{C}}H—\underbrace{\overset{O}{\overset{\Vert}{C}}—\overset{H}{\overset{\vert}{N}}}_{\text{peptide bond}}—\overset{R_2}{\overset{\vert}{C}}H—COO^-$$

- Short chains of amino acids are called peptides. Long chains of amino acids are called proteins.

> ***MasteringChemistry***
>
> **Self Study Activity: Structure of Proteins**
>
> **Tutorial: Peptides are Chains of Amino Acids**

◆ Learning Exercise 19.3

Draw the ionized condensed structural formulas of the following dipeptides and tripeptides:

1. serylglycine

2. cystylvaline

3. Gly-Ser-Cys

Answers

1. 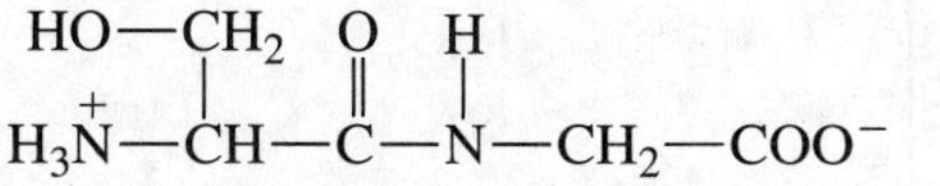
$$\begin{array}{l} \quad\quad\ \ HO{-}CH_2 \ \ O \ \ \ H \\ \quad\quad\quad\quad\quad | \quad\ \ \| \quad\ | \\ H_3\overset{+}{N}{-}CH{-}C{-}N{-}CH_2{-}COO^- \end{array}$$

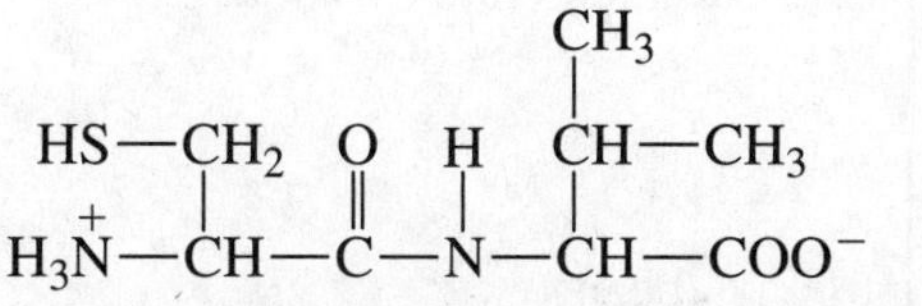

2.
$$\begin{array}{l} \quad\quad\quad\quad\quad\quad\quad\quad\quad\quad CH_3 \\ \quad\quad\quad\quad\quad\quad\quad\quad\quad\quad | \\ \quad\quad\ \ HS{-}CH_2 \ \ O \ \ \ H \ \ CH{-}CH_3 \\ \quad\quad\quad\quad\quad | \quad\ \ \| \quad\ | \quad\ \ | \\ H_3\overset{+}{N}{-}CH{-}C{-}N{-}CH{-}COO^- \end{array}$$

3.
$$\begin{array}{l} \quad\quad\quad\quad\quad\quad\ \ O \ \ HO{-}CH_2 \ \ O \quad\quad\quad\ CH_2{-}SH \\ \quad\quad\quad\quad\quad\quad\ \ \| \quad\quad\quad\ | \quad\ \ \| \quad\quad\quad\ | \\ H_3\overset{+}{N}{-}CH_2{-}C{-}N{-}CH{-}C{-}N{-}CH{-}COO^- \\ \quad\quad\quad\quad\quad\quad\quad\quad\ | \quad\quad\quad\quad\quad\ | \\ \quad\quad\quad\quad\quad\quad\quad\quad H \quad\quad\quad\quad\quad\ H \end{array}$$

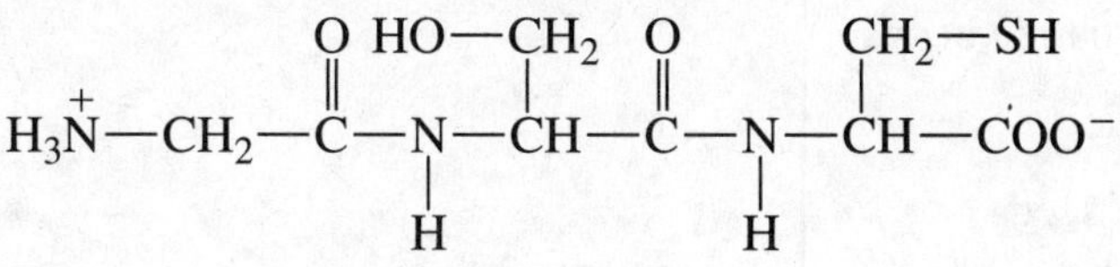

19.4 Protein Structure: Primary and Secondary Levels

- The primary structure of a protein is the sequence of amino acids connected by peptide bonds.
- In the secondary structure, hydrogen bonds between different sections of the peptide produce a characteristic shape such as an α helix, β-pleated sheet, or a triple helix.
- Certain combinations of vegetables are complementary when the protein from one provides the missing amino acid in the other. For example, garbanzo beans and rice have complementary proteins because tryptophan, which is low in garbanzo beans, is provided by rice, and lysine, which is low in rice, is provided by garbanzo beans.

MasteringChemistry

Self Study Activity: Primary and Secondary Structure

Tutorial: The Shapes of Protein Chains: Helices and Sheets

◆ Learning Exercise 19.4A

Identify the following descriptions of protein structure as primary or secondary structure:

1. ________ Hydrogen bonding forms an alpha (α)-helix.

2. ________ Hydrogen bonding occurs between C═O and N—H within a peptide chain.

3. ________ The type of protein structure that gives the sequence of amino acids that are linked by peptide bonds.

4. ________ Hydrogen bonds between protein chains form a pleated-sheet structure.

Answers **1.** secondary **2.** secondary **3.** primary **4.** secondary

◆ Learning Exercise 19.4B

Seeds, vegetables, and legumes are typically low in one or more of the essential amino acids, tryptophan, isoleucine, and lysine.

	Tryptophan	Isoleucine	Lysine
Sesame seeds	OK	low	low
Sunflower seeds	OK	OK	low
Garbanzo beans	low	OK	OK
Rice	OK	OK	low
Cornmeal	low	OK	low

Indicate whether the following protein combinations are complementary or not:

1. ________ sesame seeds and sunflower seeds

2. ________ sunflower seeds and garbanzo beans

3. ________ sunflower seeds, sesame seeds, and garbanzo beans

4. ________ sesame seeds and garbanzo beans

5. ________ garbanzo beans and rice

6. ________ cornmeal and sesame seeds

7. ________ rice and cornmeal

Answers
1. not complementary; both are low in lysine **2.** complementary
3. complementary **4.** complementary
5. complementary **6.** complementary
7. not complementary; both are low in lysine

19.5 Protein Structure: Primary and Secondary Levels

- In globular proteins, the polypeptide chain, including its α-helical and β-pleated sheet regions, folds upon itself to form a tertiary structure.
- In a tertiary structure, hydrophobic R groups are found on the inside and hydrophilic R groups on the outside surface. The tertiary structure is stabilized by interactions between R groups.
- In a quaternary structure, two or more subunits must combine for biological activity. They are held together by the same interactions found in tertiary structures.

MasteringChemistry

Self Study Activity: Tertiary and Quaternary Structure
Tutorial: Levels of Structure in Proteins

◆ Learning Exercise 19.5

Identify the following descriptions of protein structure as tertiary, quaternary, or both:

1. ____________ a disulfide bond joining distant parts of a peptide
2. ____________ the combination of four protein subunits
3. ____________ hydrophilic side groups seeking contact with water
4. ____________ a salt bridge forms between two oppositely charged side chains
5. ____________ hydrophobic side groups forming a nonpolar center

Answers **1.** tertiary **2.** quaternary **3.** both tertiary and quaternary
4. both tertiary and quaternary **5.** both tertiary and quaternary

19.6 Protein Hydrolysis and Denaturation

- Denaturation of a protein occurs when heat or other denaturing agents destroy the secondary, tertiary, and quaternary structures (but not the primary structure) of the protein until biological activity is lost.
- Denaturing agents include heat, acid, base, organic solvents, agitation, and heavy metal ions.

MasteringChemistry

Tutorial: Protein Demolition

◆ Learning Exercise 19.6

Indicate the denaturing agent in the following examples:

A. heat or UV light **B.** pH change **C.** organic solvent
D. heavy metal ions **E.** agitation

1. ____ placing surgical instruments in a 120 °C autoclave
2. ____ whipping cream to make a dessert topping
3. ____ applying tannic acid to a burn
4. ____ placing $AgNO_3$ drops in the eyes of newborns
5. ____ using alcohol to disinfect a wound
6. ____ using *Lactobacillus* bacteria culture to produce acid that converts milk to yogurt

Answers **1.** A **2.** E **3.** B **4.** D **5.** C **6.** B

Checklist for Chapter 19

You are ready to take the Practice Test for Chapter 19. Be sure that you have accomplished the following learning goals for this chapter. If you are not sure, review the section listed at the end of the goal. Then apply your new skills and understanding to the Practice Test.

After studying Chapter 19, I can successfully:

____ Classify proteins by their functions in the body (19.1).

____ Draw the ionized structural formula for an amino acid (19.1).

____ Draw the ionized structural formulas for an amino acid at its isoelectric point (pI), above and below the pI (19.2).

____ Describe a peptide bond; draw the ionized structural formulas for a peptide (19.3).

____ Distinguish between the primary and secondary structures of a protein (19.4).

____ Distinguish between the tertiary and quaternary structures of a protein (19.5).

____ Describe the ways that denaturation affects the structure of a protein (19.6).

Practice Test for Chapter 19

1. Which amino acid is nonpolar?

   A. serine **B.** aspartic acid **C.** valine **D.** cysteine **E.** glutamine

2. Which amino acid will form disulfide cross-links in a tertiary structure?

   A. serine **B.** aspartic acid **C.** valine **D.** cysteine **E.** glutamine

3. Which amino acid has a basic side chain?

   A. serine **B.** aspartic acid **C.** valine **D.** cysteine **E.** glutamine

4. All amino acids

   A. have the same side chains
   B. form zwitterions
   C. have the same isoelectric points
   D. show hydrophobic tendencies
   E. are essential amino acids

5. Essential amino acids

   A. are the amino acids that must be supplied by the diet
   B. are not synthesized by the body
   C. are missing in incomplete proteins
   D. are present in proteins from animal sources
   E. all of the above

For questions 6 through 9, use the following condensed structural formulas for alanine:

A. $H_3\overset{+}{N}-\underset{}{\overset{CH_3}{\overset{|}{C}}}H-COO^-$ **B.** $H_2N-\overset{CH_3}{\overset{|}{C}}H-COO^-$ **C.** $H_3\overset{+}{N}-\overset{CH_3}{\overset{|}{C}}H-COOH$

6. ____ alanine in its zwitterion form

7. ____ alanine at a low pH

8. ____ alanine at a high pH

9. ____ alanine at its isoelectric point

10. The sequence Tyr-Ala-Gly

A. is a tripeptide
B. has two peptide bonds
C. has tyrosine with free —NH_3^+ end
D. has glycine with the free —COO^- end
E. all of these

11. The type of bonding expected between lysine and aspartic acid is a

A. salt bridge **B.** hydrogen bond **C.** disulfide bond
D. hydrophobic interaction **E.** hydrophilic attraction

12. What type of bond is used to form the α helix structure of a protein?

A. peptide bond **B.** hydrogen bond **C.** salt bridge
D. disulfide bond **E.** hydrophobic attraction

13. What type of bonding places portions of the protein chain in the center of a tertiary structure?

A. peptide bonds **B.** salt bridges **C.** disulfide bonds
D. hydrophobic interactions **E.** hydrophilic attractions

For questions 14 through 18, identify the protein structural levels that each of the following statements describe:

A. primary **B.** secondary **C.** tertiary **D.** quaternary **E.** pentenary

14. ____ peptide bonds **15.** ____ a β–pleated sheet

16. ____ two or more protein subunits **17.** ____ an α helix **18.** ____ disulfide bonds

For questions 19 through 22, match the function of a protein with one of the examples A–D:

19. ____ enzyme **A.** myoglobin in muscle

20. ____ structural **B.** α–keratin in skin

21. ____ transport **C.** peptidase for protein hydrolysis

22. ____ storage **D.** casein in milk

23. Denaturation of a protein

A. occurs at a pH of 7 **B.** causes a change in protein structure
C. hydrolyzes a protein **D.** oxidizes the protein **E.** adds amino acids to a protein

24. Which of the following will not cause denaturation?

A. 0 °C **B.** $AgNO_3$ **C.** 80 °C **D.** ethanol **E.** pH 1

Answers to the Practice Test

1. C	**2.** D	**3.** E	**4.** B	**5.** E
6. A	**7.** C	**8.** B	**9.** A	**10.** E
11. A	**12.** B	**13.** D	**14.** A	**15.** B
16. D	**17.** B	**18.** C	**19.** C	**20.** B
21. A	**22.** D	**23.** B	**24.** A	

20
Enzymes and Vitamins

Study Goals

- Classify enzymes according to the type of reaction they catalyze.
- Describe the lock-and-key and induced-fit models of enzyme action.
- Discuss the effect of changes in temperature, pH, concentration of substrate, and concentration of enzyme on enzymatic activity.
- Describe the competitive, noncompetitive, and irreversible inhibition of enzymes.
- Discuss feedback control and regulation of enzyme activity by allosteric enzymes.
- Identify the types of cofactors that are necessary for enzyme activity.
- Describe the functions of vitamins and coenzymes.

Think About It

1. What are some functions of enzymes in the cells of the body?

2. Why are enzymes sensitive to high temperatures and low or high pH levels?

3. Why do we need vitamins?

Key Terms

Match the following key terms with the correct statement shown below:

a. lock-and-key model **b.** vitamin **c.** inhibitor
d. enzyme **e.** active site

1. ____ The portion of an enzyme structure where a substrate undergoes reaction

2. ____ A protein that catalyzes a biological reaction in the cells

3. ____ A model of enzyme action in which the substrate exactly fits the shape of the active site of an enzyme

4. ____ A substance that makes an enzyme inactive by interfering with its ability to react with a substrate

5. ____ An organic compound essential for normal health and growth that must be obtained from the diet

Answers **1.** e **2.** d **3.** a **4.** c **5.** b

20.1 Enzymes

- Enzymes are globular proteins that act as biological catalysts.
- Enzymes accelerate the rate of biological reactions by lowering the activation energy of a reaction.
- The names of many enzymes end with *ase*.
- Enzymes are classified by the type of reaction they catalyze: oxidoreductases, transferases, hydrolases, lyases, isomerases, or ligases.

MasteringChemistry
Tutorial: Enzymes and Activation Energy

◆ Learning Exercise 20.1A

Indicate whether each of the following characteristics of an enzyme is true (T) or false (F):

An enzyme

1. ____ is a biological catalyst
2. ____ functions at a low pH
3. ____ usually does not change the equilibrium position of a reaction
4. ____ is obtained from the diet
5. ____ greatly increases the rate of a cellular reaction
6. ____ is needed for every reaction that takes place in the cell
7. ____ catalyzes at a slower rate at lower temperatures
8. ____ functions best at mild conditions of pH 7.4 and 37 °C
9. ____ lowers the activation energy of a biological reaction
10. ____ increases the rate of the forward reaction, but not the reverse

Answers **1.** T **2.** F **3.** T **4.** F **5.** T
6. T **7.** T **8.** T **9.** T **10.** F

◆ Learning Exercise 20.1B

Match the common name of each of the following enzymes with the description of the reaction:

a. dehydrogenase **b.** oxidase **c.** peptidase
d. decarboxylase **e.** esterase **f.** transaminase

1. ____ hydrolyzes the ester bonds in triacylglycerols to yield fatty acids and glycerol
2. ____ removes hydrogen from a substrate
3. ____ removes CO_2 from a substrate
4. ____ decomposes hydrogen peroxide to water and oxygen
5. ____ hydrolyzes peptide bonds during the digestion of proteins
6. ____ transfers an amino ($-NH_2$) group from an amino acid to an α-keto acid

Answers **1.** e **2.** a **3.** d **4.** b **5.** c **6.** f

◆ Learning Exercise 20.1C

Match the IUPAC classification for enzymes with each of the following types of reactions:

a. oxidoreductase **b.** transferase **c.** hydrolase
d. lyase **e.** isomerase **f.** ligase

1. ____ combines small molecules using energy from ATP
2. ____ transfers phosphate groups
3. ____ hydrolyzes a disaccharide into two glucose units
4. ____ converts a substrate to an isomer of the substrate
5. ____ adds hydrogen to a substrate
6. ____ removes H_2O from a substrate
7. ____ adds oxygen to a substrate
8. ____ converts a cis structure to a trans structure

Answers **1.** f **2.** b **3.** c **4.** e **5.** a **6.** d **7.** a **8.** e

20.2 Enzyme Action

- Within the structure of the enzyme, there is a small pocket called the active site, which has a specific shape that fits a specific substrate.
- In the lock-and-key model or the induced-fit model, an enzyme and substrate form an enzyme–substrate complex so the reaction of the substrate can be catalyzed at the active site.

MasteringChemistry

Self Study Activity: How Enzymes Work

◆ Learning Exercise 20.2A

Match the terms active site (A), substrate (B), enzyme–substrate complex (C), lock-and-key model (D), and induced-fit model (E) with the following descriptions:

1. ____ the combination of an enzyme with a substrate
2. ____ a model of enzyme action in which the rigid shape of the active site exactly fits the shape of the substrate

3. ____ has a structure that fits the tertiary structure of the active site

4. ____ a model of enzyme action in which the shape of the active site adjusts to fit the shape of a substrate

5. ____ the portion of an enzyme that binds to the substrate and catalyzes the reaction

Answers **1.** C **2.** D **3.** B **4.** E **5.** A

◆ Learning Exercise 20.2B

Write an equation to illustrate the following:

1. the formation of an enzyme–substrate complex ____________

2. the conversion of enzyme–substrate complex to product ____________

Answers **1.** $E + S \rightleftharpoons ES$ **2.** $ES \rightarrow E + P$

20.3 Factors Affecting Enzyme Activity

- Enzymes are most effective at optimum temperature and pH. The rate of an enzyme reaction decreases considerably at temperatures and pH above or below the optimum.
- An enzyme can be made inactive by changes in pH, temperature, or chemical compounds called inhibitors.
- An increase in substrate concentration increases the reaction rate of an enzyme-catalyzed reaction until all the enzyme molecules combine with substrate.

MasteringChemistry

Tutorial: Denaturation and Enzyme Activity

Tutorial: Enzyme and Substrate Concentrations

◆ Learning Exercise 20.3A

Urease, which has an optimum pH of 7.0, catalyzes the hydrolysis of urea to ammonia and CO_2 in the liver. Draw a graph to represent the effects of each of the following on enzyme activity. Indicate the optimum pH and optimum temperature.

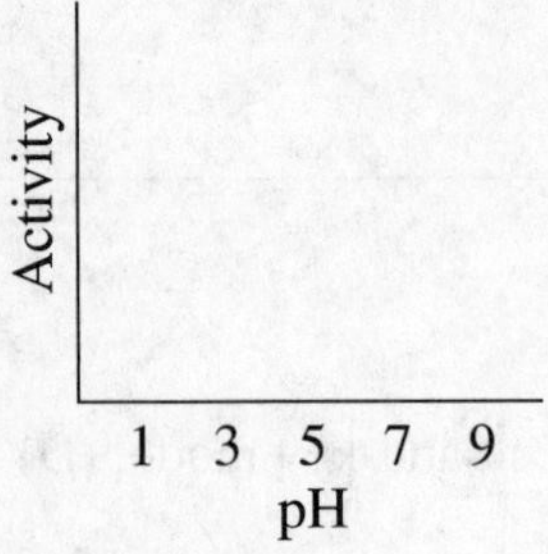

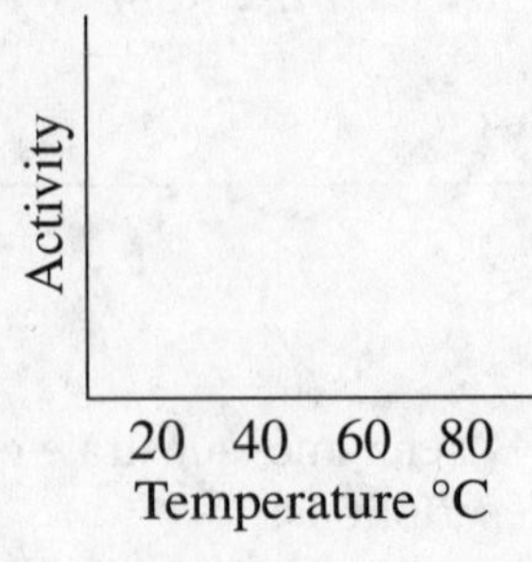

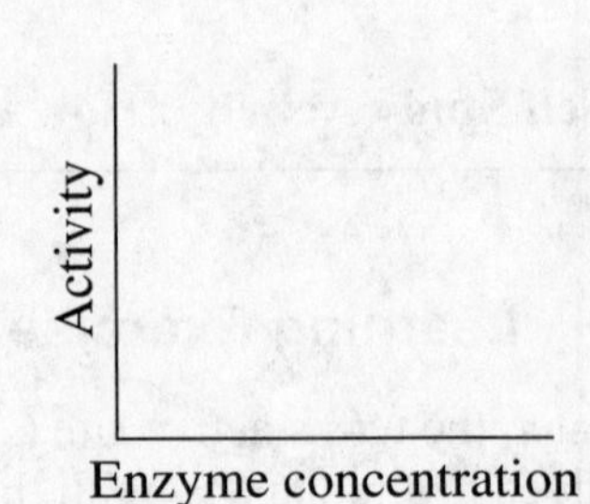

Answers

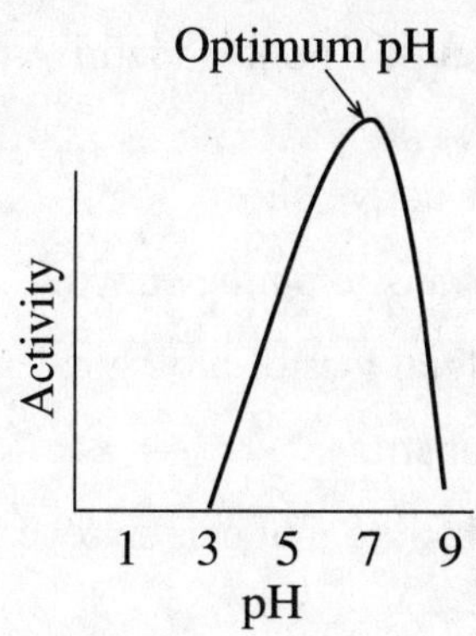

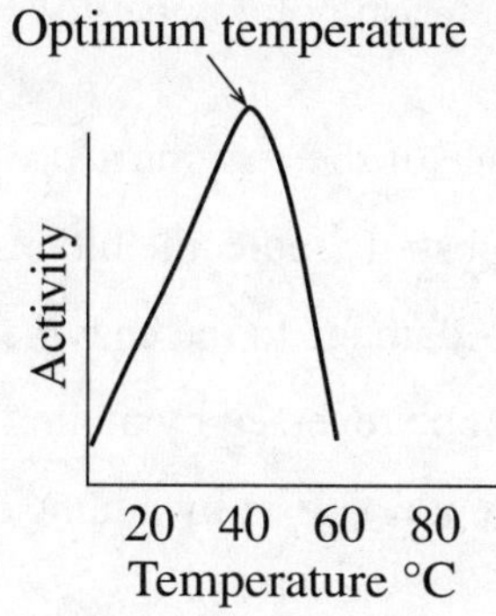

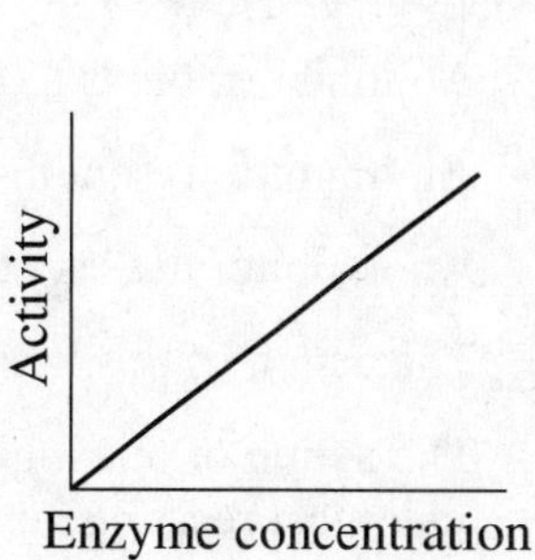

◆ Learning Exercise 20.3B

How is the rate of the urease-catalyzed reaction in Learning Exercise 20.3A affected by each of the following?

a. increases **b.** decreases **c.** not changed

1. ____ adding more urea when an excess of enzyme is present

2. ____ running the reaction at pH 10

3. ____ lowering the temperature to 0 °C

4. ____ running the reaction at 85 °C

5. ____ increasing the concentration of urease for a specific amount of urea

6. ____ adjusting pH to the optimum

Answers **1.** a **2.** b **3.** b **4.** b **5.** a **6.** a

20.4 Enzyme Inhibition

- A competitive inhibitor has a structure similar to the substrate and competes for the active site. When the active site is occupied by a competitive inhibitor, the enzyme cannot catalyze the reaction of the substrate.
- A noncompetitive inhibitor attaches elsewhere on the enzyme, changing the shape of both the enzyme and the active site. As long as the noncompetitive inhibitor is attached to the enzyme, the altered active site cannot bind with substrate.
- An irreversible inhibitor forms a permanent covalent bond with an amino acid side group in the active site of the enzyme, which prevents enzymatic activity.

MasteringChemistry

Tutorial: Enzyme Inhibition

Self Study Activity: Enzyme Inhibition

◆ Learning Exercise 20.4

Identify each of the following as characteristic of competitive inhibition (C), noncompetitive inhibition (N), or irreversible inhibition (I):

1. ____ An inhibitor binds to the surface of the enzyme away from the active site.
2. ____ An inhibitor resembling the substrate molecule blocks the active site on the enzyme.
3. ____ An inhibitor causes permanent damage to the enzyme with a total loss of biological activity.
4. ____ The action of this inhibitor can be reversed by adding more substrate.
5. ____ The action of this inhibitor is not reversed by adding more substrate, but can be reversed when chemical reagents remove the inhibitor.
6. ____ Sulfanilamide stops bacterial infections because its structure is similar to PABA (*p*-aminobenzoic acid), which is essential for bacterial growth.

Answers **1.** N **2.** C **3.** I **4.** C **5.** N **6.** C

20.5 Regulation of Enzyme Activity

- Many digestive enzymes are produced and stored as inactive forms called zymogens, which are activated at a later time.
- Hormones such as insulin and enzymes that catalyze blood clotting are synthesized as zymogens.
- When allosteric enzymes bind regulator molecules on a different part of the enzyme, there is a change in the shape of the enzyme and the active site. A positive regulator speeds up a reaction, and a negative regulator slows down a reaction.
- In feedback control, the end product of an enzyme-catalyzed sequence acts as a negative regulator and binds to the first enzyme in the sequence, which slows the rate of catalytic activity.

MasteringChemistry

Tutorial: Regulating Enzyme Action

◆ Learning Exercise 20.5

Match the following characteristics of types of enzyme regulation:

(Z) zymogen (A) allosteric enzyme (P) positive regulator
(N) negative regulator (F) feedback control

1. ____ an enzyme that binds molecules at a site that is not the active site to increase the rate of enzyme activity
2. ____ the end product of a reaction sequence binds to the first enzyme in the pathway
3. ____ a molecule that slows down reaction by preventing proper binding to the substrate
4. ____ an inactive form of an enzyme that is activated by removing a peptide section
5. ____ a molecule that binds at a site different than the active site to speed up the reaction

Answers **1.** A **2.** F **3.** N **4.** Z **5.** P

20.6 Enzyme Cofactors and Vitamins

- Simple enzymes are biologically active as a protein only, whereas other enzymes require a cofactor.
- A cofactor may be a metal ion, such as Cu^{2+} or Fe^{2+}, or an organic compound called a coenzyme, usually a vitamin.
- Vitamins are organic molecules that are essential for proper health.
- Vitamins must be obtained from the diet because they are not synthesized in the body.
- Vitamins B and C are classified as water-soluble; vitamins A, D, E, and K are fat-soluble vitamins.
- Many water-soluble vitamins function as coenzymes.

MasteringChemistry

Tutorial: Enzyme Cofactors and Vitamins

◆ Learning Exercise 20.6A

Indicate whether each statement describes a simple enzyme or a protein that requires a cofactor.

1. _______________ an enzyme consisting only of protein

2. _______________ an enzyme requiring magnesium ion for activity

3. _______________ an enzyme containing a sugar group

4. _______________ an enzyme that gives only amino acids upon hydrolysis

5. _______________ an enzyme that requires zinc ions for activity

Answers **1.** simple **2.** requires a cofactor **3.** requires a cofactor
4. simple **5.** requires a cofactor

◆ Learning Exercise 20.6B

Identify the water-soluble vitamin associated with each of the following:

a. thiamine (B_1) **b.** riboflavin (B_2) **c.** niacin (B_3)
d. cobalamin (B_{12}) **e.** ascorbic acid (C) **f.** pantothenic acid (B_5)

1. ____ collagen formation **2.** ____ part of the coenzyme for NAD^+

3. ____ pellagra **4.** ____ part of coenzyme A

5. ____ FAD and FMN **6.** ____ scurvy

Answers **1.** e **2.** c **3.** c **4.** f **5.** b **6.** e

◆ Learning Exercise 20.6C

Identify the fat-soluble vitamin associated with each of the following:

a. vitamin A **b.** vitamin D **c.** vitamin E **d.** vitamin K

1. ____ prevents oxidation of fatty acids **2.** ____ blood clotting

3. ____ night vision **4.** ____ rickets

5. ____ formed in skin by sunlight

6. ____ derived from cholesterol

Answers **1.** c **2.** d **3.** a **4.** b **5.** b **6.** b

Checklist for Chapter 20

You are ready to take the Practice Test for Chapter 20. Be sure that you have accomplished the following learning goals for this chapter. If you are not sure, review the section listed at the end of the goal. Then apply your new skills and understanding to the Practice Test.

After studying Chapter 20, I can successfully:

____ Classify enzymes according to the type of reaction they catalyze (20.1).

____ Describe the lock-and-key and induced-fit models of enzyme action (20.2).

____ Discuss the effect of changes in temperature, pH, concentration of enzyme, and concentration of substrate on enzyme action (20.3).

____ Describe the reversible and irreversible inhibition of enzymes (20.4).

____ Discuss feedback control and regulation of enzyme activity (20.5).

____ Identify the types of cofactors that are necessary for enzyme activity (20.6).

____ Describe the functions of vitamins as coenzymes (20.7).

Practice Test for Chapter 20

1. Enzymes

A. are biological catalysts
B. are polysaccharides
C. are insoluble in water
D. always contain a cofactor
E. are named with an *ose* ending

For questions 2 through 5, classify the enzymes as simple (S) or requiring a cofactor (C).

2. an enzyme that yields amino acids and a glucose molecule on analysis

3. an enzyme consisting of protein only

4. an enzyme requiring zinc ion for activation

5. an enzyme containing vitamin K

For questions 6 through 10, select answers from the following (E = enzyme; S = substrate; P = product):

A. $S \rightarrow P$
B. $EP \rightarrow E + P$
C. $E + S \rightarrow ES$
D. $ES \rightarrow EP$
E. $EP \rightarrow ES$

6. ____ the enzymatic reaction occurring at the active site

7. ____ the release of product from the enzyme

8. ____ the first step in the lock-and-key model of enzyme action

9. ____ the formation of the enzyme–substrate complex

10. ____ the final step in the lock-and-key model of enzyme action

For questions 11 through 15, match the names of enzymes with a reaction they each catalyze:

A. decarboxylase **B.** isomerase **C.** dehydrogenase
D. lipase **E.** sucrase

11. ____ $CH_3-CH(OH)-COOH \rightarrow CH_3-C(=O)-COOH$

12. ____ sucrose + $H_2O \rightarrow$ glucose and fructose

13. ____ $CH_3-C(=O)-COOH \rightarrow CH_3COOH + CO_2$

14. ____ fructose $\rightarrow$ glucose

15. ____ triglyceride + $3H_2O \rightarrow$ fatty acids and glycerol

For questions 16 through 20, select your answers from the following:

A. increases the rate of reaction
B. decreases the rate of reaction
C. denatures the enzyme, and no reaction occurs

16. ____ setting the reaction tube in a beaker of water at 100 °C

17. ____ adding substrate to the reaction vessel

18. ____ running the reaction at 10 °C

19. ____ adding ethanol to the reaction system

20. ____ adjusting the pH to optimum pH

For questions 21 through 25, identify each description of inhibition as one of the following:

A. competitive **B.** noncompetitive

21. ____ An alteration that affects the overall shape of the enzyme.

22. ____ A molecule, which closely resembles the substrate, interferes with enzymatic activity.

23. ____ The inhibition can be reversed by increasing substrate concentration.

24. ____ The heavy metal ion, Pb^{2+}, bonds with an –SH side group.

25. ____ The inhibition is not affected by increased substrate concentration.

Answers to the Practice Test

1. A	**2.** C	**3.** S	**4.** C	**5.** C
6. D	**7.** B	**8.** C	**9.** C	**10.** B
11. C	**12.** E	**13.** A	**14.** B	**15.** D
16. C	**17.** A	**18.** B	**19.** C	**20.** A
21. B	**22.** A	**23.** A	**24.** B	**25.** B

21

Nucleic Acids and Protein Synthesis

Study Goals

- Draw the structures of the bases, sugars, and nucleotides in DNA and RNA.
- Describe the structures of DNA and RNA.
- Explain the process of DNA replication.
- Describe the preparation of recombinant DNA.
- Describe the transcription process during the synthesis of mRNA.
- Use the codons in the genetic code to describe protein synthesis.
- Describe the regulation of protein synthesis in the cells.
- Explain how an alteration in the DNA sequence can lead to mutations in proteins.
- Describe the preparation of recombinant DNA.
- Explain how retroviruses use reverse transcription to synthesize DNA.

Think About It

1. Where is DNA in your cells?

2. How does DNA determine your height or the color of your hair or eyes?

3. What is the genetic code?

4. How does a mutation occur?

5. What is recombinant DNA?

Key Terms

Match the following key terms with the correct statement shown below.

a. DNA **b.** RNA **c.** double helix **d.** mutation **e.** transcription

1. _____ the formation of mRNA to carry genetic information from DNA to protein synthesis

2. _____ the genetic material containing nucleotides and bases adenine, cytosine, guanine, and thymine

3. _____ the shape of DNA with a sugar-phosphate backbone and base pairs linked in the center

4. _____ a change in the DNA base sequence that may alter the shape and function of a protein

5. _____ a type of nucleic acid with a single strand of nucleotides of adenine, cytosine, guanine, and uracil

Answers **1.** e **2.**a **3.** c **4.** d **5.** b

21.1 Components of Nucleic Acids

- Nucleic acids are composed of four bases, five-carbon sugars, and a phosphate group.
- In DNA, the bases are adenine, thymine, guanine, or cytosine. In RNA, uracil replaces thymine.
- In DNA, the sugar is deoxyribose; in RNA, the sugar is ribose.
- A nucleoside is composed of a base and a sugar.
- A nucleotide is composed of three parts: a base, a sugar, and a phosphate group.
- Deoxyribonucleic acid (DNA) and ribonucleic acid (RNA) are polymers of nucleotides.

MasteringChemistry

Tutorial: Nucleic Acid Building Blocks

◆ Learning Exercise 21.1A

1. Write the names and abbreviations for the bases in each of the following:

DNA ______________________________

RNA ______________________________

2. Write the name of the sugar in each of the following nucleotides:

DNA ______________________________

RNA ______________________________

Answers

1. DNA: adenine (A), thymine (T), guanine (G), cytosine (C)
   RNA: adenine (A), uracil (U), guanine (G), cytosine (C)
2. DNA: deoxyribose
   RNA: ribose

◆ Learning Exercise 21.1B

Name each of the following and classify it as a purine or a pyrimidine:

1. [structure: pyrimidine ring with NH_2, =O, N–H]
2. [structure: purine ring with NH_2, N–H]
3. [structure: purine ring with O, N–H, NH_2]
4. [structure: pyrimidine ring with H_3C, O, N–H, =O]

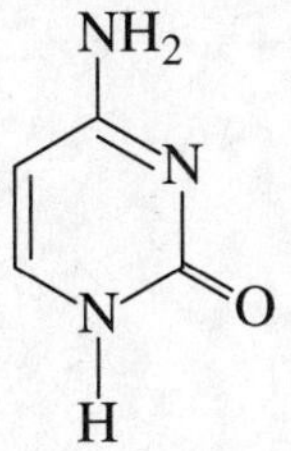

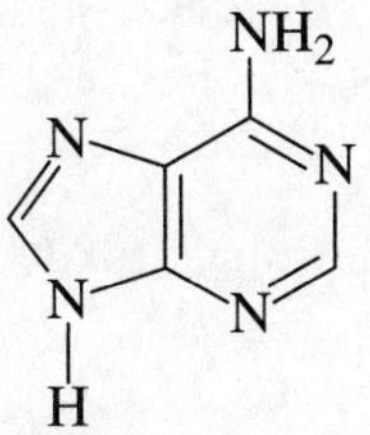

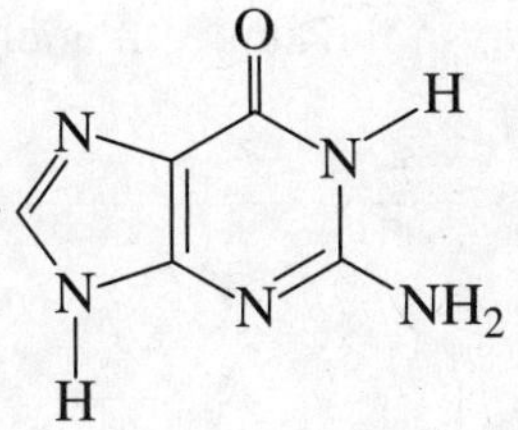

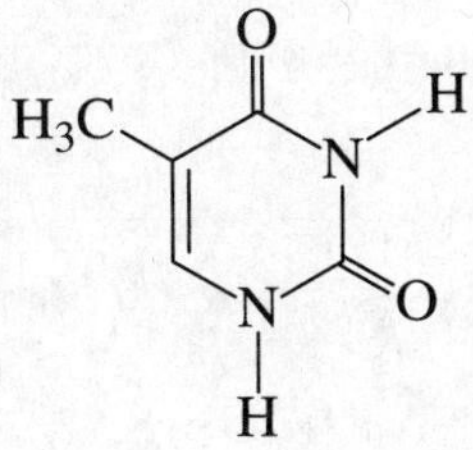

Answers

1. cytosine, pyrimidine
2. adenine; purine
3. guanine, purine
4. thymine, pyrimidine

◆ Learning Exercise 21.1C

Identify the nucleic acid (DNA or RNA) in which each of the following are found:

1. ______ adenosine-5′-monophosphate
2. ______ dCMP
3. ______ deoxythymidine-5′-monophosphate
4. ______ dGMP
5. ______ guanosine-5′-monophosphate
6. ______ cytidine-5′-monophosphate
7. ______ UMP
8. ______ deoxyadenosine-5′-monophosphate

Answers

1. RNA	2. DNA	3. DNA	4. DNA
5. RNA	6. RNA	7. RNA	8. DNA

◆ Learning Exercise 21.1D

Write the structural formula for deoxyadenosine-5′-monophosphate. Indicate the 5′- and the 3′-carbon atoms on the sugar.

Answer

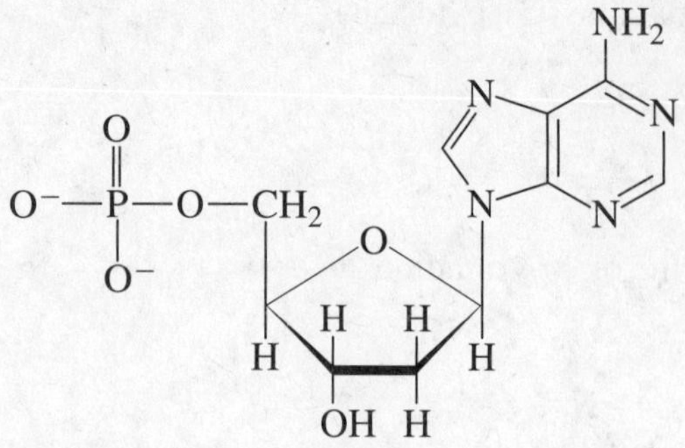

NH_2, N, N, O, $O^-—P—O—CH_2$, N, N, O, O^-, H, H, H, H, OH H

Deoxyadenosine 5′-monophosphate (dAMP)

21.2 Primary Structures of Nucleic Acids

- Nucleic acids are polymers of nucleotides in which the —OH group on the 3′-carbon of a sugar in one nucleotide bonds to the phosphate group attached to the 5′-carbon of a sugar in the adjacent nucleotide.

MasteringChemistry
Self Study Activity: DNA and RNA Structure

◆ Learning Exercise 21.2A

In the following dinucleotide, identify each nucleotide, the phosphodiester bond, the 5′-free phosphate group, and the free 3′-hydroxyl group.

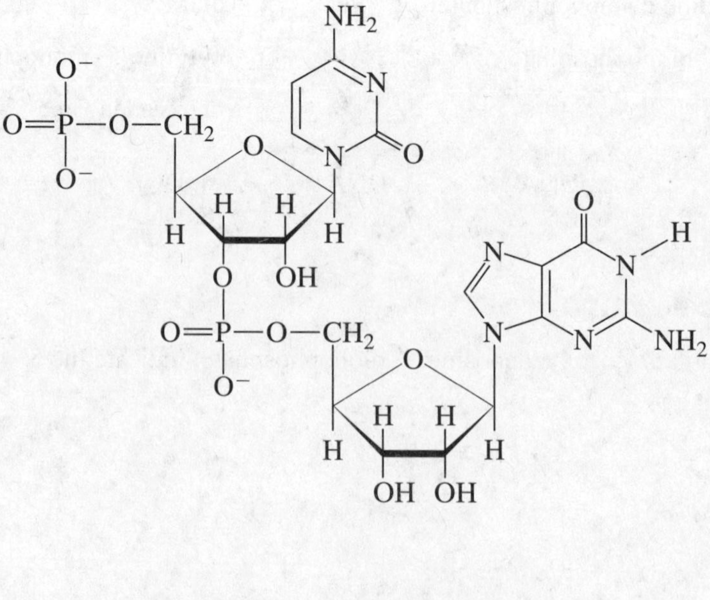

NH_2, O^-, N, $O{=}P—O—CH_2$, O, N, O, O^-, O, H, H, H, H, H, N, N, O, OH, $O{=}P—O—CH_2$, N, N, NH_2, O, O^-, H, H, H, H, OH OH

Answer

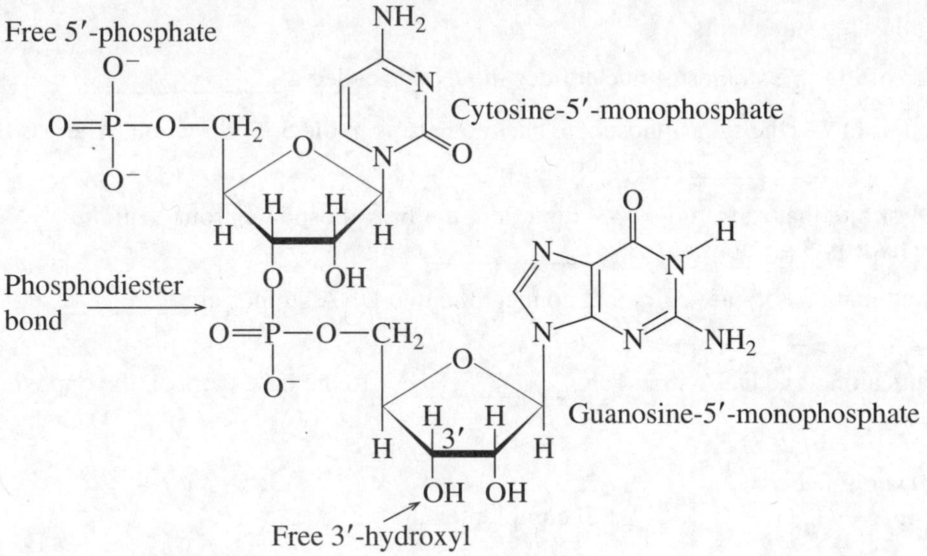

Free 5′-phosphate

Cytosine-5′-monophosphate

Phosphodiester bond

Guanosine-5′-monophosphate

Free 3′-hydroxyl

◆ Learning Exercise 21.2B

Consider the following sequence of nucleotides in RNA: —A—G—U—C—

1. What are the names of the nucleotides in this sequence?

2. Which nucleotide has the free 5′-phosphate group? ______________________

3. Which nucleotide has the free 3′-hydroxyl group? ______________________

Answer

1. adenosine-5′-monophosphate, guanosine-5′-monophosphate, uridine-5′-monophosphate, cytosine-5′-monophosphate
2. adenosine-5′-monophosphate (AMP) read as 5′—A—G—C—T—3′
3. cytosine-5′-monophosphate (CMP)

21.3 DNA Double Helix

- The two strands in DNA are held together by hydrogen bonds between complementary base pairs, A with T and G with C.
- One DNA strand runs in the 5′-3′ direction with a free 5′ phosphate, and the other strand runs in the 3′-5′ direction with a free 3′ phosphate.

MasteringChemistry

Tutorial: The Double Helix

◆ Learning Exercise 21.3A

Complete the following statements:

1. The structure of the two strands of nucleotides in DNA is called a ____________.
2. In one strand of DNA, the sugar-phosphate backbone runs in the 5′-3′ direction, whereas the opposite strand goes in the ____________ direction.
3. On the DNA strand that runs in the 5′-3′ direction, the free phosphate group is at the ____________ end and the free hydroxyl group is at the ____________ end.
4. The only combinations of base pairs that connect the two DNA strands are ____________ and ____________.
5. The base pairs along one DNA strand are ____________ to the base pairs on the opposite strand.

Answers **1.** double helix **2.** 3′-5′ **3.** 5′- 3′
4. A—T; G—C **5.** complementary

◆ Learning Exercise 21.3B

Complete each DNA section by writing the complementary strand.

1. 5′—A—T—G—C—T—T—G—G—C—T—C—C—3′

2. 5′—A—A—A—T—T—T—C—C—C—G—G—G—3′

3. 5′—G—C—G—C—T—C—A—A—A—T—G—C—3′

Answers
1. 3′—T—A—C—G—A—A—C—C—G—A—G—G—5′
2. 3′—T—T—T—A—A—A—G—G—G—C—C—C—5′
3. 3′—C—G—C—G—A—G—T—T—T—A—C—G—5′

21.4 DNA Replication

- During DNA replication, DNA polymerase makes new DNA strands along each of the original DNA strands that serve as templates.
- Complementary base pairing ensures the correct pairing of bases to give identical copies of the original DNA.

MasteringChemistry

Tutorial: DNA Replication

Self Study Activity: DNA Replication

◆ Learning Exercise 21.4A

How does the replication of DNA produce identical copies of the DNA?

Answer In the replication process, the bases on each strand of the separated parent DNA are paired with their complementary bases. Because each complementary base is specific for a base in DNA, the new DNA strands exactly duplicate the original strands of DNA.

◆ Learning Exercise 21.4B

Match each of the following terms with components or events in DNA replication:

a. replication fork	**b.** Okazaki fragment	**c.** DNA polymerase
d. helicase	**e.** leading strand	**f.** lagging strand

1. _______ the enzyme that catalyzes the unwinding of a section of the DNA double helix

2. _______ the points in open sections of DNA where replication begins

3. _______ the enzyme that catalyzes the formation of phosphodiester bonds between nucleotides

4. _______ short segments produced in the formation of the 3′-5′ daughter DNA strand

5. _______ the new DNA strand that grows in the 5′ to 3′ direction during the formation of daughter DNA

6. _______ the new DNA strand that is synthesized in the 3′ to 5′ direction.

Answers **1.** d **2.** a **3.** c **4.** b **5.** e **6.** f

21.5 RNA and Transcription

- The three types of RNA differ by function in the cell: ribosomal RNA makes up most of the structure of the ribosomes, messenger RNA carries genetic information from the DNA to the ribosomes, and transfer RNA places the correct amino acids in the protein.
- Transcription is the process by which RNA polymerase produces mRNA from one strand of DNA.
- The bases in the mRNA are complementary to the DNA, except U is paired with A in DNA.
- The polymerase enzyme moves along an unwound section of DNA in a 3′ to 5′ direction.
- In eukaryotes, initial RNA includes noncoding sections, which are removed before the RNA leaves the nucleus.
- The production of mRNA occurs when certain proteins are needed in the cell.
- In enzyme induction, the appearance of a substrate in a cell removes a repressor, which allows RNA polymerase to produce mRNA at the structural genes.

MasteringChemistry

Tutorial: Types of RNA

Self Study Activity: Transcription

Self Study Activity: The *lactose* Operon in *E. coli*

Tutorial: Activating and Inhibiting Genes

◆ Learning Exercise 21.5A

Match each of the following characteristics with a specific type of RNA: mRNA, tRNA, or rRNA.

1. the most abundant type of RNA in a cell ____________

2. the RNA that has the shortest chain of nucleotides ____________

3. the RNA that carries information from DNA to the ribosomes for protein synthesis ____________

4. the RNA that is the major component of ribosomes ____________

5. the RNA that carries specific amino acids to the ribosome for protein synthesis ____________

6. the RNA that consists of a large and a small subunit ____________

Answers **1.** rRNA **2.** tRNA **3.** mRNA
4. rRNA **5.** tRNA **6.** rRNA

◆ Learning Exercise 21.5B

Fill in the blanks with a word or phrase that answers each of the following questions:

1. Where in the cell does transcription take place? ________________________

2. How many strands of the DNA molecules are involved? ________________________

3. sections in genes that code for proteins ________________________

4. sections in genes that do not code for proteins ________________________

5. the abbreviations for the four nucleotides in mRNA ________________________

6. Write the corresponding section of a mRNA produced from each of the following:

A. 3′—C—A—T—T—C—G—G—T—A—5′

B. 3′—G—T—A—C—C—T—A—A—C—G—T—C—C—G—5′

Answers **1.** nucleus **2.** one **3.** exons **4.** introns **5.** A, U, G, C
6. A. 5′—G—U—A—A—G—C—C—A—U—3′
B. 5′—C—A—U—G—G—A—U—U—G—C—A—G—G—C—3′

◆ Learning Exercise 21.5C

Match the following descriptions of cellular control with the terms:

a. repressor **b.** operon **c.** structural gene
d. feedback control **e.** enzyme induction

______ **1.** the production of an enzyme caused by the appearance of a substrate

______ **2.** a unit formed by a structural gene and a control site

______ **3.** high levels of an end product stop the production of the enzymes in that pathway

______ **4.** a protein that binds to the control site on the gene to block protein synthesis

______ **5.** the portion of DNA that produces the mRNA for protein synthesis

Answers **1.** e **2.** b **3.** d **4.** a **5.** c

21.6 The Genetic Code

- The genetic code consists of a sequence of three bases (triplet) that specifies the order for the amino acids in a protein.
- The 64 codons for 20 amino acids allow several codons for most amino acids.
- The codon AUG signals the start of transcription, and codons UAG, UGA, and UAA signal the stop.

MasteringChemistry

Tutorial: Genetic Code

◆ Learning Exercise 21.6

Give the abbreviation for each of the amino acids coded for by the following mRNA codons:

1. UUU ______________ **2.** GCG ______________

3. AGC ______________ **4.** CCA ______________

5. GGA ______________ **6.** ACA ______________

7. AUG ______________ **8.** CUC ______________

9. CAU ______________ **10.** GUU ______________

Answers **1.** Phe **2.** Ala **3.** Ser **4.** Pro **5.** Gly
6. Thr **7.** Start/Met **8.** Leu **9.** His **10.** Val

21.7 Protein Synthesis: Translation

- Proteins are synthesized at the ribosomes in a translation process that includes three steps: initiation, elongation, and termination.
- During translation, the different tRNA molecules bring the appropriate amino acids to the ribosome, where the amino acid is bonded by a peptide bond to the growing peptide chain.
- When the polypeptide is released, it takes on its secondary and tertiary structures to become a functional protein in the cell.

MasteringChemistry

Self Study Activity: Overview of Protein Synthesis

Self Study Activity: Translation

Tutorial: Following the Instructions in DNA

◆ Learning Exercise 21.7A

Match each of the following descriptions with a step of the translation process:

a. initiation **b.** activation **c.** anticodon **d.** translocation **e.** termination

1. ____ the three bases in each tRNA that complement a codon on the mRNA
2. ____ the combining of an amino acid with a specific tRNA
3. ____ the placement of methionine on the large ribosomal subunit
4. ____ the shift of the ribosome from one codon on mRNA to the next
5. ____ the process that occurs when the ribosome reaches a UAA, UGA, or UAG codon on mRNA

Answers **1.** c **2.** b **3.** a **4.** d **5.** e

◆ Learning Exercise 21.7B

Write the mRNA that would form for the following section of DNA. For each codon in the mRNA, write the amino acid that would be placed in the protein by a tRNA.

1. DNA strand: 3′—CCC—TCA—GGG—CGC—5′

mRNA: _______—_______—_______—_______

Amino acids: _______—_______—_______—_______

2. DNA: 3′—ATA—GCC—TTT—GGC—AAC—5′

mRNA: _______—_______—_______—_______—_______

Amino acids: _______—_______—_______—_______—_______

Answers **1.** mRNA: 5′—GGG—AGU—CCC—GCG—3′
—Gly—Ser—Pro—Ala—
2. mRNA: 5′—UAU—CGG—AAA—CCG—UUG—3′
—Tyr—Arg—Lys—Pro—Leu—

◆ Learning Exercise 21.7C

A segment of DNA that codes for a protein contains 270 nucleic acids. How many amino acids would be present in the protein for this DNA segment?

Answer Assuming that the entire segment codes for a protein, there would be 90 (270 ÷ 3) amino acids in the protein produced.

21.8 Genetic Mutations

- A genetic mutation is a change of one or more bases in the DNA sequence that may alter the structure and ability of the resulting protein to function properly.
- In a substitution, one base is altered, which may code for a different amino acid.

- In a frameshift mutation, the insertion or deletion of one base alters all of the codons following the base change, which affects the amino acid sequence that follows the mutation.

MasteringChemistry
Tutorial: Genetic Mutations

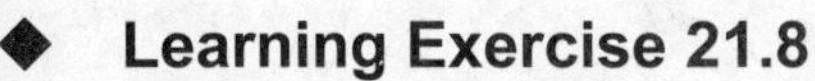

◆ Learning Exercise 21.8

Consider a segment of a DNA template of 3′—AAT—CCC—GGG—5′.

1. Write the mRNA segment produced.

_______—_______—_______

2. Write the amino acid order produced from the segment of mRNA codons.

_______—_______—_______

3. Suppose a mutation replaces the thymine in this segment of the DNA template with a guanine. Write the mRNA segment it produces.

_______—_______—_______

4. What is the new amino acid order?

_______—_______—_______

5. Why is this mutation referred to as a substitution?

6. How is a substitution different from an insertion or deletion mutation?

7. What are some possible causes of genetic mutations?

Answers

1. 5′—UUA—GGG—CCC—3′ **2.** Leu–Gly–Pro
3. 5′—UUC—GGG—CCC—3′ **4.** Phe–Gly–Pro

5. In a mutation that is a base substitution, only one codon is affected, and one amino acid may be different.
6. In an insertion or deletion mutation, the triplet codes that follow the mutation point are shifted by one base, which leads to a different amino acid order in the remaining sequence of the protein.
7. X–rays, UV light, chemicals called mutagens, and some viruses are possible causes of mutations.

21.9 Recombinant DNA

- Recombinant DNA is DNA that has been synthesized by opening a piece of DNA and inserting a DNA section from another source.
- Much of the work in recombinant DNA is done with the small circular DNA molecules called plasmids found in *Escherichia coli* bacteria.
- Recombinant DNA is used to produce large numbers of copies of foreign DNA that is useful in genetic engineering techniques.

MasteringChemistry

Self Study Activity: Applications of DNA Technology

Self Study Activity: Restriction Enzymes

Self Study Activity: Cloning a Gene in Bacteria

Self Study Activity: Analyzing DNA Fragments Using Gel Electrophoresis

Self Study Activity: DNA Fingerprinting

Self Study Activity: The Human Genome Project: Human Chromosome 17

◆ Learning Exercise 21.9

Match the statements shown below with the following terms:

a. plasmids **b.** restriction enzymes **c.** polymerase chain reaction
d. recombinant DNA **e.** Human Genome Project

1. ______ a synthetic form of DNA that contains a piece of foreign DNA

2. ______ research that determined the DNA sequences for all the genes in a human cell

3. ______ small, circular, DNA molecules found in *E. coli* bacteria

4. ______ a process that makes multiple copies of DNA in a short amount of time

5. ______ enzymes that cut open the DNA strands in the plasmids

Answers **1.** d **2.** e **3.** a **4.** c **5.** b

21.10 Viruses

- Viruses are small particles of 3–200 genes that cannot replicate unless they invade a host cell.
- A viral infection involves using the host cell machinery to replicate the viral nucleic acid
- A retrovirus contains RNA as its genetic material

MasteringChemistry
Self Study Activity: HIV Reproductive Cycle

◆ Learning Exercise 21.10

Match the key terms with the statements shown below:

a. host cell **b.** retrovirus **c.** vaccine **d.** protease **e.** virus

1. ____ the enzyme inhibited by drugs that prevent the synthesis of viral proteins

2. ____ a small, disease-causing particle that contains either DNA or RNA as its genetic material

3. ____ a type of virus that must use reverse transcriptase to make a viral DNA.

4. ____ required by viruses to replicate

5. ____ inactive form of viruses that boosts the immune response by causing the body to produce antibodies

Answers **1.** d **2.** e **3.** b **4.** a **5.** c

Checklist for Chapter 21

You are ready to take the Practice Test for Chapter 21. Be sure that you have accomplished the following learning goals for this chapter. If you are not sure, review the section listed at the end of the goal. Then apply your new skills and understanding to the practice test.

After studying Chapter 21, I can successfully:

______ Identify the components of nucleic acids RNA and DNA (21.1).

______ Describe the nucleotides contained in DNA and RNA (21.1).

______ Describe the primary structure of nucleic acids (21.2).

______ Describe the structures of RNA and DNA; show the relationship between the bases in the double helix (21.3).

______ Explain the process of DNA replication (21.4).

______ Describe the structure and characteristics of the three types of RNA (21.5).

______ Describe the synthesis of mRNA (transcription) (21.5).

______ Describe the function of the codons in the genetic code (21.6).

______ Describe the role of translation in protein synthesis (21.7).

______ Describe some ways in which DNA is altered to cause mutations (21.8).

______ Describe the process used to prepare recombinant DNA (21.9).

______ Explain how retroviruses use reverse transcription to synthesize DNA (21.10).

Practice Test for Chapter 21

1. A nucleotide contains

A. a base
B. a base and a sugar
C. a phosphoryl group and a sugar
D. a base and deoxyribose
E. a base, a sugar, and a phosphoryl group

2. The double helix in DNA is held together by

A. hydrogen bonds
B. ester linkages
C. peptide bonds
D. salt bridges
E. disulfide bonds

3. The process of producing DNA in the nucleus is called

A. complementation
B. replication
C. translation
D. transcription
E. mutation

4. Which occurs in RNA but **NOT** in DNA?

A. thymine
B. cytosine
C. adenine
D. phosphate
E. uracil

5. Which molecule determines protein structure in protein synthesis?

A. DNA **B.** mRNA **C.** tRNA **D.** rRNA **E.** ribosomes

6. Which type of molecule carries amino acids to the ribosomes?

A. DNA **B.** mRNA **C.** tRNA **D.** rRNA **E.** protein

For questions 7 through 15, select answers from the following nucleic acids:

A. DNA **B.** mRNA **C.** tRNA **D.** rRNA

7. ____ Along with protein, it is a major component of the ribosomes.

8. ____ A double helix consisting of two chains of nucleotides held together by hydrogen bonds between bases.

9. ____ A nucleic acid that uses deoxyribose as the sugar.

10. ____ A nucleic acid produced in the nucleus that migrates to the ribosomes to direct the formation of a protein.

11. ____ It can place the proper amino acid into the peptide chain.

12. ____ It has bases of adenine, cytosine, guanine, and thymine.

13. ____ It contains the codons for the amino acid order.

14. ____ It contains a triplet called an anticodon.

15. ____ This nucleic acid is replicated during cellular division.

For questions 16 through 20, select answers from the following:

A.
```
—A—G—C—C—T—A—
 |  |  |  |  |  |
—T—C—G—G—A—T—
```

B. —A—U—U—G—C—U—C—

C.
```
—A—G—T—U—G—U—
 |  |  |  |  |  |
—T—C—A—A—C—A—
```

D. —G—U—A—

E. —A—T—G—T—A—T—

16. ____ a section of an mRNA

17. ____ an impossible section of DNA

18. ____ a codon

19. ____ a section from a DNA molecule

20. ____ a single strand that would not be possible for mRNA

For questions 21 through 25, select the correct order of protein synthesis from the following statements A to E:

A. tRNA assembles the amino acids at the ribosomes.
B. DNA forms a complementary copy of itself called mRNA.
C. Protein is formed and breaks away.
D. tRNA picks up specific amino acids.
E. mRNA goes to the ribosomes.

21. ____ first step

22. ____ second step

23. ____ third step

24. ____ fourth step

25. ____ fifth step

For questions 26 through 30, select an answer from the following:

A. mutation
B. enzyme induction
C. inducer
D. operon
E. repressor

26. ____ a unit that attaches to the control site and blocks the synthesis of a protein

27. ____ an error in the transmission of the base sequence of DNA

28. ____ a portion of a gene composed of the control site and the structural genes

29. ____ a substrate that promotes the synthesis of the enzymes necessary for its metabolism

30. ____ the level of end product regulates the synthesis of the enzymes in that metabolic pathway

Answers to the Practice Test

1. E	**2.** A	**3.** B	**4.** E	**5.** A
6. C	**7.** D	**8.** A	**9.** A	**10.** B
11. C	**12.** A	**13.** B	**14.** C	**15.** A
16. B, D	**17.** C	**18.** D	**19.** A	**20.** E
21. B	**22.** E	**23.** D	**24.** A	**25.** C
26. E	**27.** A	**28.** D	**29.** B	**30.** C

22

Metabolic Pathways for Carbohydrates

Study Goals

- Explain the role of ATP in anabolic and catabolic reactions.
- Compare the structure and function of the coenzymes NAD^+, FAD, and coenzyme A.
- Give the sites, enzymes, and products for the digestion of carbohydrates.
- Describe the key reactions in the degradation of glucose in glycolysis.
- Describe the three possible pathways for pyruvate.
- Discuss the impact of ATP levels on glycogen metabolism.
- Describe gluconeogenesis and the Cori cycle.

Think About It

1. Why do you need ATP in your cells?

2. What monosaccharides are produced when carbohydrates undergo digestion?

3. What is meant by *aerobic* and *anaerobic* conditions in the cells?

4. How does glycogen help maintain blood glucose level?

Key Terms

Match the following key terms with the correct statement shown below.

a. ATP **b.** glycogen **c.** glycolysis
d. catabolic reaction **e.** mitochondria

1. _____ The storage form of glucose in the muscle and liver

2. _____ A metabolic reaction that produces energy for the cell by degrading large molecules

3. _____ A high-energy compound produced from energy-releasing processes that provides energy for energy-requiring reactions

4. _____ The degradation reactions of glucose that yield two pyruvate molecules

5. _____ The organelles in the cells where energy-producing reactions take place

Answers **1.** b **2.** d **3.** a **4.** c **5.** e

22.1 Metabolism and Cell Structure

- Metabolism is all of the chemical reactions that provide energy and substances for cell growth.
- Catabolic reactions degrade large molecules to produce energy.
- Anabolic reactions utilize energy in the cell to build large molecules for the cells.
- In cells, different organelles contain the enzymes and coenzymes for the various catabolic and anabolic reactions.

◆ Learning Exercise 22.1A

Match each of the following organelles with their description or cellular function:

a. lysosomes **b.** ribosomes **c.** mitochondria
d. Golgi complex **e.** cytoplasm **f.** cell membrane

1. ____ separates the contents of a cell from the external environment

2. ____ contain enzymes that catalyze energy-producing reactions

3. ____ the cellular material between the plasma membrane and the nucleus

4. ____ modifies proteins from the endoplasmic reticulum for cell membranes

5. ____ sites of protein synthesis

6. ____ contain hydrolytic enzymes that digest old cell structures

Answers **1.** f **2.** c **3.** e **4.** d **5.** b **6.** a

◆ Learning Exercise 22.1B

Identify the stages of metabolism for each of the following processes:

a. stage 1 **b.** stage 2 **c.** stage 3

1. ____ oxidation of two-carbon acetyl CoA, which enters a series of reactions that provide most of the energy for ATP synthesis

2. ____ polysaccharides undergo digestion to monosaccharides, such as glucose

3. ____ digestion products such as glucose are degraded to two- or three-carbon compounds

Answers **1.** c **2.** a **3.** b

22.2 ATP and Energy

- Energy is stored in ATP, a high-energy compound that is hydrolyzed when energy is required for the anabolic reactions that do work in the cells.
- The hydrolysis of ATP, which releases energy, is linked with many anabolic reactions in the cell.

MasteringChemistry

Self Study Activity: ATP

Tutorial: ATP: Energy Rich

◆ Learning Exercise 22.2

Complete the following statements for ATP:

The ATP molecule is composed of a nitrogen base (1) ____________, a (2) ____________ sugar, and three (3) ____________. ATP undergoes (4)____________, which cleaves a (5) ____________ and releases (6) ____________. For this reason, ATP is called a (7) ____________ compound. The resulting phosphate group called inorganic phosphate is abbreviated as (8) ____________. This equation can be written as (9) ____.

The energy from ATP is linked to cellular reactions that are (10) ____________.

Answers
1. adenine **2.** ribose **3.** phosphoryl groups **4.** hydrolysis
5. phosphoryl group **6.** energy **7.** high-energy **8.** P_i
9. $ATP + H_2O \rightarrow ADP + P_i + \text{energy}$ (7.3 kcal/mole) **10.** energy requiring

22.3 Important Coenzymes in Metabolic Pathways

- Coenzymes such as FAD and NAD^+ pick up hydrogen ions and electrons during oxidative processes.
- Coenzyme A is a coenzyme that carries acetyl (two-carbon) groups produced when glucose, fatty acids, and amino acids are degraded.

◆ Learning Exercise 22.3

Select the coenzyme that matches each of the following descriptions:

a. NAD^+ **b.** NADH **c.** FAD **d.** $FADH_2$ **e.** coenzyme A

1. ____ participates in reactions that convert a hydroxyl group to a C=O group

2. ____ contains riboflavin (vitamin B_2)

3. ____ reduced form of nicotinamide adenine dinucleotide

4. ____ contains the vitamin niacin

5. ____ oxidized form of flavin adenine dinucleotide

6. ____ contains the vitamin pantothenic acid, ADP, and an aminoethanethiol

7. ____ participates in oxidation reactions that produce a carbon–carbon double bond (C=C)

8. ____ transfers acyl groups such as the two-carbon acetyl group

9. ____ reduced form of flavin adenine dinucleotide

Answers **1.** a **2.** c, d **3.** b **4.** a, b **5.** c
6. e **7.** c **8.** e **9.** d

22.4 Digestion of Carbohydrates

- Digestion is a series of reactions that break down large food molecules of carbohydrates, lipids, and proteins into smaller molecules that can be absorbed and used by the cells.
- The end products of digestion of polysaccharides are monosaccharides glucose, fructose, and galactose.

MasteringChemistry

Tutorial: Breakdown of Carbohydrates

◆ Learning Exercise 22.4

Complete the table to describe sites, enzymes, and products for the digestion of carbohydrates.

Food	Digestion Site(s)	Enzyme	Products
1. Amylose			
2. Amylopectin			
3. Maltose			
4. Lactose			
5. Sucrose			

Answers

Food	Digestion Site(s)	Enzyme	Products
1. Amylose	**a.** mouth **b.** small intestine (mucosa)	**a.** salivary amylase **b.** pancreatic amylase	**a.** smaller polysaccharides (dextrins), some maltose and glucose **b.** maltose, glucose
2. Amylopectin	**a.** mouth **b.** small intestine (mucosa)	**a.** salivary amylase **b.** pancreatic amylase, branching enzyme	**a.** smaller polysaccharides (dextrins), some maltose and glucose **b.** maltose, glucose
3. Maltose	small intestine (mucosa)	maltase	glucose and glucose
4. Lactose	small intestine (mucosa)	lactase	glucose and galactose
5. Sucrose	small intestine (mucosa)	sucrase	glucose and fructose

22.5 Glycolysis: Oxidation of Glucose

- Glycolysis is the primary anaerobic pathway for the degradation of glucose to yield pyruvate. Glucose is converted to fructose-1,6-bisphosphate that is split into two triose phosphate molecules.
- The oxidation of each three-carbon sugar yields the reduced coenzyme 2 NADH and 2 ATP.

MasteringChemistry

Self Study Activity: Glycolysis

Tutorial: The Glycolysis Pathway

◆ Learning Exercise 22.5

Match each of the following terms of glycolysis with the best description:

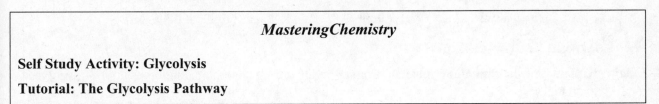

a. 2 NADH　**b.** anaerobic　**c.** glucose　**d.** two pyruvate
e. energy invested　**f.** energy generated　**g.** 2 ATP　**h.** 4 ATP

1. ____ the starting material for glycolysis

2. ____ steps 1–5 of glycolysis

3. ____ operates without oxygen

4. ____ net ATP energy produced

5. ____ number of reduced coenzymes produced

6. ____ steps 6–10 of glycolysis

7. ____ end product of glycolysis

8. ____ number of ATP required

Answers　**1.** c　**2.** e　**3.** b　**4.** g
5. a　**6.** f　**7.** d, a, g　**8.** g

22.6 Pathways for Pyruvate

- In the absence of oxygen, pyruvate is reduced to lactate and NAD^+ is regenerated for the continuation of glycolysis.
- Under aerobic conditions, pyruvate is oxidized in the mitochondria to acetyl CoA, which enters the citric acid cycle.

MasteringChemistry

Tutorial: Pathways for Pyruvate

Self Study Activity: Fermentation

◆ Learning Exercise 22.6A

Fill in the blanks with the following terms:

lactate	NAD^+	fermentation	NADH
aerobic	anaerobic	acetyl CoA	

When oxygen is available during glycolysis, the three-carbon pyruvate may be oxidized to form (1) __________ + CO_2. The coenzyme (2) __________ is reduced to (3) __________. Under (4) __________ conditions, pyruvate is reduced to (5) __________. In yeast, pyruvate forms ethanol in a process known as (6) __________.

Answers	**1.** acetyl CoA	**2.** NAD^+	**3.** NADH
	4. anaerobic	**5.** lactate	**6.** fermentation

◆ Learning Exercise 22.6B

Essay Explain how the formation of lactate from pyruvate during anaerobic conditions allows glycolysis to continue.

Answer Under anaerobic conditions, the oxidation of pyruvate to acetyl CoA to regenerate NAD^+ cannot take place. Then pyruvate is reduced to lactate using NADH in the cytoplasm and regenerating NAD^+.

22.7 Glycogen Metabolism

- Glycogen, the storage form of glucose, is synthesized when blood glucose levels are high.
- In the *glycogenesis* pathway, glucose units are added to a glycogen chain.
- *Glycogenolysis*, the breakdown of glycogen, occurs when blood glucose levels are depleted and glucose is required for energy by muscles and the brain.

MasteringChemistry

Tutorial: Glycogen Metabolism

◆ Learning Exercise 22.7

Associate each of the following descriptions with pathways in glycogen metabolism:

a. glycogenesis **b.** glycogenolysis

1.____ breakdown of glycogen to glucose
2.____ activated by glucagon
3.____ starting material is glucose-6-phosphate
4.____ synthesis of glycogen from glucose
5.____ activated by insulin
6.____ UDP activates glucose

Answers **1.** b **2.** b **3.** a **4.** a **5.** a **6.** a

22.8 Gluconeogenesis: Glucose Synthesis

- In *gluconeogenesis*, glucose is synthesized from noncarbohydrate precursors such as lactate, pyruvate, citric acid cycle intermediates, and the carbon atoms of amino acids.
- Most of the enzymes used in gluconeogenesis are the same as the enzymes from glycolysis except for hexokinase, phosphofructokinase, and pyruvate kinase.
- In the *Cori cycle*, lactate formed in the muscles is transported to the liver, where it is converted to pyruvate and then to glucose.

MasteringChemistry

Tutorial: Gluconeogenesis

◆ Learning Exercise 22.8

Match each of the following with the descriptions below:

a. gluconeogenesis **b.** pyruvate **c.** pyruvate kinase
d. pyruvate carboxylase **e.** Cori cycle

1. ____ an enzyme in glycolysis that cannot be used in gluconeogenesis
2. ____ a typical noncarbohydrate source of carbon atoms for glucose synthesis
3. ____ a process whereby lactate produced in muscle is used for glucose synthesis in the liver and used again by the muscle
4. ____ the metabolic pathway that converts noncarbohydrate sources to glucose

5. ____ an enzyme used in gluconeogenesis that is not used in glycolysis

6. ____ a metabolic pathway that is activated when glycogen reserves are depleted

Answers **1.** c **2.** b **3.** e **4.** a **5.** d **6.** a

Checklist for Chapter 22

You are ready to take the Practice Test for Chapter 22. Be sure that you have accomplished the following learning goals for this chapter. If you are not sure, review the section listed at the end of the goal. Then apply your new skills and understanding to the practice test.

After studying Chapter 22, I can successfully:

_____ Associate catabolic and anabolic reactions with organelles in the cell (22.1).

_____ Describe the role of ATP in catabolic and anabolic reactions (22.2).

_____ Describe the coenzymes NAD^+, FAD, and coenzyme A (22.3).

_____ Describe the sites, enzymes, and products of digestion for carbohydrates (22.4).

_____ Describe the conversion of glucose to pyruvate in glycolysis (22.5).

_____ Give the conditions for the conversion of pyruvate to lactate, ethanol, and acetyl coenzyme A (22.6).

_____ Describe the formation and breakdown of glycogen (22.7).

_____ Describe the reactions in which noncarbohydrate sources are used to synthesize glucose (22.8).

Practice Test for Chapter 22

1. The main function of the mitochondria is

A. energy production **B.** protein synthesis **C.** glycolysis
D. genetic instructions **E.** waste disposal

2. ATP is a(n)

A. nucleotide unit in RNA and DNA
B. end product of glycogenolysis
C. end product of transamination
D. enzyme
E. energy storage molecule

For each of the substances in questions 3 through 6, match with one of the following enzymes and end products for their digestion:

A. maltase **B.** glucose **C.** fructose **D.** sucrase
E. galactose **F.** lactase **G.** pancreatic amylase

3. sucrose __________________ **4.** lactose __________________

5. small polysaccharides __________________ **6.** maltose __________________

For questions 7 through 11, match the descriptions below with one of the following cell components:

A. mitochondria **B.** lyzosomes **C.** cytosol
D. ribosomes **E.** cell membrane

7. ____ protein synthesis

8. ____ fluid part of the cytoplasm

9. ____ separates cell contents from external fluids

10. ____ energy-producing reactions

11. ____ hydrolytic enzymes degrade old cell structures

12. Glycolysis

A. requires oxygen for the catabolism of glucose
B. represents the aerobic sequence for glucose anabolism and ATP production
C. represents the splitting off of glucose residues from glycogen
D. represents the anaerobic catabolism of glucose to pyruvate
E. produces acetyl units and ATP as end products

13. Which does *not* appear in the glycolysis pathway?

A. dihydroxyacetone phosphate **B.** pyruvate **C.** NAD
D. acetyl CoA **E.** lactate

For questions 14 through 18, match each description with one of the following metabolic pathways:

A. glycolysis **B.** glycogenolysis **C.** gluconeogenesis
D. glycogenesis **E.** fermentation

14. ____ conversion of pyruvate to alcohol

15. ____ breakdown of glucose to pyruvate

16. ____ formation of glycogen

17. ____ synthesis of glucose

18. ____ breakdown of glycogen to glucose

For questions 19 through 25, match the following coenzymes with the descriptions below:

A. NAD^+ **B.** NADH **C.** FAD **D.** $FADH_2$ **E.** coenzyme A

19. ____ converts a hydroxyl group to a C=O group

20. ____ reduced form of nicotinamide adenine dinucleotide

21. ____ oxidized form of flavin adenine dinucleotide

22. ____ contains the vitamin pantothenic acid, ADP, and an aminoethanethiol

23. ____ participates in oxidation reactions that produce a carbon–carbon (C=C) double bond

24. ____ transfers acyl groups such as the two-carbon acetyl group

25. ____ reduced form of flavin adenine dinucleotide

For questions 26 through 28, answer the following for glycolysis:

26. ____ number of ATP invested for the oxidation of one glucose molecule

27. ____ number of ATP (net) produced from one glucose molecule

28. ____ number of NADH produced from the degradation of one glucose molecule

Answers to the Practice Test

1. A	**2.** E	**3.** B, C, D	**4.** B, E, F	**5.** B, G
6. A, B	**7.** D	**8.** C	**9.** E	**10.** A
11. B	**12.** D	**13.** D, E	**14.** E	**15.** A
16. D	**17.** C	**18.** B	**19.** A	**20.** B
21. C	**22.** E	**23.** C	**24.** E	**25.** D
26. 2	**27.** 2	**28.** 2		

23
Metabolism and Energy Production

Study Goals

- Describe the reactions in the citric acid cycle that oxidize acetyl CoA.
- Explain how electrons from NADH and H^+ and FAD move along the electron transport chain to form H_2O.
- Describe the role of oxidative phosphorylation in ATP synthesis.
- Calculate the ATP produced by the complete combustion of glucose.

Think About It

1. Why is the citric acid cycle considered a central pathway in metabolism?

2. How is the citric acid cycle connected to electron transport?

3. Which stage of metabolism produces most of the ATP for the cells?

Key Words

Match the following key terms with the correct statement shown below.

a. citric acid cycle **b.** oxidative phosphorylation **c.** coenyzme Q
d. cytochromes **e.** proton pump **f.** tricarboxylic acid cycle

1. ________ a mobile carrier that passes electrons from NADH and $FADH_2$ to cytochrome *b* in complex III

2. ________ proteins containing iron as Fe^{3+} or Fe^{2+} that transfer electrons from QH_2 to oxygen

3. ________ protons utilizing the complexes I, II, and III move from the matrix into the intermembrane space

4. ________ the synthesis of ATP from ADP and P_i using energy generated from electron transport

5. ________ oxidation reactions that convert acetyl CoA to CO_2, producing reduced coenzymes for energy production via the electron transport

6. ________ another name for the citric acid cycle

Answers **1.** c **2.** d **3.** e **4.** b **5.** a, f **6.** f

23.1 The Citric Acid Cycle

- Under aerobic conditions, pyruvate is oxidized in the mitochondria to acetyl CoA, which enters the citric acid cycle.
- In a sequence of reactions called the citric acid cycle, acetyl CoA combines with oxaloacetate to yield citrate.
- In one turn of the citric acid cycle, the oxidation of acetyl CoA yields two CO_2, GTP, three NADH, and $FADH_2$. The phosphorylation of ADP by GTP yields ATP.

MasteringChemistry

Self Study Activity: Krebs Cycle

Tutorial: The Citric Acid Cycle

◆ Learning Exercise 23.1A

Match the name of the enzymes with the following steps in the citric acid cycle:

a. isocitrate dehydrogenase
b. α-ketoglutarate dehydrogenase
c. fumarase
d. succinate dehydrogenase
e. malate dehydrogenase
f. aconitase
g. succinyl CoA synthetase
h. citrate synthase

1. ____ acetyl CoA + oxaloacetate → citrate

2. ____ citrate → isocitrate

3. ____ isocitrate → α-ketoglutarate

4. ____ α-ketoglutarate → succinyl CoA

5. ____ succinyl CoA → succinate

6. ____ succinate → fumarate

7. ____ fumarate → malate

8. ____ malate → oxaloacetate

9. ____ allosteric enzymes that regulate the citric acid cycle

Answers **1.** h **2.** f **3.** a **4.** b **5.** g
6. d **7.** c **8.** e **9.** a, b

◆ Learning Exercise 23.1B

In each of the following steps of the citric acid cycle, indicate if oxidation occurs (yes or no) and any coenzyme or direct phosphorylation product produced (NADH + H^+, $FADH_2$, GTP).

Step in Citric Acid Cycle	Oxidation	Coenzyme
1. Acetyl CoA + oxaloacetate → citrate	________	________
2. Citrate → isocitrate	________	________
3. Isocitrate → α-ketoglutarate	________	________
4. α-Ketoglutarate → succinyl CoA	________	________
5. Succinyl CoA → succinate	________	________
6. Succinate → fumarate	________	________
7. Fumarate → malate	________	________
8. Malate → oxaloacetate	________	________

Answers

1. no **2.** no **3.** yes, NADH + H^+ **4.** yes, NADH + H^+
5. no, GTP **6.** yes, $FADH_2$ **7.** no **8.** yes, NADH + H^+

23.2 Electron Carriers

- The reduced coenzymes from glycolysis and the citric acid cycle are oxidized to NAD^+ and FAD by transferring hydrogen ion and electrons to the electron transport system.

> ***MasteringChemistry***
>
> **Tutorial: Electron Carriers**
>
> **Tutorial: Oxidation and Reduction of Electron Carriers**

◆ Learning Exercise 23.2

Write the oxidized and reduced forms of each of the following electron carriers:

1. Flavin mononucleotide oxidized ____________ reduced ____________

2. Coenzyme Q oxidized ____________ reduced ____________

3. Iron–protein clusters oxidized ____________ reduced ____________

4. Cytochrome *b* oxidized ____________ reduced ____________

Answers

1. oxidized: FMN reduced: $FMNH_2$
2. oxidized: Q reduced: QH_2
3. oxidized: Fe^{3+}–S cluster reduced Fe^{2+}–S cluster
4. oxidized: Cyt *b* (Fe^{3+}) reduced: Cyt *b* (Fe^{2+})

23.3 Electron Transport

- In the electron transport system or the respiratory chain, electrons are transferred to electron carriers, including flavins, coenzyme Q, iron–sulfur proteins, and cytochromes with Fe^{3+}/Fe^{2+}.
- The final acceptor, O_2, combines with hydrogen ions and electrons to yield H_2O.

MasteringChemistry
Self Study Activity: Electron Transport
Tutorial: Electron Transport

◆ Learning Exercise 23.3A

Identify the protein complexes and mobile carriers involved in electron transport.

a. Cytochrome *c* oxidase (IV)
b. NADH dehydrogenase (I)
c. Cytochrome *c*
d. Coenzyme Q–cytochrome *c* reductase (III)
e. Succinate dehydrogenase (II)
f. Q

1. ____ FMN and Fe–S clusters

2. ____ $FADH_2 + Q \rightarrow FAD + QH_2$

3. ____ mobile carrier from complex I or complex II to complex III

4. ____ used to move electrons from cyt *a* and a_3 to O_2 and $2H^+$ to yield H_2O

5. ____ mobile carrier between complex III and IV

6. ____ cyt *b*, Fe–S clusters, and cyt c_1

Answers **1.** b **2.** e **3.** f **4.** a **5.** c **6.** d

◆ Learning Exercise 23.3B

1. Write an equation for the transfer of hydrogen from $FMNH_2$ to Q.

2. What is the function of coenzyme Q in electron transport?

3. What are the end products of electron transport?

Answers

1. $FMNH_2 + Q \rightarrow FMN + QH_2$

2. Q accepts hydrogen atoms from $FMNH_2$ or $FADH_2$. From QH_2, the hydrogen atoms are separated into hydrogen ions and electrons, with the electrons being passed on to the cytochromes.

3. $CO_2 + H_2O$

23.4 Oxidation Phosphorylation and ATP

- The flow of electrons in electron transport pumps protons across the inner membrane, which produces a high-energy proton gradient that provides energy for the synthesis of ATP.
- The process of using the energy of electron transport to synthesize ATP is called oxidative phosphorylation.

MasteringChemistry

Tutorial: Power from Protons: ATP Synthase

Tutorial: The Chemiostatic Model

◆ Learning Exercise 23.4

Match the following terms with the correct description below:

a. oxidative phosphorylation **b.** tight (T) site **c.** ATP synthase
d. proton pumps **e.** loose (L) site **f.** open (O) site
g. proton gradient

1. ____ the complexes I, III, and IV, through which H^+ ions move out of the matrix into the intermembrane space

2. ____ the protein tunnel where protons flow from the intermembrane space back to the matrix to generate energy for ATP synthesis

3. ____ energy from electron transport is used to form a proton gradient that drives ATP synthesis

4. ____ the conformation of the F_1 section of ATP synthase that binds ADP and P_i

5. ____ the accumulation of protons in the intermembrane space that lowers pH

6. ____ the conformation of the F_1 section of ATP synthase that releases ATP

7. ____ the conformation of the F_1 section of ATP synthase where ATP forms

Answers **1.** d **2.** c **3.** a **4.** e **5.** g **6.** f **7.** b

23.5 ATP Energy from Glucose

- The oxidation of NADH yields three ATP molecules, whereas the oxidation of $FADH_2$ yields two ATP molecules.
- The complete oxidation of glucose yields a total of 36 ATP from direct phosphorylation and the oxidation of the reduced coenzymes NADH and $FADH_2$ from electron transport and oxidative phosphorylation.

MasteringChemistry
Tutorial: ATP Energy from Glucose

◆ Learning Exercise 23.5

Complete the following:

Substrate	**Reaction**	**Products**	**Amount of ATP Produced**
1. Glucose	glycolysis (aerobic)		
2. Pyruvate	Oxidation		
3. Acetyl CoA	citric acid cycle		
4. Glucose	glycolysis (anaerobic)		
5. Glucose	complete oxidation		

Answers

Substrate	**Reaction**	**Products**	**Amount of ATP**
1. Glucose	glycolysis (aerobic)	2 pyruvate	6
2. Pyruvate	oxidation	acetyl CoA + CO_2	3
3. Acetyl CoA	citric acid cycle	$2CO_2$	12
4. Glucose	glycolysis (anaerobic)	2 lactate	2
5. Glucose	complete oxidation	$6CO_2 + 6H_2O$	36

Checklist for Chapter 23

You are ready to take the Practice Test for Chapter 23. Be sure that you have accomplished the following learning goals for this chapter. If you are not sure, review the section listed at the end of the goal. Then apply your new skills and understanding to the practice test.

After studying Chapter 23, I can successfully:

_______ Describe the oxidation of acetyl CoA in the citric acid cycle (23.1).

_______ Identify the electron carriers in the electron transport system (23.2).

_______ Describe the process of electron transport (23.3).

_______ Explain the chemiosmotic theory whereby ATP synthesis is linked to the energy of electron transport and a proton gradient (23.4).

_______ Account for the ATP produced by the complete oxidation of glucose (23.5).

Practice Test for Chapter 23

1. Which is true of the citric acid cycle?

A. Acetyl CoA is converted to CO_2 and H_2O.
B. Oxaloacetate combines with acetyl units to form citric acid.
C. The coenzymes are NAD^+ and FAD.
D. ATP is produced by direct phosphorylation.
E. All of the above.

For questions 2 through 6, match the types of reactions with each of the following:

A. malate **B.** fumarate **C.** succinate
D. citrate **E.** oxaloacetate

2. ____ formed when oxaloacetate combines with acetyl CoA

3. ____ H_2O adds to its double bond to form malate

4. ____ FAD removes hydrogen from it to form a double bond

5. ____ formed when the hydroxyl group in malate is oxidized

6. ____ the compound that is regenerated in the citric acid cycle

7. One turn of the citric acid cycle produces

A. 3 NADH **B.** 3 NADH, 1 $FADH_2$ **C.** 3 $FADH_2$, 1 NADH, 1 ATP
D. 3 NADH, 1 $FADH_2$, 1 ATP **E.** 1 NADH, 1 $FADH_2$, 1 ATP

8. The citric acid cycle is activated by

A. high ATP levels **B.** NADH **C.** high ADP levels
D. low ATP levels **E.** succinyl CoA.

9. The end products of electron transport are

A. H_2O + ATP **B.** CO_2 + H_2O **C.** NH_3 + CO_2 + H_2O
D. H_2 + O_2 **E.** urea (NH_2CONH_2)

10. How many electron transfers in electron transport provide sufficient energy for ATP synthesis?

A. none **B.** 1 **C.** 2 **D.** 3 **E.** 4

11. The electron transport system

A. produces most of the ATP in the body
B. carries oxygen to the cells
C. produces $CO_2 + H_2O$
D. is only involved in the citric acid cycle
E. operates during fermentation

For questions 12 through 20, match the metabolic processes with one of the following components of the electron transport system:

A. NAD^+ **B.** FMN **C.** FAD **D.** Q **E.** cytochromes

12. ____ a mobile carrier that transfers electrons from $FMNH_2$ and $FADH_2$ to cytochromes

13. ____ the coenzyme that accepts hydrogen atoms from NADH

14. ____ a coenzyme derived from niacin

15. ____ the coenzyme used to remove hydrogen atoms from two adjacent carbon atoms to form carbon–carbon double bonds

16. ____ the electron acceptors containing iron

17. ____ a coenzyme derived from quinone

18. ____ coenzymes that contain flavin

19. ____ the reduced form of this coenzyme generates three molecules of ATP

20. ____ the reduced form of this coenzyme generates two molecules of ATP

For questions 21 through 25, match the descriptions below with one of the following components of ATP synthase:

A. F_0 **B.** F_1 **C.** loose (L) site **D.** tight (T) site **E.** open (O) site

21. ____ consists of the channel for the return of protons to the matrix

22. ____ binds ADP + P_i

23. ____ consists of a center subunit and three subunits that change conformation

24. ____ $ADP + P_i \rightarrow ATP$

25. ____ releases ATP from ATP synthase

For questions 26 through 30, indicate the number of ATPs produced for each of the following:

A. 2 ATP **B.** 3 ATP **C.** 6 ATP **D.** 12 ATP **E.** 24 ATP **F.** 36 ATP

26. one turn of the citric acid cycle $(\text{acetyl CoA} \rightarrow 2CO_2)$

27. complete combustion of glucose $(\text{glucose} + 6O_2 \rightarrow 6H_2O + 6CO_2)$

28. produced when NADH enters electron transport

29. glycolysis $(\text{glucose} + O_2 \rightarrow 2\ \text{pyruvate} + 2H_2O)$

30. oxidation of 2 pyruvate $(2\ \text{pyruvate} \rightarrow 2\ \text{acetyl CoA} + 2CO_2)$

Answers to the Practice Test

1. E	**2.** D	**3.** B	**4.** C	**5.** E
6. E	**7.** D	**8.** C, D	**9.** B	**10.** D
11. A	**12.** D	**13.** B	**14.** A	**15.** C
16. E	**17.** D	**18.** B, C	**19.** A	**20.** C
21. A	**22.** C	**23.** B	**24.** D	**25.** E
26. D	**27.** F	**28.** B	**29.** C	**30.** C

24

Metabolic Pathways for Lipids and Amino Acids

Study Goals

- Describe the sites, enzymes, and products for the digestion of triacylglycerols.
- Describe the oxidation of fatty acids via β oxidation.
- Calculate the ATP produced by the complete oxidation of a fatty acid.
- Explain ketogenesis and the conditions in the cell that form ketone bodies.
- Describe the biosynthesis of fatty acids from acetyl CoA.
- Describe the sites, enzymes, and products of the digestion of dietary protein.
- Explain the role of transamination and oxidative deamination in the degradation of amino acids.
- Describe the formation of urea from ammonium ion.
- Explain how carbon atoms from amino acids are prepared to enter the citric acid cycle or other pathways.
- Show how nonessential amino acids are synthesized from substances used in the citric acid cycle and other pathways.

Think About It

1. What are the products from the digestion of triacylglycerols and proteins?

2. In what form is most of the energy stored in the body?

3. When do you utilize fats and proteins for energy?

Key Words

Match the following key terms with the correct statement shown below.

a. essential amino acid **b.** transamination **c.** lipogenesis
d. ketosis **e.** beta (β) oxidation

1. _____ a reaction cycle that oxidizes fatty acids by removing acetyl CoA units

2. _____ the synthesis of fatty acids by linking two-carbon acetyl units

3. _____ a condition in which high levels of ketone bodies lower blood pH

4. _____ an amino acid that must be obtained from the diet

5. _____ the transfer of an amino group from an amino acid to an α-keto acid

Answers **1.** e **2.** c **3.** d **4.** a **5.** b

24.1 Digestion of Triacylglycerols

- Dietary fats begin digestion in the small intestine, where they are emulsified by bile salts.
- Pancreatic lipases catalyze the hydrolysis of triacylglycerols to yield monoacylglycerols and free fatty acids.
- The triacylglycerols reformed in the intestinal lining combine with proteins to form chylomicrons for transport through the lymphatic system and bloodstream.
- In the cells, triacylglycerols are hydrolyzed to glycerol and fatty acids, which can be used for energy.

MasteringChemistry

Tutorial: Digestion of Triacylglycerols

◆ Learning Exercise 24.1

Match each of the following terms with the descriptions below:

a. chylomicrons **b.** lipases **c.** fat mobilization
d. monoacylglycerols and fatty acids **e.** emulsification

1. _____ the hydrolysis of triacylglycerols in adipose tissues to produce energy

2. _____ lipoproteins formed when triacylglycerols are coated with proteins

3. _____ the breakup of fat globules in the small intestine by bile salts

4. _____ enzymes released from the pancreas that hydrolyze triacylglycerols

5. _____ the products of lipase hydrolysis of triacylglycerols in the small intestine

Answers **1.** c **2.** a **3.** e **4.** b **5.** d

24.2 Oxidation of Fatty Acids

- When needed for energy, fatty acids link to coenzyme A for transport to the mitochondria, where they undergo β oxidation.
- In β oxidation, a fatty acyl chain is oxidized to yield a shortened fatty acid, acetyl CoA, and the reduced coenzymes NADH and $FADH_2$.

> ***MasteringChemistry***
>
> **Tutorial: Oxidation of Fatty Acids**

◆ Learning Exercise 24.2A

Match each of the following terms with the descriptions that follow:

a. activation　**b.** fatty acyl carnitine　**c.** β oxidation
d. NAD^+ and FAD　**e.** mitochondria

1. _____ coenzymes needed for β oxidation

2. _____ site in the cell where β oxidation of fatty acids takes place

3. _____ a fatty acid combines with HS–CoA to form fatty acyl CoA

4. _____ carrier that moves the fatty acyl group into the mitochondria matrix

5. _____ the sequential removal of two-carbon sections from fatty acids

Answers　**1.** d　**2.** e　**3.** a　**4.** b　**5.** c

◆ Learning Exercise 24.2B

1. Write an equation for the activation of myristic (C_{14}) acid: $CH_3-(CH_2)_{12}-\overset{O}{\overset{\|}{C}}-OH$

2. Write an equation for the first oxidation of myristyl CoA.

3. Write an equation for the hydration of the double bond.

4. Write the overall equation for the complete oxidation of myristyl CoA.

5. a. How many cycles of β oxidation are needed for complete oxidation?

b. How many acetyl CoA units will be produced by complete oxidation?

Answers

1. $CH_3{-}(CH_2)_{12}{-}\overset{\overset{\displaystyle O}{\|}}{C}{-}OH + HS{-}CoA + ATP \xrightarrow[\text{synthetase}]{\text{Acyl CoA}} CH_3{-}(CH_2)_{12}{-}\overset{\overset{\displaystyle O}{\|}}{C}{-}S{-}CoA + AMP + 2P_i$

2. $CH_3{-}(CH_2)_{12}{-}\overset{\overset{\displaystyle O}{\|}}{C}{-}S{-}CoA + FAD \xrightarrow[\text{dehydrogenase}]{\text{Acyl CoA}} CH_3{-}(CH_2)_{10}{-}CH{=}CH{-}\overset{\overset{\displaystyle O}{\|}}{C}{-}S{-}CoA + FADH_2$

3. $CH_3{-}(CH_2)_{10}{-}CH{=}CH{-}\overset{\overset{\displaystyle O}{\|}}{C}{-}S{-}CoA + H_2O \xrightarrow{\text{Thiolase}} CH_3{-}(CH_2)_{10}{-}\overset{\overset{\displaystyle OH}{|}}{CH}{-}CH_2{-}\overset{\overset{\displaystyle O}{\|}}{C}{-}S{-}CoA$

4. Myristyl (C_{14}) CoA $+ 6HS-CoA + 6FAD + 6NAD^+ + 6H_2O \rightarrow$

$$7 \text{ acetyl CoA} + 6FADH_2 + 6NADH + 6H^+$$

5. a. 6 cycles **b.** 7 acetyl CoA units are produced

24.3 ATP and Fatty Acid Oxidation

- The energy obtained from a particular fatty acid depends on the number of carbon atoms.
- Two ATP are required for activation. Then each acetyl CoA produces 12 ATP via the citric acid cycle; each NADH gives 3 ATP and each FADH gives 2 ATP from electron transport.

◆ Learning Exercise 24.3

Lauric acid is a 12 carbon saturated fatty acid: $CH_3{-}(CH_2)_{10}{-}COOH$

1. How many ATP are needed for activation?

2. How many cycles of β oxidation are needed for complete oxidation?

3. How many NADH and $FADH_2$ are produced during β oxidation?

4. How many acetyl CoA units are produced?

5. What is the total ATP produced from the citric acid cycle and electron transport?

Answers

1. 2 ATP
2. 5 cycles
3. 5 cycles produce 5 NADH and 5 $FADH_2$
4. 6 acetyl CoA
5. 5 NADH × 3 ATP = 15 ATP; 5 $FADH_2$ × 2 ATP = 10 ATP;
6 acetyl CoA × 12 ATP = 72 ATP;
Total ATP = 15 ATP + 10 ATP + 72 ATP – 2 ATP (for activation) = 95 ATP

24.4 Digestion of Triacylglycerols

- When the oxidation of large amounts of fatty acids cause high levels of acetyl CoA, the acetyl CoA undergoes ketogenesis.
- Two molecules of acetyl CoA form acetoacetyl CoA, which is converted to acetoacetate, β-hydroxybutyrate, and acetone.

MasteringChemistry

Tutorial: Ketogenesis and Ketone Bodies

◆ Learning Exercise 24.4

Match each of the following terms with the correct description:

a. ketone bodies **b.** ketogenesis **c.** ketosis
d. liver **e.** acidosis

1. _____ high levels of ketone bodies in the blood

2. _____ a metabolic pathway that produces ketone bodies

3. _____ β-hydroxybutyrate, acetoacetate, and acetone

4. _____ the condition whereby ketone bodies lower the blood pH below 7.4

5. _____ site where ketone bodies form

Answers **1.** c **2.** b **3.** a **4.** e **5.** d

24.5 Fatty Acid Synthesis

- When all energy needs have been met and glycogen stores are full, excess acetyl CoA is used to synthesize fatty acids that are stored in the adipose tissue.
- Two-carbon acetyl CoA units link together to give palmitic (C16) acid and other fatty acids.

> ***MasteringChemistry***
>
> **Tutorial: Fatty Acid Synthesis**

◆ Learning Exercise 24.5

Indicate if each of the following is characteristic of lipogenesis (L) or β oxidation (O).

1. _____ occurs in the matrix of mitochondria
2. _____ occurs in the cytosol of mitochondria
3. _____ activated by insulin
4. _____ activated by glucagon
5. _____ starts with fatty acids
6. _____ starts with acetyl CoA units
7. _____ produces fatty acids
8. _____ produces acetyl CoA units
9. _____ requires NADPH coenzyme
10. _____ requires FAD and NAD^+ coenzymes
11. _____ activated with CoA
12. _____ activated by ACP

Answers
1. O **2.** L **3.** L **4.** O
5. O **6.** L **7.** L **8.** O
9. L **10.** O **11.** O **12.** L

24.6 Digestion of Proteins

- Proteins begin digestion in the stomach, where HCl denatures proteins and activates peptidases that hydrolyze peptide bonds.
- In the small intestine, trypsin and chymotrypsin complete the hydrolysis of peptides to amino acids.

> ***MasteringChemistry***
>
> **Tutorial: Nitrogen in the Body**

◆ Learning Exercise 24.6

Match each of the following terms with the correct description:

a. nitrogen-containing compounds **b.** protein turnover **c.** stomach
d. nitrogen balance **e.** small intestine

1. ____ HCl activates enzymes that hydrolyze peptide bonds in proteins
2. ____ trypsin and chymotrypsin convert peptides to amino acids
3. ____ include amino acids, amino alcohols, proteins, hormones, and nucleic acids
4. ____ the process of synthesizing protein and breaking them down
5. ____ the amount of protein hydrolyzed is equal to the amount of protein used in the body

Answers **1.** c **2.** e **3.** a **4.** b **5.** d

24.7 Degradation of Amino Acids

- Amino acids are normally used for protein synthesis.
- Amino acids are degraded by transferring an amino group from an amino acid to an α-keto acid to yield a different amino acid and α-keto acid.
- In oxidative deamination, the amino group in glutamate is removed as an ammonium ion, NH_4^+.

MasteringChemistry
Tutorial: Transamination and Deamination

◆ Learning Exercise 24.7A

Match each of the following descriptions with transamination (T) or oxidative deamination (D):

1. ____ produces an ammonium ion, NH_4^+
2. ____ transfers an amino group to an α-keto acid
3. ____ usually involves the degradation of glutamate
4. ____ requires NAD^+ or $NADP^+$
5. ____ produces another amino acid and α-keto acid
6. ____ usually produces α-ketoglutarate

Answers **1.** D **2.** T **3.** D **4.** D **5.** T **6.** D

◆ Learning Exercise 24.7B

1. Write an equation for the transamination reaction of serine and oxaloacetate.

2. Write an equation for the oxidative deamination of glutamate.

Answers

1. $HO{-}CH_2{-}\underset{}{\overset{NH_3^+}{\overset{|}{C}H}}{-}COO^- + {}^-OOC{-}\overset{O}{\overset{\|}{C}}{-}CH_2{-}COO^- \longrightarrow$

$$HO{-}CH_2{-}\overset{O}{\overset{\|}{C}}{-}COO^- + {}^-OOC{-}\overset{NH_3^+}{\overset{|}{C}H}{-}CH_2{-}COO^-$$

2. ${}^-OOC{-}\overset{NH_3^+}{\overset{|}{C}H}{-}CH_2{-}CH_2{-}COO^- + NAD^+ \text{ (or } NADP^+) + H_2O \longrightarrow$

$${}^-OOC{-}\overset{O}{\overset{\|}{C}}{-}CH_2{-}CH_2{-}COO^- + NH_4^+ + NADH \text{ (or NADPH)} + H^+$$

24.8 Urea Cycle

- The ammonium ion, NH_4^+, from amino acid degradation is toxic if allowed to accumulate.
- The urea cycle converts ammonium ion to urea, which forms urine in the kidneys.

MasteringChemistry

Tutorial: Detoxifying Ammonia in the Body

◆ Learning Exercise 24.8

Arrange the following reactions in the order they occur in the urea cycle:

Step 1. _____ **Step 2.** ______ **Step 3.** ______ **Step 4.** ______

a. argininosuccinate is split to yield arginine and fumarate

b. aspartate condenses with citrulline to yield argininosuccinate

c. arginine is hydrolyzed to yield urea and regenerates ornithine

d. ornithine combines with the carbamoyl group from carbamoyl phosphate

Answers **Step 1.** d **Step 2.** b **Step 3.** a **Step 4.** c

24.9 Fates of the Carbon Atoms from Amino Acids

- α-Keto acids resulting from transamination can be used as intermediates in the citric acid cycle or in the synthesis of lipids or glucose or oxidized for energy.

◆ Learning Exercise 24.9

Match each of the following terms with the correct description:

a. Glucogenic **b.** ketogenic **c.** oxaloacetate
d. acetyl CoA **e.** α-ketoglutarate **f.** pyruvate

1. _____ amino acids that generate pyruvate or oxaloacetate, which can be used to synthesize glucose

2. _____ keto acid obtained from carbon atoms of alanine and serine

3. _____ keto acid obtained from carbon atoms of glutamine and glutamate

4. _____ keto acid obtained from carbon atoms from aspartate and asparagine

5. _____ amino acids that generate compounds that can produce ketone bodies

6. _____ compound obtained from carbon atoms of leucine and isoleucine

Answers **1.** a **2.** f **3.** e **4.** c **5.** b **6.** d

24.10 Synthesis of Amino Acids

- Humans synthesize only 10 amino acids. The other 10, called essential amino acids, must be obtained from the diet.

◆ Learning Exercise 24.10

Match each of the following terms with the correct description:

a. essential amino acids **b.** nonessential amino acids
c. transamination **d.** phenylketonuria (PKU)

1. _____ amino acids synthesized in humans

2. _____ a genetic condition when phenylalanine is not converted to tyrosine

3. _____ amino acids that must be supplied by the diet

4. _____ reaction that produces some nonessential amino acids

Answers **1.** b **2.** d **3.** a **4.** c

Checklist for Chapter 24

You are ready to take the Practice Test for Chapter 24. Be sure that you have accomplished the following learning goals for this chapter. If you are not sure, review the section listed at the end of the goal. Then apply your new skills and understanding to the practice test.

After studying Chapter 24, I can successfully:

____ Describe the sites, enzymes, and products for the digestion of triacylglycerols (24.1).

____ Describe the oxidation of fatty acids via β oxidation (24.2).

____ Calculate the ATP produced by the complete oxidation of a fatty acid (24.3).

____ Explain ketogenesis and the conditions in the cell that form ketone bodies (24.4).

____ Describe the biosynthesis of fatty acids from acetyl CoA (24.5).

____ Describe the sites, enzymes, and products of the digestion of dietary proteins (24.6).

____ Explain the role of transamination and oxidative deamination in degrading amino acids (24.7).

____ Describe the formation of urea from ammonium ion (24.8).

____ Explain how carbon atoms from amino acids are prepared to enter the citric acid cycle or other pathways (24.9).

____ Show how nonessential amino acids are synthesized from substances used in the citric acid cycle and other pathways (24.10).

Practice Test for Chapter 24

1. The digestion of triacylglycerols takes place in the ________ by enzymes called ________.

A. small intestine; peptidases **B.** stomach; lipases **C.** stomach; peptidases
D. small intestine; lipases **E.** all of these

2. The products of the digestion of triacylglycerols are

A. fatty acids **B.** monoacylglycerols **C.** glycerol
D. diacylglycerols **E.** all of these

3. The function of the bile salts in the digestion of fats is

A. emulsification **B.** hydration **C.** dehydration
D. oxidation **E.** reduction

4. Chylomicrons formed in the intestinal lining

A. are lipoproteins
B. are triacylglycerols coated with proteins
C. transport fats into the lymphatic system and bloodstream
D. carry triacylglycerols to the cells of the heart, muscle, and adipose tissues
E. all of these

5. Glycerol obtained from the hydrolysis of triacylglycerols enters glycolysis when converted to

A. glucose **B.** fatty acids **C.** dihydroxyacetone phosphate
D. pyruvate **E.** glycerol-3-phosphate

6. Fatty acids are prepared for β oxidation by forming

A. carnitine **B.** fatty acyl carnitine **C.** acetyl CoA
D. fatty acyl CoA **E.** pyruvate

7. The reactions in the β oxidation cycle do *not* involve

A. reduction **B.** hydration **C.** dehydrogenation
D. oxidation **E.** cleavage of acetyl CoA

For questions 8 through 11, consider the β oxidation of palmitic (C_{16}) acid:

8. The number of β oxidation cycles required to oxidize palmitic acid is

A. 16 **B.** 9 **C.** 8 **D.** 7 **E.** 6

9. The number of acetyl CoA groups produced by the β oxidation of palmitic (C_{16}) acid is

A. 16 **B.** 9 **C.** 8 **D.** 7 **E.** 6

10. The number of NADH and $FADH_2$ produced by the β oxidation of palmitic (C_{16}) acid is

A. 16 **B.** 9 **C.** 8 **D.** 7 **E.** 6

11. The total ATP produced by the β oxidation of palmitic (C_{16}) acid is

A. 96 **B.** 129 **C.** 131 **D.** 134 **E.** 136

12. The oxidation of large amounts of fatty acids can produce

A. ketone bodies **B.** glucose **C.** low pH level in the blood
D. acetone **E.** pyruvate

13. The metabolic pathway of lipogenesis requires

A. fatty acids **B.** acetyl CoA **C.** FAD and NAD^+
D. glucagon **E.** ketone bodies

14. The digestion of proteins takes place in the ________ by enzymes called ________.

A. small intestine; peptidases **B.** stomach; lipases **C.** stomach; peptidases
D. small intestine; lipases **E.** stomach and small intestine; proteases and peptidases

15. The process of transamination

A. is part of the citric acid cycle **B.** converts α-amino acids to β-keto acids
C. produces new amino acids **D.** is not used in the metabolism of amino acids
E. is part of the β oxidation of fats

16. The oxidative deamination of glutamate produces

A. a new amino acid **B.** a new α-keto acid **C.** ammonia, NH_3
D. ammonium ion, NH_4^+ **E.** urea

17. The purpose of the urea cycle in the liver is to

A. synthesize urea
B. convert urea to ammonium ion, NH_4^+
C. convert ammonium ion NH_4^+ to urea
D. synthesize new amino acids
E. take part in the β oxidation of fats

18. The urea cycle begins with the conversion of NH_4^+ to

A. aspartate **B.** carbamoyl phosphate **C.** citrulline **D.** argininosuccinate **E.** urea

19. The carbon atoms from a ketogenic amino acid can be used to

A. synthesize ketone bodies **B.** convert urea to ammonium ion, NH_4^+
C. synthesize fatty acids **D.** produce energy
E. synthesize proteins

20. The carbon atoms from various amino acids can be used in several ways, such as

A. intermediates of the citric acid cycle **B.** formation of pyruvate
C. synthesis of glucose **D.** formation of ketone bodies
E. all of these

21. Essential amino acids

A. are not synthesized by humans
B. are required in the diet
C. are excreted if in excess
D. include leucine, lysine, and valine
E. all of these

22. When the quantity of amino acids in the diet exceeds the needs of the cells, the excess amino acids

A. are stored for use at a later time
B. are used to synthesize glycogen
C. excreted
D. are converted to fat
E. are used to make more protein

23. Phenylketonuria is a condition

A. abbreviated as PKU
B. where a person does not synthesize tyrosine
C. that can be detected at birth
D. that can cause severe mental retardation
E. all of these

Answers to the Practice Test

1. D	**2.** E	**3.** A	**4.** E	**5.** C
6. D	**7.** A	**8.** D	**9.** C	**10.** D
11. B	**12.** A, C, D	**13.** B	**14.** E	**15.** C
16. D	**17.** C	**18.** B	**19.** A, C	**20.** E
21. E	**22.** C	**23.** E		